What's So Funny?

MURRAY S. DAVIS

What's So Funny?

THE COMIC CONCEPTION OF CULTURE AND SOCIETY

THE UNIVERSITY OF CHICAGO PRESS / CHICAGO AND LONDON

Murray S. Davis is the author of *Intimate Relations* (1973) and *Smut: Erotic Reality / Obscene Ideology* (1983), the latter published by the University of Chicago Press.

The University of Chicago Press, Chicago 60637
The University of Chicago Press, Ltd., London
© 1993 by The University of Chicago
All rights reserved. Published 1993
Printed in the United States of America
02 01 00 99 98 97 96 95 94 93 1 2 3 4 5

ISBN: 0-226-13810-0 (cloth)

Library of Congress Cataloging-in-Publication Data

Davis, Murray S., 1940–
    What's so funny? : the comic conception of culture and society /
Murray S. Davis.
        p.   cm.
    Includes bibliographical references and index.
    1. Wit and humor—Social aspects.   2. Wit and humor—Psychology.
I. Title.
PN6149.S62D38   1993
302.2—dc20   93-10217
                                                                                       CIP

⊗ The paper used in this publication meets the minimum requirements of the American National Standard for Information Sciences—Permanence of Paper for Printed Library Materials, ANSI Z39.48–1984.

For my parents, William Davis and Reva Lippard Davis,

who showed me that humor
makes life endurable

and inspired me to find out why.

I have tried too in my time to be a philosopher; but, I don't know how,

cheerfulness was always breaking in.

—Oliver Edwards to Samuel Johnson

17 April 1778

Contents

Preface

My conception of society was formed primarily from joke books. While I was growing up, my father displayed a "joke du jour" blackboard in his storefront window, wrote a humor column for a professional association's newsletter, and was the anecdotic master of ceremonies at its banquets. Our house was cluttered with the joke books that stimulated much of his material. Having nothing better to do as his only child, I read them all. When he died many years later, I inherited his large collection. After reexamining these joke books for possible disposal, I decided that they were too interesting to throw away and that I should to try to discover the source of their appeal, which had skewed my world view so permanently.

Important as these joke books from the 1930s through the 1960s were, I knew that a more compelling investigation of humor would have to include more recent examples. Expanding my humor resources beyond my inherited data base was easy—too easy!—because provocations for laughter, disseminated through the mass media, pervade our society. From network television sitcoms to specials by famous comedians, from all-comedy cable channels to showcases for upcoming comics, from movie comedies to children's cartoons, from newspaper comic strips and satirical columns to magazine column fillers and syndicated cartoons, from comic books to joke collections—each mass medium (with the current exception of radio) is saturated with humor. And ever since comedy replaced poetry in the 1970s as the main avant-garde verbal performance art—a little-noted but significant cultural shift—local comedy clubs have become an evening's entertainment. Soon my files were overflowing with jokes.

I chose to collect these jokes without following a formal method because humor was a fairly new academic field. Since uniform data collection methods inflexibly restrict attention, I prefer to approach fresh topics with as broad a perspective as possible. Otherwise, a researcher overly concerned with methodological rigor may overlook a topic's most thought-provoking features—whose fuzzy implications make them inherently difficult to circumscribe—before ascertaining their importance (see Davis 1971). Later methodologists can delineate a topic more precisely, but only after its original explorers have revealed those of its features worth clarifying.

To maximize these insights, then, I decided to increase my joke data base serendipitously rather than systematically. But because each joke represents a class of jokes, a different collection of jokes (say, one derived partly from newspapers in other regions of the country) should produce only a slightly different analysis of humor. Later researchers who collect jokes more rigorously than I did will certainly sharpen my classification scheme, but probably not change its fundamental organization.

I had hoped to include only jokes that made me laugh ("good jokes"), but sometimes I had to include those that didn't ("bad jokes") because they were logically necessary or were "classics." Although the latter's popularity indicates that they have tapped essential and enduring cultural and social issues, their familiarity has decreased their humor. On the other hand, unfunny jokes are easier to analyze than funny jokes because their out-of-phase components decrease their dazzle.

I also included offensive jokes. Except for purely linguistic jokes, most jokes offend someone or some group. Those that don't few find funny. Rather than produce a "politically correct" analysis of humor that would be humorous only in its lack of humor, I have tried to produce one whose illustrative jokes would offend everyone and every group equally. An *egalitarianly offensive* humor analysis can reveal the dynamic forces that produce our society's funniest jokes whereas an inoffensive one can reveal only the mildest motivations of its blandest jokes.

Although the jokes in this book are intrinsically enjoyable, they are only the raisins that make palatable the bran of abstract cultural and social theory—whose reconceptualization is my goal. Comedy has been a nonsystematic and noncumulative form of knowledge. I wanted to see what would result if its knowledge could be systematized and cumulated. My collection of humor data may be haphazard, but I tried to abstract cultural and social theory from it more rigorously through both inductive and deductive methods. A joke I encountered serendipitously would imply a basic cultural or social category, which would generate an abstract set of potential subtypes, which motivated me to search intentionally for other concrete jokes to complete this set. When I couldn't find the required joke in my resources, I made it up.

Although fabricating data, especially as blatantly as I have done it, would normally scandalize the scientific community (and rightly so), I believe making up jokes is justified here *if they're funny*. Since humor is one of the few topics whose existence depends solely on audience response, it's a joke—and thus illustrates the negation of the cultural or social feature I am describing—if it gets a laugh, regardless of its source.

I originally felt morally obligated to acknowledge the author of every joke I used because of my belief in its social importance. But this proved impossible because a joke's true creator is usually unknown. So I reluctantly decided to omit most joke citations, except for noting whoever disseminated it widely enough for me to encounter it. (But even when told by a famous comic, a joke is frequently produced by an anonymous writer.) Besides my own relatively rare ad hoc ones, then, I did not attribute jokes I considered in the public domain, which includes those found in the humor collections or quoted by the humor theorists referenced in the bibliography.

Ultimately, I clarified my objectives: not merely to locate comedy in the cultural and social worlds but to describe the cultural and social worlds from the comic perspective; not merely to apply a sociology of comedy *to* my humor data base but to generate a sociology of culture and society *from* it; not merely to bring ready-made cultural and social theory to bear on comedy but to use comedy to create more sophisticated cultural and social theory. For what sociology can teach us about comedy came to seem less important than what comedy can teach us about culture and society.

Determining the significance of humor for cultural and social theory, moreover, would greatly benefit sociology. Among the many intellectual perspectives that observe the dance of life, sociology has been the most awkward wallflower; but adding the perspicacity and vitality of wit to her repertoire might entice the dancers to pay her the attention she deserves.

Humor analysis, however, has one liability that partially offsets its benefits, for "slowing down" jokes to illuminate their operation spoils their surprise: the sudden shift of meaning that produces a laugh. Although the scientific analysis of humor does indeed destroy the effectiveness of particular jokes, it does not have to undermine humor in general. Jokes may become less amusing but society's serious side may become more amusing. Humor analysis need kill humor no more than artistic analysis need kill art. On the contrary, both sciences can actually enhance the appreciation of their respective humanities by pointing out the elements that compose a total effect. With both humor and art, however, it is better to articulate these elements *after* the audience's immediate naive reaction to the joke or the artwork than before.

I am grateful to those who supported this project primarily during its pre- and earlier-production stages: the San Francisco Bay Area for supplying all the resources my research required, from sitdown humorists in newspapers to standup comics in clubs, Dr. Catherine Schmidt for continually being curious enough to ask her inexplicably smiling husband "What's so funny?" and perceptive enough to supplement his thoughts about the nature of humor with her own; Doug Mitchell, editor extraordinaire, for sustaining his encouragement of a seemingly desultory author during this book's long gestation; and my muses Athena (wisdom) and her half-sister Thalia (comedy) for putting up with my attempt to reconcile them after their long estrangement.

I am also grateful to those who supported this project primarily during its later- and postproduction stages: the National Endowment for the Humanities, which awarded me a fellowship to complete this book, subverting my belief in the inevitable philistinism of government; the National Coalition of Independent Scholars, which suggested a strategy to elicit this fellowship from the NEH that proved successful; professors Fred Davis of the University of California at San Diego, Don Levine of the University of Chicago, Gary Marx of the Massachusetts Institute of Technology, and Eviatar Zerubavel of Rutgers University for recommending this project as a whole, which helped me obtain financing and publication, or criticizing its details, which helped me avoid embarrassment.

Finally, I hope my potential audience will not react to my book as Groucho Marx did to his friend S. J. Perelman's new book:

> From the moment I picked it up until I laid it down I was convulsed with laughter. Someday I intend reading it.

Illuminating how Groucho amuses us by pivoting his own amusement from the content to the authorship of Perelman's book illustrates the inquiry of my book.

Introduction

Comedy is the flip side of culture and society.[1]

Before elaborating this aphorism (and its pivotal pun) in the rest of this book, I feel obligated to justify the entire endeavor. Many researchers have regarded comedy as an unsuitable topic for "serious" study ever since the Greek philosophers restricted comic objects to the inconsequential actions of insignificant persons.[2] Even today, it still seems frivolous to spend time and money investigating comedy rather than the "major" aspects of society like government, business, education, and family, or the "critical" social problems like war, crime, drug abuse, and poverty. Yet the persistence with which some scholars have continued to study this disreputable research topic indicates that comedy must contain certain truths about human existence they find more compelling than even the status and tenure they could have acquired by investigating more reputable subjects.

What truths? For one, humor can reveal the truth about a person. As Thomas Carlyle observed in 1833, "Laughter [is] the cipher-key wherewith we decipher the whole man!" (1908:24). Like his dreams, a person's sense of humor opens a window into his unconscious (Freud 1963). If a person *is* what he worries about, if his character's core is its deficiencies, then the idiosyncratic topics he laughs at can indicate the weak points in his psychological structure. Conversely, what a person *does not* laugh at can also indicate his vulnerabilities. In 1790 G. C. Lichtenberg reflected, "Nothing better reveals a man's character than the joke he takes in bad part." The individual, then, delineates much of his essential self (to both himself and others) by what he does, and does not, find funny.[3]

For another, humor can reveal the truth about a society. Critic Louis Kronenberger (quoted in Hertzler 1970:18) observed "how frequently a joke can catch, better than a dozen treatises, the essence of a people, a period, an entire civilization." And sociologist Joyce Hertzler added that humor can serve "as a kind of sociocultural index of the culture or society, the groups and population segments, the communities or localities, and the eras in which it occurs. . . . What a people laugh at at any given time can reveal what they perceive socially, what they are interested in, concerned about, amused by, disgusted with, preoccupied with" (1970:58–59).[4] In today's terms, jokes are the *fractals* of society.

Humor, in short, may seem trivial, but it provides an inconspicuous back entrance to a person's, group's, or society's innermost chamber, which continually knocking on their front door may never disclose. More generally, intellectual advances have occurred whenever thinkers have rechristened what their time dismissed as trivial into the key for understanding the world. The same kind of revaluation Marx did for the lower class, Freud did for sex, and feminist, gay, and ethnic historians did for oppressed groups, we should now do for humor.

Those convinced that humor is worth knowing still face the question of whether it is knowable. Many humor theorists—and many humorists—believe it isn't. They feel that humor, like some delicate insect under a magnifying glass, will be incinerated when touched by the sunlight over the investigator's shoulder.

Ever since the Roman rhetoricians failed to explain why humor helped speeches succeed,[5] scientific attempts to analyze humor have been held in contempt:

> What Humor is, not all the Tribe
> of Logick-mongers can describe.
> [Jonathan Swift]

Mark Twain once portrayed an academic lecture on humor thus: "The professor got the subject down on the floor and broke its back." Perhaps the best known rejection of the scientific analysis of humor is E. B. White's: "Humor can be dissected, as a frog can, but the thing dies in the process and the innards are discouraging to any but the pure scientific mind" (1941:xvii). Max Eastman, the socialist who was also—incongruously—America's foremost humor theorist in 1920s and 1930s, called these skeptics "humor agnostics": "There is no other subject . . . besides God and laughter, toward which the scientific mind has ever advocated so explicit and particular a humility" (1921:134).[6] Some humor agnostics have even gone so far as to reverse the relative dominance between the scientist and his subject: "The learned and philosophic have given laughter their most serious consideration, and as they pore over the spritely and elusive thing, testing it with the dry and colourless terms of science and philosophy, the tables are frequently turned on them and the Ariel which they are anatomizing so absorbedly shakes himself free, straps them upon the operating table and sets about anatomizing them in turn, and the earnest analysts of laughter become themselves laughable" (M. Armstrong, quoted in Keith-Spiegel 1972:34).

Science not only can't understand humor, it also can't be as entertaining as humor. Those who equate science with seriousness believe a scientific analysis of humor cannot, by definition, be amusing. "People who sit down to write books on humor are scientific people, philosophical analyzers who feel that they must make something serious, something real out of it, and show us that humor can, in proper hands, be made as dull and as respectable as philology or epistemology" (Stephen Leacock, quoted in Raskin 1985:7). Expecting the science to be as funny as its subject will inevitably disappoint. *Time* magazine, in an egregiously unfair and erroneous report, ridiculed the first International Symposium on Humor for precisely this deficiency: "Psychiatrist William Fry . . . several years ago developed a theory that laughter is physically harmful and can actually kill you. That might still be a· better fate than sitting through an academic conference on humor" (*Time*, 2 Aug. 1976:58).

Humor researchers usually feel compelled to respond to the potential criticism that their work is duller than their lively topic led its audience to expect. Anticipating this criticism, most major treatises on humor, including the premier issue of the journal *Humor* (Raskin 1988:3), have begun by justifying or apologizing for their serious tone. Eastman, however, manages to deflect this accusation by accepting it in the extreme—thereby making funny at least the criticism of not being funny: "I must warn you, reader, that it is not the purpose of this book to make you laugh. As you know, nothing kills the laugh quicker than to explain a joke. I intend to explain all jokes, and the proper and logical outcome will be, not only that you will not laugh now, but that you will never laugh again. So prepare for the descending gloom" (1939:xv).

The scientific analysis of humor, in short, has been criticized for being a self-negating oxymoron because its comic content clashes with its scientific form, causing it to fail both as science (understanding) and as humor (entertainment).[7]

Why should this particular discrepancy between method and topic provoke so much complaint from critics and resignation from researchers? After all, no one complains when a scientific analysis of sex fails to arouse its readers (and some object when it does). Conversely, no one complains when a humorous treatment of science isn't informative.

This criticism—that a scientific discussion of humor is neither fruitful nor funny—provides a clue to its own correction. It suggests that we can investigate humor without destroying it by focusing on the differences (and similarities) between science and humor. Science and humor are two alternative modes of understanding the world, sharing some features—particularly their disrespect for appearances—but contrasted in others—particularly their respect for underlying systems. Of the two, many believe that humor's insights are the more profound but the more delicate. Consequently, those humorists—like E. B. White and Robert Benchley—who disparage the scientific analysis of humor and defame those who try to explain it secretly *hope* that humor will remain inexplicable: "Humor won't stand much blowing up, and it won't stand much poking. It has a certain fragility, an evasiveness, which one had best respect" (White 1941:xviii); "There seems to be no lengths to which humorless people will not go to analyze humor. It seems to worry them. They can't believe that anything could be funny just on its own hook" (Benchley 1983:92). Humor will lose its potency, they fear, unless it retains its mystery.

Even those who believe comedy can be understood admit it will not be easy. Comedy, like obscenity (with which it shares other characteristics [see Davis 1983]) is easier to experience than to define, prompting the response, "I know it when I laugh at it." More than almost all other human phenomena, humor is ambiguous, variable, enigmatic. But since the ultimate goal of science is to express the inexpressible, humor presents it with a worthy challenge. And the best place for humor researchers to begin is with their topic's very ambiguities—of which there are many. Some of its ambiguities this book attempts to clarify are whether humor inheres in mind or nature, system or incongruity, sound or meaning, words or logic, the typical or the ideal, individuals or society.

After defending their own lack of humor, most modern treatises on comedy begin with a history of humor theories from Plato to Bergson and beyond. But I want this book to be more than merely a survey of past theorists. Eastman (1921:3–4) complained that most past theorists discussed the comic as a "side show" to their main concern. But I believe, with Eastman, that humor belongs in the center stage of human life. Consequently, I will integrate these past theorists' ideas around humor rather than the more common approach of *dis*integrating humor around the history of theories about it. Rather than locate the comic in a theorist's overall approach, then, I will drag in the theorist's entire worldview when necessary to explain various aspects of comedy.[8]

Like sex, humor does not appear to fit readily into any intellectual scheme that explains the rest of life. Even those who minimize humor's importance usually find it enigmatic enough to try to explain it. Consequently, Western civilization has accumulated a sizable literature of humor interpretation, whose growth has recently accelerated but whose common thread has increasingly unraveled into distinct lines: venerable disciplinary traditions like the literary, philosophical, and psychological; newer ones in anthropology, mathematics, linguistics, and theology; practical ones by professional comedians and comedy writers; and last, and so far regrettably least, the sociology of humor, whose unrealized potential I hope to bring out.[9]

In the 1960s, Peter Berger eloquently called on his colleagues to consider the importance of comedy for sociology: "Indeed, an argument could be made that the social scientist who does not perceive this comic dimension of social reality is going to miss essential features of it. . . . These remarks, needless to say, are not meant to denigrate the serious study of society but simply to suggest that such study itself will profit greatly from those insights that one can obtain only while laughing" (1963:165). At the same time, William Cameron was pointing out the profession's resistance to such a call:

> The work on humor has been done for the most part by psychologists and philosophers. Some sociologists have dabbled around the edges, mostly concerned with particular situations giving rise to humor or with the uses of humor as a weapon in racial and minority disputes. No one has attempted an overall analysis of broad categories of humor (such as the joke, the cartoon, and the wisecrack) in the light of a carefully elaborated sociological or socio-psychological theory. It is just not the sort of thing sociologists officially favor. . . .
>
> Editors love to read a funny essay themselves, but few will risk publishing it in *their* journal. It would seem that among sociologists humor is to be enjoyed only clandestinely, like sex. [1963:80]

After languishing for a long time, interest in the sociology of humor has begun to increase.[10] It has, a sociology of sociology suggests, because the topic itself has become more respectable among the general public. Previously, many sociologists were so uncertain about the worth of their approach that they feared it would be contaminated by applying it to a lowly valued topic like humor, degrading their discipline's status even further. Recently, however, the prevalence and prestige of humor in society today—not to mention the money earned by those who produce it—has greatly increased. As humor's public status has risen, the contamination fears that had prevented many sociologists from studying it have diminished.

Unfortunately, each of the intellectual disciplines that treat humor has evolved along divergent paths, aware of the others only enough to inadvertently translate into its own jargon the same unresolvable controversies that have already bogged down theirs. To try to overcome the intellectual fragmentation of humor theory today, then, I will combine the insights into humor I found most provocative from all these disciplines (though giving more weight to sociology's to bring out comedy's overlooked but important implications about the social world). This united front approach will at least have the virtue of facilitating communication among intellectual disciplines that have been investigating separate sides of the same subject.

Most of the previous humor theories within these intellectual disciplines have tried to explain too much. Whenever true believers claim a theory can explain *all* instances of humor, skeptics criticize their extreme claims by citing counterexamples that the presumptuous theory cannot easily explain (for example, "*X* is an incongruity but it isn't funny"; "*X* is funny but it isn't an incongruity"). Some explanations of the comic also apply to the serious: Kant's theory, which defines humor mainly as "disappointed expectation," cannot explain why someone who expects to make love with a beautiful woman but is unexpectedly shot by her jealous husband fails to find it funny. Other explanations of the comic do not even apply to all comic phenomena: Hobbes's theory, which defines humor mainly as "sudden superiority," implies the difficult-to-prove assumption that *every* instance of humor disparages somebody. As Peter de Vries somewhere puts it, "Talking about theories of comedy is like a woman squeezing into a girdle that's too small. There are so many things to laugh at, nothing fits. There's always an overflow."

But just because these particular humor theories have claimed too much does not mean they are worthless. Maurice Charney (1978:3–4) suggests that each theory may explain a specific kind of comedy very well. Thus it is fruitful to apply Hobbes's superiority theory to aggressive jokes, Bergson's mechanization theory to farce, Freud's sexual theory to dirty jokes, and Northrop Frye's anthropological theory to Aristophanic Old Comedy. Apparently, each of these kinds of comedy had served as the particular paradigm from which the theorist constructed his general model of all comedy. Unfortunately, this procedure has led each of these humor theories to focus on only one of the comic's many aspects while contemplating the whole from the point of view of this part, for which it claims principal importance.

But humor is too complicated to be comprehended by such single-factor theories, no matter how well they explain one of its aspects. Although few theories of humor have ever been wholly wrong, many just haven't learned their place. I will try to avoid the synecdoches of these past theories by finding the proper place for each in the larger scheme of their subject.[11]

Monistic humor theories have now developed to a stage where we can put aside their continual controversies over which aspect of the comic is primary. The humor theory elaborated here will be pluralistic, designed to specify the ways most of these monistic humor theories are complementary rather than contradictory (except in the relatively few instances where two opposing theories comment on exactly the same aspect of the comic). I will try to discover where their particular insights into the comic fit into an overall conception of comedy, much as one might place the pieces of a puzzle. Merging all the particular theories about the comic to create this overall conception of comedy should be more enlightening than continuing to look at comedy through the narrow slits of each of their distinct viewpoints.[12]

All these previous particular humor theories that I will be synthesizing into a more modern and general humor theory have been traditionally classified into three main groups: *incongruity theories,* developed by Kant and Schopenhauer; *release from restraint (tension relief) theories,* developed by Herbert Spencer and Freud; and *superiority theories,* developed by Aristotle and Hobbes.[13] Although these three theory groups seem to compete with one another, they actually supplement one another by dealing with different aspects of the same basic but complex process: *An individual (1) who perceives through humor an "incongruity" in the outer world, (2) expresses through laughter the "release" or "relief" of being subjectively unaffected by this objective contradiction, and (3) consequently feels his laughingly sustained subjective integration manifests his "superiority" to the humorously disintegrated object.*

This book will explore the first part of this general model: the causes of humor in the incongruities of the external world. I hope someday to be able to explore the rest: the causes of laughter in the response of the inner self to these outer incongruities, and the effects of comedy on various kinds of culture and levels of society.

PART ONE

THE COMIC ATTACK ON CULTURE

Wit's Weapons:
Incongruity and Ambiguity

Those who examine laughter behaviorally might infer that laughter is related to orgasm, for both display similar respiratory staccato, muscular spasms, postural contortions, and facial grimaces. But those who examine laughter phenomenologically will conclude that the laugher and the copulator (see Davis 1983: part 1) have vastly different inner experiences, even if their outer expressions are similar.

Near the beginning of the nineteenth century, the ascendance of a new basic conceptual paradigm—initiated in philosophy and aesthetics mainly by Immanuel Kant—motivated the major thinkers of the time to shift their focus from the objective to the subjective world. The objective world could not be understood in itself, they now felt, because it was determined as much—if not more—by the subject. This Copernican revolution in the history of ideas influenced comic theorists to begin to look for the source of laughter not in the comic object but in the comic subject, shifting their attention from the funny something to the person who finds something funny. The new subjectivist view of comedy was succinctly summed up by Baudelaire: "The comic, the power of laughter, is in the laugher, not at all in the object of laughter" (1972:148). Even today most comic theorists no longer regard the objective world as intrinsically funny but as somehow made funny by its human observers.

In an ancillary section of the *Critique of Judgement* in 1793, Kant himself felt the need to extend his humorless philosophy to laughter, whose source he located in the subject's temporal *expectation:* "Laughter is an affection arising from the sudden transformation of a strained expectation into nothing" (1951:177). From the kernel of this brief definition evolved "incongruity theory," the most influential theory of humor in cognitive psychology today, and the psychological underpinnings for the sociological analysis of humor I will develop here.[1]

In 1819 William Hazlitt elaborated Kant's conception of the comic by contrasting it with its opposite: "To understand or define the ludicrous, we must first know what the serious is." Hazlitt proceeded to identify the serious with the *expected:* "Now the serious is the habitual stress which the mind lays upon the expectation of a given order of events, following one another with a certain regularity and weight of interest attached to them." And the comic with the *unexpected:* "The ludicrous, or comic, is the unexpected loosening or relaxing this stress [on the expected] below its usual pitch of intensity, by such an abrupt transposition of the order of our ideas, as taking the mind unawares, throws it off its guard, startles it into a lively sense of pleasure, and leaves no time nor inclination for painful reflections" (1930; 6:7).

Since the unexpected is an essential feature of humor, comics continually try to undercut their audience's expectations; for instance, by refusing to follow commonplace sentiments:

> My job is simply bringing joy to the wealthy.
>
> [Martin Mull]

emotional presumptions:

> My wife comes home and says, "Pack your bags. I just won $20 million in the California lottery." "Where are we going, Hawaii, Europe?" I ask jubilantly. "I don't know where you're going, Doug, as long as it's out of here."
>
> [Doug Ferrari]

or political platitudes:

> When [Reagan] came into office in 1981, he took an idle nation and restored it to its former glory. Unfortunately, the idle nation was Japan.
>
> [Johnny Steele]

System and Incongruity

For us to be able to expect that "a given order of events follow[s] one another with a certain regularity," the set of events must be arranged according to an orderly plan or *system* in which each element is related to all the others. Systems may be subjective (exist in the mind) or objective (exist in the world). Subjective systems whose interrelated elements cluster coherently have been termed "universes" (Monro 1951:45–46), "frames" (Bateson 1972:177–93; Goffman 1974), "meaning structures" (Zijderveld 1968:290), "associative contexts" (Koestler 1974:6), "scripts" (Raskin 1985:81), as well as "gestalts," "realms," "planes," "grounds," or "schema." (I will usually use all these terms interchangeably, though sometimes employing *system* to emphasize the internal elements' interconnection and *frame* to emphasize their disconnection from external elements.)

If we know the state of one element in a system and the interrelation between all of them, we can anticipate the state of any other element in the system. All the elements of a system, therefore, are potentially predictable.

But the success of our prediction depends on the correlation between our subjective "expectation system" and the objective "real system." [2] For the particular systems I will examine in this book this correlation is far from perfect. The earthquake of humor makes us suddenly conscious of the chasm between them.

"The essence of the laughable," concludes Hazlitt, one of the first to apply the term to humor, "is the *incongruous*" (1930; 6:7). An "incongruity" is supposed to be an element of a system but turns out to be unrelated to all the other interrelated elements of the system. [3] (Thus incongruity is a relational concept: Nothing can be incongruous in itself but only by standing out phenomenologically from an otherwise congruous system.) A real incongruity that deviates from prediction will collapse an orderly expectation system, causing those who had viewed the objective world through this particular subjective frame to laugh. [4]

The mental gestalt of an expectation system is usually delicate. For the system to continue to exist the gestalt must remain whole. Those whose expectation system gestalt becomes incomplete or partial may break up into laughter, as Ralph Waldo Emerson tried to say in the prepsychological vocabulary of the nineteenth century: "It is in comparing fractions with essential integers or wholes that laughter begins. . . . The essence of all jokes, of all comedy, seems to be an honest or well-intended halfness. . . . The balking of the intellect, the frustrated expectation, the break of continuity in the intellect, is comedy; and it announces itself physically in the pleasant spasms we call laughter" (1946:205). By replacing only one congruous element with an incongruous element, humor can disintegrate an expectation system. The humorous incongruity disorders what had been ordered, breaking open the frame and scattering its elements. Erving Goffman calls this loss of frame "negative experience" (1974:378–438), for it takes its character from what it is not—that is, ordered, and therefore expected, experience.

Several characteristics of incongruities and systems *intensify* humor's negative experience. The more incongruities that explode a given expectation system, the funnier. Ethnic jokes, for instance, have been perennially popular in part because they are multi-incongruous, simultaneously undermining egalitarian ideology ("they are as good as us") *and* either cognitive rationality:

> Did you hear about the Pole who locked his family in the car? He had to find a coat hanger to get them out.

or normative mores:

> A Pole walks into a local bar and goes straight up to the bartender, who turns away in disgust at the handful of horseshit the Pole is holding. "Hey, Harry," says the Pole, "look what I almost stepped in."

The correlation between number of incongruities and degree of funniness, however, holds only up to a point. Beyond that point, the audience will no longer be able to figure out what system all these incongruities are supposed to be incongruous to. Psychologist Paul McGhee, a leading expert on children's humor, agrees that too many incongruities spoil the joke:

> Up to a point, the greater the number of characteristics of the object violated, the more incongruous it is (it is not yet clear whether funniness increases directly as a function of the number of incongruous elements).
>
> Beyond this unspecified point, so many elements have been distorted or changed that the child has difficulty recognizing the object; rather than becoming an incongruous depiction of a familiar object, the extremely discrepant depiction of the object is simply perceived as a totally novel and unfamiliar object. This eliminates the funniness. [1979:73]

Not just any incongruous element will detonate a system into laughter. We distinguish "quality humor," in which incongruous elements clash with a system's core characteristics, from "mere silliness," in which they clash with its peripheral aspects. More precisely, rather than being either essential or inessential, a system's elements have *degrees* of essentiality; consequently, the various incongruities that annihilate them produce *degrees* of funniness. Conversely, the larger the laugh, the more essential the system's aspect that must have been annihilated. Mort Sahl, for instance, cuts to the (bleeding) heart of one ideological system:

> A liberal newspaper is one that would report a nuclear exchange between the United States and the Soviet Union with a headline reading, "WORLD ENDS: WOMEN AND MINORITIES HARDEST HIT."

The better-known the system an incongruity makes strange, the more our amusement. Consequently, humor often deforms proverbs and clichés:

> What we do practice extensively in our age is the twisting of proverbs to suit new purposes. . . . As Jacobs recognizes, "a proverb, being a highly conventionalized, fixed formulation, lends itself to distortion." . . . Jacobs quotes as an example, "Many are called but few get the right number." He adds that "the literal significance of a common phrase or proverb can also be evoked by placing it in an unexpected context; as Hamlet's 'O that this too, too solid flesh should melt' sometimes found on weighing scales." [Redfern 1986:150]

How funny we find an incongruity also depends on how firmly we are attached to the expectation system it attacks If we find incongruities that temporarily annihilate our *cognitive* expectation system to be funny, we may find those that temporarily annihilate our *moral* expectation system even funnier. Before the recent liberalization, the emigre Andrei Siniavski reported, Russians valued humor so greatly because Soviet society prohibited so much:

> Perhaps nowhere in the history of letters has the theme of prohibition been so fundamental and forceful as in the Soviet joke. . . . There are taboos on obscenity, political subversion, truth, the state of affairs in general, government secrets. . . . Numerous jokes are structured like taboos, which are then subjected to unceremonious transgression. . . . The joke . . . simply does not exist without crossing into forbidden territory. [1984:356–60]

Normative prohibitions, however, can be too strong for humor just as they can be too weak. We do not find funny an incongruity that breaks up an expectation system to which we are morally committed either very much or very little. Christopher Wilson puts this proposition more technically: "[Social Psychological experiments indicate] an inverted-U shaped relationship of funniness and degree of incongruity. Jokes are moderately incongruous; minimal or extremely high levels of incongruity are unfunny" (1979:150–52).

In short, how funny we find an attempt at humor depends in part on the quantity and quality of its incongruities as well as on our familiarity with and commitment to the expectation system to which they are incongruent.

Systems and Ambiguity

We have located humor's epicenter in the *incongruous* element that shatters an expectation system into nothing. This model of humor focuses on a single system. But many jokes are based on two systems. Since every congruous element can be incongruous somewhere else, humorists also ply their trade by interpolating an element congruous with the other elements of one system into another system where it is *less* congruous or even incongruous. For instance, a humorist may imagine Evelyn Wood expanding her "speed reading" techniques from their original literary home into the realms of art and music:

> Try to grasp the essence of a picture or a piece of music as fast as you can; forget the irrelevant details. You should be able to view an average size museum in fifteen minutes, or hear a Beethoven symphony in ten.

Although it may be appropriate to approach literature (especially nonfiction and light fiction) in such a hasty instrumental way, approaching art or music in this way is ludicrously incongruous with the leisurely aesthetic contemplation usually associated with these quasi-sacred activities.

We can also locate humor's epicenter, then, in the *congruous* element that connects two opposing expectation systems or frames. In this second model, humorists proceed first by showing an element to be congruous with other elements in one system, and then by suddenly showing it to be congruous or even *more* congruous with those in another system:

> A man comes home from work early and takes the elevator up to his seventh-floor apartment. When he gets off the elevator, he notices a smiling man with a big cigar getting on. When he goes into his apartment, he smells smoke and sees some ashes in an ashtray. Since neither he nor his wife smoke, he becomes very suspicious. His suspicions are confirmed when he goes to the bedroom and sees both his bed and his wife in disarray. He runs to the balcony, and sees the smiling man with the big cigar walking out of the building below. Blinded by rage, he picks up a refrigerator (for he is a very strong man) and throws it down on the man with the big cigar, flattening him. His wife runs out of the bedroom and over to the balcony, looks down, sees the dead man, and cries to her husband, "What have you done? I've never seen that man before in my life!" Con-

sumed with remorse for killing an innocent man, the jealous husband jumps over the balcony to his death.

Next scene: the entrance to heaven. Three men encounter St. Peter, who asks them to describe the moment of their death.

First man: I was walking along smoking my favorite cigar, thinking of how good my life is when—bang!—out of the blue something hits me on the head and I'm dead.

Second man: I had just killed a man who I thought had been sleeping with my wife, but discovering I was wrong made me so upset that I killed myself in remorse.

Third man: I don't know what happened. I was hiding in this refrigerator. . . .

In the "single system" model, humor shifts its audience's attention from one system into no system via an *incongruity;* in the "double system" model, humor shifts its audience's attention from one system into another system via an *ambiguity,* an element congruous with both systems—their "overlap point" (Davis 1983:57–58): the refrigerator in the above joke, for example.

Since every *thing* is a nexus of attributes, *everything* is potentially ambiguous, and therefore potentially humorous. For a joke can rotate its audience's attention around an ambiguous object from one attribute (and the entire system associated with it) to another attribute (and the different system associated with it). In the above joke, the second use of "refrigerator" suddenly shifts its audience's focus from its heaviness to its hollowness (and between the systems associated with each). And the following joke hinges on the ambiguity of a grocery store's attributes:

My grandfather was into nostalgia: "I remember when I could go to the corner store and pick up a bag of potato chips and a can of beer and a *Jet Magazine* for 5 cents." "Can't do that now, Grampa, they've got those video surveillance cameras."

[Al Clethen]

As the joke's specification of the store's attributes rotates from its merchandise to its monitors, the frame in which we locate them suddenly shifts from sentimental to larcenous.

Frequently, a joke's attribute rotation will convert a seemingly irrelevant detail into a crucial one:

A Pole who finds himself in Moscow [in the mid-1980's] wants to know the time. He sees a man approaching him carrying two heavy suitcases and asks the fellow if he knows the correct time.

"Certainly," says the Russian, setting down the two bags and looking at his wrist. "It is 11:43 and 17 seconds. The date is Feb. 13, the moon is nearing its full phase and the atmospheric pressure stands at 992 hecto-pascals and is rising."

The Polish visitor is dumbfounded but manages to ask if the watch that provides all this information is Japanese. No, he is told, it is "our own, a product of Soviet technology."

"Well," says the Pole, "that is wonderful, you are to be congratulated."

"Yes," the Russian answers, straining to pick up the suitcases, "but these batteries are still a little heavy."

Here, the transformation of the suitcases from implied travel accessor-ies to revealed watch batteries suddenly shifts our interpretive frame of the society that produced them from hypercompetent to incom-petent.

In brief: *from an expected continuation within one system, the comic mind pivots around an ambiguity to branch off into another system.* In the next chapter, we will see that many ambiguous pivots are merely phonetic:

How many Californians does it take to screw in a light bulb? None. They screw in hot tubs.

The subtler ones, however, are more semantic:

Well, it's hard to find a good relationship. Recently, I took this one girl home and put on "We Are the World," hoping it would put her in a giving mood. Instead, she got hungry."

[Garry Shandling]

Arthur Koestler was the best-known modern exponent of the view that humor is produced by the intersection of systems or frames,[5] which he called "associative contexts":

It is the sudden clash between these two mutually exclusive codes of rules—or associative contexts—that produces the comic effect. It compels the listener to perceive the situation in two self-consistent but incompatible frames of reference at the same time; his mind has to operate simultaneously on two dif-ferent wavelengths. While this unusual condition lasts, the event is not only, as is normally the case, associated with a single frame of reference, but "bisociated" with two. The term bisociation was coined by the present writer to make a distinc-tion between the routines of disciplined thinking within a single universe of discourse—on a single plane, as it were—and the creative types of mental activity that always operate on more than one plane. In humor, both the *creation* of a subtle joke and the *re-creative* act of perceiving the joke involve the delightful mental jolt of a sudden leap from one plane or asso-ciative context to another. [1974: 5-6]

Sociologists have tried to sociologize the humorous shift between frames of reference. William Cameron provided an example of a humorous shift between the frames of urban and rural reference groups:

> A fundamental concept in social psychology is that of the frame of reference, and related to it, the reference group. These twin notions are highly useful in examining jokes. Many jokes derive their effect by contrasting two different frames of reference in which something would be appropriate to one is mistaken and inappropriate to the other. . . .
>
> > There was a young man from the city,
> > Who saw what he thought was a kitty.
> > He gave it a pat, but it wasn't a cat,
> > And we buried his clothes out of pity.
>
> The man from the city, with an urban frame of reference, wrongly defined the real situation involving the skunk, with disastrous results. . . . Perhaps the reader identifies with the rural population and exults when vaunted urban superiority takes a fall. [1963:85–86][6]

A few years later, Anton Zijderveld provided an example of a humorous shift between the frames of adult and child social categories (although his example shifts them not within the joke itself but between its tellers).

> Joking is defined as the conscious or unconscious transition from one institutionalized meaning structure to another, without changing much of the original role behavior and logic. . . .
>
> A zote is a risqué, sexual joke. . . . An old and stale zote told by somebody who obviously tries to be funny . . . is nothing to laugh about. Such a stale joke is common property, whereas a joke, on the contrary, draws its power from being new and rare. If, however, this stale zote is all of a sudden told by a child of five or six, who obviously does not know what he is talking about, but tells it in order to look like an adult, the entire situation changes completely. . . . the stale joke is transported by the child from one frame of reference to another and gains by that new substance and meaning. The old zote has become a joke again. It is funny not because of the original substance and meaning, but because the narrator is still a child. [1968:290–91]

Unfortunately, neither Cameron nor Zijderveld were able to convince other social scientists to examine the social implications of humorous shifts between systems or frames.

The linguist Victor Raskin recently translated Koestler's gestalt-based psychological theory of humor into a "script-based semantic theory" of humor, which has been far more influential: "first, in order to be a joke, any text should be partially or fully compatible with two different scripts and secondly, a special relation of script oppositeness should obtain between the two scripts" (1985:xiii).[7] Raskin analyzes jokes into the paired opposing scripts whose conjunction produces them; for instance finding a Doctor [instrumental] script and a Lover [erotic] script in the following example:

> "Is the doctor at home?" the patient asked in his bronchial whisper: "No," the doctor's young and pretty wife whispered in reply: "Come right in."

The semantic "trigger" for switching scripts is the joke's *ambiguity* (or negatively its *contradiction*) (1985:114ff.). Raskin applies his theory specifically to sexual, ethnic, and political humor to "disambiguate" them into their various paired opposite scripts.[8]
I will contribute to this tradition by distinguishing more abstract oppositional entities than Raskin does when he analyzes humor into the opposing scripts whose conjunction creates it.

Several characteristics of ambiguities and systems *intensify* humor's dislocatory experience. Compared to more contemplative activities like art or science, comedy pivots its audience's attention between systems *quickly*. Wit, in particular, is the ability to rapidly discover and articulate the common ambiguous element in seemingly different systems. In 1690, John Locke (following Hobbes) compared synthetic "wit" to analytic "judgement" (which he clearly preferred) in a definition which would be influential, if not fully accepted (see Martin 1974), for two hundred years:

> [Wit lies] most in the assemblage of ideas, and putting those together with quickness and variety wherein can be found any resemblance or congruity, thereby to make up pleasant pictures and agreeable visions in the fancy; judgement, on the contrary, lies quite on the other side, in separating carefully one from another ideas wherein can be found the least difference, thereby to avoid being misled by similitude and by affinity to take one thing for another. [1939:280][9]

In 1711, Addison in *The Spectator* (no. 62) supplemented Locke's definition of wit by stressing that the resemblance must be unexpected: "It is necessary that the Ideas should not lie too near one another in the Nature of things; for where the Likeness is obvious, it gives no Surprize" (1965:264). An article in the *British Quarterly Review* a century later reverses perspective on wit's perspective reversal, from what wit combines to what had kept them apart. The anonymous author finds exactly the right image for the "shock of agreeable surprise" produced by wit's "original and striking comparison": "It is as if a partition-wall in our intellect was suddenly blown out; two things formerly strange to one another have flashed together" (quoted in Martin 1974:43).[10]

Comics need find only one element that ambiguously connects two seemingly different systems to raise a laugh. For instance, those who use the term *nail* metaphorically as sexual slang to describe an erotic coupling in terms of a mechanical one may provoke a slight smirk (at least among adolescent boys preoccupied with both kinds of couplings, however contradictory the mind-set each requires). But those who attempt to extend the comparison between the two systems over more than one element may prolong a larger laugh.[11] One comic connected two types of intimate relations with two types of metallic fasteners:

> Girls used to get *pinned* in high school, now they get *nailed.*
>
> [Bill Maher]

And this apocryphal newspaper headline managed to connect an escaped mental patient who raped a woman with three types of metallic fasteners: Nut Bolts and Screws (Redfern 1986:120). Koestler observed that the archetypical, if not the longest, sustained humorous comparison between two incompatible realms—fantasy and reality—is *Don Quixote:*

> Jokes and anecdotes have a single point of culmination. The literary forms of *sustained humor,* such as the picaresque novel, do not rely on a single effect but on a series of minor climaxes. The narrative moves along a line of intersection of contrasted planes—e.g., the fantasy world of Don Quixote and the cunning horse-sense of Sancho Panza—or is made to oscillate between them; as a result tension is continuously generated and discharged in mild amusement. [1974:8]

Jack Mingo (1983) provides a more contemporary example of sustained humorous comparison in *The Official Couch Potato Handbook* by pointing out the isomorphism between the category of human TV watchers and the category of "potatoes." Mingo equates various types of potatoes with various types of TV viewers: "M*A*S*H Potatoes" are those addicted to that TV sitcom and other sophisticated comedy shows, "Red-Eyed Potatoes" are those addicted to late night TV viewing, etc. The comic form that transposes elements between the styles of individuals or social realms in the most sustained manner is parody.

The best parodies suggest a secret similarity between realms presumed to be very different, such as religion and computers:

> [Jeffrey Armstrong] is rewriting the Bible and recasting famous prayers. Dubbing himself St. Silicon, savior of data, he represents CHIP (Church of Heuristic Information Processing). . . .
>
> Armstrong has redone the psalms, turned the commandments into commands. . . . He said that his Eastern religion helpmates have designed the perfect new mantra for meditators too. It goes: "OEM, RAM. ROM, EPROM." . . .
>
> He plans to market a set of binary rosary beads, too. "There's a zero on one bead and a one on the other," he said. . . .
>
> One of his favorite prayers is Hail Memory:
> Hail Memory.
> Full of space.
> The motherboard is with thee.
> Blessed art thou amongst micros.
> And blessed is the fruit of thy processor: data.
> Holy memory.
> Motherboard of ROM.
> Pray for us beginners.
> Now and at the hour of our sign-off.
> Enter.
>
> All of his prayers end with "Enter" or "Return." His favorite saying is the golden rule of St. Silicon: Do unto your data that you were able to undo.
>   [John Dvorak, *San Francisco Examiner*, 9 Mar. 1986, D3]

Sex is so multifarious an activity that it is relatively easy to sustain the correspondence between its elements and those of other realms. In HBO's "This Was Burlesque" (Nov. 1983), some bellboys, listening at the door of the hotel room of a married couple, mistake the couple's conversation about trying to close a suitcase with conversation about sex:

> "You get on top."
> "No, You get on top."
> "Let's both get on top!"

Only the last line makes the bellboys realize, after momentarily trying to stretch its application, that their sexual interpretation must be inappropriate. Since Freud, in fact, it has become so common to interpret jokes sexually (more technically, to map their ambiguous elements isomorphically onto a sexual plane) that it now comes as an amusing surprise when the connection between a series of seemingly sexual elements turns out to be more innocent:

Question: "What is it that Gorbachev has a long one, Bush has a short one, the Pope has one but doesn't use it, and Madonna doesn't have one?"
Answer: "A last name."

[Leslie Gibbon]

Amateur comedians usually joke about a variety of topics; professionals who have their act together often restrict their humor to variations on a single theme. Those unable to sustain the systematic comparison between two realms (as above) may maintain the easier comparison between a single realm and various other realms—sandblasting the base realm with elements derived from the secondary realms. By using these external elements to bring out ambiguities, the comic can chisel away at a topic from various directions like a sculptor. But unlike the sculptor who begins with a formless matter and gradually clarifies its edges, the comedian begins with what his audience believed to be a clear subject matter and proceeds to blur its edges, making ambiguous what his audience thought they clearly understood. With this defocusing comic technique in mind, listen to Lenny Bruce destabilize his early 1960s audience's already precarious puritanical views even further:

> That's why they don't like Americans anywhere . . . —because [in World War II] we fucked all of their mothers for chocolate bars. . . .
> If this society was the least little bit correct, if religion helped it out a little bit, and that act was the least bit the antithesis of what is perverse, and you felt that it was a true Christian act of procreation, if it was sweet hugging and kissing—watch. The fellow comes off the plane:
> *British voice:* Is that the fellow who fucked Mother? Oh, yes! How are you? *Damn,* I haven't seen you in *so* long, and you're such a *wonderful* person. You certainly made Mother feel *good.* I certainly would like to *thank* you—that certainly was a nice thing to do. And I understand you gave her some candy besides.
> But we don't agree that it's a nice act. It's a filthy, dirty act. In fact, that's what any eighteen-year-old chick or thirty-year-old chick will tell you when you take her out:
> "You don't *love* me, you just want to *ball* me."
> Boy! Listen to that:
> *Girl:* He was a *nice* guy—he didn't try to fool around with me. But *you* don't love me, you just want to ball me.
> *Guy: What?* Of course I love you—I wouldn't want to sleep with you if I didn't love you.
> *Girl:* No, no. If you loved me you'd drive me to Wisconsin; punch me in the mouth; read the Bible to me all night; you'd borrow money from me.

> You wouldn't want to ball me. You don't do that to someone you love—
> you do that to somebody you hate. Really *hate*.
> In fact, when you *really* hate them, what's the vernacular we use?
> "*Screw you*, mister!"
> If you were taught it was a sweet Christian act of procreation, it was the
> nicest thing we can do for each other, you'd use the term correctly, and
> say
> "*Unscrew you*, mister!"
>
> [Lenny Bruce]

The audience's response to the monologist's humor mirrors the children's response to the psychologist's humor encountered in the previous section. The psychologist presented the children with many incongruities simultaneously, *before* they were able to recognize what these incongruities were supposed to be incongruous to. Unable to construct a coherent expectation system, the children didn't find funny the incongruities that undermined it. The monologist articulated many ambiguities that undermined his topic sequentially, *after* his audience had already possessed a coherent expectation system for it. By the end of his monologue, much of his audience could no longer recognize what they had been laughing at.

Incongruities and Ambiguities

The comic has been difficult to comprehend because it conflates the two models implicit in the following eighteenth-century aphorism: "Wit consists in discerning the resemblance between diverse things, and the difference between similar things" (Montesquieu [?]). *Incongruity* is related to the second part of this definition: the real difference between things that seem alike. An element of a system that is sufficiently unlike its other elements can destroy an audience's perception of the system's integrity. *Ambiguity* is related to the first part of this definition: the real resemblance between things that seem to differ. An element of one system that is sufficiently like the elements of a second system can also destroy an audience's perception of the first system's integrity. In short, incongruities, which emphasize internal differences, produce humor by fitting too poorly in a system; ambiguities, which emphasize external similarities, produce humor by fitting too well in too many systems. Most people find the combination of incongruity and ambiguity (ordinary jokes) funnier than either incongruity (nonsense humor) or ambiguity (bad puns) alone.

Some humor, then, annihilates a single system with an *incongruity*. The audience for this "annihilated single system" model of humor suddenly sees that one element in an otherwise coherent system is incongruous with it. But they never resolved the incongruity, for the system is destroyed without being replaced by another one. Consequently, the audience never restores its cognitive equilibrium.[12] Other humor transposes a double system with an *ambiguity*. The audience for this "transposed double system" model of humor also suddenly sees that one element in an otherwise coherent system is not as congruous with it as they believed, at least not uniquely so. But they resolve the incongruity by reconceiving the element from the perspective of a second system, to which the element is ambiguously related. (Most of the other elements of the second system, however, are incongruous with the first.) Consequently, the audience restores its cognitive equilibrium by switching systems.[13]

"Shaggy dog stories," by the way, are those drawn-out pointless jokes that continually imply that their tellers will soon shift the system, soon resolve the incongruity, soon restore the audience's cognitive equilibrium—but they never do. Thus shaggy dog stories transform the expected "transposed double system" humor into "annihilated single system" humor.

It is easier to distinguish these two models in theory than in practice because it is sometimes difficult to distinguish incongruities within each system from incongruities between each system. It is more productive to distinguish these two models according to whether the difference or similarity, frames or switch point, incongruity or ambiguity stands out phenomenologically in a particular instance of humor. In general, it is better to analyze humor whose *form* is more prominent (for example, linguistic humor) in terms of ambiguity, and humor whose *content* is more prominent (ethnic humor) in terms of incongruity. Consequently, I will employ both these models, pointing out incongruities or ambiguities, depending on the particular type or aspect of humor I am dealing with.

The Humorizer

The general technique comics use to explode phenomena into laughter I will call the "humorizer," as in "Let's put it through the humorizer to see if we can make it funny." Humorists use the humorizer to rub various things against their topic until they find one that can scratch off its attributes into incongruities or ambiguities or preferably both, generating the spark of laughter.

The humorizer may produce humor by continually juxtaposing phenomena until a pair appears whose attributes are incongruous. For example, a computer that randomly joins objects or processes assembled the following novel pairs:

Comic Headlines:
  Scientists Discover New Moon Orbiting Kate Smith
  Tornado Kills Five, Self
Diseases:
  Athlete's Brain
  Cheese-in-Mouth Disease
New Inventions:
  Emergency Dribble Mug
  I. Q. Retardant
Gourmet Items:
  Insect Brittle
  Endangered Species Au Gratin
  Fur-Ball Shortcake

[John Swartzwelder, *Playboy*, Dec. 1982, 32]

Since most paired objects or processes randomly joined by a computer are irrelevant to each other, their juxtaposition produces at best nonsense humor. But I selected the above pairs from the author's selection of the computer's random output because I felt they were funnier than mere nonsense. Each pair contains subtle congruous elements that hold it together, implying an encompassing system that articulates its incongruous elements. This use of the humorizer recalls Kenneth Burke's "perspective by incongruity" (1965:71–124), which involves "the merging of categories once felt to be mutually exclusive" (69).[14]

The humorizer may also produce humor by searching out a topic's ambiguities, which relate it to other phenomena, especially those differently evaluated. In the above monologue Lenny Bruce articulated the ambiguities that connect problematic copulation to pleasurable procreation. This use of the humorizer employs what I will call "perspective by ambiguity." Sociologist Donald Levine has argued most persuasively that modern science, especially modern social science, has overlooked ambiguity's heuristic value:

> Literary ambiguity signifies the property of words or sentences of admitting more than one interpretation; experiential ambiguity signifies a property possessed by any stimuli of having two or more meanings or even simply of being unclear as to meaning. . . . Now I wish to posit a connection between the two modalities of ambiguity by asserting that the ambiguities of life are systematically underrepresented, when they are not ignored altogether, by methodologies oriented to constructing facts through strictly univocal modes of representation. [1985:8]

More than any other kind of current commentator on human existence, humorists bring out its multiple interpretations and meanings.

In the 1930s Burke analogized perspective by incongruity to "the same 'cracking' process that chemists now use in their refining of oil" (1965:119).[15] I would also analogize perspective by ambiguity to the same process, though it produces different distillates. Today we would compare both perspectives to a particle accelerator that splits apart a physical phenomenon to reveal its components. Humor, in short, can reveal the components of a nonphysical phenomenon by exploding it; the humorizer is the closest thing to an atom smasher the nonphysical sciences have.

Comic Defects of Particular Systems

Although this book is neither a history nor an anthropology of humor, let me briefly and broadly delineate humor's cross-temporal and cross-social generality to locate this book's approach to humor on these dimensions. Obviously, different periods, subgroups, and societies find different things funny: they designate different elements incongruous and ambiguous because they have different expectations systems these elements violate. Yet this temporal and social variability does not preclude the possibility that at least *some* aspects of the expectation systems violated by incongruities and ambiguities are enduring and universal. Joyce Hertzler distinguishes humor found funny by only specific eras and groups, which he terms "laughter singularities," from humor found funny by almost everyone, which he terms "laughter universals" (1970:61).

Since expectation systems change, the incongruities and ambiguities that once made them funny are ephemeral. Either figure or ground in humor may become obsolete. The wit who epigrammatized, "Harold Garfinkle is the Charles Manson of sociology," won't live to know whether the twenty-first century has ever have heard of Harold Garfinkle, has to look up Charles Manson, or even knows what sociology is. No area of a used bookstore is more joyless than its humor section, whose once-brightly colored now-faded books are rarely perused. Although new humor books sell better than nearly any other book category, old ones retain little interest. Even those who intellectually understand their references often find their humor more annoying than amusing. Their authors now seem to try too hard to be funny—though of course they didn't then—because the expectation systems they tried to explode now lack the immediacy and relevance of living expectation systems. The tragedy of comedy is that it helps bring about the very social change that renders it passé.

Hertzler describes the humor based on these ephemeral expectation systems: "each era . . . has its own conditions and themes for laughter—its own run of attention—because of the major preoccupations, concerns, interests, activities, relations, and modes prevailing at the time. . . . There are . . . vogue and fad themes of the moment: what is fashionable or 'in' as humorous or ludicrous" (1970:56, 58). He traces out the succession of transient humor themes in American society: from the "hunters, frontiersmen, and backwoodsmen" jokes of the early nineteenth century, through the urban versus rural jokes of the late nineteenth century ("country rubes or bumpkins, hayseeds, and clodhoppers" versus "city slickers and smart alecks"), through the immigrant and dialect jokes of the early twentieth century, to the war jokes periodically punctuating the midtwentieth century—to mention only a few (1970:56–58).[16] On the other hand, Hertzler also lists some lasting subjects of hilarity in American society, "such as insults, sex, vanity, masqueraders and pompous persons, matrimonial relations, bad manners, scatological acts, foreigners, sometimes categories of persons, such as priests and preachers or teachers" (1970:61–62). Thus, at any one time, American humor comprises both "topical humor," based on transient surface incongruities and ambiguities in our society, and "perennial humor," based on its enduring structural incongruities and ambiguities (see Freud 1963:122). Bridging topical and perennial humor are what Cameron calls "retreads," in which the comic dresses traditional incongruities and ambiguities in contemporary clothes. "He mentions that old military jokes are reissued with each war (reflecting new conditions, personnel, enemy, material, etc.), and some drunk jokes have been rerun as narcotic jokes and beatnik jokes" (Cameron 1963:93; Hertzler 1970:62). Other retreads have been noted: "The moron jokes of the 40's . . . became, with little alteration, the Polish jokes of the 70's, just as the sick jokes of the 50's became the dead-baby jokes of the 80's" (Jack Rosenthal, New York Times, 31 Aug. 1983, 24).

Contemporary American society has increasingly differentiated into antagonistic sociological categories—especially ages, genders (including sexual orientations), races, and ethnic groups (particularly the newer nonwhite ethnics)—and inward looking "life-style" associations (yuppies, joggers, computer hackers, etc.). This social segmentation, together with specialized magazines and newsletters that cater to each of these population segments, has increased indigenous laughter singularities. Conversely, the growing dominance of national television and cable networks over regional media, metropolitan areas over small towns, the middle class over other classes, and the assimilated over the ethnic (particularly the older white ethnics) has increased laughter universals encompassing our whole society. Thus today American comedy schizophrenically encompasses both the humor that appeals only to "laughter sects" and the humor that results in "choral laughter" (Hertzler 1970:202).

Bridging laughter sects and choral laughter are what I will call "rezones," the spatial analog of Cameron's temporal retreads, in which the traveling comic translates jokes between laughter sects by localizing their references. The separate humors of the parts and the whole also feed on one another, for each sect laughs at the ignorance of all outsiders while the overall chorus laughs at the narrowness of each sect.

Hertzler pursues the issue of humor's generality to the world level, distinguishing the worldwide factors that increase laughter singularities—the rise of new nations and regional blocks—from those that increase laughter universals: "the modern technologies of mass communication, mass production, distribution, advertising, and consumption, and the increasing and areally extending mobility of people and things, increasing urbanization, mass leisure, mass entertainment and amusement, mass art, and even mass government create common situations prevailing over great areas that inevitably produce common types of humorous reactions" (1970:201). Although refraining from declaring laughter universals the winner, Hertzler does point to the growing number of "world jokes," which concern urban life (crowding, traffic, etc.), new gadgets and "technoways," clothing, stratification, and sports (1970:201).

Today, expectation systems are still so various that not everything is funny to everyone. There is always someone trying seriously to defend or indifferently to ignore what someone else is trying humorously to undermine. But if in the future a single expectation system were ever to become dominant worldwide (as in some science fiction scenarios), mankind's entire mental life could become vulnerable to sudden and total collapse by a joke.

Comic Defects of General Systems

Since humor breaks down an expectation system by replacing congruous elements with incongruous ones, it informs us—indirectly— which elements belong in the system and which do not. Whatever threatens the system's continued existence is obviously out of place in it. As the phenomenological psychologist Kurt Riezler pointed out,

> incongruity presupposes an order relative to which it is incongruous. Nightshirt and sword, dignity and slippers are incongruous. The fat man does not fit the small chair. In life man,

the miserable and awkward being, is tripped ever and again in such discrepancies. A dignitary should be dignified even in slippers. A man solemnly uses words he does not know how to pronounce. Finding such discrepancies ridiculous, we assume that man's things and acts should fit one another; that the fat man should sit in a large chair and that men's ambitions should correspond with their stature. [1950:171]

But Riezler continues: "Since the . . . kinds of order we accept in finding incongruities ridiculous are not of equal rank, the ridiculous itself is not of equal rank. . . . Though humor denies that the customary order is a matter of course, it need not make explicit the order on the basis of which it denies the customary order" (1950:173–74). One task of the humor theorist is to discover the order attacked by the humorous incongruity. This order may be on the level of the particular phenomenon or the general system.

Because humorists have had relatively low status and philosophers relatively high status (at least until recently), most people—including most philosophers and humorists—have been unaware of their similarities. But like philosophers, humorists try to discover the essential nature of phenomena. By using the humorizer technique, humorists become, in effect, dialectical phenomenologists. Unlike traditional phenomenologists who slowly and deliberately pare away a phenomenon's unnecessary attributes to reveal its essence, dialectical phenomenologists continually juxtapose one phenomenon's attributes with another's to find its "anti-essence," the attribute that differs so much from the other attributes that it detonates the phenomenon into laughter. The explosion of laughter that results from adding an incongruous element to a phenomenon indicates that the opposite element must be essential to the perception of that phenomenon.

Consider, for example, what the following pieces of humor reveal about the role of the psychiatrist:

> I was a psychiatrist, but that didn't work because I really hated people. My motto was "I have my own problems. If you can't handle yours, try alcohol. I do."
>
> [Geoff Bold]

> I don't get no respect. My psychiatrist said to me, "Maybe life isn't for everyone."
>
> [Rodney Dangerfield]

Those who laugh at these jokes must characterize a psychiatrist as altruistic rather than egoistic, philanthropic rather than misanthropic, realistic rather than escapist, and life-affirming rather than life-denying. Their contradistinctions manifest the humanism inherent in the core definition of the psychiatric role far more forcefully than any direct description of its nature would have done.[17]

Humorists determine a phenomenon's essential characteristics through ambiguity as well as incongruity. If humorists show a phenomenon's *incongruous* attributes to be *not innate,* they show its *ambiguous* attributes to be *not unique.* An ambiguous attribute cannot characterize a particular phenomenon essentially because it also belongs to other phenomena.

More explicitly than the humorists themselves, humor theorists can articulate the particular phenomenon disintegrated by comic incongruities and ambiguities, and locate it in the larger orders that humor threatens.[18] In the last section, we examined historical and anthropological humor research that used humor to uncover the values, manners, concerns, and conditions of a specific society. (Most nonpsychological and nonlinguistic humor research is of this kind.) But humor often goes beyond the local time and place in which it appeared. "Through their peculiar closeness to the circumstances that produced them, comedies have registered the imprint of their times and places. . . . Devised to meet particular occasions, comedy outlives them by appealing to broad universals" (Levin 1987:5). I will study instances of humor, then, less to discover the features of our specific society that led to their special creation than to discover the abstract universal properties of society that allow the creation of humor in general.[19]

In the rest of this book, I will try to delineate the larger orders comedy undermines, which can be discovered even in its very origins: "Recent research into the actors of ancient Greece suggests that in its earliest sense the *komos* (the word which gave rise to the term "comedy") was a drunken phallus-bearing procession in honor of Dionysus, involving merry "disordered" songs and dances as well as ritualized insults directed at unpopular members of the population" (Palmer 1988:120). Analyzing this image into the orders it contradicts, we find:

1. "songs and dances" imply *linguistic* (including kinesic) disorder
2. "drunkenness" implies *logical* disorder
3. humanization and sexualization of the Gods implies *anthropological* disorder
4. "ritualized insults directed at unpopular members of the population" implies *social* disorder

Thus comedy, from its inception, has undermined the cultural order—particularly its linguistic, logical, and anthropological systems—and the social order.[20]

Describing humor's assault on the *social* order will be the chief concern of this book. But because any particular joke may threaten several systems simultaneously, and because the collapse of some has repercussions on the stability of others, part 1 will describe humor's assault on the *cultural* order that overlays it.

Let's get cracking!

1

Unstable Meanings

We saw in the introduction to this part that whatever disrupts an interconnected expectation system can be funny. We will examine in this chapter the features of language that humorously disrupt linguistic systems. Linguistic humor deserves prime position in chapter 1 because it underlies all the humor that disrupts other cultural and social systems. If the pun is "the lowest form of humor," it is the foundation of all wit (see Redfern 1986:7–8; Nilsen 1989).

Linguistic humor is basic because the humor of these other systems is expressed largely through language. But language is not merely a medium for extralinguistic humor, it possesses intrinsic humor-producing properties—far more than other media whose humor emanates mainly from extrinsic sources, such as the *performance* incongruities of music (for example, Victor Borge's pratfalls while playing "serious" piano pieces) and the *content* incongruities of art (for example, the earthy mustache on the saintly Mona Lisa). Although important for humor theory, I will consider the humor-producing properties of language more cursorily than those of the other systems, not because I'm "anti-semantic" (see below), but because more researchers are currently studying linguistic humor than other kinds of humor.[1]

Despite the doubts of children and foreigners trying to learn it, language is generally an ordered system: a structured, rule-governed combination of elements (Hertzler 1970:176; Pepicello and Weisberg 1983:74). Language, however, also comprises some exceptions to and equivocalities in its rules. These very incongruities and ambiguities, which make language so exasperatingly unintelligible for novices, make it so potentially funny for advanced students.

Since we can discover the rules of a system by observing their humorous violations, as we saw in the introduction to part 1, we can discover the rules of the linguistic system by observing the ways certain usages of language generate laughter by violating them:

> So an investigation of what verbal performances we find amusing may be expected to lead to the discovery of the rules being violated. What is interesting about taking this route is that the point of a joke or of a humorous remark may not always be explicable in terms of *antecedently* understood rules. In many cases, rules, conventions, maxims, and other aspects of language are *brought to light* in the process of providing a satisfactory explanation of what makes something funny. [Goldstein 1990:39][2]

The main rule of language violated by linguistic humor, we shall see, was first proposed, to my knowledge, by the poet W. H. Auden: "It is a law of language that any given verbal sound always means the same thing and only that thing" (1962:379–80).[3] Those who want to analyze linguistic humor, then, must show how it violates Auden's "one sound, one meaning" rule by being either "one sound, several meanings" or "several sounds, one meaning."

In the first section, we will examine violations of this rule at various linguistic levels. In the second section, we will examine how punsters and antipunsters react to these rule violations.

Levels of Linguistic Humor

As the heterogeneous composite of several relatively homogeneous languages, English is more amenable to word play than other European tongues, which are more monomorphic.[4] The historical development of English encouraged punning by producing many homonyms:

> During the Middle English period the possibilities of punning had been vastly increased as a result of the wholesale importation of Romance loan-words into the language. The excessive Latinization of the vocabulary during the Renaissance had the same effect. The consequent wealth of synonyms, which from then on became a permanent characteristic of English, brought with it an increasing differentiation in usage as well as in meaning and connotation, which was eminently favorable to punning and other forms of conscious or unconscious verbal ambiguity including malapropisms. No less is this true of the

revolutionary changes in pronunciation that English under-
went at the beginning of the fifteenth century and through
which it acquired many new homonyms. [Helge Kökeritz,
quoted in Redfern 1986:47]

and many paranyms (near homonyms): "One significant outcome [of
being a linguistic melting pot] is the availability of numerous similar
monosyllabic words (e.g., pat, pet, pit, pot, put) which obviously facilitate approximate wordplay" (Redfern 1986:160). English reached its
current potential to generate a plethora of puns when printing imposed on this verbal profusion its visual constraints: "As Hugh Kenner
points out, 'Printing and its by-product lexicography enforced a uni-
formity of spelling which gave each word a stable identity to the eye,
whatever it equivocal status for the ear'" (Redfern 1986:28).

The pun, Walter Redfern notes, "is a post-Renaissance word, and an
inaccurate but convenient tag for a whole variety of rhetorical devices
which play on words" (1986:6). These rhetorical devices that constitute
punning are difficult to distinguish, but recent advances in linguistics
have clarified some of them. Language, we now understand, is a complex but ordered system, organized on several different levels: phonological (sound), morphological (meaning), lexical (word), syntactical
(sentence structure), and semantic (sentence meaning) (Hertzler
1970:176). Each level is a uniquely organized system whose characteristic ambiguities and incongruities produce its distinctive kinds of humor (Pepicello and Weisberg 1983:66–67). Unfortunately, different linguists distinguish slightly different linguistic levels, and therefore
analyze a particular piece of humor into different ambiguities and incongruities. Rather than try to resolve their disagreement over the correct classification system (see Pepicello and Weisberg 1983 and Attardo
1988), I will assemble a simple heuristic one that systematically accounts for the most provocative examples.

Humorous Sounds

Some human sounds, of course, are funny in themselves: the "k"-
sound (Fry 1968:33) (a back-of-the-mouth sound incongruous to the
more frequent front-of-the-mouth sounds), imitating natural or mechanical sounds (inhuman sounds incongruous to human ones),
speaking too loud or soft or too high or low (extremes incongruous to
the vocal mean), or rhyming excessively:

I talk too much so I joined a self-help group: *On and On Anon.*
[Evan Davis]

Humorous Meanings

Extreme amounts of meaning can produce the equivalent morphological incongruities. Hertzler gives an example of too little meaning: "Verbosity itself—a muchness of language, a blitz of words—may be funny to many":

> A man who lisped was telling an acquaintance about a third man who "talked and talked and talked!' The acquaintance asked: "What did he talk about?' The lisped reply: "He didn't thay!"
>
> [1970:185]

The opposite of such verbosity is taciturnity, primarily found in old jokes about President Calvin Coolidge:

> A Washington matron once boasted she could make President Calvin Coolidge talk. Cornering him at a dinner, she sought to make good her boast. "Oh, Mr. President," she said, trying to disarm him with frankness, "I have made a bet that I can make you say at least three words." "You lose," Coolidge replied."

Humorous Words

Language, however, derives most of its unique humor from *ambiguity* of form, unlike other systems whose main sources of humor are incongruities of content. Language humor is centered in the ambiguous *word*, at the junction between its sound and its meaning—in the "pun" in its purest sense. "When the ambiguity in a sentence can be isolated in one word, then we have a pun; for example, 'Australians are the finest people in the world because they were chosen by the best *judges* in England'" [L. G. Kelly, quoted in Redfern 1986:10; emphasis added]. Freud gives many examples of puns. For instance:

> A doctor, as he came away from a lady's bedside, said to her husband with a shake of his head, "I don't like her *looks*." "I've not liked her looks for a long time," the husband hastened to agree
>
> [1963:37; emphasis added].

The pun, Freud observes, shifts our usual focus of attention from a word's meaning to its sound. "In one group of these jokes (play upon words) the technique consisted in focusing our psychical attitude upon the *sound* of the word instead of upon its *meaning*—in making the (acoustic) word-presentation itself take the place of its significance as given by its relations to thing-presentations" (1963:119). Putting the matter more clearly, psychotherapist Silvano Arieti describes the pun as "focusing on the . . . verbalization and giving less importance to the connotation" or as an "altered connotation-verbalization balance" (1976:77–82, 107).

Koestler defines the pun as "two disparate strings of thought tied with an acoustic knot" (1974:8).[5] Developing his metaphor, we may distinguish word-based puns according to the "tightness" of the acoustic knot. The less similar the sounds, the looser the meanings, the weaker the ambiguity, and the poorer the pun. Consequently, I will classify word-based linguistic humor according to the closeness of the sounds that connect meanings. Since inconsistencies in terminology have obscured the relation between these categories, I will standardize their names to show their systematic relation (while giving their more common names in parentheses).

A. Monophones (polysemes): one word, one sound, different meanings.[6] The dictionary definition of a word usually lists several meanings, sometimes unrelated to one another.[7] In ordinary language, only one meaning of a word is relevant. In the pun, two (or more) meanings are relevant. "If it were true that a word always offered all its meanings at the same time, we would experience nonstop in conversation the irritating impression produced by a string of puns" (J. Vendryès, quoted in Redfern 1986:180–81). Each meaning of the punned word makes sense in the sentence, although very different sense. In Freud's joke above, as Arieti points out (1976:107), the doctor uses the word looks to mean "physical health" whereas the husband uses the same word to mean "attractiveness." "Punning," observes Redfern, "is the art of superimposing. . . . Like a bus or a sandwich, the pun is a double-decker. As in an air-jam, meanings are stratified, stacked vertically. As a result, we get simultaneous, competing references in the same unit" (1986:26). (Children, in fact, learn that words have more than one meaning largely through their linguistic humor.)

Usually we have little trouble deciding which meaning of a word its speaker intends because some of its meanings are more common than others. Consider the ubiquitous contest phrase "Void where prohibited." The contest organizers intend us to understand void in its frequently used contractual meaning, "of no legal force; not binding; invalid." But void also has a less frequently used biological meaning, "to discharge urine or feces," tempting unintended interpretations of the contest rules.

Sexual connotations, which lurk in many secondary meanings (especially of transitive verbs [Redfern 1986:170]), often take precedence unexpectedly, as in these inadvertent puns:

> A contestant on a quiz program was asked, "What do you find on pool tables that you find in men's trousers?" The answer should have been pockets.

> "Friday is poultry night—remember all ladies present will get a free goose. That is, all ladies will get a goose for free."

Indeed, "Berloquin detects the strength of a pun as lying in 'the gap [that is, incongruity] between the banality of what is said and the shock of what is hinted'" (Redfern 1986:154). An austere admonition, for instance, can be undercut by a lascivious implication:

> Bill Alvarado caught Dr. Dean Edell on KGO radio answering a question about genital enlargement surgery thisaway: "Before subjecting yourself to such a procedure, think about it long and hard."
>
> [Herb Caen]

When none of the meanings of a word is primary, the context or situation determines the intended meaning.[8] Thus *reservations* means "qualms," except in settings where it means "set aside and held for." A comedian who disregards these locational cues can opt for its psychological meaning:

> *Maitre de:* "Do you have any reservations?"
> *Customer:* "No, I'm fairly certain I want to eat here."

Wit is, in part, the facility to show that a secondary meaning of a word is more appropriate to the immediate situation than its primary meaning—Groucho Marx's forte. "Groucho Marx is generally acknowledged to have been a gifted wit, and a great deal of his humor—like that of the comic genius S. J. Perelman—involved nothing more than the manipulation of words, or the sudden revelation that a word has more than one meaning."

> When a young Dick Cavett told Groucho, on the occasion of their first meeting on a hot afternoon in New York, that he was a big fan of the older humorist, Groucho responded by saying, "I could *use* a big fan in weather like this."
>
> [Steve Allen 1987:31]

Related to the distinction between primary and secondary meanings is the distinction between literal and figurative meanings.[9] Originally the literal meaning was primary and the figurative meaning secondary; over time this relation may reverse as the figurative meaning becomes more common than the literal meaning. Punsters, consequently, often take literally what most people mean figuratively:[10]

I didn't really lose my job. I know where it is, but there's this new guy doing it.

[Bob Goldthwait]

When I was 18, I got a girl in trouble. I framed her for murder.

[Bruce Baum]

Likewise, those more punned against than punning may discover that
they themselves have punned inadvertently when their audience takes
literally what they intended only figuratively:

Singer Kaye Stevens, making her first TV appearance on the "Jack Paar"
late night show, was obviously very nervous after her debut. Paar asked
her if this was truly her first appearance on television, to which she replied,
"I was a virgin until I appeared on your program, Mr. Paar!"

Occasionally, however, punsters take figuratively what others mean literally:

A man applying for work in a Florida lemon grove seemed rather well
bred for such a job. "Look, Mac," said the foreman, "have you actually
had experience picking lemons?" "I certainly have," replied the applicant.
"I've been divorced four times."

  B. *Homophones (homonyms): two words, same sound, different meanings.*
"To pun," Redfern suggests, "is to treat homonyms as synonyms"
(1986:17)—which is technically true only for this category of puns. The
ambiguity of these puns connects meanings somewhat less tightly
than the above category because their words (like *scent* and *cent* or *bear*
and *bare*), though pronounced the same, are spelled differently.

Whenever Richard Lambert [a geology professor at Skyline College] is
asked, "Where's the safest place to be during a quake?" he replies, "In a
stationery store."

[Herb Caen]

A man fleeing the Soviet invasion of Czechoslovakia tried to take refuge
from the soldiers in a store near the border. "I'm sorry, sir," said the owner,
"No Czechs cashed here."

Because homonyms widen the scope of meanings attached to a sound,
even distant unintended meanings can upstage intended ones: "As an
example of the traditional British enjoyment of the double-meaning
joke, the former film-censor John Trevelyan cites the case of Marie
Lloyd changing the words of her song 'She Sits Among the Cabbages
and Peas,' after complaints from a watchdog committee, to 'She Sits
Among the Cabbages and Leeks'" (Redfern 1986:159). Words distin-

guishable only in print may be confused when pronounced, a frequent source of embarrassment to radio and television newsreaders:

> "Final results of the FFA contest are: Apple picking won by Dick Jones. Tractor driving award to Jack Davis. One of our own girls, Miss Betty Smith, was chosen as the best hoer."

And words distinguishable in careful speech (like *major* and *made your*) may be less easily distinguished in the slur of everyday speech:

> *Vivian:* Last night I had a date with a very important guy—an air force general.
> *Melba:* Major-general?
> *Vivian:* Not yet.

If category A ambiguities are full puns, category B ambiguities are three-quarters puns.

C. *Paraphones (paranyms, homonoids): two words, similar sound, different meanings.* The complex etymologies of English words facilitate the looser type of puns of category C, which try to pass off "similarity as identity" (Redfern 1986:15; Nilsen 1989:398). English contains many similar sounding words (such as *creditor* and *predator*) whose primary meanings are very different but whose secondary meanings may be related (mostly because their underlying processes are parallel).

Compared to the above, these weaker category C ambiguities are half-puns. Pepicello and Weisberg characterize this linguistic strategy as "minimal pairs," which they define as "pairs of words that differ by only one phoneme in pronunciation" (1983:67). Maxwell Droke, in his manual for public speakers (1956:61), suggests some examples:

> Beauty is only skin dope.
> Inflation is a stab in the buck.
> Alimony is a matter of wife and debt.

Slightly weaker minimal pair puns differ by slightly more than one phoneme, such as the *anti-semantic/anti-Semitic* one above, and the *Baroque/broke* one here:

> I used to be a Renaissance Man, but then I went Baroque.

Since the sounds are not *that* similar and the connections between meanings farfetched, puns based on paranyms are often called "groaners"—for obvious reasons:

> A man forgets to buy his wife her favorite anemones for her birthday. The shop has only some greenery left, which he purchases. But the forgiving wife exclaims on his return: "With fronds like these, who need anemones?"

Rhymes are half puns whose minimal pair differences are found only in their beginnings and middles, not in their endings, which must match:

When I am dead,
I hope it may be said:
"His sins were scarlet,
but his books were read."

[Hilaire Belloc]

In this example, *dead, said,* and *read* are half-puns; *read* and the implicit *red* are three-quarters puns. "The pun is like the rhyme," Redfern notes, "in that it calls the sense by the sound; it brings together words which are often thought separate" (1986: 99). Hazlitt elaborates: "Rhymes are sometimes a species of wit where there is an alternate combination and resolution or decomposition of the elements of sound, contrary to our usual division and classification of them in ordinary speech, not unlike the sudden separation and re-union of the component parts of the machinery in a pantomime" (1930, 6:21).[11] Such phonetic recombinations leads us to our next category.

D. *Allophones: two words, shifted sounds, different meanings.* Allophones are alternative (*allo-*) sounds (*phones*). Shifting the sounds of two words in the same direction, say from *r* to *l,* can be funny if their meanings also shift, say from politics to sex:

Eleanor Roosevelt, discussing democracy with an oriental ambassador, asked: "And when did you last have an election?" The diplomat, with some embarrassment, answered, "Before blekfust."

especially if the transformed words recall a well-known cliché:

Do you know what the philosopher's wife shouted at her husband who was too busy reading to discuss their strained relationship? "Stop putting Descartés before divorce!"

When parts of two words are not merely shifted but reversed (as in one of the first network radio bloopers, "And now—the president of the United States: Hoobert Heever"), their morphemes are linked by their interchanged phonemes. These reversals are more commonly known as "spoonerisms," after Reverend W. A. Spooner of Oxford (1844–1930) who was notorious for such slips.[12] Today, he would be diagnosed as having a speech defect rather than perceived as having a comic talent:

The substitution blunders that occur in these cases . . . appear to be due to interference of the preparatory processing of sounds soon *to be* produced on the mechanism producing the instant speech. How else could we account for the Reverend Spooner's outburst in chapel: "Excuse me, sir, you appear to be occupewing my pie"? [Goldstein 1990:40–41]

Most "tongue twisters" trick their speakers into committing the phonemic substitution errors of spoonerisms, like this obscenifying graffito:

I am not the fig plucker but the fig plucker's son, and I can pluck figs until the fig plucker comes.

These category D ambiguities are merely one-quarter puns, for symmetrical sounds connect meanings only weakly and are appreciated mostly by children. Pepicello and Weisberg (1983:66–67), who characterize this linguistic strategy as "metathesis," give the example of this childish riddle:

What's the difference between a midget witch and a deer fleeing from hunters? One's a stunted hag, the other a hunted stag.

Some spoonerisms, however, can be appreciated by adults:

A behavioral psychologist pulls habits out of a rat.[13]

Many spoonerisms involve names, which obviates the nonsense to which phonetic reversal usually leads.

Eddie Peabody, the great banjoist, was introduced thus:
Announcer: "Ladies and Gentlemen: Mr. Eddie Playbody will now pee for you."

Local news: So, remember . . . we want all of you to turn out for the Peter pulling contest at St. Taffy's Church . . . ugh . . . that should be the *taffy* pulling contest at St. *Peter's* Church this Sunday!"

The best examples reverse more than one set of sounds while maintaining parallel meanings:

I'd rather have a free bottle in front of me than a pre-frontal lobotomy.
[Fred Allen]

A larger form of allophonic humor, technically known as "chiasmus," reverses entire words:

Dr. Churchill was walking down the hospital corridor when suddenly his patient Mr. Barnes came running by, his hands cupping his genitals. Hot on his heels was Nurse Torquemada carrying a still-steaming tea kettle.
Catching the nurse by the arm, the doctor yelled, "Hold it, nurse, you misunderstood! I said *prick* his *boil!*"

E. Allo-aphones (junctions): two words, shifted silences, different meanings. Ambiguity may reside not only in sounds or words but in the silences within and between them. Ambiguities in these brief indicators of separation allow alternate groupings of sounds or words and consequently alternate meanings, as in this graffito:

> It is better to have loved a short man,
> than never to have loved a tall [at all].

Since no one else has named them (though several linguists have described them), I will call these ambiguous silent separations that can create humor "allo-aphones": alternative (*allo-*) lack (*a-*) of sounds (*phones*) or silences. If positive puns are words that convey varying degrees of connection, negative puns are silences within and between words that convey varying degrees of separation. Allo-aphones, Goldstein notes, reveal neglected aspects of language:

> The example [given below] draws our attention to that much-neglected phoneme (if phoneme it be), the *juncture* (the time gap between spoken words), and in particular, to the way in which different *lengths* of pause determine different senses. Pause length is clearly an important phonological feature of spoken language . . . , but, to my knowledge, precious little work has been done in the *semantic* importance of the lengths of junctures in spoken English. Yet an appreciation of the rules governing pauses is essential not just in odd cases of possible ambiguity, such as the example, but for all speech performances. . . .
> It may be natural to suppose, and many philosophical theorists of language have proposed, that the meaning of a sentence is composed wholly of the meanings of its constituent words. But [the example] shows this to be false. [1990:41–42]

Pepicello and Weisberg (1983:67–68), who characterize this linguistic strategy as "stress and juncture," give an *analytic* example:

> Two men were in a bar. One said, glancing at a girl, "Say, isn't that Hortense?" The other replied, "She looks perfectly relaxed to me" [whore tense].

Redfern gives a *synthetic* example:

> Britons never shall be slaves, only Europe peons [Europeans].

Harvey Mindess (1971:85) shows how linguistic stress can separate the parts of a word, creating new *internal* junctions and consequently new meanings:

Did you hear what happened when the butcher's wife backed into the meat slicer? Disaster! [dis-assed her].

Humorists often split compound words along their main internal junctures to play off the meanings of the simple new words against the meaning of the compound old one, a favorite formula of Steve Allen:

My agent and I have never had a contract. We just have a handshake deal. And whenever I think of that deal—my hands shake.

More complex allo-aphones split words not along their main fault line between syllables but along minor fissures within them:

Discovering your roof leaks sure brings out the moan in homeowner.

The following commercial blooper shows how an inadvertent *external* junction between words can create an unintended meaning:

So stop by our downtown store and visit our fashion center. You will see our lovely models in heat [*pause, turns page*] resistant fabrics which will keep you cooler this summer.

Conversely, the hearer may deliberately disregard the stress cue about how to interpret an external junction, as in Goldstein's example (omitted above):

My first example is stolen from the popular TV comedy show *Benson*. Benson (B) is a black man, and in this scene he is a guest at an otherwise all-white gathering. The following dialogue ensues between the white hostess (A) and Benson:
A: How do you like your coffee, black?
B: Us niggers do have names, ma'am.

Although the above list of elemental ambiguities may be incomplete, we can still use it to analyze very complex phonetic and morphemic humor. Full, three-quarters, half, one-quarter, and negative puns can all be found in the following verse:

She offered her honor,
he honored her offer,
and all night long,
it was on her and off her.

Humorous Sentences

We have examined the ambiguity of words, and the different ways context, sounds, and silence select one of their multiple meanings, which is potentially humorous when the choice is unexpected. We will now examine how this unexpectedly selected meaning of one word changes the meaning of the other words in the sentence, which actualizes the potential humor.

Like Locke and Addison, Freud describes how humor shifts its audience between two very different circles of ideas—though adding that this shift occurs at an ambiguous word:

> If, therefore, we derive unmistakable enjoyment in jokes from being transported *by the use of the same or a similar word* from one circle of ideas to another, remote one . . . , this enjoyment is no doubt correctly to be attributed to economy in psychical expenditure. The pleasure in a joke arising from a "short-circuit" like this seems to be the greater the more alien the two circles of ideas that are brought together by the same word— the further apart they are, and thus the greater the economy which the joke's technical method provides in the train of thought. [1963: 120; emphasis added]

In ordinary speech, our focus usually stays on the primary meaning of each word in a sentence. In the pun, however, our focus *pivots* from the primary to the secondary meaning at the critical ambiguous word and remains on the secondary meanings of the rest of the words in the sentence. Some examples:

> A man went to see a girl, and she called down from upstairs that she was not dressed. "Can't you slip on something and come down?" he called.
> So she slipped on the top step and came down.

This pun pivots *slip on* from its meaning of "dress in" to its meaning of "stumble over," and consequently changes the meaning of how she "came down."

> Milton Berle, being honored as the first recipient of the "Comedy Legends" award at a Tuesday luncheon, was asked how he was informed he had been chosen. "Budd Friedman called me up and asked if I believed in free speech. I said 'Of course.' He said, 'Good. You're making one in Vegas on June 14.'"

This pun pivots "free" from its meaning of "unfettered" to its meaning of "unrenumerated," and consequently changes the meaning of the request. Note that a later word can switch the punned word to its secondary meaning retroactively:

> Now we're at Toys R Us in Salinas, where Steve Barclay, buying a Barbie doll for his 2-year-old daughter, asked a saleswoman: "Does Barbie come with Ken?" Salesperson: "Barbie comes with GI Joe—she fakes it with Ken," and everybody fell down.
>
> [Herb Caen]

In this example, *fakes it* makes sense only with the secondary sexual meaning of the preceding "comes."

Another aspect of wit is the facility to pivot not merely to the appropriate (or extremely inappropriate) secondary meaning of one word—as Groucho Marx did in the "fan" pun above—but also to the related secondary (and if possible primary) meaning of another word—Robin Williams's forte:

> "It's so hard shooting in a mental hospital," [Penny Marshall] said [on the set of the movie *Awakenings* in which she directed Robin Williams], except that the phrase, slurred by fatigue, came out as "menstrual hospital."
>
> "Yes, and shooting a period picture," Williams chimed in brightly, no pause to ponder the play on words, no more than nanoseconds between her slip and his lip.
>
> [*New York Times Magazine*, 11 Nov. 1990, 34][14]

To pun, in short, is to go into a word through one meaning and out another.

The pun, then, is a *trope*—a point at which an ambiguous word shifts the meaning of the rest of the sentence.[15] (*Pun* itself comes from the Italian *puntiglio* ["fine point" or "quibble"] and ultimately from the Latin *punctum* ["point"].) Redfern elaborates the pun's "trope" with his own "trope," that is, elaborates trope's classical rhetorical sense—"place where meanings change"—by using trope's current literary sense—"figure of speech": "Wordplay, or turns on words. The key movement of the pun is pivotal. The second meaning of a word or phrase rotates around the first one. Or branches off from it; puns are switch words, like pointsmen at a junction. . . . The pivotal wordplay enables the story to bifurcate. . . . Trains of thought benefit from being rerouted" (Redfern 1986:23). "We are already familiar with the pun as an agent of deflection or bifurcation," Redfern continues later to account for the comic effect of a linguistic humorist's well-known work: "In [Lewis Carroll's] *Alice*, no argument is ever developed. It is immediately undercut, often by a misinterpretation. The word which is misinterpreted acts as a pivot. . . . The pun is invaluable as a pivot for redirection" (Martin Gardner, quoted in Redfern 1986:65). Since "to misinterpret" is to select the wrong meaning of a word, and consequently of a sentence, some humorists, like Steve Allen, deliberately misinterpret meanings to veer the conversation through non sequitur:

> A certain percentage of jokes—though very far from all—involve some type of wordplay—for example, a deliberate misunderstanding of the meaning of a common or idiomatic combination of words. . . .

Many of my ad-lib studio audience interviews over the years have involved deliberately selecting the less reasonable interpretation of a phrase and pretending that it was properly operative. . . .

Almost anything that is said can be interpreted in more than one way (a fact semanticists bemoan), and so I am able at almost any point in a conversation to deliberately derail the train of logical thought. For example, here is a bit of dialogue from one of our interviews:

> Q: What is your name, sir?
> A: Tom Francis, Central Tool and Die Works, Pittsburgh, Pennsylvania.
> Q: That's a rather long name, Mr. Pennsylvania. How did you happen to come by it?
> A: I'm not sure I follow you.
> Q: Well, I'm not so sure you don't follow me. *Somebody's* been following me for the past five days . . a short, dark man in a green sweater. However, it may be a case of mistaken identity.
>
> [1987:20, 32, 57]

More than any other modern comedian, Groucho Marx specialized in pivoting dialogues and monologues through secondary meanings:

> *Young girl:* "I would say it's what's upstairs that counts."
> *Groucho:* "Well, I have something upstairs—my upstairs maid, and that's not easy because I only have a one story house. And the one story you're *not* going to hear about is my upstairs maid."

If the humor of the word occurs at the junction between the phonological and the morphological, the humor of the sentence occurs at the junction between the syntactic and the semantic. Just as phonological pivots create morphological ambiguity, syntactic pivots create semantic ambiguity. English possesses several syntactic ambiguities that comics often exploit, which the nineteenth-century American humorist Artemus Ward ungrammatically called "ingrammaticisms" (Eastman 1939:128).

Syntactic pivots create humor by changing not merely the meaning of the word but its part of speech. For instance, from noun to verb:

> "Did you see her dress?"
> "No, she wouldn't let me."

or from verb to noun:

> *Question:* How do you make an elephant fly?
> *Answer:* Well, first you take a gr-r-r-reat big zipper.

Some syntactical pivots create even cleverer humor by changing the parts of speech of *two* words in a sentence; for instance, by changing *flies* from a verb to a noun while changing *like* from a preposition to a verb in the following:

> Time flies like an arrow
> but fruit flies like a banana.

["Stupid Mac Tricks"]

The potential confusion in English between signifiers and signifieds permits comedians to explore the consequences of using various parts of speech as proper nouns, as in Abbott and Costello's classic "Who's on First" routine:

> A: You know, strange as it may seem, they give baseball players peculiar names nowadays. On the St. Louis team Who's on first, What's on second, I-Don't-Know's on third.
> C: That's what I want to find out. I want you to tell me the names of the fellows on the St. Louis team.
> A: I'm telling you. Who's on first, What's on second, I-Don't-Know's on third.
> C: Yeah, you know the fellows' names?
> A: Yes.
> C: Well, who's on first?
> A: Yes.
> C: I mean the fellow's name.
> A: Yes.
> C: I mean the guy playing first.
> A: Who.
> C: The fellow playing first.
> A: Who.
> C: The first baseman.
> A: Who.
> C: The guy playing first.
> A: Who is on first!
> C: What are you asking *me* for?

Costello is confounded because the same signifiers ("who," "what," "I don't know") that Abbot uses to refer to his signifieds (baseball players) more commonly perform other syntactic functions in the English language signifier system.[16]

Linguistic humor not only alters parts of speech, it brings out the ambiguity of their references. Humor frequently uses ambiguity of pronoun reference as another syntactic source of semantic confusion:

> Mrs. S. was the last to enter the dirigible. Slowly, with her huge nose pointed skyward, she headed for the distant horizon.

Pronoun ambiguity is prevalent because their particular reference depends on who is using them:

Two clergymen were discussing the current sad state of sexual morality. "I didn't sleep with my wife before we were married." one clergyman stated self-righteously. "Did you?" "I'm not sure," said the other. "What was her maiden name?"

Humor can also exploit the ambiguity of common noun reference because, like pronouns, they are also general:

The visitor, who is named Bob Green, Jr., asks [a supposedly omniscient computer]: "Where is my father right this minute?"
"Sitting in O'Malley's having a beer," the computer replies.
"My father died in Memphis, Tennessee, in 1977," the visitor says triumphantly.
"Bob Green Sr. died in Memphis, Tennessee, in 1977," the computer retorts. "Your father is sitting in O'Malley's having a beer."

Often amusingly ambiguous too is the reference of possessives—both *of*:

Teacher: William, what was George Washington most famous for?
William: His memory.
Teacher: That's an odd answer . . . What makes you think Washington's memory was so remarkable?
William: Well, they sure put up a lot of monuments to it.

and *have:*

Question: Does your wife have any Chinese blood? (His wife was born in Wuchang, China.)
Steve Allen: Yes, she keeps a small jar of it in the garage.

Deliberately or inadvertently mixing up direct and indirect objects may also result in humor:

Byron R. Skinner, president of San Jose City College, publishes a "President's Newsletter," and I found his April 25 issue especially newsy. For instance: "Graduates Breakfast: Members of the administrative council will cook and serve the graduates." Summa cum cannibalism?
[Herb Caen]

Finally, modifiers, especially slippery in English, are easily misplaced, resulting in comic confusion over what or whom they are attached to:

During a trip to Africa I shot an elephant in my pajamas. How he got into my pajamas I'll never know.
[Groucho Marx]

On "The Joey Bishop Show," Senator Barry Goldwater had been asked by Joey if he would like to be on the show twice a week. The senator replied, "No, thank you. I'd much rather watch you in bed with my wife."

Since the syntax of silences as well as words can be ambiguous, humor can alter semantics by subtly shifting the stress that creates junctures:

Can you tell me how long cows should be milked?
The same as short ones.

The reply forces us to retravel the question, this time changing course at the point of ambiguity from joining *long* adverbially with *how* to joining *long* adjectivally with *cows*, which flips the interpretation from temporal to spatial. Henny Youngman's syntactical humor deserves special mention for the way he alters stress to reshuffle junctures:

My wife will buy anything marked down. Yesterday, she brought home an escalator.

Again, the second sentence forces us to return to the first to increase the stress on *down*, which inserts a wider juncture between *marked* and *down*, thus transforming the combination "marked-down" (that is, cheap) to "marked 'down'" (that is, a sign for a direction). And in his famous throwaway line—"Take my wife, please!"—the juncture pause between *wife* and *please*, created by the degree of stress on each word, retroactively determines the precise meaning of *take:*

A classic example of this type of joke is Henny Youngman's famous "Take my wife—please." I've seen critics knock an entire class of jokes by citing that joke as a *bad* example. Precisely the reverse is true. It's a terrific joke. It's hardly ever quoted properly, by the way. To be amused by that line, you have to understand that Henny has just said, "Women are crazy today." Then he adds, "Take my wife—please." It's a wonderful play on two separate meanings of the verb "to take": "to consider" and "to physically carry or move from place to place." [Steve Allen 1987:32][17]

Humorous Communication

So far, my analysis of linguistic humor has regarded language as an isolated system. But language is also part of a larger communication system between senders and receivers: speakers and hearers on the micro level, broadcasters and audiences on the macro level. Some forms of humor derive from these interactive, rather than structural, aspects of language.

Expression without communication produces one of the most poignant kinds of comedy. Those who believe they are communicating with others but aren't teeter between comedy and tragedy. From

Chekhov to Ionesco, Breton to Beckett, *humour noir* to black humor, writers and especially dramatists (those most concerned with verbal interaction) have portrayed the ironies of our inability to (truly) communicate with others. In his study of the historic roots of black comedy, Mathew Winston comments, "The characters are unable to communicate; words become cliché, babel, or a refuge from experience. The absurd detaches itself from the language of rational discourse because such language posits a rational world. The resultant breakdown of language is both funny as verbal play and threatening because it indicates an inability to comprehend the world or to control one's life" (1972:279).

One can cease to communicate through the various forms of wordplay discussed above. Winston continues in a later work, "wordplay . . . is the perfect means to convey disorder, for it breaks the accepted linguistic conventions of normal speech" (1978:39). The verbal ambiguities of wordplay, we will see, shift attention from *what* is communicated to the language *through which* it is communicated, the noise of the form drowning out the information of the content. "Verbal play reminds us of the artifice of the work we are experiencing, distances us from its mimetic referents. Although we may be moved by the characters and their predicaments, by the story told and the world depicted, we are repeatedly made aware that what we are dealing with is not reality but language" (Winston 1978: 39).

One can also noncommunicate by speaking out of turn, which contradicts perhaps the most important requirement of human communication: the "turn-taking" rule. When two people are transmitting concurrently, neither can be receiving. Those aware that their simultaneous transmission is creating mutual interference usually stop sending until they can work out their speaking schedule ("You go first.").[18] (If they shift into the reception mode at exactly the same time, they may be further embarrassed if not amused by the ensuing silence—suddenly incongruous with their previous talk activity.) In surrealistic comic drama, however, they keep talking, communication be damned. In musical comedy and comic opera, simultaneous speech is differentiated by separate musical lines—communicating clearly at least each character's different personality and emotion (Hoy 1974:966).

When communication from sender to receiver gets through but is distorted, we have miscommunication rather than noncommunication. Impaired speech or hearing apparatus may contribute to comic miscommunication by making ambiguous a word ordinarily assumed to be unambiguous. Emily Litella, Gilda Radner's partially deaf "editorial respondent" on "Saturday Night Live," continually misunderstood the news and editorials to which she was responding: "What's all this stuff I've been hearing about too much violins on television?"

Students unable to hear, comprehend, or spell correctly often make laughable mistakes when forced to translate into written assignments what they have only heard spoken. Here are some of the mistranslations of high school students, which have been collected as the "Pullet Surprises":

> Frank Furter was a Supreme Court justice.
>
> It's hard to imagine, but someday I'll be a mother. First, I'll get pregnant; then, I'll spend nine months in hard labor.
>
> When two people are in love, they should share a lot of infection.
>
> A problem driver is unpredictable and erotic.
>
> Everyone is a human bean.
>
> [Jack Smith, *San Francisco Chronicle*, 14 May 1985, 35]

College students misunderstand their lecturers almost as much, as shown by these freshman history papers collected and woven together by a college professor:

> During the Middle Ages, everybody was middle aged. Church and state were co-operatic. Middle evil society was made up of monks, lords, and surfs. . . . The Crusades were a series of military expanditions made by Christians seeking to free the holy land (the "Home Town" of Christ) from the Islams. . . . Victims of the Black Death grew boobs on their necks. . . . The Middle Ages slimpared to a halt. The renascence bolted in from the blue. Life reeked with joy. Italy became robust, and more individuals felt the value of their human being. . . . The Reformation happened when German nobles resented the idea that tithes were going to Papal France or the Pope thus enriching Catholic coiffures. . . . An angry Martin Luther nailed 95 theocrats to a church door. . . . Louise XIV became King of the Sun. He gave the people food and artillery. If he didn't like someone, he sent them to the gallows to row for the rest of their lives.
>
> [Anders Henricksson, *San Francisco Chronicle*, "Sunday Punch," 27 May 1983, 7]

Such mishearing can be involuntary or willful. In comedy, the willful mishearer usually exhibits false naiveté by choosing the simplest, most literal interpretation (or misinterpretation) of a question. Here is an exchange between a medical officer and a new recruit in the Second World War:

> M.O.: How are your bowels working?
> R.: Haven't been issued with any, sir.

M.O.: I mean, are you constipated?
R.: No, sir, I volunteered.
M.O.: Heavens, man, don't you know the King's English?
R.: No, sir, is he?"

The willful mishearer may also violate discourse norms by responding to aspects of the discourse not intended to elicit a response, or at least not currently, as in this sequence from the 1975 film *Monty Python and the Holy Grail:*

Arthur: Old woman!
Man: Man.
Arthur: Man, sorry. What knight lives in that castle over there?
Man: I'm thirty-seven.
Arthur: What?
Man: I'm thirty-seven I'm not old.
Arthur: Well, I can't just call you man.
Man: You could say Denis.
Arthur: I didn't know you were called Denis.
Man: Well, you didn't bother to find out, did you?[19]

Mistranslations between foreign languages also produce many humorous miscommunications. Humorous mistranslations often occur when we translate the figurative expressions of one language into another language literally. An early computer translation program became notorious for translating the English platitude "the spirit is willing but the flesh is weak" into Russian as "the vodka is robust but the meat is tasteless." And the Pepsi slogan "Come Alive—You're in the Pepsi Generation!" appeared briefly in China as "Pepsi Brings Your Ancestors Back from the Dead!" Those learning English as a second language (as well as English speakers learning another language) often assemble an amusing mélange by trying to impose on their second language the unique grammatical structure of their original language (Zijderveld 1968:301). Leo Rosten reports the following conversation in a train station in Paris between himself and a ticket clerk whose tourist English was no better than Rosten's tourist French:

I: Bonjour, m'sieur! Is not this day reliable?
Ticketeer: You speak *French!* What joys! *Vive* the States United! May I wax your elbow?
I: Voila! To affairs?
Ticketeer: Advance.
I: I demand you: When, dear Amy [*cher ami*], do gentleman trains go toward Lady Nice?
Ticketeer: They are *very* nice chemises of iron, wet knight.

I: I fear I have been soft. What I intended to choke you is: "What *time* do such trains arrive Nice?"
Ticketeer: The *time?!* Smite my neck for buttering your confusion. It takes twelve hours from Paris.

[1958:334–35]

We usually find it much funnier to encounter actual verbal mistakes than their artificial *re*presentation in linguistic humor, for we know that only the former requires real effort to undo their damage. It is easier to contrive ambiguities and incongruities into a joke than to circumvent them in reality without continual mental monitoring. Should they nevertheless occur, those who failed to expend enough energy to avoid them must now expend much more energy to remedy their negative repercussions—especially on their speaker's status as a verbally competent individual. Audience awareness of how much real energy must now be wasted trying to repair the consequences intensifies these inadvertent puns into howlers. Some of the funniest linguistic lapses occur in mass communications, for they cannot easily be taken back—like the typos and bloopers below.

Errors in printed communication create ambiguities of reference or spelling that, in transforming one word into another, redirect the sentence away from its intended meaning toward another, incongruous meaning. "Typographical errors, editorial oversights, and copyreaders' misses have a humorous appeal for many."

A small-town weekly provides the following public announcement: "The ladies of the Plum Street Church have discarded clothing of all kinds. They ask that you come and inspect them." A current events item: "Mrs. Alice Sommes, the club president, then rapped her navel and the meeting came to order."

[Hertzler 1970:183]

Although most typos create only nonsense, some make partial sense:

The proprietor said he would allow no woman in the bra without a man.

He heard himself assailed as a self-centered financial executive who buttered his own beard.

Before the verdict was rendered this morning, "Miss Mexico" told interviewers that if the court freed her, she would become a nut.

A few typos even yield more insightful sense than the original:

Wanted: Lawyer is searching for accomplished, well-recommended deceptionist.

James Melville, the district attorney, then forcefully addressed the jury and gummed up the case.

Mr. and Mrs. Oliver Sloane request the pleasure of your presents at the marriage of their daughter.

The report was signed by five faulty members of the university.

Since radio is a focused medium, what is supposed to be outside the broadcast frame ("off mike") is often humorously incongruous to what is supposed to be inside it ("on mike"):

> One lesson an announcer learns is to make sure he is off the air before he makes any private comments. But even the greatest sometimes slip. A legend is Uncle Don's remark after he had closed his famous children's program. He thought his mike was cut off the air when he said, "I guess that will hold the little bastards."

Television, with more dimensions than radio, has more potential to produce discordant juxtapositions. Humorous incongruities and hypercongruities can occur (1) between picture and sound:

> Camel's News Reel had a mix-up due to an AT&T switching error, when John Cameron Swayze said, "And now to Roy Neal in Philadelphia." Roy Neal's voice came on, but the picture was of a Washington correspondent, sitting back in a swivel chair, his heels on a desk, reading a newspaper. Suddenly a voice cut in, "Good grief, we've got Washington!"

(2) between parts of the picture:

> Viewers were watching the exciting Western film titled *Broken Arrows*, which was being presented on "Monday Night at the Movies." A typical scene was being shown where the good guys were huddled around a burning covered wagon shooting frantically at the encircling Apaches, who were getting knocked off with great precision. At this point, superimposed over the action, the following latest football score was shown: "Cowboys 36—Redskins 6"

(3) between types of programs:

> The 1986 Home Box Office comedy program *Not Necessarily the News*, in a segment entitled "Days of the News," combined newscast and soap opera by presenting the "on air" stormy love affairs between anchorpersons and their field reporters;[20]

(4) between the sequence of programs and commercials:

> "There's excitement in store on our *Million Dollar Movie* tonight with Ann Sheridan—stay tuned as Phillips Milk of Magnesia brings you *Woman on the Run*."

Reactions to Linguistic Humor

In a study of Chesterton, Hugh Kenner points out our schizophrenic reaction to punning and wordplay: " 'The pun is the foundation of his humor and through his analogical perceptions inextricably mixed with his thought; dangerous because word-play of all the forms of paradox balances most precariously on *the knife-edge between the perfunctory and the profound"* (quoted in Redfern 1986: 45; emphasis added).

On the one hand, many regard wordplay as the lowest form of thought: "There is a form of wit which is like the excrement of the mind" (Friedrich Schlegel, quoted in Redfern 1986:176); "The pun is the guano of the winged mind" (Victor Hugo, quoted in Redfern 1986:141). To illustrate the extremity of pun loathing, Redfern also mentions "the probably apocryphal Congressman who proposed a constitutional amendment to ban puns" (1986: 176). Finally, "Puns, paradoxes and riddles do to language what pies do to faces and prat-falls to bottoms—destroy its dignity. R. B. Blackmur has called punning 'the onomatopoeia of meaning,' or we might say that punning is sound whacking sense" (B. Fussell, quoted in Redfern 1986:146).

On the other hand, despite this disapproval, and "whatever the risks involved, many [punners] persist. It could be that, obscurely, wordplayers sense that they tread on very basic territory: meaning, communication, the nature of reality itself" (Redfern 1986:31). The overwhelming desire to pun is indicated by its seemingly inappropriate appearance in extreme situations, like dying—"Puns are frequently used in very serious, even morbid, situations. Shakespeare's Mercutio is bleeding to death when he says, 'Ask for me tomorrow and you shall find me a grave man'" (Nilsen 1989: 398–99)—and death, as in this tombstone epitaph:

> Stranger, tread
> this ground with gravity:
> Dentist Brown is filling
> His last cavity.[21]

Not only individuals but entire historical periods had different opinions on punning. As William Empson notes, the Elizabethans produced puns without the guilt of later generations:

> It is partly this tact which makes Marvell's puns charming and not detached from his poetry. . . . He manages . . . to imply that it was quite easy to produce puns and one need not worry about one's dignity in the matter. It became harder as the language was tidied up, and one's dignity was more seriously engaged. For the Elizabethans were quite prepared, for instance, to make a pun by a mispronunciation, would treat puns as mere casual bricks, requiring no great refinement. [quoted in Redfern 1986: 51]

After the Elizabethans, punning began to fall into disfavor as "England caught the virus of decorum": "The Restoration dramatists were admirably lucid, but their use of language was, in the last resort, unimaginative. The banishing of the pun, except for comic purposes, was the symbol of a radical defect: it was a turning away from the genius of language" (Kenneth Muir, quoted in Redfern 1986:52). Punning was ostracized from serious literature: "'As a neoclassical theory of decorum began to take shape, conceits were excluded from the sublime style and relegated to the low style' [R. Queneau]. In that backlash . . . much the same fate befell puns" (Redfern 1986:98). The Victorians exiled puns still further. They "banished puns to the parlour or the nursery, and we are still sheepish about serious wordplay" (Eric Korn, quoted in Redfern 1986:181). Only in the twentieth century, Korn goes on to note, have Joyce and Nabokov restored to serious literature the possibility of punning.

Punning has been both admired and despised because, by accentuating verbal ambiguity and incongruity, it emphasizes the language system over the "higher" cultural and social systems.

Ambivalence about Ambiguity

Linguistic humor makes us realize how capricious language is. It is far easier to rearrange the language system than any other system. Words and sentences could easily mean something other than what we intend them to mean. We become especially aware of the instability of language when encountering puns (Redfern 1986:14), which imply we cannot rely on words' meanings. "I suspect puns are rejected because it is neater and less threatening to believe that every word has a reliable signification, that it is not suddenly taking on a will of its own and attaching itself ad lib to other suppressed meanings" (Helen McNeil, quoted in Redfern 1986:118). Puns commit, in Oliver Wendell Holmes term, "verbicide—violent treatment of a word with fatal results to its legitimate meaning" (quoted in Redfern 1986:67). A punned word is never the same again, for one cannot use it in its primary sense without being aware of its secondary meanings.

One feels about puns, in part, the way one feels about ambiguity. Those who dislike ambiguity also dislike puns, which debase language away from its univocal ideal. "Ambiguity is a vice of words. . . . A scientific age like ours tends to worry about this aspect of language. Meaning should be mathematical, unambiguous. But this plurality of reference is in the very nature of language, and its management and exploitation is one of the joys of writing" (Anthony Burgess, quoted in

Redfern 1986:131). In logic, "to expose a sophism [is] to detect the equivocal or double meaning of a word" (Coleridge, quoted in Redfern 1986:41). In other words, arguments make their mistaken turns at inadvertent puns—as analytical philosophers love to point out. But a person can dislike the ambiguity of puns not only because of the ideal it falls away from but also because of the negative ideal it falls toward. The "singleness of apprehension [of the antipunster] cannot stand the shock of a double meaning" (anonymous, quoted in Redfern 1986:59). Especially for authoritarian personalities who dislike ambiguity (Redfern 1986:10), "punning offers the constant lesson that we can keep nothing in neat categories. Slips remind us of the verge of madness, the loss of control" (Redfern 1986: 123).

On the other hand, those who like puns see the world as an ambiguous place whose essence can be caught *only* through linguistic ambiguity. Puns free them from the tyranny of language whose rules are designed to say only one thing at a time. "Puns appeal to those who want to say several things at once, and for whom unambiguous utterance is too linear and restricting" (Redfern 1986:177). Thus punning appeals both to the culturally naive and the culturally sophisticated. Applying his "liberationist" conception of humor to language restrictions,[22] Harvey Mindess concludes that intellectuals who try to explain the world's ambiguous nature have the least qualms about punning: "Inveterate punsters tend to be highly literate people: teachers, writers, and other intellectuals who frequently resort to words to communicate their subtlest thoughts. One needs to be immersed in verbalization to feel free to pun with impunity" (1971:88). The great religious figures and cultural commentators, in particular, often resort to puns as the only way to express their heightened awareness of the ambiguities of human existence: "The pun, dropped from the sky, should not be greeted with too much amazement. Far be it from me to insult the pun! I respect it for what it is. The most august, sublime and delightful examples of mankind, and perhaps beyond, have made plays on words. Jesus Christ made a pun on Peter, Moses on Isaac, Aeschylus on Polynices, Cleopatra on Octavian" (Victor Hugo, quoted in Redfern 1986:69).

Irony about Incongruity

If the ambiguity of puns breaks apart what has been connected, the incongruity of puns brings together what has been unconnected. Puniphobes fear puns will bring together what shouldn't be together, for verbal incongruities are the linguistic equivalent of sexual perversions.

"We may say that puns and ambiguities are to common language what adultery and perversion are to 'chaste' (i.e., socially orthodox) sexual relations. They both bring together entities (meanings/people) that have 'conventionally' been differentiated and kept apart; and they bring them together in deviant ways, bypassing the orthodox rules governing communications and relationships." [Tony Tanner, quoted in Redfern 1986:174; see also Davis 1983: parts 2, 3]

Puniphiles, however, hope puns will bring together what hadn't been considered together, for "creativity" means in part to assemble pairs whose seeming incongruities turn out not to be incongruities at all. Even such seemingly accidental attributes as people's names can be seen as puns that bring together actors and activities:

This whole complex of beliefs runs counter to the "conventional" view of language (i.e., that all names and indeed all words are only arbitrary conventions), for such a theory rules out predestined proper names. . . . It does in fact seem likely to me that legends were invented to explain names and vice versa; names devised to suit the legendary adventures of eponymous heros. . . . The belief in significant names is an attempt to create a fully significant universe, from which the arbitrary or the meaningless are banished. Puns, by finding relationships everywhere, operate in this *pantheistic* fashion. [Redfern 1986:38–40; emphasis added]

This pantheism implicit in puns combats the chance and chaos implicit in the rest of the world. "Jean-Paul Richter . . . was perhaps the first to wax lyrical, and indeed cosmic, about the whole phenomenon [of wordplay]. Jean Paul located one of the seductions of puns in the 'surprise at the element of chance which runs through the world playing with sound and parts of the world. As a wild coupling without priest, every coincidence pleases us, perhaps because the very idea of causality half-hiding and half-revealing itself seems like wit to wed the dissimilar'" (Redfern 1986:56). In short, puns overcome the randomness of experience by revealing some underlying design to the world, if only linguistic.

Humorous signs versus Serious signifying

The most conspicuous effect of puns is to call attention to language as an autonomous system, separate from the other systems of the world. How one feels about puns also depends on how one feels about becoming conscious of the difference between language and these other systems.

Those who like puns enjoy the awareness of language they create vis-à-vis these other systems. By interrupting its smooth flow, which seems to make language transparent to these other systems, puns offer language itself as a spectacle for contemplation. Language, pun lovers believe, not only differs from these other systems, but determines them. Language itself influences how we view these other systems— a fact brought home especially to cultural exiles: "Punning appeals particularly to exiles (whether external or inner) for, having two homes and languages, the exile has a binary, split perspective . . . on his adopted culture: Ionesco, Beckett, Nabokov, Joyce. . . . It is hard to be entirely serious in your non-native tongue. . . . You see the second language from the outside, and its mechanisms, its automatisms, are that much more apparent to you" (Redfern 1986:164).

On the other hand, those who dislike puns despise the linguistic self-consciousness they produce, which Redfern (1986:15) calls " 'foregrounding,' that is, calling attention more to language than to what it signifies." Pun haters regard language as a transparent medium, which should be used only to operate on other, more "substantial," systems. If the aesthetic puniphile regards language as superior to other systems, the utilitarian puniphobe regards it as inferior, for wordplay *distracts* from language's operational point. "Nothing is more futile than the irrelevant pun that is based on only a verbal similarity and brings out no contrast, innuendo, or congruity of meaning. Nothing is a clearer sign of incompetent writing than word-play that distracts rather than concentrates the reader's attention" (W. B. Stanford, quoted in Redfern 1986:20).[23] Puns make utilitarian puniphobes realize that this supposedly transparent medium of language has characteristics of its own, which may distort their view of other systems and in which they may become ensnarled.

The transparency of language is sustained by its order. By violating linguistic expectations, however, puns disrupt this order and, as in a chemical precipitation, suddenly transform language from transparent to opaque. The seemingly trivial assumptions about language undermined by puns constitute the unthinking bases of thought. Without taking its conventional aspects for granted, puniphobes fear they cannot use language for "serious" thinking. They especially despise partial puns that break the language rules too easily. If one need not spell or even pronounce two words exactly the same to equate their meanings, one can connect almost any word with almost any meaning— overthrowing all linguistic order.

By separating sign from signified, puns question its referential character (Redfern 1986:122). By accentuating language as an autonomous system, puns disconnect it from other systems. "Such a diversion," Redfern points out, "such a reminder that words can come adrift of their bases, is precisely what anti-punners object to" (1986:57). Anti-punners, like the early eighteenth-century Augustans, fear this separation's consequent lawlessness: "For the Augustans, . . . 'words were responsible to things; or it was dangerous to think otherwise. The pun . . . is a step in this subversive direction'" (Denis Donoghue, quoted in Redfern 1986:54). But propunners, like the late eighteenth- and early nineteenth-century Jean Paul Richter, approve this separation's consequent freedom: "a third ground for pleasure in puns is the evidence it gives of intellectual freedom, which can turn our glance from the object to its sign" (quoted in Redfern 1986:57). If puniphobes fear that puns allow *language* to control people by entrapping them in its internal complexities, puniphiles hope that puns allow *people* to control language by freeing them from its external constraints: "When we make a pun, when we play with words, we are making them our own. Not for us alone, of course, as we can then display them as trophies to others, as proofs of that mastery over language about which we need to reassure ourselves every bit as much as the child apprentice" (Redfern 1986:153).

Linguistic humor versus "Higher" humor

Contemporary puniphobes are not alone. There has been a long tradition of disparaging "mere" linguistic humor relative to some "higher" conception of humor ever since Cicero distinguished humor based on words from humor based on things: "a witty saying has its point sometimes in facts, sometimes in words, though people are most particularly amused whenever laughter is excited by the union of the two" (1942:383). Seventeen centuries later, Addison (1965; no. 62:267) devalued purely linguistic humor still further by distinguishing "true Wit," which "consists in the Resemblance of Ideas," from "false Wit," which consists "in the Resemblance of Words," and located "Punns" among the species of "false Wit":

> There is no kind of false Wit which has been so recommended by the Practice of all Ages, as that which consists in a Jingle of Words, and is comprehended under the general Name of *Punning*. It is indeed impossible to kill a Weed, which the Soil has a natural Disposition to produce. The Seeds of Punning are in the Minds of all Men, and tho' they may be subdued by

Reason, Reflection and good Sense, they will be very apt to shoot up in the greatest Genius, that is not broken and cultivated by the Rules of Art. Imitation is natural to us, and when it does not raise the Mind to Poetry, Painting, Musick, or other more noble Arts, it often breaks out in Punns. [1965; no. 61:259]

After reviewing the "History of Punning," Addison, even in 1711, could worry, "I do very much apprehend . . . that our Posterity will in a few Years degenerate into a Race of Punnsters" (1965; no. 61:262). Because phonetic similarity is shallower than semantic, Hazlitt observed a century later, resemblance between words produces less profound humor than resemblance between things or ideas:

Mere wit, as opposed to reason or argument, consists in striking out some casual and partial coincidence which has nothing to do . . . with the nature of the things, which are forced into a seeming analogy by a play upon words, or some irrelevant conceit, as in puns, riddles, alliteration, &c. The jest . . . lies in the sort of mock-identity, or nominal resemblance, established by the intervention of the same words expressing different ideas. . . . verbal and accidental strokes of wit, though the most surprising and laughable, are not the best and most lasting. That wit is the most refined and effectual, which is founded on the detection of unexpected likeness or distinction in things, rather than in words. [1930; 6:19–22]

At the beginning of the twentieth century Bergson argued that purely linguistic humor uncouples the formal language system from more substantial systems:

there is often only a slight difference between the play upon words on the one hand, and a poetic metaphor or an illuminating comparison on the other. Whereas an illuminating comparison and a striking image always seem to reveal the close harmony that exists between language and nature, regarded as two parallel forms of life, the play upon words makes us think somehow of a negligence on the part of language, which . . . seems to have forgotten its real function and now claims to accommodate things to itself instead of accommodating itself to things. And so the play upon words always betrays a momentary *lapse of attention* in language, and it is precisely on that account that it is amusing. [1956:139][24]

But it was Dorothy Parker, in a 1956 *Paris Review* interview, who denigrated linguistic humor most succinctly by aphorizing, "Wit has truth in it, wisecracking is merely calisthenics with words."

Proponents of supralinguistic humor have offered several ways to distinguish purely verbal humor from the humor of higher systems. Cicero suggests the negative test of translating the funny story into different words: "the joke which still remains witty, in whatever words it is couched, has its germ in the facts; that which loses its pungency, as soon as it is differently worded, owes all its humor to the language" (1942:387). Addison also suggests translating it into a different—foreign?—language: "I shall here define it to be a Conceit arising from the use of two Words that agree in the Sound, but differ in the Sense. The only way therefore to try a Piece of Wit is to translate it into a different Language, if it bears the Test you may pronounce it true; but if it vanishes in the Experiment, you may conclude it to have been a Punn" (1965; no. 62: 262–63). (If purely linguistic humor so depends on the unique structure of its original language that it ceases to be funny when translated into a foreign language, perhaps "seriousness" is also largely—if not merely—linguistic if it so depends on the unique structure of its original language that it *becomes* funny when translated into a foreign language.) Those who teach comic technique, such as Maxwell Droke (1956:10, 76) and Gene Perret (1982:61), suggest the positive test of whether the funny story produces a visual image—a lesson which comedienne Rita Rudner seems to have taken to heart:

> I had the worst birthday party ever as a child. Because my parents hired a pony to give rides. And these ponies are never in good health. But this one dropped dead. It wasn't much fun after that. One kid would sit on him and the rest of us would drag him around in a circle.

The image need not even be visual. Redfern (1986:138) reports a visceral graffito scrawled on the side of a condom machine: "This is the worst chewing gum I ever tasted!"

Nevertheless, the distinction between verbal and conceptual humor is not clear cut, for there are intermediate examples that connect phenomena more than verbally though less than conceptually. The following parody begins with the merely phonetic resemblance between drinking and thinking. By sustaining the comparison between the parallel progression of each dependency, however, the author implies that the seemingly opposite lifestyles associated with heavy drinking and heavy thinking possess unsuspected similarities.

> Confessions of a Heavy Thinker
> by Frank M.

> It started out innocently enough. I began to think at parties now and then, to loosen up. Inevitably though, one thought led to another and soon I was more than just a social thinker.

I began to think alone—"to relax," I told myself—but I knew it wasn't true. Thinking became more and more important to me, and finally I was thinking all the time. . . .

I began to think on the job. I knew that thinking and employment don't mix, but I couldn't stop myself. . . .

I began to avoid friends at lunchtime so I could read Thoreau and Kafka. I would return to the office dizzied and confused, asking, "What is it exactly we do here?" . . .

I soon had a reputation as a heavy thinker. . . . One day the boss called me in. He said, "Skippy, I like you, and it hurts me to say this, but your thinking has become a real problem. If you don't stop thinking on the job, you'll have to find another job." This gave me a lot to think about.

Things weren't going so great at home either. . . . One evening I turned off the TV and asked [my wife] about the meaning of life. She spent the night at her mother's.

I came home early after my conversation with the boss. "Lambchop," I confessed. "I've been thinking. . . ."

"I know you've been thinking," she said, "and I want a divorce."

"But Poopsie, surely it's not that serious."

"It is serious," she said, lower lip aquiver. "You think as much as college professors, and college professors don't make any money, so if you keep on thinking we won't have any money!"

"That's a faulty syllogism." I said impatiently, and she began to cry. I'd had enough. "I'm going to the library," I snarled, as I slammed out the door. . . .

I headed for the library, in the mood for some Nietzsche, with [a PBS station] on the radio. I roared into the parking lot and ran up to the big glass doors . . . and they didn't open. The library was closed.

To this day I believe that a Higher Power was looking out for me that night.

As I sank to the ground scrabbling at the unfeeling glass, whimpering for Zarathustra, a poster caught my eye. "Friend, is heavy thinking ruining your life?" it asked. You probably recognize that line. It comes from the standard Thinker's Anonymous poster. . . .

Which is why I am what I am today: a recovering thinker. I never miss a TA meeting. At each meeting we watch a noneducational video; last week it was "Porky's." Then we share experiences about how we avoided thinking since the last meeting. . . .

I still have my job and things are a lot better at home. Life just seemed . . . easier, somehow, as soon as I stopped thinking. . . .

[Angus Stocking, *San Francisco Chronicle*,
"Sunday Punch," 5 Nov. 1989, 2]

Puns, in short, "may serve to reveal real relationships of considerably greater importance than the mere chance likeness of sound shared by two words or phrases" (Robert B. Martin, quoted in Redfern 1986:59).

Although all humor makes us aware of ambiguities and incongruities in supposedly coherent systems, "bad" puns makes us aware of those we already know and would prefer to forget: the imperfections of language. "Good" puns, on the other hand, also make us aware of the imperfections of the higher cultural and social systems, of which we often need to be reminded.

2

Irrational Logics

If the locus of linguistic humor is the single term (or homophone) whose meaning is *ambiguous,* the locus of logical humor is two (or more) terms whose relation is *irrational.* Since humor undermines logical rationality the same way it undermines linguistic meaningfulness—by denying its defining features—we can use humor to discover what logical rationality's defining features are. "Wittgenstein once said that 'a serious and good philosophic work could be written that would consist entirely of jokes (without being facetious)'" (Malcolm 1958:29). Wittgenstein suggests we could use jokes to display the fundamental philosophical paradoxes to which our language and our logic lead us. Despite the fresh insights frequently obtained by applying a high status form (like philosophizing) to a low status content (like jokes), neither he nor his students, to my knowledge, ever tried to write such a work.[1] His Viennese contemporary Freud also thought jokes, like dreams, use "methods of inference that are rejected by logic" (1963:125). Unlike Wittgenstein, however, Freud devoted much of his book on humor (1963: esp. 60ff., 124ff., 203ff.) to analyzing the ways specific jokes employ "faulty reasoning."

Faulty reasoning, colloquially called "bullshit,"[2] underlies a large class of jokes. Since attributing faulty reasoning to someone is pejorative, some jokes depend on how innately it characterizes a person as much as on the type of faulty reasoning attributed.

Many jokes have depicted the temporary episodes of faulty logic that afflict the inebriated or the stoned, whose ability to follow the rigors of rationality is muddled by alcohol or drugs. For instance, they may be unable to comprehend a phenomenon correctly from its characteristics:

> Two inebriated gents were weaving their way down a railroad track. "Golly," complained one, "this is a long flight of steps." "I don't mind the steps so much," countered the other. "It's the low railings that get me."

But they may then proceed rationally from their initial misconception:

> The court house at Stephenville, Texas, has a large clock that is the pride of the town. It is illuminated at night. One citizen staggered up to a mail box, dropped a penny in the slot, glanced at the clock, and exclaimed, "Jehoshaphat, I'm nine pounds overweight."

Other jokes imply that faulty logic is intrinsic to certain outgroups, against whom teller and audience define themselves, such as "the dumb":

> Two dumb guys show up at Halloween with burnt faces. They'd been bobbing for French fries.
>
> [Henny Youngman]

In this example, the "dumb" do not realize that two kinds of objects (apples and french fries), which seem to them similar (because both float on liquids), are actually so different that an activity (bobbing) appropriate for one kind of object may be inappropriate or even dangerous when attempted with the other.

Comics malign certain ethnic groups by insinuating they employ faulty logic habitually:

> Did you hear about the Polish mob that kidnapped a son of a Polish businessman? They sent the son home to deliver the ransom note. And the father paid it by sending his son back with the money.

This joke implies that true reasoning takes into account factors overlooked by faulty reasoning. The Polish kidnappers were so focused on following a secondary tactic of kidnapping (sending ransom notes) that they neglected its primary strategy (keeping control over their hostage). The Polish businessman was so focused on following the standard response to this tactic (paying the ransom) that he did not realize he no longer needed to do so.

Since reasoning that contains too much logic (like many Jewish jokes) can be as faulty as reasoning that contains too little (like absurd elephant jokes), jokes may be based on both these "deviations from our established logic" (Zijderveld 1968:301–2). For example, Freud's overly rational approach to irrationality has itself become an object of humor, in which irrationality triumphs over rationality and its hyper-rational ally psychotherapy. In most jokes on psychotherapy, "insanity or absurdity prevails over reason":

> A lady visits an analyst to discuss her husband's problem. "It's terrible," she says. "He thinks he's a horse. He lives in a stable, he walks on all fours, and he even eats hay. Please tell me, doctor—can you cure him?" "Yes, I believe I can," says the analyst. "But I have to warn you, the treatment will be long and expensive." "Oh, money's no object," the lady replies. "He's already won two races."
>
> [Mindess 1971:224]

As we saw in the introduction to part 1, humor presupposes the very expectation system it repudiates. Irrational humor, premised on our belief that events in the *objective* world are not random (see Brown 1977:216; Charney 1978:5), demonstrates that its order is less rational than we had thought. Likewise irrational humor demonstrates that our *subjective* views are also less rational than we presume, as Pirandello observed: "The humorist is well aware that the claim that man has a logical mind is much too exaggerated if compared with his actual logical coherence, and that, if we imagine ourselves as capable of logical thought on the speculative level, the logic of our actions can belie the logic of our thought and show that it is fictitious to believe in its absolute sincerity" (1974:135).

Some philosophers and scientists have attempted to reduce rationality to a single system. But because they have been unable to prove that an overall scheme connects all the logical relations composing what Western society has traditionally regarded as "rationality," it is more plausible to assume that Western rationality comprises merely *clusters* of logical relations. Although each cluster connects its own internal elements rigorously, its external links to the other clusters are more tenuous. The unity of our society's conception of rationality may lie less in the single structural skeleton presumed to hold it all together than in the common vulnerability of each logical ligament to being fractured by the comic. Let us proceed, then, to examine how humor ruptures the logical relations in each of these clusters.

Binary Incongruities

The simplest way for humorists to wrench rationality is to *reverse* the traditional ways it has joined things. If reason requires us to connect things one way, the humorist will reconnect them the opposite way. The Russian emigré Andrei Siniavski calls this comic inversion "reverse logic," "spite logic," and even "feminine logic":

The joke is in no way a mere reflection of life in its normal flow, its logical and visual consistency. It is constructed to spite logic and that which we gain from our immediate life experience. I don't know whether there is such a concept as reverse logical connection; if not, it should be introduced in relation to the theory of the joke. The analogy with anecdotal "feminine logic" can be applied here: "My husband has been cheating on me so much that I don't know anymore who got me pregnant!" A person intends to say one thing and says something very different. It is the "other" or different reason which ends up being the real one, reestablishing the logical connection but in a reversed direction. For the speaker this is the only "logic." [1984:361][3]

Though currently common in the humorless context of computers, the most encompassing term for this mode of comic thinking is "binary logic." Binary logic generates different kinds of humor depending on the different ways things can be reversed.

   The comic mind automatically reverses every category it encounters (A) to determine whether its binary category (not-A) is funny. If there are comedy clubs, why aren't there "tragedy clubs"? If bars have happy hours, why don't they have "gloomy hours" (when they raise the price of their drinks). If we celebrate birthdays, why don't we celebrate "deathdays" (by, for instance, taking away a child's favorite toy six months after his or her birthday)? If we can have accidental war, why can't we have—as Art Buchwald suggested in 1982—"accidental peace" (which in fact broke out several years later, evincing the prescience of the comic approach). The "drive-in movie" critic Joe Bob Briggs once cleverly took on the serious (if not sober) advocacy organization MADD (Mothers Against Drunk Drivers) by urging the formation of the counteradvocacy organization DAMM (Drunks Against Mad Mothers).

   Besides reversing entire categories, the comic mind can interchange their characteristics (A_{a1}, $B_{b1} \rightarrow A_{b1}$, B_{a1}). Humorists have employed this technique to switch distinctive features between object types:

I bought a box of razor blades, and I found an apple in it. Can't trust anybody anymore.

[Brian Copeland]

between biological species:

Today was a bad day for me. My dog left me and my wife pooped on the floor.

[Mike Meehan]

and between social institutions:

> I recently went on tour of movie stars homes. Did you know they have pictures of famous delicatessens on their walls?
>
> [Elayne Boosler]

Moreover, the comic mind can reverse category and characteristic with each other, as in the childhood classic:

> Two flies were talking and suddenly one points to the other and says, "Your man is open."

Such whole-part reversals are funnier when the characteristics are lower status than those they characterize:

> *Question:* What did Mickey Mouse get for Christmas?
> *Answer:* A Dan Quayle watch.

Spatially transferring something (say, an answering machine) from its commonplace setting (home) to the opposite setting (not home) may also estrange the familiar phrases associated with it.

> A friend of mine has an answering machine on his car phone. The message is "Hi. I'm home right now . . . so I can't come to the phone . . . but if you leave your name and number, I'll call you when I'm out."
>
> [Steven Wright]

The more expected two elements' customary order (A, B), the more effectively the comic can transpose them (B, A).

> Joke'm if they can't take a fuck.
>
> [Robin Williams]

A more complex comic transposition—

> If life is a cabaret, is death a Dennys?
>
> [Doug Ferrari]

—follows the form: If A, B; then if not-A, not-B. When one ordering of elements has existed long enough to become a cliché—for example, "Necessity is the mother of invention"—permuting it may reveal a surprising truth—for example, "Invention is the mother of necessity." (Once started, the comic mind may keep spinning until it exhausts the possibilities. Revolving the elements of this cliché once more gives us the Freudian insight "Mother is the invention of necessity.")

Humorists can also alter the meaning of a cliché by shifting its attribution from those who usually say it to those it is usually said about:

> Old Jewish couple, about 90 years old, go to a divorce lawyer and say they want to get divorced. The lawyer says, "You're 90 years old. You

want to be divorced now?" "Yes, we've always wanted to be. We've never enjoyed being with each other. Been married 60 years." Lawyer: "Why'd you wait so long?" "We were waiting for the children to die."

[Billy Crystal]

Finally, it may be amusing to reverse not only the formal elements of a cliché but also its content, as in this parody of Allen Ginsberg's poem *Howl:*

I saw the worst minds of my generation
destroyed by sanity,
stuffed, tranquilized, overdressed,
jogging through the Caucasian streets at dusk, looking for an
affectionate fix.

The humorist's compulsion to reverse everything forms the core of Pirandello's theory of humor, which he calls "the feeling of the opposite":

Every feeling, every thought, or every impulse that arises in the humorist immediately splits into its contrary: every affirmative into a negative, which finally ends up assuming the same value as the affirmative. . . . [The humorist is] a man who is constantly somewhat off key, who is like a violin and double bass at the same time; . . . a man in which a thought cannot originate without the opposite or contrary thought originating at the same time, and who finds that for each reason he has to say *yes,* there arise one or more that compel him to say *no* and keep him suspended in perplexity for the rest of his life. [1974:125, 124]

Harvey Mindess provides a rare self-conscious description of the comic mind shifting into reverse: "A while ago, on entering a library, I had an odd experience. My eyes scanned a shelf labeled Recent Books, but what registered in my mind was Decent Books. My brain immediately clicked through a deductive process, reasoning that the rest of the shelves must be filled with Indecent Books, and I found the thought so funny that I almost laughed out loud" (1971:140).[4]

Much humor, then, transposes elements between things that are different or opposite. In the following chapters I will describe the comic reversals of relatively concrete anthropological and sociological entities. In this chapter I will describe the comic reversals of the relatively abstract logical processes that tie them together.

Perspective Reversal

What primarily determines how we conceive of a phenomenon is the standpoint from which we view it. One way comics change our view of things is to reverse our perspective on them. Henny Youngman, for instance, literally reverses the perspective with which we identify in a stereotypical situation:

> The place I worked in last week is kind of run-down. Between my dressing room and the room where all the chorus girls change clothes there's actually a hole in the wall. But I don't care; I let 'em look.
>
> [Henny Youngman]

By shifting the point around which we organize the components of a phenomenon, perspective reversal changes its entire organization— often revealing new components or new relations between old ones:

> An optimist claims that we live in the best of all possible worlds. A pessimist fears that it's true.
>
> [Peter Anthony]

Reversing perspectives relativizes them (fig. 1), which produces more extreme comic contradictions when the perspectives reversed claim to be absolute, as in the following "definition":

> *Infidel:* In New York, one who does not believe in the Christian religion; in Constantinople, one who does.
>
> [Ambrose Bierce]

Comics who reverse perspectives from dominant to subordinate undermine the former's moral authority, especially if it has already been weakened for other reasons. Like prey after a wounded animal, comics have exploited the recent vulnerability of savings and loans by employing perspective reversal to lessen their legitimacy still further:

> It turns out the best way to rob a bank is to own one. The security cameras have all been pointed the wrong way! When I make a deposit now, I ask the teller for ID.
>
> [Will Durst]

Conversely, even more cynical comics can shift perspective from the exploited to the exploiters, as in this T-shirt slogan:

> A Fool and His Money . . .
> Are Fun to Go Out With.

Humorists reverse not only the perspectives *of* the viewers but also the perspectives *on* the viewed, which alters the relative priority of its attributes. If we customarily emphasize *primary* attributes, comics reverse perspectives to shift the accent to *secondary* ones:

> Leonard Bernstein uses music to accompany his conducting.
>
> [Oscar Levant]

Figure 1

More profoundly, comics reverse perspectives to reprioritize entire world views; for instance, replacing our traditional deference to *objectivity* with new respect for *subjectivity:*

Reality. What a concept!

[Robin Williams]

Reality is just a crutch for those afraid to face drugs.

(These affirmations of subjectivity over objectivity rank with Bishop George Berkeley's "The brain is in the mind.")

Comedians, like mathematicians (Paulos 1980:11), believe the perspective that examines a problem *directly* frequently produces less insight than the perspective that examines it *indirectly* by focusing on its theoretical negative:

The professional arsonist builds vacant lots for money.

[Jimmy Breslin]

In this example, Breslin transforms a phenomenon into its negative (buildings into vacant lots) in order to turn the activity that creates it from negative to positive (destroying into building)—providing us with a new perspective from which to reappreciate, if not reevaluate, the occupation of professional arsonist. Leo Rosten offers an even more complex example that works out the negative implications of one negation:

A note I once received from Groucho Marx. I had written him, and I didn't get an answer until months later. Here was his answer. Dear Junior: Excuse me for not answering you sooner. But I have been so busy not answering letters lately that I have not been able to get around to not answering yours in time.

Causation Reversal

Our perspective reveals not only the internal organization of a phenomenon but also its external connection with other phenomena through its location in a causal chain. Humorists frequently create humor by reversing this causal chain's direction. If we have traditionally expected one cause-effect sequence, the humorist can point out that the opposite sequence is now more likely:

The nation's financial troubles did not escape attention. "I mean the thrift industry is really in terrible shape," said Senator Bentsen, who is chairman of the Senate Finance Committee. "It's reached the point where if you buy a toaster, you get a free savings and loan."

[*New York Times*, 30 Nov. 1989, A6]

Or if someone asserts one cause-effect sequence, a humorist can assert the opposite:

> A toastmaster once introduced the humorist Irvin S. Cobb at a dinner party, saying: "All you have to do is put a dinner in his mouth, and out comes a speech." Cobb thanked the toastmaster for his gracious introduction, acknowledged the compliment, and added, "Your toastmaster is far more remarkable. All you have to do is put a speech in his mouth, and out comes your dinner."
>
> [Bergler 1956:190]

Since some cause-effect sequences can be reversed only in extreme situations, any situation that can reverse one of these cause-effect sequences must be extreme:

> I drive a beat-up old VW bug. A burglar felt so sorry for me he broke into my car and installed a tape player.
>
> [Frank Prinzi]

Causation can be complex. Aristotle distinguished four types of causes: material, efficient, formal, and final. Those who seek the relatively profound final cause may encounter those who think it witty to reply with the relatively petty efficient cause:

> When John Brodie was the star quarterback of the 49ers, he always held the ball for points after a touchdown. "Why does a high-priced star like you do that?" he was asked by a reporter. "Because if I don't," replied Brodie, "the ball falls over."
>
> [Herb Caen]

Seldom simple and direct, moreover, causation usually comprises a chain of lesser intermediate causes. Besides merely reversing cause and effect, then, comics can shift our focus to these intermediate causes. Rather than state the expected—most important original—cause, they can retrace the chain of causation only part way to a less important intermediate cause:

> Where does electricity come from?
> The wall.
>
> [Doug Kehoe]

Or the comic can short-circuit a causal chain by omitting its intermediate causes entirely, making a drastic effect appear uncaused:

> Rather than get divorced again, I'll just go find a woman I don't like and give her a house.
>
> [Lewis Grizzard]

Philosopher David Hume suggested that causation is merely a conventional concept, for we actually experience only correlation and temporal sequence. Even so, the humorist can still amuse by reversing correlation,

> as in a *Guindon* cartoon (1984) showing a man looking at a bathroom scale. The caption reads: Harry has a height problem. According to the weight chart he should be seven feet tall.

Or by reversing temporal sequence:

> There ought to be a *divorce ceremony* . . . paid for by the husband's parents . . . the couple walks backward through the church . . . they take off the ring and give it to the worst man . . . before the excouple goes off in their separate cars, the audience throws cooked rice.
>
> [Rick Reynolds]

If Western humorists reverse straight-line temporal sequences, Marxist humorists reverse dialectical ones, as in this recent Eastern European witticism:

> It turns out that Communism is the longest and most painful path from Capitalism to Capitalism.

Intention Reversal

Intention is a weaker form of causation. When people intend for something to happen, it usually does—but not always. Intention is what distinguishes people from objects, which presumably lack it. People intend; in consequence, the objects of their intentions are transferred or transformed. But when it appears as though objects are doing the intending and people are being moved or altered, comedy ensues. W. H. Auden describes two common reversals of intention that have been found funny. A comic contradiction results when

> the operation of physical laws upon inorganic objects associated with a human being [occurs] in such a way that it is they who appear to be acting from personal volition and their owner who appears to be a passive thing. [For example,] a man is walking in a storm protected by an umbrella when a sudden gust of wind blows it inside out. This is funny for two reasons: [1. The umbrella is supposed to be under the control of its owner. 2. The activating agent (the wind) is invisible.]. . . . The same contradiction is the basis of most of the comic effects of the clown. In appearance he is the clumsy man whom inanimate objects conspire against to torment.
>
> [1962:373]

Reversing customary temporal sequences, for instance, can appear to give objects intention:

> You know the highlight of a bulimic's birthday party?
> The cake jumps out of the girl.
>
> [Burt Katz]

Showing film in reverse also produces the humorous "special effect" of animating inanimate objects and deanimating animate ones, as in an early Chaplin film in which a hat appears of its own volition to draw itself into a hand. Modern technology (namely, "reverse scan" on the better video recorders) has democratized the ability to watch film backward, effectively doubling the number of movies that have ever been made as well as transforming comedies into tragedies and trage- dies into comedies:

> If you're bored with old movies, try watching them backwards on the
> VCR. . . . *Jaws* is the best. *Jaws* becomes a film about a giant shark that
> keeps throwing up people until they open the beach.
>
> [Howard Budgay]

Beside making natural objects appear intentional, comedians make natural processes appear humanly planned:

> A terrorist group in Beirut is taking responsibility for the earthquake.
>
> [Steve Allen]

They also portray apparent human control over fixed social processes:

> My recipe for inexpensive phone sex: Call for the time of day and start
> shouting, "All right, slut, say it again, only add 10 seconds."
>
> [Jim Samuels]

And they make the accidental appear intentional:

> I flew in from New York on a plane and I said to the clerk, "I have three
> pieces of luggage. I want this piece of luggage to go to Toronto. I want
> this piece of luggage to go to Cleveland. And I want this piece of lug-
> gage to go to Miami. He said, "We can't do that." I said, "Why not? You
> did it last week."
>
> [Henny Youngman]

Practical jokers, in particular, try to make their designed objects or planned events seem natural to prevent the butts of their jokes from becoming suspicious:

> My eye doctor is a practical joker. He has pictures of his family on his
> desk—all blurred.
>
> [Garry Shandling]

Conversely, we may also be amused by those who claim that natural human behaviors, particularly those of despised outgroups, are planned. In this pre-civil rights joke, a Southern sheriff attributed an implausible intention to a human being, who had been treated as an object, to restore to him enough human status to make him responsible for his own demise:

> The body of a Negro man was dragged from a river in Mississippi; almost sixty pounds of steel chain was wrapped around the body. These events occasioned the sheriff to remark: "Just like a colored man; steals more chain than he can swim the river with."

Responsibility is the downside of intentionality, especially when leading to negative events. Jews, in particular, have been held responsible for negative events, even when this attribution requires convoluted justification:

> The car of Rabbi Golden was stopped at the traffic light, waiting for the red to change to green, when the coupe driven by Father Mitchell crashed into him.
> At once, traffic cop Kelley hastened over, "Well now, father. . . . How fast would you say the good rabbi was going when he backed into you?"

Jews have even been held liable for the "benefits" of being discriminated against:

> Long line for milk in Russia. Not enough milk. Jews told to leave the line. Still not enough milk. Other non-Russians told to leave the line. Still not enough milk. Noncommunists told to leave the line. Actually, no milk at all. One communist to another as they were dispersing, "How about those Jews, they get all the breaks!"

Since most people try to avoid disreputable behaviors, it can be funny to do them *intentionally*. For example, a *Bizarro* cartoon (1989) shows a man talking to a woman in an upscale restaurant; the caption reads:

> I'm tired of good food and stimulating conversation. Let's criticize other people's clothing.

It can also be funny when means do not accomplish their intended ends:

> Don't you feel sorry for the men who had vasectomies in the 1970s who ended up having to wear condoms in the 1980s?
>
> [Mike Binder]

Misalignment between means and ends is a classic plot device in theatrical comedy.[5]

Statistical Incongruities

The comic compromises another set of connections within Western rationality: the cluster of logical relations between comparable things, particularly those similar on every dimension except magnitude. Through his authoritative textbook distinctions between various types of scales, sociological statistician Hubert Blalock (1960: esp. 11–16) taught a generation of social scientists how to describe the possible logical relations between things that differ in magnitude.

Nominal Interchange

Beyond mere dichotomies (which I have termed "binary logic"), Blalock calls the simplest relation between categories a "nominal scale." Categories related nominally may be exhaustive and nonoverlapping, but their difference in magnitude is irrelevant and unspecified. All comparable nominal categories (for example, Catholics, Protestants, and Jews) belong to the same larger set (religious groups) but each differs from the others most crucially in ways other than magnitude. Humor blurs the borders between nominal categories by switching traits between the members of each category:

> Father Malachy was walking down a street in Boston when he saw a large banner over a store:
>> Greenberg and O'Sullivan
> Father Malachy hastened in with a broad, broad smile. He was greeted by a bearded man wearing a *yarmulke.*
> "Well, sir," beamed Father Malachy, "I jist want ye t' know how foine it is afther all these years, for a simple Irishman to see your people and mine working together—and as partners! What a sorprise. What a sorprise!"
> "Father, I thank you. But I'll give you a bigger surprise," said the old man. *"I'm* O'Sullivan."

I will examine humorous trait switching between various nominal *social* categories in chapters 4 and 5.

Blalock goes on to compare to this nominal scale baseline the relations between categories whose differences in magnitude are relevant and specified.

Ordinal Disproportion

We may order categories by magnitude according to the *degree* they possess a certain characteristic, even if it's impossible to specify this degree precisely. One category may possess more or less of a given characteristic relative to other categories, though we do not know exactly how much more or less. Blalock calls the relation between categories by degrees along a single continuum an "ordinal scale" (better known today by Lofti Zadeh's term "fuzzy logic"). An ordinal ranking of groups according to their income, for example, might comprise the upper class, the middle class, and the lower class.

In keeping with their hierarchical world view, classical Greek comic theorists began to conceive of comedy as an ordinal relation by focusing on its vertical rather than horizontal incongruities. Although Aristotle's crucial treatise on comedy has been lost, Umberto Eco plausibly reconstructs its beginning in his novel *The Name of the Rose*, whose plot hinges on its imaginary rediscovery:

> In the first book [of the *Poetics*] we dealt with tragedy and saw how, by arousing pity and fear, it produces catharsis, the purification of those feelings. As we promised, we will now deal with comedy (as well as with satire and mime) and see how, in inspiring the pleasure of the ridiculous, it arrives at the purification of that passion. . . . We will show how the ridiculousness of actions is born from the likening of the best to the worst, . . . from the debasing of the characters. [1984:569]

Modern attempts to analyze comedy as an ordinal relation characterized by *vertical* incongruities began with Francis Hutcheson. In 1750 Hutcheson contrasted comedy (low) to Addison's conception of heroic poetry (high), which "gives us pleasure by filling the mind with great conceptions" using "similitudes and metaphors from objects of dignity and grandeur":

> That then which seems generally the cause of laughter is the bringing together of images which have contrary additional ideas, as well as some resemblance in the principal idea: *this contrast between the ideas of grandeur, dignity, sanctity, perfection, and the ideas of meanness, baseness, profanity,* seems to be the very spirit of burlesque; and the greatest part of our raillery and jest is founded upon it. [1987:32; emphasis added]

Herbert Spencer, though now known primarily for his humorless theory of social evolution, developed the most influential conception of ordinal comedy a century later. In 1860 Spencer (1910:452–66) published an article entitled "The Physiology of Laughter," which expounded his "surplus excitation" view of humor. Whoever encounters an incongruity experiences a surge of "nervous energy." Normally, a person would dissipate his suddenly increased nervous energy by generating new ideas and feelings. But when this direction is blocked (for instance "when the short silence between the *andante* and *allegro* in one of Beethoven's symphonies, is broken by a loud sneeze" [460]), his excess energy must discharge itself somewhere else: "an efflux through the motor nerves to various classes of the muscles, producing the half-convulsive actions we term laughter" (462). This "deflected discharge" or "relief" aspect of Spencer's theory of laughter has influenced psychologists (especially Freud [1963:146]) more than sociologists. But when Spencer specifies the cause of this surplus mental excitation, implications for the social sciences become broader. Examining a list of "nonludicrous incongruities," Spencer concludes that not every incongruity is humorous. To be funny, an incongruity must possess an additional property: it must *descend:* "Laughter naturally results only when consciousness is unawares transferred from great things to small— only when there is what we may call a *descending* incongruity" (1910:463). The antecedent part of a humorous incongruity must stimulate mental excitation, along with the expectation that it will continue and be resolved; the subsequent (or descending) part must not continue or resolve it satisfactorily. The two categories form an ordinal relation: we expected the second to be equal to the first; we are amused when it turns out to be less than the first.

In 1903 Theodor Lipps (1964:393–97) elaborated Spencer's adumbrated comic theory by defining the comical as "the surprisingly insignificant." We prepare ourselves for much conceptual activity, but encounter something demanding little conceptual activity. After a lengthy tiring hike to see what our guidebook described as a mountain's epic grandeur, we laugh upon discovering only a molehill there instead. In 1905 Freud (1963:69), strongly influenced by Lipps as well as Spencer, repeats a remark by Heinrich Heine as an example of what Lipps called "joking enumeration"—"Speaking generally, the inhabitants of Göttingen are divided into students, professors, philistines and donkeys"—a seemingly human series suddenly descending into an incongruous animal. A more recent joking enumeration that unexpectedly descends from the spirit to the body is Alexander Woollcott's oft quoted remark, "Everything I like is either illegal, immoral, or fattening."[6]

The comic mind, then, may feel compelled to complete a set of prestigious items with their *lowest* common denominator. If the best college football teams compete in the Rose Bowl, the Orange Bowl, and the Cotton Bowl, the comic mind will suggest that the worst ones should compete in the Toilet Bowl.

Many humorists have produced descending incongruities in which the last element is much lower than the first in sublimity, quality, importance, dignity, esteem, value, expense, etc. But no one has perfected the descending incongruity better than Rabelais, whose writings pull the exhilarated reader along a cognitive roller coaster, continually descending from high to low, lofty to grotesque, serious to comic (see Frame 1977:199–200). We best remember Rabelais for his smutty and scatological passages, but often forget how their placement—usually following a lofty philosophic or emotional passage—enhances their humor. In one passage, the giant Gargantua laments for his wife Badebec, who died giving birth to his son Pantagruel:

> Never shall I see her, never shall I find one like her; it's an inestimable loss to me! O my God, what had I done to you for you to punish me so? Why did you not send death to me earlier than to her? Ah, Badebec, my darling, my love, my little cunt (to be sure, hers was a good three acres and two sesterees in size).
>
> [Frame 1977:xv]

Descending incongruities are so humorous per se that a reader may be unable to keep from laughing at writers who alternate philosophical with sexual or scatological passages—like the Marquis de Sade—no matter how serious their intentions.

Modern humor abounds in examples of incongruities that descend from such momentous concerns as marital problems:

> There are big signs in Las Vegas that say,"Divorces, $65; with Salad Bar, $75."
>
> [Cathy Ladman]

global harmony:

> Recounting an engagement in Atlantic City that coincided with the Miss America Pageant, Jay Leno recalled with awe the aspirations of the newly crowned queen as put forth in her acceptance speech, "As Miss America, my goal is to bring peace to the entire world, and then to get my own apartment."

or religious belief:

> I used to be an atheist, but I gave it up. No holidays.

After awesome events subside into mundanity, the humor of descending incongruities reflects their spectators' efforts to reorient to everyday life. The great San Francisco earthquake of 1989 inspired the following:

> Moments after a part of the Bay Bridge had nearly collapsed on them, two house painters were sitting in their truck stunned, but in good humor, "I want my dollar [toll] back," said one.
>
> [San Francisco Examiner, 29 Oct. 1989, A19]

Since death is the most awesome event a human being encounters, juxtaposing it with almost any other aspect of human life—no matter how ordinarily important—creates a descending incongruity. Juxtaposing the morbid with the mundane underlies "the so-called humor of the gallows,"

> like the famous answer of the condemned criminal who was offered his last cigarette, "No, thank you. I've made up my mind to quit smoking" or the reply of the man who has just heard his death sentence, "Let that be a lesson to me."
>
> [Želvys 1990:330]

Holocaust humor is gallows humor writ large:

> A Jewish friend of mine told me a story in the early 1950's—a time not terribly long after the world learned of the horrors of Hitler's extermination camps—about two Jewish inmates who were being marched to the gas chamber by Nazi guards.
>
> One of the men was suddenly overcome by a wave of anger and began to shout at his oppressors, calling them every vulgar name he could think of.
>
> "Max," his companion whispered, "you'd better shut up or you're going to get us in trouble."
>
> [Steve Allen 1987:13]

Humor based on the relations between cause and effect as well as between means and ends is ordinal rather than binary when it results from disproportion rather than reversal or unintended consequence. Bergson (1956:112–16) describes the humor produced by "a great effect springing from a small cause" (like a rolling snowball):

> a caller rushing violently into a drawing room; he knocks against a lady, who upsets her cup of tea over an old gentleman, who slips against a glass window which falls in the street on to the head of a constable, who sets the whole police force agog, etc.

Bergson also describes the humor produced by "a great cause resulting in a small effect" (like a ball, after much movement, returning to its starting point):

> We have the same circular effect, the same return to the starting point, in a more recent play [*Les Surprises du divorce*]. A henpecked husband imagines he has escaped by divorce from the clutches of his wife and his mother-in-law. He marries again, when, lo and behold, the double combination of marriage and divorce brings back to him his former wife in the aggravated form of a second mother-in-law. [1956:115][7]

A more modern example of great effort for little effect, suggested during an energy crisis:

> Some ways to conserve energy: only plug in the electric clock when you want to know what time it is.
>
> [Peter Anthony]

Hegel examines the humor produced by the disproportion between means and ends:

> [Two] kinds of situations . . . lend themselves to comic treatment. . . . There is first of all the case of ends essentially trivial in themselves that come to be pursued with great shows of earnestness and elaborate preparations. Precisely because his purpose has been from the beginning essentially trivial, the fellow around whom such a situation develops can hardly be *personally ruined,* in any significant sense, by its inevitable collapse. . . .
>
> A situation the reverse of this develops when people adopt aims of real substance, hoping thereby to make themselves seem important, when in fact their characters and capacities are precisely the opposite of what success in such ventures demands. We have an instance in the *Ecclessiazuzae* of Aristophanes, where the women who are determined to frame and establish a new political constitution still retain all [their] capriciousness and passionate wilfulness. [Hegel 1979:182–83]

Eastman gives an example of how elaborate means may be humorously undercut by a trivial end:

> A man went to a baker and asked him to bake a cake in the form of the letter S. The baker said he had never baked such a cake but thought he could manage it, if the customer would give him a week to prepare the necessary tins. The customer agreed, the tins were prepared, the cake baked, and proudly shown to the customer when he returned a week later. "Oh, but you misunderstood me," the customer said. "You made it as a block letter, but I wanted script." "Oh well, that's all right," the baker said, "if you have the time to wait, I can make one in script. It will take me another week, however, as the tins will have to be made all over again." The customer agreed, and again the tins were prepared and the cake baked. When the customer returned a week later and saw the cake, he was delighted. "That's exactly what I wanted," he said. "I'm very glad," said the baker, preparing to wrap up the cake. "Now would you like to take it with you, or shall I send it to your house?" "Oh no, don't bother," the customer said. "I'll eat it right here."
>
> [1939:65–66; see also Fry 1968:150ff.]

What happens when incongruities go up instead of down? Spencer considered that effect too by contrasting "descending incongruities" with "ascending incongruities," which "not only fail to cause laughter, but work on the muscular system an effect of the reverse kind. When after something very insignificant there arises without anticipation something very great, the emotion we call wonder results; and this emotion is accompanied not by contraction of the muscles, but by relaxation of them. In children and country people, that falling of the jaw which occurs on witnessing an imposing and unexpected change, exemplifies this effect" (1910:464). If we are amused by an upper-class opera goer who sneaks away during intermissions to rob banks (à la James Bond movies), we are awed by a lower-class bank robber who listens to opera between crimes (à la *The Godfather* movies).

Interval-Ratio Excess and Insufficiency

The ordinal relation between categories described above highlights their *relative* magnitude; the following intercategory relations highlight their *absolute* magnitude. Categories related by a standard unit of measurement, such as a meter or a degree, form what Blalock calls an "interval scale." Categories related by an interval scale that also includes a zero point, such as the metric system for lengths or the Celsius system for temperatures, form what Blalock calls a "ratio scale." (In practice, Blalock hedges, all interval scales are also ratio scales, for we can always conceive of a zero point in theory if not always find one in reality.)

Those who push something to its comic extreme implicitly assume that the conventional view of it forms a zero point from which deviations are absolute.[8] Consequently, they *exaggerate* or *minimize* a phenomenon to make it funny by increasing or decreasing the degree of one of its characteristics *beyond the maximum-minimum band of variation allowed by the conventional conception of that phenomenon*. Of course, it is usually difficult to specify these zero points or the precise distances from them where exaggeration or minimization become humorous.

No theorist has been more insightful about the humor that manipulates absolute size, quantity, or degree than Max Eastman (1921:49–57), who considers the humors of both "overstatement" and "understatement."

The humor of overstatement or exaggeration evokes laughter not at much but at *too* much—at that which goes beyond the limiting distance of variation allowed by conventional views. (Unlike the humor of incongruity, which pulls apart its objects, the humor of overstatement merely stretches and distorts them—elongations most apparent in their visual form of caricature.) A second source of Rabelais's comedy is the humorous hyperbole:

> the enormous size of vaginas and their availability on the market, the dimensions of appetite for eating and drinking; the millions that a giant (or his mare) can drown in his (or her) urine. [Frame 1977:105–6]

In his later book on humor, Eastman (1939:152) quotes "Noel Coward's famous postcard from Paris with a picture of the Venus de Milo—'You see what will happen to you if you keep on biting your nails.'" Following Constance Rourke, Eastman (1939:149–55, 167–68) finds exaggeration to be the distinguishing characteristic of American humor, particularly of the South and West during the 1830s and 1840s. Not "mere exaggeration" (within the limiting distances allowed by convention), but "humorous exaggeration" (beyond these limits). All mythical heroes are exaggerations, but American mythical heroes like Paul Bunyan are humorous exaggerations. Unlike other countries, America has always regarded its legendary heros as a joke. American humor of overstatement reached its zenith toward the end of the nineteenth century in Mark Twain (1939:156–58). Unfortunately, Eastman complains, the humor of overstatement is so easy to overuse that American humor has begun to decline: "The easiest way to make things laughable is to exaggerate to the point of absurdity their salient traits. . . . since imitation is an easy and apelike trick and exaggeration a rather mechanical process, exaggerative imitation is within the scope of mediocre minds, and is more often a tedious perpetration than other forms of comic art. It is something that people who have no playful gift, but think they have, can learn to do" (1939:156–58). Eastman implies that the zero point is also surrounded by an outer band *beyond which* exaggeration is no longer funny; only "gifted" humorists can keep their exaggerations between these inner and outer bands.

Humorous exaggeration becomes evaluative when the exaggerator—explicitly or implicitly—locates something or someone on the extreme (usually negative) end of a scale that ranges from good to bad. Some comic exaggerators specify a generally accepted low point and then claim that their subject falls below even that nadir:

> When I was younger, it was said I resembled Al Capone, but I lacked his compassion.
>
> [Oscar Levant]

More extreme comic exaggerators claim that their subject is awful enough to alter well-established processes, such as by reversing a social custom (fig. 2).[9] The most extreme comic exaggerators claim that their subject is so negative it can cancel out the strongest positive; inept enough, for instance, to discredit even the saintly:

> In Carmel Valley last Saturday, Merv Griffin told about Pia Zadora starring in "The Diary of Anne Frank" in Dallas. "She was so bad," he reports, "that when the German soldiers arrived, everybody in the audience called out, 'She's upstairs!'"

> [Herb Caen]

The antithesis of the humor of overstatement is the humor of understatement. Eastman observes that we laugh not at little, but at *too* little:

Figure 2

"anything that does not measure up to some accepted standard of size, degree, quantity or intensity, can be the cause of laughter. . . . the sole thing laughter requires of an understatement is that it should be so far under as to be, for the real business of saying the thing, no good" (1921:49–57; 1939:179–80).[10] Eastman, however, points out the difficulty of specifying the tipping point where humorists minimize a character-istic's degree beneath its norm enough to make it funny:

> Of course the "quantities" we treat here are not usually of the kind contemplated by science. They are "intensive" rather than "extensive" quantities. When Mark Twain speaks of "a misunderstanding conducted with crowbars," you cannot put that word *misunderstanding* on the scales and determine just how much less it weighs than it ought to. You do, however, instantly perceive it not as an inappropriate, but as an inade-quate word. It belongs to a series—misunderstanding, dis-pute, altercation, quarrel, row, set-to, scrap, fight, battle—whose scope of meaning, or whose "psychic weight," varies on a scale. The series as a whole is appropriate, but this mem-ber stands low—it stands too low—in the scale. [1939:181]

Eastman quotes another example of understatement humor from P. G. Wodehouse:

> Few things so speedily modify an uncle's love as a nephew's air-gun bullet in the fleshy part of the leg.
>
> [1939:185]

"Modify . . . love" is certainly a weaker response to that situation than usually occurs. The main repository for the humor of understatement in America has been *The New Yorker*: "That is why it is dear to the heart of the New Yorkers, who are so given over to the ideal of 'playing down' jokes—a decadent ideal, although productive of the best cap-tion writing yet achieved—that they would almost feel pained if they saw somebody laugh out loud while reading their magazine. They go in for the reserved smile" (1939:182). This was true in Eastman's day, and is still true in ours; though the humor of the average New Yorker, as opposed to the humor of the literary New Yorker, is generally the opposite of understatement—indicating that the elite who read *The New Yorker* are still trying to distance themselves from their churlish neighbors. Since the end of the eighteenth century, the humor of under-statement has been the humor of the aristocratic class. Zijderveld be-lieves this dry euphemistic humor is dying out in "modern society, fond of slogans and slapstick" (1968:302–3). But understated humor has never been popular in America, whose humor has historically been skewed toward overstatement because its aristocratic class has been relatively small.

What makes exaggeration or minimization funny? Both the humors of overstatement and understatement are ironic because each *implies* the opposite of what it ostensibly *asserts* (Eastman 1921:55). Augmenting or diminishing a characteristic's magnitude to the extreme transforms it into something incongruous with its original state. For instance, increasing an event's frequency beyond a certain point negates and reverses its character. Clichés, not funny when used occasionally, become funny when used continually. *Beyond the Valley of the Dolls*, a 1970 film designed to consist entirely of seemingly sincere clichés, has become a comic cult classic. Likewise we may take seriously problems encountered singularly, but be unable to refrain from laughing at those encountered en masse. A common spoof of soap opera or country music squeezes almost every problem they portray—for example, alcoholism, crime, death—into a single episode or song:

I was drunk the day my mom got out of prison.
And I went to pick her up in the rain.
But before I could get to the station in my pick-up truck,
She got run over by a damn old train.

[Merle Haggard]

These forms of humor function homeostatically to support the conventional position by denigrating deviations. By drawing out minor deviations from the norm to an absurd extreme, either overtly through overstatement or covertly through understatement, exaggeration or minimization humor continually attempts to rescue and revive the conventional position before the natural tendency to drift away from it goes too far.

Dialectical Incongruities

Comedy sabotages a third cluster of logical relations within Western rationality: those between things related by more than reversal and differing by more than magnitude. The conceptions of the comic discussed above play off the monolectical logic of science, which formalizes symmetrical and complementary relations; those discussed below play off the dialectical logic of the humanities, which formalizes conflictual relations. Kant was the first modern philosopher to distinguish key pairs of antithetical concepts and to describe their logical relations in detail. Although Kant developed his own theory of the comic along different lines, those influenced by his distinctions (acknowledged or not) have tried to demonstrate how the comic complicates the logical relations between his disparate conceptual pairs in aesthetic, intellectual, and moral realms.

Aesthetic Paradox

Kant distinguishes between the form and the content of phenomena—a division humor tries to confuse by applying to the form what is usually applied to the content:

> You can't throw away garbage cans. They won't take them. . . . I even put up a sign that said, "Take this." They took the sign.
>
> [Haywood Banks]

Using Bertrand Russell's equivalent distinction between metalevel and object-level (first applied to humor by William Fry [1968: esp. 119–36]), John Allen Paulos differentiates two logical types of statements—"Object-level statements are statements *within* a (usually) formal system which is the object of study. . . . Metalevel statements are statements *about* the formal system or about the object level statements within it" (1985:39; see also 1980:23, 41–55)—then provides an illustrative joke:

> Groucho says to an acquaintance, "Did you hear the one about the organization for people whose IQs are in the bottom 2%? I was just looking at its newsletter called *Densa*." Groucho stops, bends closer, and says casually, "Do you get it?" The acquaintance, thinking he's being asked if he understands the joke, answers "Yes" to which Groucho rejoins, "I'm surprised. I thought you were a little brighter than that." [1985:40]

Finally, he interprets the joke in terms of this distinction: "Risking a charge of pedantry, I'll note that Groucho's acquaintance misinterprets 'Do you get it?' to be a metalevel question about the joke and not an object-level question that is part of the joke" (1985:40).[11]

The form or metalevel is usually invisible or irrelevant to the content or object-level. Self-referential humor, however, *refers* the metalevel form to the object-level content, reinforcing or contradicting it.

The form reinforces its content in *positive* self-referential humor, as when a car's bumper sticker reads Bumper Sticker or a truck's reads Keep on Truckin'. Or when an autobiographical book is entitled *My Life Is in Your Hands*. Two other examples of positive self-referential humor, literary:

> Once again there is no there there in Oakland. The "THERE" banner that has been flapping atop the Tribune tower blew away last week in a high wind.
>
> [Herb Caen]

and political:

> during the Irangate investigations a reporter asked President Reagan if William Casey, the director of the C.I.A., had carried on covert operations without the president knowing about it. President Reagan's exact response was, "Not to my knowledge."
>
> [Mark Russell][12]

The form contradicts its content in *negative* self-referential humor, which Paulos calls the humor of paradox:

> Modal jokes result when the content of a statement is incongruous with its form or mode of expression. That is, the statement's mode of expression belies its content, and the resulting incongruity is often humorous. . . . Examples are deskplates with "Plan Ahead" squeezed onto them, lapel buttons with the message "Support Mental Health or I'll Kill You," or a hysteric screaming "Relax!" [1980:42]

A more subtle example:

> I want to have a license plate that reads IFORGOT. That way, if I'm involved in a hit-and-run, the witnesses won't be able to tell the police my license number.
>
> [Guichy Guy]

Harvey Mindess points out that psychotherapy provides many examples of self-referential humor, both positive:

> *Patient:* Please help me doctor. I'm afraid I'm losing my memory.
> *Doctor:* Mmm-mmm. And how long have you had this problem?
> *Patient:* What problem?
>
> Are you a psychiatrist?
> Why do you ask?
> You *are* a psychiatrist.
>
> [1971:177, 107]

and negative:

> "Okay group," proclaims one encounter therapist, "we're going to keep practicing spontaneity until we get it right!"
>
> [1971:226]

Psychotherapy has become a frequent topic of self-referential humor by being a self-referential activity, obsessively probing behind object-level statements to find their metalevel self-reference. More generally, an egocentric age like ours, strongly influenced by psychotherapeutic conceptions, encourages self-referential humor, especially the negative form that manifests the paradoxes to which such an orientation leads ("I'm not insecure, am I?").

Although the classical Greek logicians often discussed the paradoxes inherent in negative self-reference, the oldest actual joke based on them I've been able to find comes from Cicero:

> [Nasica] had called upon the poet Ennius and, when he inquired for him at his front door, had been told by the housemaid that her master was not at home, which reply Nasica perceived to have been given by the master's order, he being in fact in the house. A few days later Ennius called at Nasica's, and asked for him at the entrance, whereupon Nasica called out that he was not at home. "What?", cries Ennius, "Do I not know your voice?" To which Nasica rejoined, "You are a shameless fellow; when I asked for you, I believed your maid when she said you were not at home; do you not believe me when I tell you the same thing at first hand?"
>
> [1942:407–9]

From classical civilization to modern society, negative self-referential humor has comprised self-denying statements of varying complexity, from the simple to the abstruse, as in the caption to a 1982 cartoon in which a man is speaking to a clerk at a sign agency:

> I want a dozen Think Metric signs, each about 16-by-24 inches.
>
> [Bill Hoest]

Self-denying statements become more complicated when their components are negated not concurrently but consecutively:

> A wife laughs at her distraught husband who has a loaded revolver at his temple. "Don't laugh," he tells her. "You're next."

If positive self-referential humor can become complex—for instance, Marshall McLuhan's remark that "Mae West . . . impersonated a female impersonator" (Redfern 1986:145)—negative self-referential humor can become really convoluted, even blurring the distinction between self-affirming and self- denying statements. The following interchange, for instance, seems to deny a request at the object-level in order to affirm it at the metalevel:

> Masochist to Sadist: "Beat me!"
> Sadist to Masochist: "No!"[13]

Humorists have also contraposed form and content vertically, rekeying the form's position on the hierarchy of styles—sublime, elevated, exalted; intermediate; gross, low, humble—to the level most contradictory to the content.

For instance, a comedian can try to fill a low style with high content:

I want to sing a song [in Beachboys style] about all the world's leaders gathering at Malibu, called "Surfin' for Peace."

[Tom Sharp]

The low style of the limerick contrasts ironically with potentially serious subjects:

There once was a whore from Rockaway,
Who you could smell from a block away,
I took one whiff,
And I got the syph,
And now it's eating my cock away.

Another low style is musical comedy, which Mel Brooks applied to perhaps the gravest subject matter of the twentieth century. In his 1968 movie *The Producers,* a broadway producer tries to make a musical comedy about those responsible for the Holocaust entitled *Springtime for Hitler.* The more fragile the content and the more gross the style that expresses it, the more ridiculous the result.

Try to imagine if Camus had been born a valley girl and had written *The Stranger* in a style not of minimal affect but of emotional hyperbole: "Mom died today. Or yesterday fur sure. I like, you know, barfed out. It was grodie to the max."

Conversely, the comedian may fill high style with low content, as in parody (see Bergson 1956:140–42). Among the elevated styles especially prone to parody with vulgar content are literary forms:

Comic verse thrives on the melodious union of incongruities, such as the "cabbages and kings" in Lewis Carroll's "The Walrus and the Carpenter," and particularly on the contrast between lofty form and flat-footed content. Certain metric forms associated with heroic poetry, such as the hexameter or Alexandrine, arouse expectations of pathos, of the exalted; to pour into these epic molds some homely, trivial content—"beautiful soup, so rich and green / waiting in a hot tureen"—is an almost infallible comic device. . . .

Another type of incongruity between form and content yields the bogus proverb: "The rule is: jam tomorrow and jam yesterday—but never jam today." Two contradictory statements have been telescoped into a line whose homely, admonitory sound conveys the impression of a popular adage. [Koestler 1974:8]

scientific forms:

If everyone keeps stacking *National Geographics* in garages and attics instead of throwing them away, the magazines' weight will sink the continent 100 feet sometime soon and we will be inundated by the oceans. . . .

Welcome to the *Journal of Irreproducible Results*. . . .

The journal spoofs, parodies and satirizes what its editor calls "the verbosity, pompousness, obscurantism and sheer stupidity encountered in scientific publications and projects."

Some items and quotes are real, reprinted from legitimate journals to illustrate their fatuity. But most articles are parodies written in technical scientific language, complete with diagrams, tables, formulas, mathematical calculations—and nonsensical conclusions. Far-reaching conclusions extrapolated from limited data are a favorite target of the journal. . . .

In "Pickles & Humbug," the journal reported the striking discovery that pickles cause cancer, communism, airline tragedies, auto accidents and crime waves. About 99.9% of cancer victims had eaten pickles sometime in their lives, the article pointed out. So have 100% of all soldiers, 96.8% of communist sympathizers and 99.7% of those involved in car and air accidents. Moreover, those born in 1839 who ate pickles have suffered a 100% mortality rate. And rats force-fed 20 pounds of pickles a day for a month ended up with bulging abdomens and loss of appetite. [*Los Angeles Times*, 9 Oct. 1982, 1.1.11][14]

and religious forms:

As Irving Kristol points out, there arose [in Judaism] a humor of "pious blasphemy." In innumerable jokes, for instance, the form is that of edifying rabbinic discourse, while the content is impudent and sophistical. The following is a parody of Talmudic logic, to be sung in the prefigured melody of Talmudic study: "If I have the right to take money out of my pocket, from which the other man has no right to take money, then is not my right all the greater to take money from *his* pocket, from which even he has the right to take money?" "The form," according to Kristol, "is impeccably orthodox; only the content negates the purpose of this form, which in the Talmud aims at establishing the immutable principles of justice and piety. [Altman 1971:150; see also Stora-Sandor 1991:215–17].

Putting the most obvious or absurd contents in the most serious forms produces the humor of "pseudoprofundity": "the auditor is made to feel that he has missed something important or that he cannot fathom profoundly simple, Zen-like paradoxes because he lacks the poetic sensibility" (Charney 1978:26). For example, the inspirational "Deep Thoughts" segment of "Saturday Night Live":

It takes a big man to cry,
but it takes a bigger man
to laugh at that man.

[Jack Handey]

Although contradictions between style and content are usually sustained throughout the parody, sometimes only its ending reveals them to be mismatched retrospectively:

I can safely say I have no prejudices. Let a man be black or white, Christian, Jew, or Moslem—it's all the same to me. All I have to know is that he's a human being. He couldn't be worse.

[Mark Twain]

Twain concludes what appears to be a humanistic homily by suddenly crashing its elevated style into a misanthropic content, enhancing the humor produced by the style-content contradiction with that produced by a descending incongruity.

An increasingly common genre of content/form, object-level/meta-level, humor undermines the distinction between *reality* and *media;* more precisely, between the immediate presentation of reality and its mediated representation.[15] (This humor genre is traceable back to *Don Quixote.*) Separately, reality and media have their distinct forms of humor. Technically, satire imitates reality critically whereas parody imitates media uncritically. But satire and parody have become interchangeable in usage and difficult to distinguish in practice, in part because much satire has been directed against the media itself (see for instance Steve Allen 1987:142).

Reality/media humor disputes the traditional assumption about which should be given the "accent" of ontological priority. It is not true that reality is *given* whereas media representations of it are *socially constructed.* But it is true that, although reality may be as socially constructed as media representations of it, most people believe that reality's "construction" has ontological priority, that reality is "obviously" more "real" than representations of it by the media. Whoever does not give ontological priority to reality, they believe, is stupid or even schizophrenic.

Humorists, however, side with the stupid or schizophrenic by merging media and reality. Aspects of the media they incongruously insert into the mundane range from merely its jargon—

as in the 1986 *Gumpertz* cartoon where a man with a queasy look, having eaten some poorly digesting food, says to his wife over dinner, "Please stand by. I'm experiencing technical difficulties."—

to its actual components—

> as in the 1986 *Wm. Hamilton* cartoon, where a waking man says to his
> wife, "My dreams have started running commercials."

Beyond merely regarding some media conventions as "real," more sophisticated humorists draw the more extreme conclusion that what we
regard as "reality" is unreal, or at least no more real than its mediated version,

> as when one cartoon humanoid said to another, in a 1985 *Mal* cartoon,
> "I feel my role in life has been reduced to a cameo appearance."
>
> After Jerry Ford made his cameo appearance on "Dynasty" Wednesday
> night, Jerry Pritikin mused: "So now we have an ex-president playing an
> actor and an ex-actor playing President." As the graffitists put it, "There is
> no God, just Theater."
>
> [Herb Caen]

In the most extreme versions of this kind of humor, we laugh as
the accent of ontological priority oscillates back and forth between the
incongruous realms of media and reality. In his 1981 short story "The
Kugelmass Episode," Woody Allen describes someone who continually shifts between being a real person and being a fictional character
in *Madame Bovary*. In his 1985 movie *The Purple Rose of Cairo*, he portrays
someone who shifts between being a film character and being a real
person. Garry Shandling did for television in the late 1980s what
Woody Allen did for books and movies. Only he himself was the main
character in a television show, "It's Garry Shandling's Show," which
was about the making of that very television show.

> In fact, much is made of how his show "breaks" the fourth
> wall of TV, like the old "Burns and Allen Show," by having
> Shandling discuss the plot of the show with us, but it goes
> well beyond that. It breaks the fifth, sixth, and seventh walls
> as Shandling ambles between the show (i.e., the set), the cam-
> era, and the studio audience.
>   He doesn't just talk to us, he discusses the show itself—how
> the plot is working itself out—with the viewers but also with
> people in the studio, the characters in the show, and the actors
> *playing* the characters. It's part rehearsal, part improv session,
> yet tightly scripted and ingeniously staged, with the added
> dimension of giving the impression that we're "in" on things
> and stepping behind the scenes. They even kid their own gags,
> as when someone once yelled at Garry, "Will you *quit* talking

to that camera!" [Gerald Nachman, *San Francisco Chronicle*, "Datebook," 1 May 1988, 17][16]

And the character Garry applied such media metaphors to his everyday life on the show as "Oh-Oh, I feel a 'dissolve' coming on." Perhaps the show's best-known positive self-referential humor was its theme song:

This is the theme to Garry's show
the opening theme to Garry's show
this is the music that you hear as you watch the credits.

All this to confuse the traditional distinction between media and reality until we laugh at our inability to distinguish them.

Intellectual Fallacy

The nineteenth-century philosopher Arthur Schopenhauer, who developed the preeminent theory of humor's logic, explained the ludicrous as a fallacious relation between the general and the particular (thereby accounting for the whole of humor, he characteristically believed). In *The World as Will and Representation*, Schopenhauer laid out his biological interpretation of Kant's distinction between conceptual and perceptual. Laughter, he specified in volume 1, results from the discrepancy between abstract rational knowledge and knowledge acquired more directly from perception: "This very incongruity of knowledge from perception and abstract knowledge, by virtue of which the latter always only approximates to the former as a mosaic approximates to a painting, is the cause of a very remarkable phenomenon . . . I refer to *laughter.*" The incongruity between objects actually *perceived* and the same objects abstractly *conceived*, in short, produces laughter. We are amused whenever we suddenly equate empirically different objects by subsuming them under a single concept. "Now the more correct the subsumption of such actualities under the concept from one standpoint, and the greater and more glaring their incongruity with it from the other, the more powerful is the effect of the ludicrous which springs from this contrast."[17] "All laughter," Schopenhauer concludes with his usual conceit, "is occasioned by a paradoxical, and hence unexpected subsumption, it matters not whether this is expressed in words or in deeds. This in brief is the correct explanation of the ludicrous" (1969; 1:58–59).

Schopenhauer elaborated his subsumption theory of the ludicrous with examples in volume 2, clarifying its various types. "Wit" is the mental facility for locating an object under a concept, even though the object had seemed very different from all the other objects usually grouped under that concept (1969; 2:96; see also 1:59). For example, take

> the well-known anecdote of the Gascon at whom the king laughed on seeing him in the depth of winter in light summer clothes, and who said to the king: "If your Majesty had put on what I have put on, you would find it very warm"; then to the question what he had put on, replied: "My whole wardrobe."

"Under this latter concept is to be thought the immense wardrobe of a king as well as the single summer jacket of a poor devil, the sight of which on his freezing body appears very incongruous with the concept." (1969; 2:92–93). Schopenhauer contrasts wit, in which the mind moves from perception to conception, with "absurdity," in which it moves from conception to perception and notices "this real thing [perception] now brings to light any incongruity with the concept which was overlooked" (1969; 12:96). For example, "When someone had stated that he was fond of walking alone, an Austrian said to him: 'You like to walk alone; so do I; then we can walk together.' He starts from the concept 'A pleasure which two people like can be enjoyed by them in common,' and he subsumes under this the very case that excludes community" (1969; 2:96).[18] Absurdity in theory leads to folly in practice. Whoever subsumes under the same concept objects fundamentally different in other respects begins to treat them the same way "until, to the astonishment of the person acting, their great difference in other respects stands out; this species of the ludicrous is called *folly*. . . . As the play requires action, this species of the ludicrous is essential to comedy" (1969; 1:59–60; 2:96).[19]

The most logically rigorous form of witty subsumptions Schopenhauer discusses is the faulty syllogism. Instead of incongruously subsuming "a real object of perception" under a concept, we can also incongruously subsume a lower generality "species-concept" under a higher generality "genus-concept." "In fact, if we want to know the thing absolutely explicitly, we can refer everything ludicrous to a syllogism in the first figure, with an undisputed *major* and an unexpected *minor* maintained, to a certain extent, only by chicanery; and it is in consequence of this combination that the conclusion has the quality of the ludicrous" (1969; 2:92). Schopenhauer does not explicate the "chicanery" that maintains the faulty syllogisms of humor, but, considering its potential to clarify what our society believes to be the correct syllogisms of seriousness, such sleight of mind seems worth pursuing.

Humorous "pseudosyllogisms" appear to have the form of true syllogisms, but their premises do not actually lead to their conclusion.

A pseudosyllogism may be funny because its premises support a much *stronger* conclusion than that obtained. For instance, the syllogist may interpret each premise in isolation, without considering how their interaction affects their conclusion. Freud provides an example of a joke whose conclusion should have been more than the sum of its premises:

> The *Schadchen* was defending the girl he had proposed against the young man's protests.
>
> *Young man:* I don't care for the mother-in-law. She's a disagreeable, stupid person.
>
> *Schadchen:* But after all you're not marrying the mother-in-law. What you want is her daughter.
>
> *Young man:* Yes, but she's not young any longer, and she's not precisely a beauty.
>
> *Schadchen:* No matter. If she's neither young nor beautiful she'll be all the more faithful to you.
>
> *Young man:* And she hasn't much money.
>
> *Schadchen:* Who's talking about money? Are you marrying money then? After all it's a wife that you want.
>
> *Young man:* But she's a hunchback too.
>
> *Schadchen:* Well, what *do* you want? Isn't she to have a single fault?

Freud's analysis: "The broker behaved as though each separate defect was got rid of by his evasions, whereas in fact each one of them left a certain amount of depreciation behind which had to be added to the next one. He insisted on treating each defect in isolation and refused to add them up into a total" (1963: 61–62).

Or a pseudosyllogism may be funny because its premises support only a much *weaker* conclusion than that obtained. A joke may overderive its punch line from its setup, as well as underderive it. What at first appeared to be the conclusion of a true syllogism turns out to be part of no syllogism at all. Whoever made the following blooper intended his last statement to be unrelated to his previous statements (connected by only an *and*), but his audience interpreted his last statement as the conclusion of an enthymeme (implied syllogism) (connected by a *therefore*), whose major premise (which they inferred) is a comic, if not empirical, truth:

> Local news: "Mr. Baker, who applied for the job, seemed to be very well qualified. He is obviously a man of sound judgement and intelligence. Mr. Baker is not married."

Translated into syllogistic form:

(People of sound judgement and intelligence do not get married.)
Mr. Baker is of sound judgement and intelligence.
Therefore, Mr. Baker did not get married.

Or consider another kind of pseudosyllogism:

If you can pick your friends,
and you can pick your nose,
Why can't you pick your friend's nose?

[Soupy Sales]

Translated into syllogistic form:

A person can pick his friends.
A person can pick his nose.
Therefore a person can pick his friend's nose.

This conclusion, however, would follow only if "nose" were a subset of "friends," which it is not. Because the premises are actually unrelated, the conclusion does not follow.

These logical non sequiturs constitute nonsense humor (currently called "off the wall," after the unpredictable bounce of a ball).[20] Like the aesthetic paradoxes of self-reference or pseudoprofundity, intellectual nonsense mystifies its audience. Unable to follow its seeming logic, they are often reduced to supplying logic where none exists.

> On the simplest level of non sequiturs, verbal nonsense possesses an air of mystery and unexplored metaphoric potentiality. The displaced logic teases the imagination to complete propositions that cannot logically be completed. We search for the hidden link in the following conditional utterance: "If I had a sister, I'm sure she would love Camembert." . . . The following German proverb is familial and domestic in its imaginative thrust: "If my grandmother had wheels, she would be a bus." . . . We would like to understand the logic of this statement, just as audiences that listen to double-talk usually take an inordinately long time to figure out that they are hearing a non-language. We are hopelessly vulnerable in our inherent and automatic manufacture—nay secretion—of significance. [Charney 1978:25–26]

Since nonsense humor is nonrational, it is depreciated by those who value rationality. Even the early television comedian Sid Caesar, whose humor used to *distort* rationality, criticizes a sketch in "Saturday Night Live," and modern comedy in general, for using non sequiturs to *disrupt* rationality entirely: "The sketch did not have a beginning, a middle or an end. Everything was done for shock value . . . which we call 'off the wall.' In off-the-wall humor, which prevails today, you can use any non sequitur for shock value, though it has nothing to do with the story your sketch is trying to tell." [*TV Guide*, 5 Nov. 1983, 10] Conversely, nonsense humor is appreciated by the prerational (children), the temporarily hyporational (drunken college students), and the postrational (many intellectuals) (Freud 1963:125–27; Mindess 1971:81–82, 175).[21]

Moral Deficiency

Alongside the aesthetic distinction between form and content, and the intellectual distinction between general and particular, Kant analyzes the moral distinction between the ideal and the real. Friedrich Schiller, the first to elevate this last distinction to the most important opposition in German philosophy, was also the first (1795) to connect it with comedy. "The poet is a satirist when he takes as subject the distance at which things are from nature, and the contrast between reality and the ideal . . . In satire, the real as imperfection is opposed to the ideal, considered as the highest reality" (1964:307).[22]

The literary satire best known for deriving humor from the contrast between the ideal and actual world is, of course, *Don Quixote*. Since the discrepancy between ideal and actual has been most extreme in war, the most striking satires—from Stendhal's *The Charter House of Parma* to Joseph Heller's *Catch-22*—have juxtaposed its traditional heroic ideal with the grisly chaos of its actual battles.

Later (1819) Hazlitt brings this distinction to England in the famous introductory sentences to his *Lectures on the Comic Writers, etc. of Great Britain*: "Man is the only animal that laughs and weeps; for he is the only animal that is struck with the difference between what things are, and what they ought to be. We weep at what thwarts or exceeds our desires in serious matters; we laugh at what only disappoints our expectations in trifles" (1930; 6:5). Samuel Coleridge (1836) spiritualizes the distinction between ideal and actual (while mundanizing the descending and ascending incongruities Spencer would later discuss): "is there some one humoritic point common to all that can be called humorous? . . . I think there is;—and that it consists in a certain reference to the general and the universal, by which the finite great is brought into identity with the little, or the little with the finite great, so as to make both nothing in comparison with the infinite. The little is made great, and the great little, in order to destroy both; because all is equal in contrast with the infinite" (1951:262). Finally, the tradition that bases comedy on the distinction between ideal and real enters France with Bergson in 1900: "The most common of these contrasts is perhaps that between the real and the ideal, between what is and what ought to be. Here again transposition may take place in either direction. Sometimes we state what ought to be done, and pretend to believe that this is just what is actually being done; then we have *irony*. Sometimes, on the contrary, we describe with scrupulous minuteness what is being done, and pretend to believe that this is just what ought to be done; such is often the method of *humour*" (1956:142–43). Bergson employs this distinction particularly when speaking of how comedy corrects our "imperfections" by waking us from our "illusions" (1956:117, 181).

But the most extensive and systematic discussion of comedy's relation to the contradiction between the perfect ideal world and the imperfect actual world can be claimed by American aesthetician James Feibleman. Both comedy and tragedy, for Feibleman, "emerge from the same ontological problem: the relation of the logical to the historical order" (1949:98). Comedy emphasizes how much the world as it is falls short of the world as it ought to be—thereby hoping to reduce this gap:

> Comedy is one kind of exemplification that nothing actual is wholly logical. . . . A constant reminder of the existence of the logical order as the perfect goal of actuality, comedy continually insists upon the limitations of all experience and of all actuality. The business of comedy is to dramatize and thus make more vivid and immediate the fact that contradictions in actuality must prove insupportable. It thus admonishes against the easy acceptance of interim limitations and calls for the persistent advance toward the logical order and the final elimination of limitations. [1949:81–82]

Comedians must continually highlight the failure of the actual world to measure up to the ideal world because the routine of existence tends to obscure this discrepancy:

> Needless to say, this kind of ridicule does service to the ideal, to the truth of an ideal society, by jesting at things which in the current society have come to be taken too seriously. Customs and institutions, in virtue of their own weight, have a way of coming to be regarded as ultimates. But the comedians soon correct this error in estimation, by actually demonstrating the forgotten limitations of all actuals. In this sense the clown, the king's jester, and the film comedian . . . correct overevaluation by exhibiting current evaluations in the light of

their shortcomings. The corrosive effect of humor eats away the solemnity of accepted evaluation, and thus calls for a revaluation of values. [1949:85–86]

Feibleman mentions two specific techniques by which comedians have denigrated "the limited orders of actuality" to affirm "the ideal logical order": "It may, for example, be achieved (1) by means of direct ridicule of the categories of actuality (such as are found in current customs and institutions), or it may be achieved (2) by confusing the categories of actuality as an indication of their ultimate unimportance, and as a warning against taking them too seriously. . . . The first is the method employed by Ring Lardner; the second, that employed by Gertrude Stein" (1949:82).[23] A more recent example of the first technique ridicules the actual practice of parenthood by chronicling its humorous discrepancies from the idealized parental role in a self-help book entitled *Raising Children in a Bad Mood*. A more recent example of the second confuses modern instrumental and primitive religious categories by portraying an actual rather than idealized pilot's monologue at the beginning of an airplane flight:

> This is your captain speaking. For the next three minutes I will babble incoherently while your stewardess Nancy performs the ancient Malasian rite of the hands.
>
> [Jeremy Kramer]

I will examine how various aspects of the *social world* fall ludicrously short of their ideal in chapters 6 through 8.

Ridiculing the categories of *actuality* to show their discrepancies from the ideal, or confusing them to show their ultimate unimportance, are not the only techniques that produce axiological humor. A third technique employing "value inversion," one unmentioned by Feibleman, confuses the categories of *ideality* itself to show their relativism.

All societies organize their ideal values into hierarchies; they differ only in where they locate particular ideal values in these hierarchies. Nietzsche was one of the first modern thinkers to point out that all social values are not equal but stratified. The destiny of the *Übermensch*, goes his main theme roughly, is to revaluate, and especially to invert, the value hierarchy of his society.

Unexpectedly inverting a society's value hierarchy creates humorous incongruities as old virtues become new vices and vice versa—explaining why we frequently find Nietzsche and others who employ this technique amusing.[24] Like these philosophers, humorists revolve every ideal to reveal a counterideal:

> Did you hear about the big new prize contest? The first prize is one week in Philadelphia; the second prize is two weeks in Philadelphia.

Since the ideals people pretend to esteem may not be the ones they actually practice, it can be amusing to hear from those who speak without this hypocrisy, who "tell it like it is." In American society that might mean blatantly ranking materialistic values above nonmaterialistic ones (fig. 3). Likewise, a new form of humor captures the old Soviet Union's current value transition from once respected proletarian ideals to once derided bourgeois merchandise:

> Upon my arrival in Odessa, I mentioned my fears to one of my colleagues, whom I'd be appearing with that night at the Comedy Day performance. He responded that things had opened up tremendously, pointing out that glasnost had helped change the slogan "We will bury you" to "Do you want fries with that?"
>
> [Yakov Smirnoff]

Figure 3

More generally amusing are those who shift rapidly from aspiring for any immaterial ideal to craving for any capitalist commodity, by nature trivial and ephemeral.

Conversely, humor that inverts values can transform not only ideals into counterideals but also counterideals into ideals. Lily Tomlin, for instance, warns consumers about the coming crisis in plastics, currently a lowly valued item in our ecologically oriented age:

> "We are running out of plastics," she says. Unless something is done, she warns us, "there will be a panic on plastics. . . . Greedy people will be hoarding things like Baggies, rain bonnets, shower curtains, Astroturf, spatulas, plastic toothpicks, Parcheesi dice, and leisure suits." In addition, "Tupperware parties will have to be shut down." We are in danger of "an end to civilization as we know it."

The humorists of Western civilization frequently invert its major positive values, such as industriousness, by calling attention to those who don't share them:

> Flanagan and Monaghan were working a trench. Flanagan brings Monaghan a massive thump on the side of the head with his sledgehammer. . . . I'm afraid, Mrs. Monaghan, your husband will never work again, says the doctor. She says: I'll go in and tell him, it might cheer the poor man up a bit.

> I have a friend who's so lazy he won't even go to a ball game until the second inning. That's so he won't have to stand for the National Anthem. . . . He even married a pregnant woman.

They also invert its major negative values, such as crime, by calling attention to those who elevate them over supposedly higher values, such as intimacy. In Woody Allen's 1969 film *Take the Money and Run*, his criminal persona says of a pretty girl, "After 15 minutes I wanted to marry her. After 30 minutes I'd completely given up the idea of snatching her purse."

Sexual desire has recently risen in our society's value hierarchy. Consequently, humorists now describe those who still subordinate it to more trivial desires—like hunger:

> I was broke when I was starting out. I used to go to orgies for the grapes.
> [Rodney Dangerfield]

or more reprehensible desires—like greed:

> Donald Trump was at a party to celebrate the launching of his new Trump Shuttle air service. A beautiful young woman came over to him, told him how much she admired him, and offered to perform a blowjob on him. Trump responds, "What's in it for me?"

Turning from the basic values of our society to what inverts them, we can define an obsession as an orientation to something lowly valued by our society, like alcohol, that—as humorists show—overrides all other higher values, like sexual desire:

> Our Unabashed Dictionary defines *alcoholic* as a man who goes into a topless bar just for a drink.
>
> [*Playboy*, Jan. 1982][25]

Other devalued obsessions, like television, can also override higher values, like communicating about relationship problems:

> I'm watching TV and my husband comes in and says he wants to discuss our sexual problems. Like I'm going to turn off "Wheel of Fortune" for that.
>
> [Roseanne Barr]

Although our society does not value death per se, it does value treating death more seriously than other worldly concerns. Ridiculed, therefore, are those who treat death as less important than such relatively trivial mundane values as money:

> *Hold-up man:* "Your money or your life."
> *Jack Benny:* [*pause*] "I'm thinking it over."

theater:

> A lady sent away a year in advance for tickets to *A Chorus Line,* the smash Broadway hit. You know how hard those tickets are to get. Well, the night of the show, she was sitting in the theater with an empty seat next to her. A man seated behind her said, "Excuse me, lady. Why is that seat next to you empty?" She answered, "Well, I wrote away a year ago for tickets for my husband and myself, but unfortunately he died." The man said, "I'm sorry to hear that, but didn't you have any friends you could give the ticket to?" The lady said, "Yes, but they're all at the funeral."
>
> [Morty Gunty]

or games:

> "Eugene, you promised to be home by 2 o'clock this afternoon and now it's after six."
> "Honey, please. My best friend Wally is dead—dropped dead on the 10th green this morning."
> "Oh, how terrible."
> "It certainly was. The whole day, it's been hit the ball . . . drag Wally . . . hit the ball . . . drag Wally."
>
> [Larry Wilde]

The rational and the comic, we have seen, have distinct logics—not merely different but antithetical.[26] Unless kept separate,[27] their opposing logics can lead to mutual annihilation: (1) Rationality can nullify humor—jokes become less funny when explained, which translates comic logic into rational logic; (2) Humor can nullify rationality—rational arguments become less persuasive when ridiculed, which translates rational logic into comic logic. (Thus the use of ridicule in rhetoric to "dispel distasteful suggestions not easily weakened by reasonings" [Cicero 1942:373–75].)

As a way to interconnect the elements of the world, then, comedy is an alternative to rationality. But is it better?

Although both Wittgenstein (in theory) and Freud (in detail) (1963: esp. 60ff., 124ff., 203ff.) traced various kinds of *humor* to "faulty reasoning," I have traced various kinds of *rationality* to "faulty humor." (If humor lacks what is valuable in rationality, rationality also lacks what is valuable in humor.) I have tried to show that the logic of jokes is not only *not* inferior to the logic of rationality but may actually be superior to it. Just as non-Euclidian geometry revealed the limits of ordinary geometry, the non-Aristotelian logic of humor reveals the limits of rational logic. Both conceptual revolutions circumscribe traditional geometry or rationality by locating them within a larger set of alternative geometries or logics, articulating their relative strengths and weaknesses.

Insofar as comic connections can point up the ways that rational connections are arbitrary or spurious, and point to the larger set of logics that include both rationality and comedy, the comic unification of the world is potentially the more profound.

3

Indistinct Beings

The comic manifests not only the incongruities *within* rationality described in the last chapter. It also exposes the incongruity *between* rationality as a whole (its unified ideal, without its previously noted incoherences) and irrational existence—revealing, in short, the disparity between knowing and being, logic and life. The comic targets especially those who try to apply rational systems to reality too rigorously, observes Catholic theologian William Lynch:

> The comic is par excellence the great enemy of the univocal mind. I call univocal that kind of mind which, having won through to all the legitimate unities and orderings of the logical and rational intelligence, insists, thereafter, on descending through the diversities, densities and maelstroms of reality in such a way as to give absolute shape to it through these unities and orderings. This mentality wishes to reduce and flatten everything to the terms of its own sameness, since it cannot abide the intractable differences, zigzags and surprises of the actual. It is, therefore, impatient, rigid, inflexible, intolerant, and even ruthless. [1969:40]

But just because comedy is hostile to procrustean rational systems does not mean it is without order itself. Rather, comedy may simply organize phenomena around a different point from all logical organizations. Lynch continues, "On the surface, comedy, with its antipathy to the order of things, seems anarchic. . . . But it is not at all anarchic; it is only a defender of another and more human order. . . . Metaphysically, it is a defender of being against the pure concept or category" (1969:41). This entire book describes the differences between the logical and comical organizations of our society's major systems, between formal categories and formless being.

The relentless logical mind, however, which tries to categorize everything, has even tried to categorize amorphous being itself into its component *beings*—a categorization the even more relentless comic mind has tried to undo. This chapter will focus on their different organizations of "anthropological systems," the logical distinctions between human and other kinds of beings that comedy blurs.[1]

These beings are the primary categories of culture, the basic units of the content of linguistic and rational forms. The logical order divides being into *distinct beings* arranged in a clear hierarchy of superhuman, human, and subhuman. But "the home of the comic," Lynch points out, is the *"analogical order"*:

> Analogy . . . says . . . that being is the same and one everywhere, but everywhere profoundly different. . . . A thing need not step out of the human to be all things. . . . The mud in man, the lower-most point in the subway, is nothing to be ashamed of. It can produce . . . the face of God. . . . Things are funny, precisely because they can recall the relation between God and themselves. . . . To recall this incredible relation between mud and God is . . . the function of the comic. [1969:42–43]

The analogical order divides being into *similar beings* (both same and different) that have some (but not all) attributes in common. Comedy juxtaposes the logical and analogical orders of being, producing incongruous beings both distinct and similar, stratified and equal, whose bilevel characteristics belie cosmic clarity.

Arthur Lovejoy examined the evolution of both these cosmic schemes in the Western world under the general rubric of the "Great Chain of Being."[2]

The *superhuman* stratum of the Great Chain of Being includes a divine level, describable only as the negative of earthly existence, and an angelic level, inhabited by incorporeal beings of pure intelligence. Since we tend to laugh at belief systems when our faith in them is weakening—rather than when we believe or disbelieve in them fully— jokes about God and angels flourished when our society's religious belief system was waning during the first two-thirds of the twentieth century. But this kind of religious joke has become less popular today because the number of exbelievers, who find funny the violation of a passé system, has declined relative to the number of nonbelievers, for whom these superhuman levels have always been irrelevant, and the smaller number of believers, for whom these superhuman levels are still inviolate.

Jokes about the *subhuman* stratum of the Great Chain of Being, which comprises animal and object levels, on the other hand, seem to have increased since Darwin, Marx, and modern science described man as basically a biological or physical entity. Because modern ideas have weakened the human/subhuman boundary, jokes that identify human beings with animals and objects have become more numerous, though perhaps less humorous.

Being the "middle link" in the Chain, *human* beings possess both superhuman and subhuman characteristics. In a rare attempt to draw out the comic implications of his topic, Lovejoy notes the humor created by man's peculiar dual nature:

> The definition of him as the "middle link" . . . emphasized the peculiar duality of his constitution and the tragi-comic inner discord in him which results from this. . . . He is therefore . . . torn by conflicting desires and propensities; as a member of two orders of being at once, he wavers between both, and is not quite at home in either. . . . He is a strange hybrid monster; and if this gives him a certain pathetic sublimity, it also results in incongruities of feeling, inconsistencies of behavior, and disparities between his aspirations and his powers, which render him ridiculous. [1960:198–99]

The incongruities produced by Man's paradoxical position, sharing mind with angels and body with beasts, have made him particularly vulnerable to laughter.

Although most people today no longer conceive of their cosmos as strictly stratified, the Great Chain of Being remains a viable enough paradigm for them to find violations of its hierarchical structure funny. Upward or downward cross-breeding between its links begets the humor of anthropological systems. Just as the comic mind reverses attributes between equal but opposite phenomena, it also upshifts attributes from lower to higher beings or downshifts them from higher to lower.

Uptransformations: Appreciative ("Good") Humor

Joseph Addison was the first to note (1711) that humor about subhuman beings actually pertains to human beings: "when we laugh at a brute or even at an inanimate thing it is at some action or incident that bears a remote analogy to any blunder or absurdity in reasonable creatures" (1965; 1:203). A century later, Schopenhauer clarified the cognitive process motivating us to laugh at animals that are *partly* human: "certain animal forms, such as apes, kangaroos, rabbits, and the like, sometimes appear ludicrous, because something in them resembling man causes us to subsume them under the concept of the human form, and, starting from this concept, we perceive their incongruity with it" (1969; 2:97–98). Inanimate or animate objects that cross the subhuman/human boundary, then, become comic by acquiring human characteristics or performing human activities incongruous with their original nature.

Conversely, we can discover the essential and unique characteristics of human beings by determining which ones become funny when acquired by something subhuman. Such abstract anatomical aspects as head shape or facial texture must be essential elements of the human appearance because we are supposed to laugh at cartoons of balloons or vegetables that simulate them. For example,

> a cartoon plum says to a peach: "I don't care how late we are. You're not leaving this house until you've shaved."

Besides looking somewhat human, an inanimate object like a puppet or a marionette may move humanly. It is of course easier for animate than inanimate objects to both look and act like human beings. The Walt Disney cartoon characters have enough human features and gestures for Koestler (1974:8) to call them "man-animal hybrids." George Lucas's *Star Wars* robots likewise possess enough human features and gestures to be called "man-object hybrids." Animate objects can move in a sufficiently human-like manner to appear to be performing human activities: A. Whitney Brown once described a restaurant sign that reads:

> Steak & Lobster
> Dancing Nightly

But even inanimate objects can sometimes seem to imitate human behavior:

> You know about the earthquakes out here. But did you know they are actually part of California's unique physical fitness program. The state does the aerobics and you lie still.
>
> [Johnny Carson]

Naturalists distinguish species particularly by their mode of reproduction. Humans, of course, copulate somewhat differently from animals, moderately differently from plants, and very differently from objects, which are by definition sexless. Humorists, consequently, like to scramble this sexual scheme,

> as in the 1987 *Wheeler* cartoon that imagines inanimate intercourse between a pencil and a pencil sharpener: "Was it good for you too?"

or via interspecies perversions:

> Dale Loudermilk wants smelling flowers outlawed and asks, "Do you realize you are placing your nostrils on the sex organs of another species?"

Since their intimate relations, even more than their sexual relations, distinguish human from subhuman beings, we find funny people who treat their relations with objects as intimate:

> To get rid of renewal requests from *Time* magazine Rita Rudner wrote to them, "Look, it's over. If I knew you would be so immature about it, I wouldn't have gotten involved."
>
> [*San Francisco Chronicle*, 8 Aug. 1988, E2]

The most conspicuous characteristic that distinguishes human from subhuman beings is speech. We also laugh, therefore, at inanimate objects like ventriloquist dummies or animate objects like magpies that appear to talk. Many jokes and cartoons depict talking insects or animals in bars.[3] Subhumans meant to be funny don't just talk, however; they usually talk in clichés (fig. 4). Humorists portray subhuman beings who speak in clichés less to transform them into human beings than to imply the transformation into subhuman beings of human beings who speak in clichés—the most mechanical and therefore least (truly) human speech pattern. Since robots are more anthropomorphic than other objects, we are not surprised to hear them speak like human beings. But since they are programmed to be hyperlogical, we are surprised to hear them speak like human stereotypes. These two working-class cartoon robots are on a lunch break:

> *Robot A:* I lost my job . . .
> *Robot B:* Layoffs?
> *Robot A:* Replaced by a human . . .
> *Robot B:* How degrading.
> *Robot A:* I've got a wife and three toasters at home. How will I pay the electric bill?
>
> [*Bizarro* (1985)]

Animals, with greater potential to perform human activities, are even more prone to platitudes:

Figure 4

Two kangaroos are talking to each other, and one says "Gee, I hope it doesn't rain today, I just hate it when the children play inside."

[Henny Youngman]

Gary Larson, the best known modern cartoonist of humanized animals, has the best ear for phrasing their responses to zoological situations in contemporary human clichés.

One of his 1986 "Far Side" cartoons shows a fish bowl in which one very young fish, who has just woken up, complains about his sibling as their mother swims by: "Mom! Thereon's dried his bed again."

An article in *Time* described "The Far Side" as "an absurdist, sometimes sinister world where animals do the unnatural (i.e., act like humans) and often trump mankind along the way."

> A female moose, in a slip and curlers, hands the phone to her husband, sitting in his easy chair. "It's the call of the wild," she says. As a woman crouches to feed nuts to two squirrels, one of the furry creatures says to his companion, "I can't stand it . . . They're so *cute* when they sit like that" [1 Dec. 1986, 86].

Other human characteristics that amuse when attributed to inanimate or animate objects are psychological ones, like motivation:

> Vegetables are interesting but lack *a sense of purpose* when unaccompanied by a good cut of meat.
>
> [Fran Lebowitz; emphasis added]

and sociological ones, like social type:

> I have no religious or moral objection to vegetables but they are, as it were, dull. They are *the also-rans* of the plate. One takes an egg, or a piece of meat, or fish, with pleasure but then one has, as a kind of penance, to dilute one's pleasure with a damp lump of boskage.
>
> [Frank Muir; emphasis added]

It is also amusing to imagine a subhuman being that requires the trappings of advanced civilizations, especially the most trivial:

> A bald-headed man and his friend are standing outside a tavern after having had a couple of drinks. Just then, a seagull flies overhead and defecates on the bald pate. The friend is very much upset and exclaims, "Oh, that's awful! Can I do something? Let me get some toilet paper." The bald-headed man rumbles, "Hell, no, he's probably a quarter of a mile away by now."

Although we smile at the incongruous cuteness of subhuman beings transformed into human beings manqué, we mock the incongruous hubris of human beings who want to be transformed into superhuman beings. Unlike heroic poetry, comedy does not exalt human beings who seek to become superhuman *directly*.

> I've written comedy material for some pretty conceited stars. One guy was so bad he phones dial-A-Prayer and asks, "Any messages?"
>
> [Ray Pasquin]

Instead, comedy exalts those canonized *indirectly* for their very human failures, like the movie characters of Charlie Chaplin.

Downtransformations: Cynical ("Bad" or "Wicked") Humor

Comics can convolute the Great Chain of Being not only by elevating its lower links but also by depressing its higher links. Uplifting humor, which depicts the upward mobility of inferior beings, is "kind" and "gentle." Such *appreciative humor* ennobles objects, vegetables, animals, or humans by attributing to them even the lower human or superhuman traits. Conversely, degrading humor, which dramatizes the downward mobility of superior beings, is "contemptuous" and "caustic." Such *depreciative humor* literally "puts down" Gods or men by debasing their essential attributes.[4] This great divide cuts across the comic cosmos, splitting it into uptransformations (usually called "humor" proper) and downtransformations (usually called "wit").[5]

Many humor theorists have contrasted humor and wit, although most focus on the different characteristics of the *subjects* who produce each kind of comedy without clearly discriminating the different trajectories of their *objects*. Charles Gruner (1978:91–116), for instance, distinguishes humor and wit with the following subjective (psychological) adjectives (partial list):

Humor	Wit
emotional	intellectual
affectionate, gentle	hostile, aggressive
kindly, genial	sarcastic

Those who distinguish humor and wit often argue passionately for the one they prefer, implying the preference involves something more momentous than mere taste. Charles Brooks clearly prefers humor:

> I am not sure that I can draw an exact line between wit and humor. . . .
>
> I am quite positive [, however,] that of the two, humor is the more comfortable and more livable quality. Humorous persons . . . are always agreeable companions and they sit through the evening best. They have pleasant mouths turned up at the corners. . . . But the mouth of a merely witty man is hard and sour until the moment of its discharge. Nor is the flash from a witty man always comforting, whereas a humorous man radiates a general pleasure and is like another candle in the room.
>
> I admire wit, but I have no real liking for it. It has been too often employed against me, whereas humor is always an ally. It never points an impertinent finger into my defects. Humorous persons do not sit like explosives on a fuse. They are safe and easy comrades. But a wit's tongue is as sharp as a donkey driver's stick. . . .

> Wit is a lean creature with sharp inquiring nose, whereas humor has a kindly eye and comfortable girth. Wit, if it be necessary, uses malice to score a point ... but humor keeps the peace in an easy chair. Wit has a better voice in a solo, but humor comes into the chorus best. Wit is as sharp as a stroke of lightning, whereas humor is diffuse like sunlight. [1957:546–48]

In contrast, S. J. Perelman (and his reviewer Mordecai Richler) clearly prefer wit:

> By its very nature, Perelman felt, humor was an angry business, its office to deflate pretentiousness and expose man's follies. In an interview, he once said, "Generally speaking, I don't believe in kindly humor—I don't think it exists. One of the most shameful utterances to stem from the human mouth is Will Rogers's 'I never met a man I didn't like.' The absolute antithesis is Oscar Wilde on the fox-hunting Englishman: 'The unspeakable in full pursuit of the uneatable.' Wilde's remark contains, in briefest span, the truth, whereas Rogers's is pure flatulence, crowd-pleasing and fake humility." Bravo. [New York Times Book Review, 9 Aug. 1987, 31]

In general, idealists prefer the uptransformations of humor, realists the downtransformations of wit.

The relative popularity of humor and wit, or more objectively up- and downtransformations, has fluctuated over the last several centuries, especially in England (Levin 1987:167, 185–91, 199–200). During the early seventeenth century, the Elizabethans gradually replaced "bitter" comedy (the traditional form, stretching back to New Comedy) with "sweet" comedy (their novel form). The late seventeenth and early eighteenth centuries saw the controversy between the advocates of humor and of wit become particularly intense and explicit, though the popularity of Defoe's and Swift's satires and the increasingly influential French comedy of manners indicated the dominance of downtransformative wit.[6] In the late eighteenth and early nineteenth century, comedy "softened" into the "amiable" and "sentimental" uplifting humor exemplified by Lawrence Sterne and Charles Lamb. Comedy hardened again during the late nineteenth and early twentieth century with the wicked wit of Oscar Wilde and George Bernard Shaw. Midtwentieth-century European comedy continued this tough-minded tradition with Brecht, Beckett, Ionesco, and Pinter. Midtwentieth-century American comedy, however, encompassed both the put-down wit of the Algonquin Round Table, S. J. Perelman, and the Marx Brothers, as well as the upbeat humor of Charles Chaplin, Will Rogers, and the *New Yorker* school. Late twentieth-century American comedy still includes both styles, although those who dislike downtransformative comedy believe it dominant today and nostalgically yearn for the (somewhat imaginary) past when (they believe) genial uptransformative comedy was more popular. The following homage to the late comedienne Gilda Radner compares her comic style with the uptransformations of most American comedians of the recent past, and contrasts it with the downtransformations of most American comedians today: Radner

> seemed to have the greatest staying power [of the "Saturday Night Live" performers] because of her wholesomeness and an eagerness to please, increasingly rare in comedy today and quite the opposite of the Attack School of Comedy led by Joan Rivers, Tracy Ullmann, Eddie Murphy, Richard Pryor, Robin Williams, Roseanne Barr and Bob Goldthwait. Even Letterman goes for the gut; he just looks nice.
>
> Radner represented a less pushy humor that audiences at the recent "Night of Jewish Humor" got a sentimental glimpse of when Shelley Berman returned for half an hour of quiet comic observations—a type of humor once personified by Will Rogers, Jack Benny, Wally Cox, Sam Levenson, Myron Cohen, Herb Shriner, Edgar Bergen, Fibber McGhee and Molly, Amos 'n' Andy, Burns and Allen, et al.
>
> That friendly tradition hardly exists anymore, certainly not in TV, with the almost lone exceptions of Bob Newhart and Garry Shandling, or reruns of "The Mary Tyler Moore Show." I suspect one reason Garrison Keillor and George Burns are so beloved (which also drew viewers so easily to Gilda Radner) is that they feel no need to bully you into laughing, the mark of a comic craftsman, and a secure one. [Gerald Nachman, *San Francisco Chronicle*, "Datebook," 28 May 1989, 18]

Superhuman to Human

Most theological jokes *humanize the gods*, portraying deities who act or react as human beings would despite their enormous differences. It was easy for the ancient Greek comic playwrights to humanize their gods, Hegel tells us, for their gods already possessed many human traits: "Aristophanes had available to him material of the richest and happiest sort, drawn partly from the Greek gods and partly from the Athenians themselves. In fact, those humanized gods contain in their very concept a contrast between the divine and the human which is essentially comical, particularly when represented as acting on motives of manifestly human pride, while insisting on their divine prerogatives" (1979:192). Comedienne Judy Tenuta creates a more schizo-phrenic comic effect by simultaneously transforming herself up into an ethereal pagan goddess and down into a crass blue-collar male:

> On stage, Tenuta is adorned in a cape—gold lame and pink are favorite colors—and a white thrift-shop gown for the "Aphrodite-on-the-skids" vibe. Her vocal delivery is a strange juxtaposition of sing-song angelic and blue-collar guttural. . . . She sees nothing odd about her schizoid speech pattern. "Of course, I'm a divine living saint," she said, "but I have to deal with these dock workers in the real, mortal world. Believe me, it's a burden for the goddess to wake at 8 p.m. every night just to abuse mortals from the stage."
>
> [San Francisco Chronicle, "Datebook," 13 Nov. 1988, 65]

The pagan gods have been desecrated on a more literary level in such epic novels as John Barth's *Giles Goat-Boy*. If the traditional epic seeks to project "men to the quality of gods," the comic epic uses its conventions and themes to "profane a sacerdotal world view by depicting an absurd hero engaged in an ironic quest for an ever-elusive truth/ meaning/stability" (Varsava 1990:223).

The Judeo-Christian God has been harder to humanize, for he is beyond any human trait by definition. Though correspondences between this transcendental God and man are more difficult to discover, they are funnier when found. The anthropomorphic God depicted by humorists possesses uniquely human characteristics, such as a profession:

> God will forgive me: it is his *métier*.
>
> [Heinrich Heine][7]

or media celebrity:

> I picture God as a giant Phil Donahue, forever taking calls.
>
> [Ellen DeGeneris]

or performs uniquely human activities with his characteristic panache:

> And what about Jesus's childhood? I think he was spoiled. Imagine, you show up at a father-son picnic with God. You're gonna win every event! Nobody can eat more pie than God!
>
> [Rick Reynolds]

If it is funny to demote God by ascribing to him these higher valued human traits or activities, it is even funnier to demote even further a presumably omniscient and omnipotent God by ascribing to him humanity's lower valued aspects, such as ignorance.

A 1982 *Mad* cartoon depicts Christ, carrying a huge cross, saying to a Roman soldier, "No, I thought you were bringing the nails!"

or incompetence:

> The Reverend Abner Ravenswood was playing golf . . . with one of his parishioners, Bryan Olcutt. Olcutt missed an easy putt and exclaimed, "Goddam!"..
>
> "Now, Bryan, I really cannot allow such cursing!" said the reverend. "If you do that once more, I swear—I shall call on the Lord to strike you down!"
>
> On the eighth hole, Olcutt missed a six-inch putt. "For God's sake, can't I do *one* goddam thing right?" he exploded.
>
> At once a great cloud formed above the two golfers, a bolt of lightning flashed—and knocked the Reverend Ravenswood to the ground. As he and Olcutt stared incredulously at the cloud, an orotund voice from heaven said, "Sorry, Ravenswood. Missed my damn target!"

Most anthropomorphically degraded is the God who acts from the very lowest human motivations, such as laziness:

> God is not evil. He's just an underachiever.
>
> [Woody Allen]

peevishness:

> One of Jesus's disciples explains that he has always been "a little annoyed" that his birthday came so close to Hanukkah because he received fewer presents.
>
> ["Saturday Night Live," 26 Dec. 1987]

or outright maliciousness:

> [Evangelist] Oral Roberts [must] view God as an extortionist. [He] treats God like a Mafioso. God says to Oral: "I'll give you till March 31 to come up with $8 million. If you don't, you're a dead man." If Oral comes up with only $4 million, does that mean God will only break his kneecaps?
>
> [David Steinberg]

Indeed, for humorists, God's very humanity itself is responsible for the world's sorry state:

> Don't blame God. He's only human.
>
> [Leo Rosten]

Higher Human to Lower Human

Since the Great Chain of Being equates spiritual or mental existence with the angels and material existence with the beasts, the unique central position of human beings between angels and beasts creates an incongruity within human identity.[8] We laugh whenever suddenly forced to relocate the locus of human identity from souls or minds to bodies, Henri Bergson observes:

> Let us suppose . . . that, so far from sharing in the lightness and subtlety of the principle with which it is animated, the body is no more in our eyes than a heavy and cumbersome vesture, a kind of irksome ballast which holds down to earth a soul eager to rise aloft. Then the body will become to the soul what . . . the garment was to the body itself—inert matter dumped down upon living energy. . . . *Any incident is comic that calls our attention to the physical in a person, when it is the moral side that is concerned.*
>
> Why do we laugh at a public speaker who sneezes just at the most pathetic moment of his speech? Where lies the comic element in this sentence, taken from a funeral speech . . . "He was virtuous and plump"? It lies in the fact that our attention is suddenly recalled from the soul to the body. [1956:92–93]

The loftier the spiritual or mental activity stressed, the funnier any hint of physicality may become.[9] Bergson continues, "This is just why the tragic poet is so careful to avoid anything calculated to attract attention to the material side of his heroes. No sooner does anxiety about the body manifest itself than the intrusion of a comic element is feared. On this account, the hero of a tragedy does not eat or drink or warm himself. . . . Napoleon . . . noticed that the transition from tragedy to comedy is effected simply by sitting down" (1956:94). A modern example of the comic downshift from mind to body appears in Tom Stoppard's play *Jumpers*. The title characters are philosophy professors at one university whose extracurricular activity is incongruous to their curricular activity in content (physicality), but analogous in form (kinesics):

> *Bones:* Tell me something—Who are these acrobats?
> *George:* Logical positivists, mainly, with a linguistic analyst or two, a couple of Benthamite utilitarians . . . lapsed Kantians and empiricists generally . . . and of course the usual behaviorists . . . a mixture of the more philosophical members of the university gymnastics team and the more gymnastic members of the philosophy school. The close association between gymnastics and philosophy is I believe unique to this university and owes itself to the Vice-Chancellor, who is of course a first-rate gymnast, though an indifferent philosopher. [1973:50–51]

(Note that the image of acrobatic professors evokes less laughter today than when the play was written because gymnastics is no longer so incongruous an avocation for faculty in our more health-conscious, body-centered times.)

Humor grounds spiritual or mental activity in two distinct dimensions of the body, and through them forms two separate lines of linkage between the human and subhuman worlds. Let us examine how humor links these higher human activities first to the body's physiology and beyond it to the biological world, and second to the body's anatomy and beyond it to the physical world.

Biological Groundings

Western society has periodically equated the human with humanity's highly valued aspects. Whenever it does, however, Western comedy has tried to unmask this identification as merely *pretention* by equating the human with humanity's lowly valued aspects instead. Comedy can undermine the legitimacy of traditional forms of stratification, for instance, by identifying the human with the body—a universal human characteristic.

The most influential thinkers of the modernist period—Marx, Nietzsche, and Freud—had the same intellectual mission: to derive all spiritual and mental phenomena from the body. Since the preceding period had deemed these cultural phenomena superior to the body, reducing these "higher" human activities to the lowly valued body made their ideas seem interesting (Davis 1971) and their writings— which consequently contained many descending incongruities— sound witty.

Higher Human Characteristics to Lower Human Physiology

Since the body as a whole has only moderately lower status than spiritual and mental phenomena, relating them to it has produced only mild amusement. But since excretion and copulation have far lower status than other aspects of the body, relating the "noble" human activities to these "base" bodily behaviors has proved far funnier.

Downtransformations of spiritual and mental phenomena to the body's lower physiological aspects created the ribald laughter peculiar to the Middle Ages, which no one has analyzed more insightfully than Russian critic Mikhail Bakhtin:

> School and university recreation had great importance in the history of medieval parody ... Not only could the students relax from the official ideological system, from scholarly wisdom and academic rules, but they were allowed to transform these disciplines into gay, degrading games, and jokes. They

were first of all freed from the heavy chains of devout seriousness, from the "continual ferment of piety and the fear of
God." They were freed from the oppression of such gloomy
categories as "eternal," "immovable," "absolute," "unchange-
able" and instead were exposed to the gay and free laughing
aspect of the world, with its unfinished and open character,
with the joy of change and renewal. This is why the medieval
parodies were not formal literary and negative satires of sacred texts or of scholarly wisdom; they merely transposed
these elements into the key of gay laughter, into the positive
material bodily sphere. Everything they touched was transformed into flesh and matter and at the same time was given
a lighter tone. [1984:83; see also 86–87]

"Earthy" medieval humor culminated in Rabelais's works, whose
"downward movement" relates everything to "the material bodily
lower stratum" centering on excretion and copulation (1984:366ff.).
Since the medieval mind conceived of the body as a "microcosm" of
the universe, inverting the body's traditional hierarchy—as Rabelais
often does—in effect turned the Great Chain of Being upside down.
Rabelaisian laughter is so powerful because it reverberates with this
cosmic implication (1984:309, 336). Rabelais's technique of relating
higher phenomena to the material bodily lower stratum is best exemplified in Gargantua's search for the perfect ass wipe:

> About the end of Gargantua's fifth year, Grandgousier visited his
> son. . . . He most earnestly inquired [from his governesses] whether they
> had kept him sweet and clean. To this Gargantua answered that he had
> taken these precautions himself, and that there was not a cleaner boy in
> all the land.
> "How did you do that?" asked Grandgousier.
> "By long and curious experiments," replied Gargantua. "I have in-
> vented a method of wiping my arse which is the most lordly, the most ex-
> cellent, and the most convenient that ever was seen."
> "What's that?" asked Grandgousier. . . .
> "Once I wiped myself on a lady's velvet mask, and I found it
> good. . . . Another time on one of their hoods, and I found it just as good.
> Another time on a lady's neckerchief; another time on some earflaps of
> crimson satin. . . . After that," said Gargantua, "I wiped myself with a ker-
> chief, with a pillow, with a slipper, with a game-bag, with a basket—but
> what an unpleasant arse-wiper that was!—then with a hat. . . . then I
> wiped myself with a hen, a cock, and a chicken, with a calf's skin, a
> hare, a pigeon, and a cormorant, with a lawyer's bag, with a penitent's
> hood, with a coif, with an otter. But to conclude, I say and maintain that
> there is no arse-wiper like a well-downed goose, if you hold her neck be-
> tween your legs. . . . Do not imagine that the felicity of the heroes and

demigods in the Elysian Fields arises from their asphodel, their ambrosia, or their nectar, as those ancients say. It comes, in my opinion, from their wiping their arses with the neck of a goose, and that is the opinion of Master Duns Scotus too.

[1955: book 1, chap. 13:66–69]

In his analysis of this passage, Bakhtin (1984:71–77) notes that Gargantua tests mostly household products, head or face apparel, and domesticated animals. More generally, Rabelais anchors to the anus human material culture, the human body's upper stratum, the subhuman beings closest to humans—and ultimately even the gods.

Recent examples of humor that couples the material body's upper and lower strata juxtapose the face and the anus by transferring more modern accouterments of the upper to the lower:

Have you seen those new bathing suits? They're more like butt floss.

[Sue Murphy]

or of the lower to the upper:

Women over thirty are now using Preparation H to tighten the bags under their eyes.

[Jane Dornacker]

The more eminent the face, the more demeaned by such bipolar contact:

Reagan had a cancer taken out of his colon and a cancer off his nose. You figure out how he got them.

[Will Durst]

Unlike Rabelais, Freud believed the comic *debases* spiritual and mental—indeed all cultural—phenomena by associating them with the body's lower physiology:

Everyone has his moral backside, which he does not show except in case of need and which he covers as long as possible with the breeches of respectability.

[Lichtenberg]

Till at last, at last every button bursts on my breeches of patience."

[Heine]

These last two analogies . . . are to a degree "debasing," as we might put it. They juxtapose something of a high category, something abstract (in these instances "respectability" and "patience"), with something of a very concrete and even low kind ("breeches"). [1963:85; see also 200–201, 210–11][10]

But what is "degrading" from the higher status perspective is "equalizing" from the lower. Jokes that emphasize biologically generated human similarities are great levelers of socially generated human differences. They level politicians in particular by showing them controlled by the same biological processes as their constituents (C. Schutz 1977:67). Jokes about President Reagan, for example, continually stressed the common physiological effects of aging, like drifting off to sleep:

> The president's doing fine after surgery, but in case of any discomfort the doctors gave him something to help him sleep through foreign policy meetings.
>
> [Johnny Carson]

President Gerald Ford was commonly caricatured (particularly by Chevy Chase) as especially clumsy. (Both physical impairments, of course, parallel the mental impairments—inattention and incompetence—that presidents are not supposed to possess.) If high status people tend to separate themselves from the rest of humanity, leveling jokes pull them back across this developing rift in the Great Chain of Being to the same side as ordinary human beings—especially by emphasizing their common bestial characteristics.[11]

Incumbents of high-status institutionalized offices—"officials"— seem almost disembodied beings, for their images are shaped far more by the incorporeal conceptions of their offices than by the corporeal bodies actually occupying them. Especially excluded from the images of officials in modern Western society are their bodies' nether parts and processes (by, for instance, commonly photographing them from the waist up or behind desks). Consequently, Western humorists have been able to explode these official images by insinuating that officials actually excrete or copulate. Thus many practical jokers rely on artificial products that look or sound like excretions—woopie cushions, fake feces, and the like—but are portable enough for their unexpected obtrusion to appear to defile otherwise impeccable officials. Excretion and copulation, in short, are not merely debasers but *pan*debasers," able to debase a wide variety of officials.

Since these lowly and contaminating pandebasers can degrade whoever they touch, some comics are tempted to ply their trade almost exclusively by associating officials with pissing, shitting, or fucking— a technique derided by many humor connoisseurs for being too easy.

It's an auspicious beginning, but [Barry Diamond's comedy record] soon falls into the trap encountered by many young comedians. Simply stated, Diamond uses profanity to get laughs. He throws four-letter words into his speech with gratuitous and boring regularity, using the language to milk laughs from the crowd. And milk them he does, largely because the audience allows him to get away with it. Instead of insisting on well-crafted material, they allow Diamond to provoke laughter with several weak routines, punctuated with "fucks." [*Just for Laughs*, Oct. 1983, 9][12]

Steve Allen caricatures comics like Richard Pryor and Eddie Murphy by inserting their frequent obscenities into the renown speeches of revered figures:

Can you imagine how shocked the American people would have been . . . if Stepin Fetchit had gone up to Clark Gable in *Gone with the Wind* and said, "Massa Butler, sir, I was just hangin' around down at the stable, and some mother fucker said you wanted to see me." . . .

Can you imagine how distressed everyone would have been if [in the same movie Butterfly McQueen had] actually said to delicate, white-bread Vivien Leigh, "Oh, Miz Scarlet, we all got to get our belongin's together, ma'am, and run out of here because the fuckin' Yankees is comin'." . . .

Whoever is the most depraved young person in this audience at the moment . . . I tell you *he* would be shocked if he turned on the six o'clock news tomorrow night and heard Dan Rather say, "Well, let's see what the fuck's in the news this evening."

[1987:211–12]

By increasing the interval between high-status speakers and low-status speech, Allen accelerates these descending incongruities.

In the last chapter we saw that alcohol and drugs are pandebasers of linguistic and logical systems; in this chapter we have seen that copulation and excretion are pandebasers of anthropological systems. Both pairs of pandebasers are often grouped together, particularly by those who dislike their humor. Phenomenologically, both alcohol/drugs and copulation (though not excretion) draw their users or doers out of ordinary consciousness, which shifts their behavior from presumably rational to seemingly ridiculous (see Davis 1983). Historically, all four were associated with the primitive phallic and vegetative rituals from which some say comedy, especially ancient Greek comedy, evolved (see Frye 1971).

All officials are anti-body, we saw, but some are more anti-body than others, just as some aspects of the body are more antiofficial than others. Much of the funniest humor occurs when jokers juxtapose the most anti-body officials with the most antiofficial aspects of the body. Pan-debasers are especially effective debasers of officials who try to ignore, deny, or transcend their power.

Business officials, for instance, are supposed to be so economically focused that they ignore any broader human—let alone sexual—concerns. Consequently, it can be humorous to shatter their customary official restraint by intimating that their narrow economic blinders may not preclude all sexual feelings and activities—even extreme ones, as in the 1982 *Boston* cartoon in which the boss says to the young secretary,

> "I've just been through a brutal board meeting, Ms. Kentworth. At times like this I need solace, compassion, understanding, and the usual blowjob!"

Conversely, it can also be humorous to shift suddenly from sexual to economic concerns:

> I picked up a woman last night and took her to my house. "Make me feel like a woman," she said. So I cut her wages 40 percent.
>
> [Larry "Bubbles" Brown]

And if it is humorous to eroticize asexual economic content by describing it in pornographic form, as in this cartoon caption relating what a man in bed with a leer on his face is reading from a book:

> "She entered the office, turned on the light and saw the third quarter earnings report perched seductively on her desk. She embraced it and devoured the words she knew she'd find. The economy was surging! It was alive! It was throbbing!"
>
> [Meyer]

it is conversely humorous to de-eroticize sexual intercourse by describing it in asexual economic jargon:

> As she delightedly unwrapped each Christmas present, the grateful mistress insisted on expressing her appreciation to her generous lover with a quickie. "Darling," the man panted after the fourth, "couldn't we consider a deferred-payment plan?"
>
> [*Playboy*, Dec. 1983][13]

Although sometimes difficult to determine whether sex is debasing (downtransforming) a higher human activity or a higher human activity is elevating (uptransforming) sex, we laugh whenever the customary anthropological interval between the two suddenly contracts.

Most antagonistic to sex in Western society are religious officials, especially Christian. Clergymen, evangelists, missionaries, popes, priests, monks, and nuns are not only supposed to refrain from having sex themselves—particularly extramarital or perverse sex—but to urge others to abstain from it as well. Comedy can destroy our conception of these religious officials simply by suggesting that they perform themselves the very sexual acts they prohibit others. Chicago's "Second City" company once performed a skit about

the ineffably sleazy talk-show tyrant who . . . brings Mother Teresa into the studio for a sexual grilling: "Let me ask you the question that I'm sure is on everyone's lips—how often do you *do* it?"
[*New York Times*, Arts and Leisure, 11 Mar. 1984, 5]

The more deviant, the funnier:

While attending an ecumenical convention, a priest and a rabbi decided to do some sightseeing in nonclerical garb. Having developed a thirst, they entered a pub that turned out to be decorated in mauve and hot pink and to have fresh flowers on the tables; and while they were sipping their beers, a beautiful young man floated over and asked the Catholic clergyman if he'd care to dance. Embarrassed and upset, the latter roughly shoved the interloper away, which caused the muscle beach-type bartender to advance threateningly on the table. He was intercepted by the rabbi, however, and after listening briefly to an explanation, he smiled and waved and returned to the bar. "Whatever did you say to that bullyboy, Aaron?" inquired the relieved priest.
"Not very much, Brendan," replied the rabbi. "Just that we were on our honeymoon."
[*Playboy*, Jan. 1982]

Any sexual analogy for evangelical activities, in fact, will provoke the same amusement:

Five Jehovah Witnesses showed up at my house—tried to "gang save" me on my porch.
[A. Whitney Brown]

And sexual obscenities, of course, especially disconcert religious personnel:

Want to have some fun? Walk into a Christian bookstore and ask the clerk, "Where the fuck are your Bibles?"
[David Fulton][14]

Laity influenced by religious prohibitions against sex—prudes and prigs—have also been the butt of sexual humor. Restoration comedy, in particular, emphasized the "incongruity . . . between the reality of lust and the affectation of virtue," between man's primitive biological urges and civilization's artificial cultural restraints, and brought out the artful doges and hypocrisies people use to satisfy their natural instincts while remaining respectable in society (Lauter 1964: 191–93). The periodic waxing and waning of sexual puritanism during Western history (Davis 1983: 230–34) has generated counterrhythms of comedy that unmasks its hypocrisy: less bawdy humor in relatively coherent times when sexual puritanism is either at its zenith (for few dare to criticize it) or at its nadir (for few care to defend it); more bawdy humor in relatively schizophrenic times when sexual puritanism is either rising or fading.

At the opposite end of the human hierarchy from powerful officials are those supposedly rendered asexual by absent rather than by controlled desire, whom Western society has viewed as almost superhuman ("angelic") beings free from the stain of sex. All the humorist has to do to debase those thought to transcend sex is to show that they don't. When children were "innocent," many words were put into their mouths without concern for the sexual innuendoes our Freudian age would dig out:

> George Cukor's 1939 film, The Women, by Clare Boothe Luce, is now a gay cult classic that played before a sellout crowd at the Castro [theater] the other night. The film's best unintentionally hilarious line . . . comes when the daughter of the Norma Shearer character crawls into bed with mommy and says, "The nice thing about divorce is that you get to sleep with your mother!"
>
> [Herb Caen]

In her 1979 Broadway show Gilda Live! Gilda Radner comically profaned our society's sanctification of children by contaminating the dainty language commonly used around them with sexual obscenity. Her song "Let's Talk Dirty to the Animals" includes the sweetly sung refrain "Fuck you, Mr. Bunny!" (Her well-known uptransformative style allowed her occasionally to get away with this extreme downtransformative content.) Similarly, comics can use the most material aspects of sex to puncture the most ethereal aspects of romance, an ideology (Mindess 1971:65–66) that views women mainly as spiritual beings whose material body possesses lower parts only indistinctly:

> I believe you should place a woman on a pedestal—high enough so you can look up her dress.
>
> [Steve Martin]

and that views the relations between men and women only transcendentally:

> How can I tell you I love you when you're sitting on my face?
>
> [T-shirt slogan]

Those who spiritualize intimate relations are particularly dismayed by comics like Andrew "Dice" Clay who biologize them.

Combining sanctity *and* innocence is especially difficult for cynics to bear (for cynics combine the urge to profane with the knowledge of the ubiquity of iniquity). Hence the sustained popularity of Charles Addams's 1946 cartoon in *The New Yorker*'s Christmas issue in which a ghoulish family on the roof of their haunted-looking house is about to pour a liquid (molten lead?) on a group of carolers. A more recent example occurs in the 1978 movie *Animal House* in which an exasperated frat man, played by John Belushi, savagely smashes a sentimental folk singer's guitar.

Human to Organically Subhuman

Whoever conceives of existence as a Great Chain of Being(s) finds models for human behavior—especially its worst aspects—in animals. Medieval and postmedieval bestiaries lent themselves to comic dramatization (Levin 1987:51–52). The Darwinian version of the Great Chain of Being, which *derives* human beings *from* animals, reduced their separation further, leaving just enough of the traditional human/animal boundary intact to produce potentially comic incongruity:

> Darwinian Man, tho well-behaved
> At best is only a monkey shaved!
>
> [W. S. Gilbert, *Princess Ida*]

More recent comedians have breached the human/biological boundary even more deeply by equating human beings with sheer protoplasm:

> I was the ugliest child ever born in Larchmont, New York. . . . When I was born, my mother looked at me and looked at the afterbirth and screamed "Twins!"
>
> [Joan Rivers]

This kind of comedy points out various characteristics that human beings share with biologically subhuman species—like mode of eating:

> I like to go to 7–11 and watch the guys buying fritos and hanging out, as though it were a "salt lick."
>
> [Sue Murphy]

In the Darwinian hierarchy, higher beings eat lower ones—a criterion comics have used to downtransform its highest beings:

> To the guy who comes on to her in a punk-rock bar [Judy Tenuta] growls, "I was looking for something a little closer to the top of the food chain."
>
> [*Time*, 24 Aug. 1987, 57]

and even its lowest beings:

> Is American Processed Cheese Food what they feed to the cheese?
>
> [Dan St. Paul]

It is funny for human beings, presumably at the top of the food chain, to be turned into food. Joan Rivers continued her self-deprecating monologue by applying a food processing term to herself:

> I was the ugliest child ever born in Larchmont, New York. The doctor took one look at me and said, "She's not done yet," and shoved me back in.
>
> [Joan Rivers]

Transforming oneself into food, however, need not be demeaning to be amusing. It depends on the food's status:

> The second half [of "The Second Annual Evening of Jewish Humor"] was hosted by comedy impresario Alex Bennett, who called himself "comic sherbet," someone to cleanse our palates between acts.
>
> [Gerald Nachman, *San Francisco Chronicle*, 8 May 1989, F2.]

Anthropologists have found that most societies treat eating as a quasi-sacred activity, carefully distinguishing *what* their members should eat and controlling *how* they should eat it. Our supposedly secular society is no exception. Consequently, it can be comic to portray eating something we shouldn't, as in the 1983 Unger cartoon in which a man asks a pet store clerk carrying a fishbowl,

> "Got any more of those blue and white striped ones that taste like tuna?"

or eating something maliciously we should eat reverently:

> I'm a vegetarian: Not because I love animals, but because I hate plants.
>
> [A. Whitney Brown]

Excretory and copulatory jokes remind people that human plumbing is more like beasts' than angels' (who apparently never excrete or copulate). Though the following cartoon manifestly uptransforms its animals, it latently downtransforms certain human activities to their unsavory animal analogies (fig. 5).

Finally, humorists can equate human beings and beasts by analogizing their deaths:

Bush is anti-abortion and pro-death penalty. That's spoken like a true fisherman. Throw them back when they're small, catch them when they're bigger.

[Elayne Boosler]

Journalist joke: "What does a cabinet minister have in common with a fly? Both can be squashed by a newspaper."

"That scent! Don't tell me . . . you dunged and urinated, and then rolled in it!"

Figure 5

Bestializing comedy can view human beings as not merely *like* animals but as *inferior* to animals—especially morally questionable individuals:

> A traveler spends an evening in a bar in a strange town. After a few drinks, he becomes expansive, uninhibited, and finally exclaims, "President Nixon is a horse's ass!" At this a burly man stalks over to him and replies, "Mister, them's fightin' words 'round here." To which the traveler replies, "I'm sorry, sir. I didn't realize this was Nixon country." "It's not," grunts the burly one. "This is horse country."

and morally questionable professions:

> Q. What is the difference between a dead skunk and a dead lawyer in the middle of the road?
> A. There are skid marks before the skunk.
>
> [Michael Rafferty]

Physical Groundings

If comedy grounds higher human characteristics in the biological world for Bakhtin (1984), it grounds them in the physical world for Bergson (1956). For the Marxist Bakhtin, the body to which comedy (especially Rabelais's) reduces higher human characteristics is a vital organism. Consequently, comedy is ultimately something positive, revitalizing the inert forms of human civilization.[15] For the bourgeois Bergson, the body to which comedy reduces higher human characteristics is the inert object. Consequently, comedy is basically something negative, devitalizing the vital forms of human civilization.

How does comedy turn living human beings into dead objects? By breaking our subjective connections (*verstehen*) with them, causing us to see them only from the outside—"a momentary anesthesia of the heart," in Bergson's felicitous phrase (1956:64).[16] Aldous Huxley observes in his novel *Antic Hay* that "every man is ludicrous if you look at him from outside, without taking into account what's going on in his heart and mind" (quoted in Winston 1978:35). In fact, any phenomena is ludicrous if we blind ourselves to its human meaning and see only its bare objective husk.

> In a *Far Side* cartoon from 1984 as a concert is about to begin, one musician, pointing to his sheet music, is saying to another, "Gee, look at all the little black dots."

(Thus behaviorism, which intentionally omits the human meaning and relevance of what it studies, is potentially the funniest school of social science.)

The human/object boundary, although strong, is more easily permeable from beneath than from above. Our society's democratic orientation magnanimously confers human characteristics on subhuman things whereas its bourgeois orientation fills the world with objects against which its members must antagonistically define themselves. Anxiety that human beings may fall to the object-level has provoked not only the serious social criticisms of Marxists and feminists but also the sarcastic personal ridicule of wits. Consequently, wit that transforms humans down to objects has a harder, more dangerous edge than humor that transforms objects up to humans.

Higher Human Characteristics to Lower Human Anatomy

Since the human body possesses not only biological function but also physical form, comedy can downtransform higher human characteristics not only through the body's physiology but also through its anatomy. Ideally, the human body is an organic whole with each part in its proper relation to all other parts. Distorting this ideal physical form is this kind of comedy's principle technique.

Anatomical deformations have been known to evoke laughter ever since Aristotle in his *Poetics* (1984: chap. 4, 2319) specified the object of comedy to be an imitation of men who are "ridiculous, which is a species of the ugly" and defined the ridiculous as "a mistake or deformity not productive of pain or harm to others." It is the second subspecies "deformity" of the species "ridiculous" of the genus "ugly" that concerns us here.

The bodies Western society has defined as deformed are much taller or shorter than its vertical norm, begetting such objects of humor as giants and dwarfs, or much fatter or thinner than its horizontal norm, begetting the comically obese or emaciated:

Wit is always the opposite of grossness, so that the comic fat man always enjoys the advantages of the dualistic paradox of soul versus body. The keenness of Falstaff's intelligence, the acuity of his wit, the alertness of his replies, the sharpness of his verbal attack all belie the fatness of his body. It is as if the fat man's body were a disguise he adopted to conceal his trenchant qualities. . . .

Extremely thin, wiry persons, with infinitely sad faces, can achieve grotesque effects comparable to fat men, but they are a much rarer breed. Perhaps Don Quixote fits here, as set against his plump servant, Sancho Panza, or the brilliant comedy team of Laurel and Hardy. . . .

The intense awareness of the body that the fat man forces

on us (and the thin man, too, by default . . .) is one of the richest sources of jokes and comic situations. [Charney 1978:163]

I will add that fat and thin comedians commonly appear in pairs, like
Abbott and Costello or Gleason and Carney. Their physical eccentricity
continually reminds their audience of the bodily norm from which
each deviates in opposite ways; their asymmetry produces a visual
instability that continually reinforces the cognitive instability that underlies their humor.

Along with the absolute size of the whole body, the relative size or
disproportion of its parts is another source of physical humor. "Except
for his gruff objurgations, Bardolph has no defense against jokes about
his nose; Falstaff has endless *ripostes* to the gibes about his belly. . . .
Inasmuch as bellies and noses are bodily rather than mental, . . . they
are the stuff of humor, and once set forth, it becomes the task of wit,
as Hazlitt would argue, to perceive and expose such exaggerated ap-
purtenances" (Levin 1987:185). Fun house mirrors distort the length
and width of torsos and limbs, caricatures enlarge noses, clowns exaggerate ears, novelty shops sell "Inflatable Super Boobs":

> They grow before your very eyes. Just slip on like a bra or over one, hide
> squeeze bulb, and you're ready for a dramatic change . . . instant ba-
> zooms. $11.99 + $1.50 mailing.

Human to Materially Subhuman

Bergson observes that comics often equate human beings with complex "mechanical" objects. His best known definition of the comic is
"something mechanical in something living" (1956:110; see also 84). In
particular, "the attitudes, gestures, and movements of the human body
are laughable in exact proportion as that body reminds us of a mere
machine" (1956:79). A recent example:

> And in a Saratoga market, Richey and Lee Grude were in line as the
> beeper on a very large woman began beeping and the small girl standing
> behind her asked her mother, "Mom, does that mean she's going to back
> up?"
>
> [Herb Caen]

To be comic, more precisely, the mechanical must not supersede the
living but coexist with it. "We shall probably find that [a drawing] is
generally comic in proportion . . . with which it enables us to see a
man as a jointed puppet. . . . But the suggestion must also be a subtle
one, for the general appearance of the person, whose every limb has
been made rigid as a machine, must continue to give us the impression

of a living being. The more exactly these two images, that of a person and that of a machine, fit into each other, the more striking is the comic effect" (1956:80). Bergson summarizes his discussion of the specific aspects of machines into which comedy transforms human beings: "all these being processes that consist in looking upon life as a *repeating* mechanism, with *reversible* action and *interchangeable* parts" (1956:126; emphasis added). A modern example that reduces human beings to all three machine aspects is the pre-Rose Bowl Doo Dah Parade's "Synchronized Briefcase Drill Team."

Practicing comics know they can get a laugh simply by describing human attributes, activities, and afflictions in terms of machine parts, processes, and breakdowns:

> Not many people know this, but Evelyn Wood was involved in a big lawsuit recently. Apparently a guy had an eyeball blowout at 15,000 words per minute.
>
> [Jay Leno]

The more human the problem, the funnier the machine metaphor:

> My ex-shrink called me. She was panicked on the phone. "I made some kind of [theoretical mistake]. I have to *recall* my clients from 1981. I'm sorry."
>
> [Richard Lewis]

A would-be comic once even imagined that *Consumer Reports* tested human ideologies with the same methods it uses to test household appliances:

> We evaluated the durability of various philosophies of life by subjecting their practitioners to a "stress test." We tortured Christians, Buddhists, Existentialists, and Marxists to see how long each would adhere to their tenets until they broke down and repudiated them.

Bergson's theory that humor results from "mechanizing the organic" was part of the general intellectual movement of his time, represented by Émile Durkheim in France and Ferdinand Toennies in Germany, that contrasted organic and mechanical organizations of society and (except for Durkheim) stressed the dehumanization potential of modern machines. Today, however, there are other forces of dehumanization at work besides machines, other features of the environment that human beings can define themselves against only with difficulty. Consequently, the ground metaphors of objective humor have gradually been changing from mechanical to electronic, from machines to computers and communications. Applying computer terminology to human relationships has become funny, for it fits well enough to imply that people may be less than human and that computers may be more than objects. A 1984 cartoon by Dan de la Torre, for instance, has a panhandler saying to a businessman,

> This is a *priority interrupt*. . . . Can your *spread-sheet* support a *line-item input* while I'm in my *downtime mode* so I can *access* lunch.

The fear that computers could become not merely human but more-than-human prompts increasingly nervous laughter:

> Dundes has collected numerous riffs on what he considers the classic computer joke format.
> Premise: All the world's knowledge has been programmed into a single computer, and a visitor is allowed to ask any question he wishes.
> Version One: "Is there a God?" the visitor asks.
> "There is now." the computer replies.
> [*San Francisco Chronicle*, 24 July 1989, B3]

The ground of human/object humor has likewise shifted from the older mechanical technology to modern communication technology, like TVs:

> Why men drink: At Perry's last Thursnite, barman Cyril Boyce overheard one guy say to another "How're things with your wife?" and the other sighing "It's all picture and no sound, if you know what I mean."
> [Herb Caen]

and VCRs:

> I zapped the radio with my new all-purpose remote, but I accidentally zapped the kids, too. It's a little like freeze tag. I left them on pause while I watched a tape of yesterday's "Evening News." . . .
> I fast-forwarded the kids and put them to bed.
> [Alice Kahn]

Since the most essential human attribute lacking in both mechanical and electronic devices is sex, it can be amusing to describe human sexual activities in asexual computer terms.

> In a 1987 *Danby* cartoon, one female computer operator is gossiping with another: "Sue's all right, but I hear she interfaces on the first date!" [17]

For Bergson, comedy equates human beings not only with complex mechanical objects but also with simple physical ones (1956:85–92, 97–102). "We laugh," Bergson tells us, "every time a person gives us the impression of being a thing." A person who becomes a thing, he implies, becomes affected less by the laws of human nature than by the laws of nature, like gravity or momentum:

We laugh at Sancho Panza tumbled into a bed-quilt and tossed into the air like a football. We laugh at Baron Munchausen turned into a cannon-ball and traveling through space. . . . [Circus] clowns came and went, collided, fell, and jumped up again in a uniformly accelerated rhythm. . . . Gradually, one lost sight of the fact that they were men of flesh and blood like ourselves; one began to think of bundles of all sorts, falling and knocking against each other. . . . The forms grew rounder, the bodies rolled together and seemed to pick themselves up like balls. Then at last appeared the image towards which the whole of this scene had doubtless been unconsciously evolving—large rubber balls hurled against one another in every direction. [1956:97–98][18]

Bergson adds another aspect of simple thingness that human beings may comically exhibit: rigidity or inelasticity (1956: esp. 66–67). Marcel Duchamp's painting *The Bride*, for example, portrays the female as plumbing. A more modern parody portrays the male as furniture:

The current *Off the Wall Street Journal II* . . . plumbs the comic possibilities of unemployed steel workers in "Lunkville, Ohio," who are filling in as temporary office furniture: "The massive steel worker, his biceps sculpted from a lifetime at the forge, nods dumbly, his arms outstretched. 'I'm a coat rack,' he offers helpfully to the reporter. He gestures to a beefy man crouched on all fours, an in/out basket perched on his back. 'Bill, over there, he's a credenza. But nights he moonlights as a water cooler.'"
[*Newsweek*, 25 Apr. 1983, 65–66]

Once rigidified, a person can be treated as a thing:

I went to a costume party last Halloween and got beat up. Last time I'll ever go as a Piñata.
[Brian Copeland]

Oscar Wilde once even compared human beings to monumental architecture:

Twenty years of romance make a woman look like a ruin, and twenty years of marriage make her look like a public building.
[quoted in Auden 1962:382]

Perhaps the least monumental rigid objects to which human beings can be comically reduced today are beer can holders:

Why are a woman's asshole and pussy so close together? So when she gets drunk you can carry her home like a six-pack.

Perverse Transformations: Grotesque ("Ugly") Humor

In 1899, retired British army officer Captain Harry Graham published
Ruthless Rhymes for Heartless Homes, which portrayed the gruesome activities of "Little Willie" in light verse:

> William, with a thirst for gore,
> Nailed a baby to the door.
> Mother said, with humor quaint,
> "Careful, Will, don't mar the paint."

Improbably, these poems became popular, and have remained so, perhaps because their logical form/content incongruity reinforced the anthropological incongruities of the perpetrator (saintly child/beastly action) and the victim (human/object). Graham's "Little Willie" jingles
began the modern humor cycles (Dundes 1987:4ff.) known as "sick
humor" in the 1950s and 1960s (Rezwin 1962), "black humor" in the
1970s (Winston 1972, 1978) and "tasteless humor" in the 1980s (Knott
1982, 1983). Yet they also exemplify an older form of the comic—the
grotesque—which goes back to Rabelais and beyond (Bakhtin
1984:303–68). If anthropological humor is the genus of comedy that
dislocates the place of human beings in the Great Chain of Being(s)
(the *cosmos* since the Middle Ages [Lovejoy 1960]), grotesque humor is
the extreme species that destroys the entire Chain by disrupting the
boundaries of their bodies (the *microcosm* since the Renaissance [Bakh-
tin 1984:336, 362–66]). "Sick," "black," or "tasteless" is what those who
still believe in the human body's microcosmic border (and consequently macrocosmic stratification) have called grotesque humor's attempt to exploit its weak points.

   Humor that portrays what Bakhtin (1984: 303–67) calls "the grotesque open body" attempts to destroy the boundary that separates
the individual body from other bodies and the world. It attacks this
boundary by exaggerating the vulnerable extremities or apertures
where the body already extrudes into the world or the world into it:

> The grotesque is interested in [bulging] eyes. It is looking for
> that which protrudes from the body, all that seeks to go out
> beyond the body's confines. Special attention is given to the
> shoots and branches, to all that prolongs the body and links it
> to other bodies or to the world outside. . . . But the most im-
> portant of all human features for the grotesque is the mouth.
> It dominates all else. The grotesque face is actually reduced to
> the gaping mouth; the other features are only a frame encasing
> this wide-open bodily abyss. . . .
> The essential role belongs to those parts of the grotesque

body in which it outgrows its own self, transgressing its own body, in which it conceives a new, second body: the bowels and the phallus. These two areas play the leading role in the grotesque image, and it is precisely for this reason that they are predominantly subject to positive exaggeration, to hyperbolization. . . . Next to the bowels and the genital organs is the mouth, through which enters the world to be swallowed up. And next is the anus. All the convexities and orifices have a common characteristic; it is within them that the confines between bodies and between the body and the world are overcome: there is an interchange and an interorientation.

Thus the artistic logic of the grotesque images ignores the closed, smooth, and impenetrable surface of the body and retains only its excrescences (sprouts, buds) and orifices, only that which leads beyond the body's limited space or into the body's depths. [1984:316–18]

Humor derived from the "grotesque open body" peaked in the sixteenth century with Rabelais (Bakhtin 1984:323), but then declined after the dominant conception of the body became the closed neoclassical ideal form:

The new bodily canon . . . presents an entirely finished, completed, strictly limited body, which is shown from the outside as something individual. That which protrudes, bulges, sprouts, or branches off (when a body transgresses its limits and a new one begins) is eliminated, hidden, or moderated. All orifices of the body are closed. The basis of the image is the individual, strictly limited mass, the impenetrable facade. The opaque surface and the body's "valleys" acquire an essen tial meaning as the border of a closed individuality that does not merge with other bodies and with the world. [1984:320; see also Douglas 1970: 137–53; Davis 1983:112–17]

Yet grotesque humor continues as a minor genre. An expert on modern black humor, Mathew Winston, summarizes the ways its grotesque form undermines this new body image:

The grotesque form of black humor is obsessed with the human body, with the ways in which it can be distorted, separated into its component parts, mutilated, and abused. . . . Bodily parts are exaggerated or distorted. The body's inability to keep to its proper confines is comic, as Henri Bergson has shown in *Le Rire*, but it also makes us fear that such horrible distortion could happen to us. The threat becomes stronger when a character is mutilated, but a comic element is added if the character is untroubled by his mishaps or if the mutilation is acted or narrated farcically. [1972:282]

It is this new "closed" conception of the body, in fact, that makes grotesque humor today seem, well, grotesque.

As Winston notes, grotesque humor can not only distort[19] but actually disintegrate the human body, that exemplary organic unity.[20] It can isolate a body part from the whole:

> I hate it when my foot falls asleep during the day. Because I know it will be up all night.
>
> [Steven Wright]

It can not merely stretch out but pull off a body part:

> How did NASA know what shampoo Christa McAuliffe used?
> They found her Head and Shoulders.

It can split the body:

> A German officer speaks to Jewish prisoners: "I have some good news and some bad news for you. First the good news. Half of you are going to Auschwitz and half of you are going to Buchenwald. Now for the bad news: This half" (indicates the torso midsection upwards) "goes to Auschwitz, and this half" (points to the lower body) "goes to Buchenwald." [21]

It can sever all the parts of the body:

> When I die, I want my remains scattered over California . . . but I don't want to be cremated.
>
> [Bob Goldthwait]

Finally, it can pulverize the body completely:

> Willie saw some dynamite,
> Couldn't understand it quite;
> Curiosity never pays:
> It rained Willie seven days.

Grotesque humorists find it especially effective to disconnect sexual parts from the body, whose integrations with it have always been problematic. They too can be isolated:

> I'm thinking of having breast implants put in my hands, so it would *feel* like I'm with someone.
>
> [Garry Shandling]

Or other body parts can be isolated from them:

> Next time you want to masturbate, sit on your hand till it goes asleep. It'll then feel like someone else is doing it.

Humorists can accentuate a part's separation from the rest of the human body by giving it the human power of speech. Martha Cornog, who calls personifying the sexual parts "genitomorphism," offers the following examples from Gershon Legman and Paul Krassner:

> Man amputates penis accidentally while shaving. Severed penis: "I know we've had lots of fist fights in our time, but I never thought you'd pull a knife on me!"
>
> A wonderful cartoon was described to me, reportedly published in *The Realist*, of a man holding his penis, which is saying (via a cartoon "balloon"), "Not tonight, dear, I have a headache!"
>
> [Cornog 1987:114]

The humor of such synecdoches, however, stems less from promoting the sexual part than from disintegrating the human whole.

Grotesque humor that disintegrates uniquely unified beings can also reintegrate them in a different way.

> The woman's husband was laid out in the funeral parlor. Suddenly she decided she didn't like the brown suit her husband had on.
>
> Walking up to the funeral director, she said, "I see another man wearing a blue suit in the next parlor. Blue was my husband's favorite color and I'd like him laid out in a blue suit."
>
> The funeral director was happy to comply, and told the woman to return in an hour and the change would be made.
>
> When the hour was up, the woman returned and happily found her husband now lying in a blue suit, the other man in a brown suit.
>
> "However did you change suits?" she asked the undertaker.
>
> "I didn't change suits," he replied. "I found it was easier just to switch heads."

More commonly, grotesque humor recombines beings from different levels of the Great Chain of Being, especially their highly organized corporeal aspects. (A fly with a human head, for instance, is more grotesque than a fly with human speech.) Grotesque humor creates even more ambiguous beings than ordinary anthropological humor, for the attributes of beings from different levels contend for dominance in its newly formed intermediate creatures, whose malintegrations are perceived as unstable gestalts continually fluctuating between levels of being. The Middle Ages distributed the visual form of this recombinative grotesque humor across Europe through the half-human, half-animal gargoyles of Gothic architecture (Feibleman 1949:84–85). Although grotesque humor usually mixes human and biological attributes, it can also mix human and physical ones. "Jokes on physical dismemberment (or its equivalent) have a long history, which turns on the shocking collocation of organic and inorganic parts. . . . The fruits of medical engineering question our vital humanity, and a person with a pacemaker, a glass eye, false teeth, a plastic knee cap, plates in his head, a Boston arm, glasses, a hearing aid, and a wig seem to attack our most cherished belief in organic integrity" (Charney 1978: 165). The classic example of organic-mechanical dismemberment-recombinative humor:

> A man in the upper berth [of a pullman sleeper train] is peeping at the woman in the lower berth undressing, and sees her take off a wig, false breasts, a glass eye. She is unscrewing a wooden leg when she catches sight of the peeper. "What do you want?" she shrills. "You know damn well what I want. Unscrew it and throw it up here."

If cynical humor exploits the weak points of the strong, grotesque humor exploits the weak points of the weak. Cynical humor tries to prevent the political, economic, or cultural elite from breaking through humanity's upper boundary and becoming too godlike; for instance, by devaluing an arrogant profession to less than a disgusting thing:

> Why does California have the most lawyers and New Jersey the most toxic-waste dumps? New Jersey had first choice.
>
> [Michael Rafferty]

Grotesque humor, conversely, tries to shove the feeblest people—the sick, the starving, the handicapped, and the helpless—through humanity's lower boundary by making them appear animal or objectlike; for instance, by devaluing an innocent infant to less than an ordinary object:

> "But Henry, that isn't our baby."
> "Shut up. It's a better carriage."

A compassionate Christian society which values, even reveres, its most vulnerable members will find the humor that accentuates their vulnerabilities especially grotesque.

Grotesque humor calls attention to the physical disabilities our society tries to disregard (see Dundes 1987:16):

> "Gosh, Dad—was that Ted Williams who just hit the home run?"
> "What do you care, Sheldon? You're blind."
>
> "Mommy, why are we having this Christmas tree in August?"
> "I've told you twenty times if I told you once, Sheldon. You've got leukemia."

or to the many mundane problems these extreme afflictions cause:

> Why don't Ethiopians [or, the most recent starving group, Somalians] go to movie theaters? Because they can't keep the seats down.

or to the inferior replacements or remedies they require:

> What do you call an Ethiopian walking his dog? A vegetarian.
>
> What do Yoko Ono and Ethiopians have in common? They both live off dead beetles.

Grotesque humor need not merely point out human frailties or privations, it can show us how to emphasize them:

> How did Helen Keller's parent's punish her? They rearranged the furniture.
>
> "Doctor, I still can't see," said the little blind girl after the operation. "April fool!"

or exploit them:

> "Mrs. Brown, can Johnny come out and play ball?"
> "But you children know he has no arms and legs."
> "That's O.K. We want to use him for second base."
>
> I've been dating a homeless woman; it's real easy to get her to stay over.
>   [Garry Shandling]

By overstating a malady's dysfunctional consequences, grotesque humor can reduce those afflicted with it from human to object:

> What do you call an Ethiopian wearing a turban? A Q-Tip.

or even to a frivolous children's game:

> Did you see the Stevie Wonder Video Game? Stevie tries to find the piano.
>   [John Means ("Dr. Gonzo")][22]

Beyond infirmity, of course, lies *death*, which transforms the body of the dying down to the object-level. Corpses produce comic incongruities by forcing us to try to integrate the human beings they were with the physical objects they have become.[23] Even cremated corpses retain enough traces of their previous humanity to contrast comically with their present objectivity.

> Little Willie, in the best of sashes,
> Fell in the fire and was burned to ashes.
> By and by the room grew chilly,
> But no one liked to poke up Willie.

But many people believe that death also uptransforms the soul of the dying toward the spiritual level. They view death as the ultimate bi-directional transformation, for it bisects a human being into his or her two most important components, then thrusts them toward opposite poles of the Great Chain of Being. Grotesque humorists employ death's bifurcations to force their audience to contemplate the incongruities between all three of the Chain's major levels—superhuman, human, and subhuman—simultaneously. As Mathew Winston puts it, "the threat to the body is part of the omnipresent threat of death in gro-tesque black humor. Death dominates, but it occurs in a ridiculous manner and is never dignified. Death is the final divorce between body and spirit, the ultimate disjunction in a form that dwells on violent incongruities. Often it is reduced to its physical manifestation, the corpse, which is man become thing; *rigor mortis* is the *reductio ad absurdum* of Bergsonian automatism" (1972:283).

The contradictory ways Western society conceives of death generate so much discordant emotion that most of its members prefer to avoid the subject. Consequently, "sick" humorists can generate a laugh, al-beit uneasy, by blatantly calling attention to our impending demise:

> Hey, you're a great lookin' crowd. I can't help thinking, "Gee, too bad they're all going to get old and die."
>
> [Larry "Bubbles" Brown]

or our loved ones:

> There was a knock at the door. Mrs. Miffin opened it. "Are you the Widow Miffin?" a small boy asked. "I'm Mrs. Miffin," she replied. "But I'm not a widow." "Oh no?" replied the little boy. "Wait till you see what they're carrying upstairs."

some sooner than others:

> "How old are you?" asked the funeral director.
> "Ninety-seven."
> "Hardly worth going home, is it?"

Conversely, sick humorists can ground death's incongruity in the opposite direction by obscuring its finality, though incompletely. On the one hand, they have depicted those who deny the existence of death by treating the dead like the living:

> The latest issue of *Spy* magazine contains a letter from a former Air Canada flight attendant describing procedures that attendants were asked to follow when a passenger died in flight:
> "Maybe it's just the Canadian way," wrote the reader from Toronto,

"but we were basically told to lie and pretend that the passenger was not dead, only ill. It seems the airline thought if we ran down the aisles screaming, 'Oh God, he's dead, Gloria!' the passengers would become alarmed and subsequently be too afraid to visit the inflight duty-free shop.

"So we were told to vacate the seat beside the deceased, put a fake oxygen mask on him, turn his face toward the window and cover him with a blanket. (So he wouldn't get cold?) The rest of the flight would be spent offering the dead man drinks and complimentary earphones to continue the charade.

"The thing I could never understand was that a flight attendant was expected to sit beside the body for landing. It's not as if they expected you to date the guy afterward or anything but really . . . how can a corpse have anything but a safe landing?"

[*San Francisco Chronicle*, 20 Dec. 1989, A9]

On the other hand, they have depicted those who acknowledge the existence of death but deny its significance by treating death as just another event of everyday life. *Deathworkers*, for instance, can complain like workers in ordinary occupations:

In a *Brian Savage* cartoon from 1982 a nineteenth-century hangman says to the criminal he is about to hang, "Oh, sure, it probably looks good to you at the moment; the pay is decent and the hours short, but I tell you, boy, it's a thankless job."

or relate to their victims with the false intimacy of modern waiters:

A similar 1985 cartoon by Rowland Wilson is captioned: "Hi! My name is Rich—I'll be your executioner today!"

or perform rites that call for total involvement while insouciantly maintaining their usual external preoccupations:

You'd better believe people in California are more laid back than those in the rest of the country. I went to a funeral in Beverly Hills last week, and three of the pall bearers were wearing Sony Walkmans.

Larry "Bubbles" Brown also reflects on *deathwork equipment* by wondering whether executions follow standard medical practice:

"Do they rub alcohol on a condemned man's arm before giving him a lethal injection?"

Black humor can even treat death as *less* significant than everyday events; for instance, as a dismissible distraction from them:

Aside from that, Mrs. Lincoln, how did you like the play?

or as not worth a petty annoyance:

One brother: "I just pushed mother off the cliff." Second brother: "Don't make me laugh; my lips are chapped."

Grotesque humorists can treat death lightly because they see it not as an end but as a beginning, for their basic human unit is not the isolated individual but all humanity and its relatively immortal succession of generations. Death horrifies only those who try to maintain their belief in the bodily integrity of the individual being (Bakhtin 1984:321–22; see also Davis 1983: part 3).

The most grotesque anthropological humor results from combining the most helpless and therefore most sacred human beings—in our society, babies—with the most dehumanizing process—death, especially one that ruptures the body. By subjecting the most uplifting beings to the most downshifting transformations, the dead baby joke juxtaposes the most contradictory cognitive categories, which in turn creates the most disorienting emotional effect:

> What's red and bubbly and scratches at windows? A baby in a microwave.
>
> Why do you put a baby in a blender feet first? So you can watch its expression.

Grotesque humor can be funnier than ordinary anthropological humor, in short, because it convolutes the Great Chain of Being more tortuously. Centrifugal organic fragmentation within the ideal of centripetal organic unity, simultaneously leading to downtransformations to the inorganic and uptransformations to the supraorganic, generates the diametrically opposed vectors that produce the extreme distortions of the grotesque. Those who need a clearly defined cosmic hierarchy for orientation will find such transformations of its beings disgustingly perverse; those who don't will find them funny.

PART TWO

THE COMIC ATTACK ON SOCIETY

We have examined how humor can disintegrate cultural systems (particularly linguistic, logical, and anthropological ones). But humor can also disintegrate social systems, and consequently threaten the integrity of the self itself.

Comedy and Sociology

Humor seems a topic better suited for psychological, rather than sociological, study because only individuals (unlike groups or institutions) laugh. But sociologists of humor (Coser 1959:171–72; Zijderveld 1968:286–87; Hertzler 1970:28–31; Fine 1983:159–60) have pointed out its many social aspects, from who laughs to what they laugh at.

Although it is true that only individuals laugh, they seldom laugh alone—and are presumed mentally ill if they do frequently. Even most seemingly solitary laughter is actually "pseudosocial," requiring a split self or imagined others. Without such self-division or self-multiplication, to tell a joke to oneself is ineffective, to play a practical joke on oneself impossible. Conversely, the individual is expected to laugh in a group of laughers. Laughter creates social reverberations that sustain and enhance it; as Henri Bergson puts it, "Laughter appears to stand in need of an echo" (1956:64). Group members scowl at whoever refuses to provide this echo—the nonlaugher in their midst—whom they regard as antisocial.

What people laugh at—when not purely cultural—is always social.

Even seemingly nonsocial objects of laughter, like individuals, are funny only because their uniquely amusing features stand out from the social norm. This entire part will examine the multifarious social objects of laughter.

Since most of its topics are inherently social, humor laughs at the same phenomena sociology investigates. Theatrical comedy, especially, has long manifested humor's social nature. Critic Northrop Frye observed that "it is a commonplace of criticism that comedy tends to deal with characters in a social group, whereas tragedy is more concentrated on a single individual" (1957:207). And even within this social ensemble, the character traits on which comedy focuses are typical rather than individual. If tragedy deals in superlatives (the unique on humanity's vertical axis), comedy deals in generalization (the common on humanity's horizontal axis) (Levin 1987:15). "Comedy," asserts Bergson (1956:157), "gives us general types"—a thesis he supports by noting that the titles of many comedies are common nouns for social types, such as *The Misanthrope, The Miser,* or *The Gambler,* (in contrast to the titles of many tragedies, which are proper nouns for individuals, such as *Othello*) (1956:70, 166; Levin 1987:66). Like comedy, sociology also focuses on social types; although unlike comic types which reinforce customary stereotypes, sociological types may crosscut and consequently undermine them.

Comedy—like sociology—also focuses on "stock situations," recurrent settings that bring out humorous behavior, currently prevalent on television. Because most continuing small scale television productions find it too difficult and expensive to construct more than one set (or "situation"), television has developed more sitcoms than "charcoms" (comedies based on typical characters who move through many different settings, such as a modern version of Don Quixote). Conversely, "sittrags" (situation tragedies) are also rare on TV because recurrent agony turns into either melodrama (soap operas) or comedy.

Besides typical characters and stock situations, another topic of both comedy and sociology is social behavior or manners. Comedy and sociology are among the few intellectual perspectives that observe everyday life. Since the Greeks, tragedy has claimed as its province the grand actions of public persons, leaving for comedy the commonplace activities of private persons. If tragedy is concerned with the extraordinary (for example, with an all-consuming impossible love affair), comedy has been concerned with the ordinary (for example, with that most mundane of institutions: the family). Cicero characterized comedy as "an imitation of life, a mirror of custom, an image of truth" (quoted by Donatus 1964:27). In the eighteenth century, there was still "wide agreement that the material of comedy be realistic, from actual life Addison said, from Nature, Fielding" (Lauter 1964:191). By the early nineteenth century, however, Charles Lamb could complain that the comedy of the time had sacrificed its dramatic interest for excessive realism:

> We have been spoiled with . . . the exclusive and all devouring drama of common life; . . . instead of the fictitious half-believed personages of the stage (the phantoms of old comedy) we recognize ourselves, our brothers, aunts, kinsfolk, allies, patrons, enemies—the same as in life. . . . We carry our fire-side concerns to the theater with us. We do not go thither, like our ancestors, to escape from the pressure of reality, so much as to confirm our experience of it. . . . We must live our toilsome lives twice over. [1964:295–96]

Today this realistic tradition is carried on by TV sitcoms, which take a common situation as their premise (such as the urban barroom in *Cheers*) to portray through slight exaggeration the manners of our time.

Comedy, then, deals with the contemporary world. But comedy's very modernity makes it more ephemeral than tragedy, whose extraordinary actions exist outside of time. "Thus the contemporaneity of comedy is one of its essential features. . . . Comedy epitomizes the height of the times, the *zeitgeist*. Hanging upon the vivid immediacy of actuality, it touches the unique particularity embodied in the passing forms of the moment. A criticism of the contradictions involved in actuality, it must inevitably be concerned with the most ephemeral of actuals" (Feibleman 1949:86–87). Sociology, which also deals largely with the contemporary world, and sometimes with its contradictions, shares with comedy the unhappy tendency to date rapidly. (Thus a sociology of comedy, like this one, faces double jeopardy, for it may go out of print when *either* its joke examples *or* its explanatory sociological concepts go out of fashion.) If the pathos of old comedians is that the young no longer find them funny, the pathos of old sociologists is that younger scholars no longer find their work interesting: for the particular social incongruities or ambiguities that motivated the elder generation in both professions have abated. (But comic or sociological geniuses who give universal form to enduring social incongruities or ambiguities can still amuse or inspire future generations.)

Comedy and sociology not only deal with the same topics—social types, situations, and manners—but also focus on the same features. The rules of the comic method, Bergson postulated, direct attention to the external:

Altogether different is the kind of observation from which comedy springs. It is directed outward. However interested a dramatist may be in the comic features of human nature, he will hardly go, I imagine, to the extent of trying to discover his own. Besides, he would not find them, for we are never ridiculous except in some point that remains hidden from our own consciousness. [1956:169][1]

and to the general:

It is on others, then, that such [comic] observation must perforce be practiced. But it will, for this very reason, assume a character of generality that it cannot have when we apply it to ourselves. Settling on the surface, it will not be more than skin-deep, dealing with persons at the point at which they come into contact and become capable of resembling one another. . . . To penetrate too far into the personality, to couple the outer effect with causes that are too deep-seated, would mean to endanger, and in the end to sacrifice all that was laughable in the effect. In order that we may be tempted to laugh at it, we must localize its cause in some intermediate region of the soul. Consequently, the effect must appear to us as an average effect, as expressing an average of mankind. And, like all averages, this one is obtained by bringing together scattered data, by comparing analogous cases and extracting their essence; in short by a process of abstraction and generalization similar to that which the physicist brings to bear upon facts with the object of grouping them under laws. In a word, method and object are here of the same nature as in the inductive sciences, in that observation is always external and the result is always general. [1956:169–70][2]

Exactly the same orientation to the "external" and the "general" underlies *The Rules of the Sociological Method,* a treatise written a few years earlier by Bergson's humorless classmate and rival at the École Normale Supérieure, sociologist Émile Durkheim.

The modern sociologist Talcott Parsons took the final step in this intellectual tradition by viewing all social phenomena *systematically.* In a book appropriately entitled *The Social System* (1951) and elsewhere, Parsons tried to describe the systemic characteristics of the social world, just as linguists, logicians, and cosmological anthropologists have tried to describe the systemic characteristics of their respective fields. *Systemic social theory* assumes that society, and each of its major components, is "ordered,"[3] that each social element is related to all the others in a comprehensible way accessible to science. If we know the state of one social element and the interrelation of all of them, we can develop an "expectation system" that comprehends them all. Systemic social theory, in short, views the entire social world as predictable (at least theoretically). Comic incongruities and ambiguities play off this predictability of social systems—like cultural systems—by negating it.

Construction and Deconstruction

A dissident school of sociologists, however, has viewed social systems (as well as all three cultural systems) not as naturally given but as socially *constructed*. These *constructionist social theorists* have shifted attention away from the static interrelation of social system elements toward their temporal interrelating by human beings both biographically and historically. The social philosopher George Herbert Mead (1934; see also Davis 1979), who founded the American wing of this school, detailed the way children organize the particular social elements they randomly experience into larger, more general, and more abstract social units that operate predictably: from individuals through social roles through social institutions to entire societies. The more pessimistic Germanic social constructionists, like Georg Simmel (1950:40–43; 1968:27–46) and Peter Berger and Thomas Luckmann (1967), added that these humanly created social (and cultural) organizations "harden" phenomenologically, escape from human control, take on a life of their own, attempt to organize human beings around themselves, and become the quasi-organic systems to which general scientific laws apply—whose very "objectivity," taken for granted by positivists, signals their alienation from their subjective creators. Implicit in constructionist social theory is the ironic explanation of humor Kurt Riezler makes explicit: "All these jokes are witty by virtue of the sudden surprise of a brief word which shows man in the snares of an order of things, assumptions, ideas, he takes for granted, though they are of his own making" (1950:174–75).

The early constructionist social theorists restricted their analyses of the social world to the formative phases of its development. But if they can describe how human beings organize the social world's haphazard particulars into predictable generals, we should also be able to describe how these same human beings react when a general social phenomenon—particularly one that has evolved away from their control—unpredictably threatens to break down into the particulars from which they had previously organized it. Under the extrasystem conditions I hope to specify elsewhere, they find it funny.

It is the humorist's task to point out or bring about this breakdown, articulating instances in which these increasingly foreign and inflexible systems disintegrate into the elements that human beings originally integrated to create them. If social (and cultural) systems have been constructed, they can also be "deconstructed."[4]

No one has stated the humorist's deconstructionist approach more insightfully than Luigi Pirandello in his 1908 essay *On Humor,* which provided the theoretical foundation for his better known later plays and short stories. Like the social constructionists whose heritage of post-Kantian idealism and romantic irony he shares, Pirandello believes that human beings impose order on their amorphous existence *artificially:* "Since life is fatally lacking in what from the point of view of human reason would be a clear and definite purpose, it becomes necessary for life, if it is not to drift aimlessly in the void, to have a particular, fictitious and illusory purpose for each human being" (1974:124; see also 137). But Pirandello goes beyond the social constructionists by noting that humor can tear apart all these illusionary human constructions: "All fictions of the spirit, all the creations of feeling are the basic material of humor; [humorous] reflection becomes something resembling a diabolical imp that takes apart the mechanism of each image, of each phantasm produced by the emotions . . . to see how it is made" (1974:124–25). Humor's goal, Pirandello concludes, is to "disillusion" human beings both profoundly and pervasively. "In this rapid vision of humor we have seen it expand gradually, go beyond the limits of our individual being, where it is rooted, and extend itself all around us. It was discovered by reflection, which sees in everything an illusory or feigned or fictitious construction of our emotions and [which] disassembles and unmakes it with a keen, subtle and detailed analysis" (1974:141). Specifically, Pirandello shows how humor disassembles the illusionary constructions of art (whose fictive hypercoherence of the world's fictive pseudocoherence makes it the illusion of an illusion [1974:66, 142–45]), of logic (which we examined in chapter 2), and especially of our selves (which we will examine in chapters 7 and 8).

Thus Pirandello's subjectivist-phenomenological conception of comedy challenged Bergson's objectivist-positivist one[5] just as Max Weber's subjectivist-phenomenological conception of sociology challenged Durkheim's objectivist-positivist one.[6] Unlike objectivist-positivist comic and social theorists who focus on "the external and the general," subjectivist-phenomenologist ones focus on "the internal and the unique." Unfortunately, the historical ascendancy of objectivist-positivism over subjectivist-phenomenology[7] has rendered comic theory unable to comprehend certain comic phenomena and social theory unable to comprehend certain social phenomena.

Incongruous and Ambiguous Disintegrating Techniques

In part 1 we saw how humanly constructed cultural worlds "hardened" phenomenologically, interconnecting their elements in expected, even systematic, ways. In part 2 we will see how the humanly constructed social world also "hardens," systematically interconnecting its elements. These social elements cohere around *actors*—both *individuals* and *groups*—and around *actions*—both *roles* and *institutions*. We will see further in part 2 how humor breaks apart the elements that have grown together into each of these social units, motivating those who had accepted their traditional integration to laugh.

In contrast to the reinforcing comic types and undermining sociological types mentioned above, comedy can confuse the typifications of these social units that sociology has helped to establish. Sociology has articulated the somewhat amorphous social units created by lay people, sharpening and reinforcing them. Sociology's greatest achievement has been to show that social life is ordered. As the early naturalists did to the biological world, sociologists have delineated areas of the social world that "hang together." Whatever one may think of the rest of introductory sociology textbooks, their tables of contents exhibit sociology at its best, for here they delineate and organize the most significant subdivisions of social life—individuals and groups, roles and institutions.

But comedy belies sociology's organization. It manifests the residual, the exceptional, the deviant. What seems to hang together, comedy takes apart. What sociology typifies, comedy denies. Encountering an exception to a typification, which momentarily calls it into question, motivates laughter. Comedy shatters the standard sociological categories. What many believe to be a unified social self, a clearly defined social group, a coherent social role, a well bounded social institution, comedy shows not to be. (Comedy, of course, breaks down these sociological categories only conceptually not actually, though cognitive breakdown may lead to real social breakdown.) The comic shows the social world to be disordered—or at least ordered in another way than most people, especially most sociologists, believe.

How does comedy blast apart social units? We saw in the introduction to part 1 that humorists can disintegrate a gestalt by injecting into it an element *incongruous* to the other elements it integrates. On the social level, humorists can explode our conception of a social unit—an individual, group, role, or institution—by attributing to it a social element—appearance, language, behavior, value, or accouterment—conceptually alien to its other elements, much as a nuclear physicist can explode an atom by shooting into it a discordant subatomic particle. Humorists interchange the tenuously attached elements of social units. These readily detachable, movable, and reattachable attributes are the social equivalent of electrons on the atomic level. (Correspondingly, social units whose attributes are especially easy to replace are the social equivalent of "free radicals," for they make them tempting targets of humor.)

Where do humorists obtain the social elements capable of destroying our common conceptions of individuals, groups, roles, or institutions? They find elements incongruous to one social unit (for example, an institution such as the family) in those congruous to different species of the same genus (another institution such as business). A silly but suitable example is a 1985 Banx cartoon in which

> a frog says to a medieval princess, "Kiss me and I turn into a marketing consultant."

We further saw in the introduction to part 1 that humorists may also shift from one gestalt to another an element that turns out to be unexpectedly *congruous* with the second gestalt while retaining its ties to the first. Humor that stresses an element's common membership in two gestalts, rather than its greater appropriateness to one than the other, is based on *ambiguity* rather than *incongruity*. Humorists who point out a congruous element in two otherwise incongruous gestalts pivot our perception between them, negating their generally accepted distinction. On the social level, humorists can deny the difference between social units by discovering a similar social element in both. The ambiguity of their common social element weakens the distinction between their separate identities. The following 1985 *Mankoff* cartoon, for instance, suggests that family and business institutions differ less than they seem:

> One business executive says to another, "Stan, did it ever occur to you that monogamy is like a portfolio with only one investment in it?"

Humorists, in short, continually stir together the elements of different social units to scramble their traditional organization, using incongruity or ambiguity to break down both internal integration and external differentiation. Despite the seeming surface differences between social units—say, between family and business institutions—humorists suggest that they must share enough deep structural similarities to allow their elements to be interchanged.[8]

Unmasking and Ironizing Devaluating Techniques

Comedians and sociologists do more than disintegrate their subject matter cognitively; they also devalue it morally. They "unmask" their subject matter by splitting it into an apparent phenomenon (what most people believe is going on) and an actual noumenon (what is "really" going on). Peter Berger gives some examples of how sociologists unmask social phenomena:

> One cannot fully grasp the political world unless one understands it as a confidence game, or the stratification system unless one sees its character as a costume party. One cannot achieve a sociological perception of religious institutions unless one recalls how as a child one put on masks and frightened the wits out of one's contemporaries by the simple expedient of saying "boo." No one can understand any aspect of the erotic who does not grasp its fundamental quality as being that of an *opera bouffe*. . . . And a sociologist cannot understand the law who does not recollect the jurisprudence of a certain Queen in *Alice in Wonderland*. [1963:165]

Sociologists often unmask a social phenomenon by distinguishing its more important but concealed "latent function" from its more obvious but less significant "manifest function"; for example, by showing that religion's latent function of holding a social group together is more important than its manifest function of worshipping the group's gods. Unmasking is especially effective when the actual noumenon uncovered is lower status than the apparent phenomenon covering it. Consequently, both comedy (specifically "satire") and sociology can be particularly provocative by revealing "dirt" behind reputable institutions, roles, groups, and individuals: the government, the bureaucracy, the professions, the rich, the powerful, the celebrated. (Comedy and sociology can also be irreverent to each other by undermining their respective pretensions.)

Like comedians who go beyond comic unmasking to use comic irony, sociologists can show that apparent social phenomena and actual social noumena are not merely different in kind or even status but are in fact contradictory. Searching out these social ironies, Louis Schneider suggests, is a major objective of sociological research: "Irony suggests a 'mocking discrepancy' between the way things are and the way they are supposed to be, between promise and fulfillment, between appearances and reality. . . . Social life is full of ironies, paradoxes, . . . and surprises. A good part of the insight of the sociologist consists in exhibiting and penetrating these" (1975:xi, 3–4). Richard

Brown goes further to distinguish several types of "sociological irony" (1977:175ff.). A social theory is ironic, for instance, if (1) it reveals behind a seemingly coherent phenomenon an incoherent noumenon— "contradictions in the events themselves, in the expectations of the actors or the general public, in the official values of the society, or in the theories of the sociologist's professional colleagues" (181)—or (2) it reveals how a seemingly independent and stable phenomenon actually depends on, or even turns into, its opposite—"how and why Puritan ascetics become bourgeois men of affairs, how capitalism becomes socialism, how socialists become oligarchs" (174).

Irony can be a property of the subject as well as the object. Someone speaks or writes ironically whenever deeper meaning contradicts surface meaning. This split in the ironic individual's communicating self, first noticed by Kierkegaard, grounds one school of sociology, symbolic interactionism (Shalin 1984). Since both sociology and comedy unmask and thereby profane powerful individuals, groups, roles, and institutions, "both of them are forbidden in dictatorially ruled countries. Dictators, conspicuously devoid of a real sense of humor and fond of socio-political ideologies, shun sociological analysis and hate political satire" (Zijderveld 1968:288). Consequently, both the political comics and social critics of authoritarian countries must retreat to ironic communication to avoid public censure. "The ironist withdraws his commitment from a public self and thereby facilitates the downfall of the ossified social order" (Shalin 1984:54).

Typical and Ideal Social Units

Social humor cannot be sorted simply by its use of incongruity, ambiguity, unmasking, or irony, I found, because many jokes employ several of these techniques. Although unable to categorize social humor clearly by its kind of attacking technique, I was better able to categorize it by the kind of social unit these techniques attack: typical or ideal. Part of the instances of social humor I collected dismantled their audiences' very definition of a *typical social unit* by portraying an *anomalous* instance of it (created largely by incongruous or ambiguous techniques). Thus a comic can disintegrate the typical role of "doorman" by transferring to himself one of the defining activities of the doorman's role (which is of course incongruous with his own reciprocal role):

> I don't get no respect. . . . Just the other day a doorman asked me to call a cab for *him*.
>
> [Rodney Dangerfield]

The other part of my social humor collection demolished their audiences' conception of an *ideal social unit* by portraying an *actual* instance of it (created largely by unmasking or ironizing techniques). Thus a comic can devalue our idealization of the serious writers' role (not mine, I hope!) by describing how their accomplishments fall short of their aspirations:

I've written several children's books. . . . Not on purpose.

[Steven Wright]

Anomaly and actuality, then, are comedy's chief weapons against *social* systems. Chapters 4 and 5 will treat social humor that disintegrates *typical* social units with *atypical actors and actions*. Chapters 6 through 8 will treat social humor that devalues *ideal* social units with their *actual incompetence, inauthenticity, and incoherence*.

4

Atypical Actors

Humorists who shift characteristics from one typical social unit to another—individual, collectivity, role, or institution—not only blur the established borders between them but also create an atypical new intermediate social unit. It is the incongruity between the traditional homogeneous social units and the novel hybrid one that causes us to laugh. I will examine humor that transfers characteristics between individuals and between collectivities in this chapter, and between roles and between institutions in the next.

The most frequently shifted attributes of actors (both individual and collective) in comedy are their physical appearance and language. Since the mask (Latin *persona*) can transplant one person's face onto incongruous others, ordinary people sometimes don the masks of celebrities, like Jack Nicholson or Richard Nixon, for amusement at parties. Masks portrayed recognizable individuals in Greek Old Comedy but became abstracted and generalized to more collective social types in Greek New Comedy (Levin 1987:63). Humorists also frequently detach and reattach to other actors the speech styles of both individuals (as when Paul Krassner calls Carl Sagan "the Barry Manilow of science") and collectivities (as when the sociologist who became a trucker says on the CB: "Ten-four good buddy, I just saw Smokies heading our way to socially control our velocity deviance").[1]

Transferring Characteristics Between Individuals

The attributes of an individual compose his or her personal identity. To shift them is to shift it:

> Shloime Goldberg is accosted on the street by an unknown Jew: "How are you? How are you?" Politely, Goldberg answers: "Fine, thank you. And you?" The stranger says: "How much you have changed. Yossele! It was so hard to recognize you! The last time I saw you, you had such nice black hair, but now you are grey and almost bald. . . ." "Wait a minute!" Goldberg tries to interrupt him. "I am not. . . ." "You used to be so elegant, but now you neglect yourself so much. Yossele, what happened?" "But . . . ," and the stranger continues: "This is amazing, you used to be such a tall man, now you have become so short. What happened to you? Have you been sick, Yossele?" "But listen, I'm not Yossele, I am Shloime." "Hah! Shame on you! You have even changed your name!"

This joke is funny because an individual's characteristics cohere into a gestalt, which hinders their transfer and hence his or her alteration. This section will explore the humor that transfers traits between the resistant gestalts of personal identities.

W. H. Auden once defined the comic as "a contradiction in the relation of the individual or the personal to the universal or the impersonal," which leads to no real suffering (1962:371). In our society, the generality of the individual involves a precarious balance. The normal individual must have neither too few nor too many characteristics in common with others. As Auden puts it, "the [normal] human person is a unique singular, analogous to all other persons, but identical with none" (1962:379). Otherwise he or she becomes a comic figure. Those who are "too unique" are regarded as funny, especially by British humor theorists, such as Addison in *The Spectator* (no. 47): "When a Man of Wit makes us laugh, it is by betraying some Oddness . . . in his own Character, or in the Representation which he makes of others" (1965; 1:203). But those who are "too general" are also regarded as funny, especially by the French, such as Pascal in his *Pensées* (no. 133): "Two faces that resemble each other, though neither makes us laugh by itself, make us laugh when together, because of their similarity" (my translation).

It is amusing to generalize the individual not only spatially but temporally, as John Allen Paulos (following Bergson)[2] observes: "It is well known that repeated display of character traits or mannerisms often is the key to a comedic personality. Certain stock types such as the pompous braggart go back to Aristophanes, Jack Benny's cheapness, W. C. Field's misanthropy, and Charlie Chaplin's walk are more contemporary examples of the same phenomenon. Most well-known comedians, in fact, develop a persona that is to a certain extent stylized, repetitive, and predictable" (1980:36). The comic power of repetition is strong enough to humorize even tragic human events. "Northrop Frye has commented that even tragic events repeatedly enacted begin to become funny. Parents losing their child to measles, say, and their consequent grief and suffering are very sad. But if a play were to depict the death from measles each year for seven years of one of their seven children and the parents' consequent grief, the tragedy would soon turn to comedy" (1980:36). An extended sequence of suicides becomes funny to watch on stage as increasing generality begins to blur the extreme egocentricity of self-murder.

Those whose physical appearance is generalized are likely to become axes of comic ambiguity. Just as linguistic ambiguity pivots us between the definitions of a word, physical ambiguity pivots us between the identities of an individual. Because identical twins are, in Harry Levin's apt metaphor (1987:82), a "human pun," several classical comedies revolve around their ambiguous identities. In Shakespeare's *Twelfth Night* (5.1:223–24), Orinso is shocked to see characters he thought unrelated—the twins Sebastian and Viola—together:

> One face, one voice, one habit, and two persons,
> A Natural perspective that is and is not!

Shakespeare's *The Comedy of Errors* is perhaps the ultimate exploration of the comic possibilities of twinship, for it contains two sets of twins, masters and servants. Similar physical appearance, in short, can function as the ambiguous element that overrides the differences between incongruous personal identities.[3] (See Arieti 1976:114–18 on the comic confusion between identity and similarity.)

If *identical twins* comically generalize an individual unintentionally, *impressionists* do so intentionally. The impressionist may literally "put on" the facial expression, clothing, manner, accouterments—and especially try to imitate the linguistic idiosyncracies[4]—that constitute the distinctive features of someone else's identity. Impressionists derive humor from the incongruity between their own identity elements and the mimicked identity elements of their target. Denny Johnson, a fey comedian, got laughs simply by trying to talk like macho John Wayne. Impressionists also derive humor from putting their target in roles or situations that comically clash with his or her idiosyncratic personality. The same Denny Johnson portrayed Jack Nicholson running a children's show and comedian Barry Sobel portrayed Mick Jagger as a TV weather forecaster. The most artful impressionists can even imitate one person imitating another. John Lasky portrayed both Woody Allen imitating William Shatner reciting the prologue of *Star Trek* and William Shatner imitating Woody Allen reciting the epilogue of *Manhattan*. And Robin Williams portrayed Sammy Davis, Jr., as Hamlet:

> "Oh, you *know*, what *piece* of work is a *man*, how noble in reason, and I really *mean* that, sincerely."

More than other kinds of comedians, impressionists reveal how tenuously attached to us are essential parts of our identity.

Impressionists inform their audience they are trying to duplicate someone; *impostors* prevent their audience from learning of their duplications. For both impressions and imposture, the more incongruous the difference between the identities of the impersonator and the impersonated, the funnier the disguise element that ambiguously connects them. Theatrical comedies have exploited the comic potential of imposture by differentiating two sets of observers of one character disguised as another: the other characters unaware of the disguise, and the audience aware of both the disguise and the other characters' ignorance of it. The audience is amused by its proprietary knowledge that one or more characters in the play are predicating their lines of behavior on an erroneous perception of the disguised character's identity, lines of behavior that diverge increasingly away from where they would have developed with accurate awareness—but, like a stretched spring, suddenly snapping back to it during the discovery scene at the end of the play.

Finally, individuals are comically generalized by certain *institutions*. All institutions try to override the individual's identity with a collective identity to some extent, but what Erving Goffman (1961a) called "total institutions" try to replace it more completely than the others. For instance, "the army is perceived as turning men into mechanical toys. The sad sack or awkward recruit, invariably out of step, is an easy laughingstock, yes; but, following the wayward march of Good Soldier Schweik, he reaffirms humane values by setting his own pace" (Levin 1987:82). In other words, the soldier who marches to a different drummer resists the army's attempt to overgeneralize the individual, thereby provoking laughter less at those who share too few traits than at those who share too many.

Transferring Characteristics between Collectivities

Comedy that revolves around similarities in individual identities is complemented by comedy that articulates differences between individuals and between collectivities. If the ambiguous identities of comic clones are often mistaken, the distinct identifying characteristics of comic eccentrics and comic social types are easily recognized.

Comic Eccentrics

Of the many social attributes that compose an individual, the comic eccentric fosters at least one to an extreme. This, Maurice Charney points out, is why a comic character is not your average person:

> Aristotle's ideal man in the *Nicomachean Ethics*, who finds happiness and peace of mind by seeking his comfortable niche in the mean between extremes, has little place in comedy. The art of comedy is typically concerned not with the normal man, but with persons who cultivate the extremes—either excess or defect, too much or too little; it doesn't matter so long as the efforts are out of proportion, disharmonious, and incongruous. . . . Comedy does not try to create lifelike characters, but pure and intense ones, who are not moderate, mixed, or fallible, but rather extremes, freaks, and caricatures of living persons. . . . The types in comedy are not realistic portraits of average men in everyday situations. [1978:69]

(This is not to say the average person can't be comic. Jack Benny, George Burns, Mary Tyler Moore, and Garry Shandling have all prompted laughter by emphasizing the contrast between the extreme characters around them and their own relative normality.) Eccentricity is the social equivalent of cognitive exaggeration. Both amuse by contrast with the norm. In *The Dark Voyage and the Golden Mean*, Albert Cook observes that the norm comedy tries to establish is the *mean* rather than the extreme. "Social man . . . strives for comfort by following the mean and adapting himself as closely as possible to the social norm. . . . Social thought and its art form, comedy, considers not the *extreme* value of good and evil, but the pure-action *mean* of best policy. In the thought of Machiavelli, this is the basis of all action between governments; and Machiavelli holds a high position in Italian literary history as a comic writer" (1964:478). Like the sociology of deviance, comedy manifests the mean of manners indirectly by describing deviations from it.

But just as the existence of the norm leads us to laugh at the extremes of human variability, so the existence of the eccentric leads us to laugh at the norm. Allowing one's attributes to develop independently to their extreme may require less psychological energy—that is, may be more "natural"—than trying to moderate them into an harmonious whole. Furthermore, the difference between expending more and less psychological energy has great comic potential, which humor can release by ripping off the strenuously maintained social mask over the relatively effortless natural man. Our laughter at eccentrics, then, may stem from our finding them truer to human nature than "normal" people, rather than the other way around.

Comic Social Types

If the comic of the personal and idiosyncratic has distinguished British humor, the comic of the impersonal and general has distinguished French wit (Levin 1987:185).[5] The comically abnormal may be not only individuals, but social types: "collectivities of eccentrics," so to speak (see Davis and Schmidt 1977). Comedy, Cook continues, tries to typify the abnormal. "In comedy [unlike tragedy], almost never does a character represent the norm, which laughs at him and expels him as he implies it by his abnormality. . . . Comedy says, 'Even in the abnormal and the unpredictable do norms and predictability emerge.'" For the comic abnormal hero is always a type—country bumpkin, boaster, ironist, misanthrope, miser, middle-aged cuckold, young lover, foreigner. They are all funny because their abnormality implies and strengthens the norm, because even they are typical norms of abnormality" (1964:487).

Harry Levin, the most distinguished contemporary analyst of historical comedy, informs us that comedy turned from ridiculing recognizable individuals to mocking more general social types at least twice during its history: once in fifth century B.C. Greece; again in eighteenth-century England: Greek

> Old Comedy . . . left its strongest impression as a civic pillory, a vehicle for topical lampoons, and no respecter of persons in exposed positions unprotected by anything like libel laws. Gradually the personal attacks were curbed and softened into Middle Comedy, which . . . drew more upon myth and fiction, less upon current events. Seldom again would the theater, constantly subject to social pressures, address itself so boldly to personalities and politics. To be sure, Sir Robert Walpole received, from such playwrights as John Gay, the kind of taunts that Cleon had provoked from Aristophanes. Government reprisals thereupon brought about the Licensing Act of 1737, which established the long overlordship of the Lord Chamberlain's Office, and turned Henry Fielding away from the stage to the novel. Yet censorship could not always guard against resemblances that were more than coincidental, whereas Aesopian scrutiny could detect radical twists in the blandest story-line. [1987:30–31]

Politics, in short, pressured comic playwrights to generalize their targets from recognizable individuals to more universal social types (whose living paradigm, however, they often subtly suggested). This historical tendency to defocus comedy forced Fielding to disclaim, "I declare here once and for all. I describe not men but manners, not an individual but a species" (Levin 1987:198), and Diderot (as well as most French comic theorists like Bergson) to overgeneralize this feature of the comedy of his time and place: "Diderot distinguished comic from tragic characters on the basis of species and individuals. This might cover the stock characters of New Comedy but took no account of the recognizable caricatures in Old Comedy" (Levin 1987:31). Comedy that emphasizes social types implies that human nature changes little over time or space (1987:63, 69), which diffuses responsibility for errors and evils from specific individuals to their social species and even to humanity at large.

Comic Sociological Categories

Besides types of abnormality, there are also types of normality. Comic characters are members not only of the small-scale comic social types enumerated by Bergson and Cook but also of the large-scale standard sociological categories: age, gender, and class. (More precisely, they are members of sociological *sub*categories: for example, the old, women, lower class.) Not everyone belongs to a social type (like "the clumsy"), except in a negative sense (like "the nonclumsy"), whereas everyone belongs to a sociological category (that is, has a particular age, gender, and class). Ever since the Greek Menander and the Romans Terence and Plautus, comic playwrights have slotted their characters into these sociological categories and their combinations: *senex, adulescens, servus, parasitus, matrona, virgo, ancilla, meretrix* (Levin 1987:63–64; 44, 172). Modern comedy, which scrutinizes more heterogeneous societies than classical comedy, had added members of racial, ethnic, religious, and—I will show—temporal categories.

Social types (and sociological categories)[6] are comic, Bergson explains in his usual mechanical terminology, because they involve the "ready-made element in personality." "In one sense it might be said that all *character* is comic, provided we mean by character the *ready-made* element in our personality, that mechanical element which resembles a piece of clockwork wound up once for all and capable of working automatically. . . . Thus to depict characters, that is to say, general types, is the object of high-class comedy. . . . Not only are we entitled to say that comedy gives us general types, but we might add that it is the *only* one of all the arts that aims at the general" (1956:156–57).

Charney notes that the "ready-made" aspect of comic social types (and sociological categories) inheres not only in their behavior but literally in their clothing. "In comedy, the question of identity that plays such a large role in tragedy is often reduced to a matter of costume, which defines identity in unambiguous terms" (1978:53).[7] Since identity in comedy is mostly a matter of external signs, it can be altered simply by putting on a new costume. "Disguise is an aspect of costume, since a character may change his identity by the mere change of dress. It is just as easy as that. The basic rule of the disguise convention, established in the plays of New Comedy, is simple: all disguise is good disguise and all disguise is impenetrable. No thorough transformations need be made, so that the audience can easily share the irony of one character's being in another character's clothes" (1978:55). Comic characters who can change their identities so readily are often misperceived, allowing the comedy to proceed through the mechanical ramifications of mistaken identity. "Identity can be more easily mistaken if it was never too strongly asserted, and the persons of comedy, unlike those in tragedy, are frequently interchangeable types. Their integral humanity has been exchanged for a self-operating mechanism, by which they become parts of a larger mechanized unit called the play, which is a microcosm of society. . . . As Bergson has so convincingly shown, the mechanization and the denial of free humanity generate the comic action. This makes most comic plots highly schematic" (1978:85).

Impostors in comic plays duplicate not only individuals (personal identity), but also the collectivities they represent (social identity). It is easy to impersonate members of collectivities because their mere costume implies their social identity, even more than their personal identity. In the classical comedies, a male character often disguised himself as a female character, and especially vice versa (Frye 1971:183). Moreover, the Elizabethan convention in which boy actors played female characters allowed more complex permutations of identity, as when a boy actor played a girl character who disguised herself as a boy character (Auden 1962:376; Charney 1978:55; Levin 1987:82). Shakespeare's As You Like It carried these reflexive identity permutations one step further, when the boy actor who played the girl Rosalind, who had been pretending to be the boy Ganymede, further pretended to be herself. And characters in the classical comedies switched class as commonly as gender, for many a master or mistress was disguised as a servant, and vice versa. "Servants and masters often exchange roles, as in Farquhar's Beaux' Strategem, Shakespeare's Taming of the Shrew, and Goldsmith's She Stoops to Conquer, and many other comedies, and the humor arises from an ironic repetition of attitudes and remarks from one role to another. . . . There is a natural appropriateness in the reversal of roles that defies the rights of birth and social position" (Charney 1978:86; see also Levin 1987:87). (The characters of more recent comedy have also impersonated a third sociological category—race. The 1986 film *Soul Man,* whose central character is a white who pretended to be black to win a scholarship to Harvard, drew most of its laughs from misperceived racial identity.) The many classical comedies that turn on these "mistaken identities" always end with "recognition scenes" that reveal "true identities," both personal and social (Charney 1978:84; Levin 1987:79–80). The erroneous belief that the identities of two characters are different (for example, mistaking a master for a servant) is corrected by a recognition scene that proves their identities are the same. The erroneous belief that the identities of two characters are the same (for example, mistaking one identical twin for the other) is corrected by a recognition scene that proves their identities are different.[8]

Today it is common to call people's views of sociological subcategories "stereotypes," a term first applied to them in 1922 by Walter Lippmann. Since in contemporary life there is "neither time nor opportunity for intimate acquaintance, . . . we notice a trait which marks a well-known type, and fill in the rest of the picture by means of the stereotypes we carry about in our heads" (quoted by Boskin 1987:251). Lippmann restricted the term mainly to a view of a sociological subcategory that morally evaluated its characteristics, to a cognitive generalization plus a value judgment. Since most stereotypes highlight the negative features of a sociological subcategory, they are usually deplored by liberals. Lippmann, who believed stereotypes were always false (Dundes 1987:102), began the moralistic movement to purge the stereotypes used in humor.[9] One comedian, however, employs sarcastic sanctimony to unmask this antistereotype crusade as overtly romanticizing social identity while secretly despising personal identity:

> Why be prejudiced against anyone because of their race or nationality or creed, when there are so many *real* reasons to hate them.
>
> [Emo Phillips]

Two kinds of social humor exploit these stereotypes in opposite ways. The first kind *exaggerates* a sociological subcategory's negative social attributes, particularly its language, appearance, possessions, or character.

Collectivity speech style has inspired "dialect humor," which Joyce Hertzler defines broadly as humor that focuses on the unique speech of *any* group: "sub-languages with peculiarities of vocabulary and idiom, accent, intonation and pronunciation, and grammatical forms, whether of specific regions, or social classes, or of racial segments of the population, or of ethnic groups [or] the foreign born" (1970:182; see also Koziski 1984:67). The most noticeable feature that differentiated ethnic groups at the turn of the century was their dialect, which the humor of the time overstated:

> Though [the traditional dialect humor of American vaudeville] attempted to display "characteristics" of particular ethnic groups, the very basis of that humor was the fundamentally superficial attribute of mispronouncing the prevailing language. The essential implication was that if that person with the dialect were to make the correct noises he would soon be just like everybody else. And this implication was borne out by the "equalitarian" proliferation of dialects in vaudeville. Alongside the Yiddish dialect could be heard the dialects of the Scottish "Sandy MacPherrson" and the Swedish "Yohnny Yohnson," the Irish "Mick" and the Negro "Sambo," and sometimes the same comedian who "did" the Jew switched in turn to the "Dutchman" (German) and then to the Yankee. During World War I many of the Dutch comics converted to Yiddish dialect. [Altman 1971:161]

The classic dialect humor of European immigrant and ethnic groups has declined dramatically today, of course, but only to be replaced by the dialect humor of the newer ethnic collectivities.

Since we differentiate the genders mostly by the way they look, humor has traditionally overdrawn their anatomical differences:

> After [one of my shows], a woman thanked me for not making jokes about the size of Dolly [Parton's] bosom. Indeed, her name has become a national generic reference. Upon hearing "Dolly Parton," a contestant on "The New $25,000 Pyramid" blurted out her instant association: "big-busted women." Burt Reynolds, who at the time was Dolly's own inamorata . . . could not resist telling Johnny Carson and much of America that "her breasts have their own Zip Code."
>
> [Paul Krassner]

(Feminist critics have complained that these corporeal jokes degrade women by calling attention to the female body—and away from what they regard as her loftier qualities).

Humorists have also inflated the stratified life styles and cultural accouterments associated with each class level, such as the extravagance of the affluent:

Standard: Say, Mr. Poor, I'm so rich, I just bought my dog a little boy.
Poor: That's nothing, Mr. Standard. Why, I'm so rich, I don't have my Bentleys air-conditioned. I just keep a dozen cold ones in the freezer.

[*National Lampoon*, Mar. 1985, 42]

or the penury of the poor:

Burbank has a new restaurant: Two Guys from Calcutta. They give you a bowl and you beg at the next restaurant.

[Johnny Carson]

Humor differentiates ethnic groups by their dominant character trait. "Usually ethnic jokes seize on some cultural trait attributed to the subject group: the formality of Englishmen, the heaviness and drunkenness of Germans, the French instinct for sophisticated sex, the clever and ambitious practicality of Jews, the sentimental and maudlin attachment of Irishmen to home and country" (Charney 1978:70). Alan Dundes (1987:98–101) observes that many jokes articulate the most characteristic traits of ethnic (and other) groups through the "comparative method." Like a scientific experiment, these jokes contrast the ways several ethnic groups approach the same situation, usually in an isolated setting, such as a life boat, a desert island, or a boat or plane in difficulty:

The ship sinks and the survivors are left on a desert island. The Americans go into business immediately. The French begin building night clubs. The Germans build armament plants. Then one turns to the other and asks, "Who's that group standing there?" The reply: "That's the English, they're still waiting to be introduced."

Some of these characterological jokes portray stereotyped ethnic groups with *deficient* positive traits:

What are the three shortest books in the world? *Italian War Heroes, Jewish Business Ethics, Who's Who in Puerto Rico.* Other titles reported in variants include: *The Polish Mind, 200 Years of English Humor, Democracy in Germany, Negroes I Have Met Yachting,* and *La Dolce Vita in Scotland.*

But most portray stereotyped ethnic groups with *excessive* negative traits, like Jewish parsimony:

Israel has the hydrogen bomb . . . Had it for twenty years . . . Never used it . . . Cost $187,000,000 . . . Do you think they're going to throw it away on an Arab?

[Jackie Mason]

Even positive traits, like Jewish industriousness, become funny when blindly pursued to excess without regard to need:

I landed at Orly airport and discovered my luggage wasn't on the same plane. My bags were finally traced to Israel where they were opened and all my trousers were altered.

[Woody Allen]

The ordinary person is a mixture of sociological subcategories, over-identification with any one of which is prevented by the presence of the others. Exaggeration humor, however, seems to reduce a person to a single pure subcategory by isolating and enhancing its features. Phenomenologically, humor that exaggerates the stereotypical behaviors associated with one of a person's sociological subcategories suppresses his or her identification with any of the others. The extreme one-dimensional person that results is comically incongruous not only to the more moderate—typical—members of the exaggerated sociological subcategory but also to the multidimensional ordinary person.[10]

Less explored but more relevant to modern comedy (and my theme) is a second kind of social humor, which *contradicts* stereotypes instead of exaggerating them. The comic mind varies the many attributes that compose the stereotype of a subcategory one by one until it comes upon an attribute incongruous with its definition;[11] if the incongruous attribute is also congruous with another subcategory against which the first is defined, so much the funnier. For the sociological subcategories defined by their opposite—old-young, men-women, black-white, Christian-Jewish, rich-poor—the comic mind will transfer a social attribute from one subcategory to its opposite, creating humor by incongruously juxtaposing a traditional social attribute of the first subcategory with those of the second.

Age Groups

Comedy subverts age stereotypes by switching traits between age groups. Thus much humor portrays children who acquire incongruous traits from adults. Since their most conspicuous difference (besides their size) is their language, humor sometimes depicts children who speak like adults, who employ "big words" and "show-off language" (Hertzler 1970:183). Charles Schultz's *Peanuts* comic strip, for example, depicts children who employ adult vocabulary, grammar, and speech rhythms (in contrast to *Dennis the Menace*, which exaggerates the childish side of our double image of childhood). Precocious humor may depict children who dignify their puerile plight to the adult level.

In a 1984 cartoon by P. Steiner, a father looks angrily at his son and says, "I seriously doubt that Amnesty International will be interested in your case."

Such humor may also depict children who actually engage in adult activities (fig. 6). This last cartoon undermines not only our conception of children, but also our conception of adult activities. If business can be merely child's play, perhaps adults shouldn't treat it so seriously.

Conversely, much humor also portrays adults who acquire incongruous traits from children or even infants. "Postcocious" humor

Figure 6

sometimes depicts adults who speak in "baby talk" (Hertzler 1970:183), especially to attack them indirectly (Mindess 1971:47–48). (A common way to mock superiors behind their backs is to imitate them acting childish, repeating their typical expressions with the vocal rhythms and tones, facial expressions and kinesics, of children at their worst: "IwanitdonebyFriiidaaay!".) Along with size and language, adults and preadults are distinguished by their clothing. The comedian Bruce Baum is best known for his portrayal of "Babyman!" a pudgy balding middle-aged Superman clone clothed only in diapers. This kind of humor also attributes to adults other features of children, such as their distinctive diseases,

> as in the *Wall Street Journal* cartoon in which a wife says to her distinguished-looking but spotted husband lying sick in bed, "For heaven's sake, Walter, can board chairmen get measles?"

or their distinctive tastes and activities,

> as in a 1988 *Mankoff* cartoon that depicts a secretary who says to a visitor looking at a group of executives sleeping with their heads on a meeting table, "They always take a nap after their milk and cookies—otherwise they get cranky."

Note that these cartoons insert the children's trait into not just any adult but into those who exhibit adult traits—appearance or role—to the extreme (an "adult's adult," so to speak).[12] The adult speech inserted into the children's mouths in *Peanuts* cartoons also derives not from ordinary adults but from the most sophisticated—most adult-like—adults. On the other side, if it is amusingly incongruous for a child to talk like an adult, it is more so for an infant, an embryo, even a sperm, to talk like one, as in the 1989 film *Look Who's Talking*.

Humor exploits incongruities and ambiguities between age groups further advanced along the life cycle as well, usually by portraying older adults who acquire incongruous characteristics from younger adults. In a rare Biblical reference to laughter, God informs old Abraham his wife Sarah will have a baby:

> Abraham bowed to the ground, and he laughed, thinking to himself, "Is a child to be born to a man one hundred years old, and will Sarah have a child at the age of ninety?" . . . Now Abraham and Sarah were old, well on in years, and Sarah had ceased to have her monthly periods. So Sarah laughed to herself, thinking, "Now that I am past the age of childbearing, and my husband is an old man, is pleasure to come my way again!" But Yahweh asked Abraham, "Why did Sarah laugh and say, 'Am I really going to have a child now that I am old?' Is anything too won-

derful for Yahweh? At the same time next year I shall visit you again and Sarah will have a son." "I did not laugh," Sarah said, lying because she was afraid. But he replied,"Oh yes, you did laugh." . . . Abraham named the son born to him Isaac. [Isaac is a form of the Hebrew for "God has laughed."] Then Sarah said, "God has given me cause to laugh; all those who hear of it will laugh with me." [Gen. 17.17;18.11–15; 21.3, 6]

In modern times, the most common age-appropriate activity humor shifts along the life cycle is not procreation but copulation:

Old Mr. Saperstein the butcher went to confession and said, "Forgive me, father, for I have sinned. Last night a beautiful young woman came into my shop and I . . . I couldn't control myself. I seduced her, and we made love for three hours.

The priest said, "I recognize your voice. You're Saperstein, and you're Jewish. Why are you telling this to me?"

"To you?" shouted Saperstein. "Father, I'm telling everybody!"

Since the old in Western society are supposed to be asexual, many humorous folktales and comic plays have portrayed how ridiculous (that is, incongruous) they look whenever they try to pursue someone sexually as though they were young. Gabe Kaplan mocks their eroticism in the modern manner by imagining a TV show called the "Geriatric Dating Game":

"Three widowers want to meet our widow. Widower No. 1, what are your hobbies?"

"Gin rummy and Maalox."

To intensify the incongruity, current senescent sexual humor even employs adolescent sexual slang:

Reminds me of something my grandfather used to say, "I'm going upstairs and fuck your grandmother." Well, he was an honest guy. He wasn't going to lie to a little kid.

[George Carlin]

(An additional vector accelerates our amusement at Carlin's reminiscence, for sex not merely clashes with our sentimental conception of the chaste old but actually debases it.)

Finally, individual maturation and social change increasingly differentiate the characteristics derived from biological age and those derived from historical generation. Humor reveals each generation's different terms for the same concepts, as in Tom Toles's 1984 cartoon that shows a grouchy older man sitting on a comfortable chair, pontificating:

"Drugs, sex, and rock and roll. What kind of values are those? I say we go back to the *old* values. . . . Wine, women, and song."

and the slow but inexorable progression of the seemingly exclusive language, culture, and politics of younger adults to older adults. Since the very names of the young are associated with a particular historical period, their names begin to seem amusingly at odds with their setting as that generation ages.

Do you realize that in the next generation, nursing homes will be filled with ladies named Debbie and Heather and Bambi?

[Mark Russell]

The senior citizens of the early twenty-first century will no doubt complain that their grandchildren's music "isn't as good as the Rolling Stones." Because only the young are presumed radical or liberal and only the old conservative, the 1980s TV series "Family Ties" could draw much of its humor from the confrontation between aging radical parents and their conservative children, implying that even something as basic as political orientation may stem more from the contingencies of generation than from the necessities of age.[13]

Gender Groups

As with age groups, humor transfers elements closely associated with one gender to the other. Because men and women have traditionally been distinguished by their clothing (at least until recently), the most common forms of gender transference humor has been transvestism (see Davis 1988). Ever since Greek mythology, audiences have laughed at men who put on women's clothes, like Heracles "painted with his great beard and furious countenance in woman's attire spinning at Omphale's commandment" (Sidney 1970:50). One of the first memorable images on television in the early 1950s was Milton Berle in drag. "In the early TV show "Texaco Star Theater," Mr. Berle's sudden fame came partly from his manic moments in dresses and lush make-up as he did take-offs of Carmen Miranda, Cleopatra, Juanita Hall, and many other women" (*New York Times*, 16 May 1985, 25). Billy Wilder's 1959 film *Some Like It Hot* and Sydney Pollack's 1982 film *Tootsie* also employed transvestism to portray amusing gender incongruities and ambiguities. Blake Edwards carried the comic possibilities of modern transvestism one step further in his 1982 film *Victor/Victoria,* in which Julie Andrews plays a female impersonator—that is, a woman pretending to be a man pretending to be a woman. His 1991 film *Switch,* about a character who dies as a man but comes back as a woman, is best known for Ellen Barkin's performance as the reborn woman who retains many premortem masculine postures, gestures, kinesics, and speech forms.

Besides clothing and communication patterns, humor transfers the accouterments and activities of one gender to the other, such as their respective bibulous preferences (fig. 7) and culinary styles:

San Francisco is the only town where guys in motorcycle leathers trade recipes.

[Will Durst]

Pepper . . . and Salt

THE WALL STREET JOURNAL

"Well, if you don't have any 'red eye' I'll take a banana daiquiri."

Figure 7

Note that, as with age groups, combining the extremes of the gender groups—the social elements that most differentiate the genders—intensifies the incongruity and consequently the humor. In the 1970s and 1980s, the best-known comic female impersonator was the obviously masculine three-hundred-pound Divine.

> "Often garishly dressed in spangles and spike heels, he wore huge, 50-pound fake breasts fashioned of foam rubber and lentils, his face deep in stylized makeup, and with a raw and raucous voice like vodka over gravel" (*San Francisco Chronicle*, 8 Mar. 1988, B7).

Gender-inappropriate humor attributes exaggerated feminine characteristics to those with the most masculine characteristics, like size, beards, leather clothing, or virile occupations:

> I'm a lumberjack and I'm OK.
> I sleep all night and I work all day. . . .
>
> I cut down trees; I skip and jump.
> I like to press wild flowers.
> I put on women's clothing
> and hang around in bars. . . .
>
> I cut down trees; I wear high heels,
> suspenders and a bra.
> I wish I'd been a girlie
> just like my dear papa.
>
> [Monty Python]

(And vice versa, for example, the mustache on the Mona Lisa). The gender incongruities of androgynous stars like Michael Jackson, David Bowie, and other beardless youth are less amusing because their preadolescent gender characteristics are less differentiated (see Davis 1983:179; Davis 1988:28–30). Because many homosexuals also adopt traits customarily associated with women, jokes that transfer women's clothing, behavior, or personality traits to men have a homosexual implication that adds anthropological sexual debasement to more egalitarian social humor. In a Cheney cartoon (1981), for example, four prisoners on their bunks in a small cell are about to go to bed; one prisoner says,

> "Okay, guys, whose turn is it to be the sultry bitch tonight?"

These gender transference jokes imply the instability of all the elements that distinguish the genders, even their essential corporeal aspects:

In the [former] Soviet Union, if you're a male athlete and don't win, you become a female athlete. That's an incentive.

[Yakov Smirnoff]

And transfering less essential elements may be only a prelude to transfering more essential elements:

For all the praise they receive as industrial workers, doctors, engineers, most [Russian] women still come home after work to cook supper, wash dishes. The Russians have a joke: a pregnant man goes to see a doctor. "How come?" asks the doctor, amazed. "It all started," says the patient, "with my washing dishes."

[*TV Guide*, 31 Aug. 1985, 5]

Gender transference jokes seem to be especially amusing in societies, like America or Russia, where gender difference is neither completely stable nor unstable but gradually breaking down (see Davis 1983:201–34).

Our language contains many gender discriminations that humor reverses. Humorists plug each gender into the clichés associated with the other. *Titters* (1976), which claims to be "the first collection of humor by women," often substitutes "males" in clichés usually associated with females, as in their article "The Myth of the Male Orgasm" (72).

Titters also attributes to females traits traditionally possessed by males. It replaces "men" with "women" in such masculine artistic forms as war comic books—"*Babes in Arms: BC* Comics Featuring 'The Fighting Hellcats'" (179)—and it refers to women's body parts in male slang in an article on bust development entitled: "Were you . . . absent the day Mother Nature passed out the *jugs?*" (74). Feminists use this same linguistic reversal technique to elevate rather than debase women's status by substituting women in noble platitudes whose protagonists have traditionally been men, for example, "A woman's got to be what a woman's got to be." or "Tune in next week to find out what happens when a woman with a future meets a man with a past." Conversely, Barbara Bush, speaking at Wellesley, got her biggest cheer by pivoting on a pronoun the traditional reference of "spouse":

"Somewhere out in this audience may even be someone who will one day follow in my footsteps and preside over the White House as the president's spouse. I wish *him* well."

The old gender stereotypes this kind of humor has tried to break down have in fact broken down in reality, though new ones have

arisen. Women have recently acquired many attributes previously reserved for men, and vice versa. Some novel forms of humor play off
both old and new stereotypes, like the underground comic book hero
Genderman ("Strong as a woman! Sensitive as a man!"). Others exaggerate the new gender stereotypes, like the *Titters* parody of *Miz* magazine articles: "How to teach your son to wear a dress and like it" (148).
Still others contradict them. The 1987 film *Three Men and a Baby* and
the television sitcoms *My Two Dads* and *Full House* force men into situations where they must care for babies or raise children, drawing laughs
from their inability to do so as smoothly as women, despite the new
gender stereotype of the maternal male. The 1987 film *Baby Boom*, in
which a single female executive (Diane Keaton) unexpectedly inherits
a baby, portrays modern women themselves as humorously unable to
care for babies, at least at first. Humor usually contradicts a new stereotype by reemphasizing an old one, which now has become a "retro-
type": when social change has led members of a sociological subcategory far from a previous stereotype, we laugh at those who try to
return to it. In recalling the previous stereotype, retrotypical humor is
reactionary; for it undermines our current expectation that members
of a sociological subcategory will always behave according to their
new stereotype.

Racial, Religious, and Ethnic Groups

It has also become more common for humor to contradict, rather than
exaggerate, the stereotypes of racial, religious, and ethnic groups,
transferring one group's characteristics to the group it has traditionally
been defined against. Contemporary humorists often switch traits between racial groups. In Mel Brooks's 1974 film *Blazing Saddles*, the races
reverse their customary music as the blacks croon, "I get no kick from
champagne" while the whites belt out "Camptown Races." Black comedian Robert Townsend drew laughs by speaking in the high
pitched, clipped but drawling style of an upper class preppie white.
Employing the more sophisticated technique of negating a negative,
humorists have interchanged white and black traits by debunking the
white stereotype in the same understanding but condescending moral
style that debunked the black stereotype in the early 1970s, which the
National Lampoon parodies:

Our White Heritage
White Myths and Stereotypes
    Although White people have been in America for over four hundred
years, there still exists an enormous amount of misunderstanding about

Whites, some of it willfully malicious, but most of it the result of a lack of proper education or just plain ignorance. . . . You can do your part to dispel a lot of misinformation that surrounds uncolored people by "debunking" these common myths whenever and wherever you hear them voiced, or by protesting strongly whenever the media or anyone in public life resorts to one of these demeaning stereotypes to describe or portray persons of Anglo-American ancestry:

Whites have "natural reason," or extra lobes in their brains, which make them good aesthetes.

They are adult-like, brooding, and worry a great deal. . . .

They are sexually frigid, or "hung like hamsters."

They all look like Commander Whitehead or the Arrow Shirt Man, and they go around reflectively rubbing their chins and saying, "Slide rule do your stuff," or "Brain don't fail me now."

They are clean, chaste, and prudish.

[Beard et al. 1985:42]

A similar parody, Martin Mull's TV series "A History of White People in America," transfers black employment problems to whites, which become humorously incongruous with the other privileged opportunities of a group seldom discriminated against. "A White Actor" (Steve Martin) discusses his problems with being stereotyped in movies:

The biggest difficulty for me in being white is getting typecast in mostly white roles. When I first started I guess I should have done more black roles but one picture led to another and pretty soon I was known as a white person. I read for "The Wilt Chamberlain Story" and I was very good but they cast a less-experienced black person in the role. It's one of the things you have to live with as a white person in the United States.

Transcegenation humor has been complicated by the bipolar stereotype of Negroes in American, which has alternated between "Sambo" and the "Savage" (Boskin 1987:252). Throughout the nineteenth century—in fact as late as the middle of the twentieth century—"minstrel show darkies," the many white comedians who performed in "blackface," adopted and exaggerated the Sambo stereotype (Charney 1978:52).[14] Recently, however, white comedians have emphasized the savage side of the black stereotype; for instance, by transferring it to the least violent whites:

Did you ever see a tough Jew in this country? I never saw four black people walking on the street saying, "Watch out! There's a Jew over there"!

[Jackie Mason]

The same issue of National Lampoon (Mar. 1985) that treated blacks with mock condescension contains another article entitled "Are Jews White

People?" which begins (and ends): "Technically, yes, but. . . ." The Jew-ish blackface entertainers of the first half of the twentieth century, like Eddie Canter and George Jessel, furthered Jewish assimilation in America, for, if Jews could pretend to be Negroes, they must be "nor-mal" whites, at least relatively—a problematic issue at the time.

Comedians also portray Jews who acquire Christian traits:

> Did you hear about the Jewish man who takes acid and buys retail?
>
> [Robin Williams]

and even adopt them wholesale:

> I went to a reformed service the other day. It was so reformed the rabbi was a gentile.
>
> [Jackie Mason]

One reason for the relatively large amount of Jewish humor is the am-biguity whether Jews are an ethnic, religious, or even racial group—which provides a much wider range of contrast for Jews than for groups that are *only* ethnic, religious, or racial. Jewish humor fre-quently portrays the contradictions of being members of these multiple groups; for instance, between their ethnic inclination for bargains and their religious restrictions on food:

> Jewish dilemma: seeing a grocery store ad that offers pork chops at half price.
>
> [James Jackson]

Except for Jews, comics had to go outside America to find a contrast for Christians. Recently, however, indigenous contrasts have been eas-ier to find since many oriental religions have made inroads into America.

> [Jerry Brown] has a little alligator on the vest pocket of his Buddhist robe.
>
> [Mark Russell]

Mark Russell implies that yuppie Christian Americans, like ex-California governor Jerry Brown, are unable to give up their own sym-bols, no matter how incongruous and mundane, even when putting on the sacred religious clothing of the Oriental religions. The steamy excitement of America's current cultural bouillabaisse obscures the in-compatibility of some tenets of Eastern religions with certain American life-styles, which comics point out:

> San Francisco is a great place for comedy. It's the only place in the coun-try where you can see things like Buddhist motorcycle gangs.
>
> [Mike Ferrucci]

The process of ethnic assimilation, of course, always produces temporary incongruities between the traditional ethnic culture and the new American one, which disrupts both their gestalts. The incongruities become especially funny whenever the newly adopted values or practices directly contradict the old. Assimilating ethnics who adopt indigenous prejudices, for instance, may discover they are actually disparaging themselves:

> Korean comic Henry Cho loves the confusion he causes when he strolls up to the microphone on stage and greets the audience in a heavy Southern accent. As the laughter starts, he smiles and says, "Bet you're saying to yourself, what's wrong with this picture?" Growing up in the South caused some identity problems for Henry: "My daddy's from Seoul, but I'm from Tennessee, so I hate Koreans!"

Assimilating ethnic groups may also complicate American society's traditional binary oppositions:

> Childhood games were also traumatic [for Cho]: "I hated playing cowboys and Indians because I was always the cook."

Unlike racial and religious groups in America, each ethnic group is not defined binarily against a single opposite ethnic group (except perhaps unethnic Americans). Consequently, American ethnic humor usually contrasts two ethnic groups only on the few traits that are opposed enough for exchanging them to be funny:

> Canadians who enter the U.S. illegally are called "snowbacks." They take jobs from Mexicans.[15]

Class Groups

Literary historian Maurice Charney notes that comedy has traditionally portrayed society as stratified:

> Comic convention postulates a society that is rigidly hierarchical. By the laws of decorum, carefully formulated by such Roman rhetoricians as Cicero and Quintilian, different social classes have their prescribed styles, both of manners and of speech. The hierarchy is conveniently divided into three major categories: high, middle, and low, although there are also unlimited gradations in between. The high people are lords and ladies, kings and queens, princes, dukes, and other aristocrats, as well as all persons thought vaguely to be "great," either by vast wealth virtuously acquired or by some other distinction. . . .
> Middle persons are generally people like ourselves, who

constitute the vast and almost unbounded middle class in America. They are neither exalted nor base, particularly vicious nor especially virtuous, but only representative types, whose normal reactions may be counted on for comic effect. . . .

Most comic action is generated from low characters, who may be, most characteristically, servants, but could also be workingmen, . . . tramps, unemployables, professional beggars. [1978:51–52]

Sociologist Richard Stephenson, however, found that, with the *bourgeoisement* of modern society, midtwentieth-century American jokes found as much humor in the upper class as in the lower. "A cursory examination of anthologies of jokes [from the 1930s and 1940s] will reveal a considerable number of stories which might be classified as involving stratification situations. The principle emphasis of such jokes is upon status, and the subject matter is concerned primarily with income and occupation. . . . There is a general propensity to ridicule the top and bottom of the status hierarchy in a kind of leveling offensive consistent with American values" (1951:570–71). Humor exaggerates or contradicts each stratum's distinctive language (Charney 1978:51–53; Hertzler 1970:181–82; Koziski 1984:67), appearance, accouterments, or character: "The laborer is characteristically lazy and seeks to avoid work; the businessman is overbearing and of doubtful veracity; the rich are idle, tightfisted, and vain; the poor are lazy, ignorant, and stupid" (Stephenson 1951:570).

Modern humor collapses the rigid hierarchy of the social world, like that of the cosmos, by exchanging traits between its upper and lower strata.

A 1982 *Don Addis* cartoon commingles upper-class audience and lower-class entertainment. In front of a marquee advertising "Female Mud Boxing in Wet T-shirts on the Mechanical Bucking Bull with Dirty Talking," a doorman greets a well-dressed couple: "Good evening, Mr. and Mrs. First Nighter!"

"Status transfer humor" proceeds on the assumption that merely associating upper- and lower-strata personnel, language, life styles, or cultural objects—like the President (Carter) and the peanut—will rub on to one stratum the status rubbed off the other, debasing the high while elevating the low. A comic I heard who noted a newspaper ad for the Marin County Blues Festival wondered what upper-class people would sing about in this lower-class musical form: "My gardener left me today. And my wife ran off with the chauffeur." Yakov Smirnoff, the emigré comic, claims he once worked on the Black Sea on the impoverished Russian equivalent of an opulent American cruise ship known as "The Love Barge." Parodists have even transferred a sociocultural protective organization usually associated with the downtrodden to the uptrodders:

> The Pluto-American Anti-Defamation League said it will bring pressure to bear on media to up-grade the image of incredibly rich people. The newly-formed group, which hopes to combat negative portrayals of incredibly rich people on television and in print, cited the crucial role that incredibly rich people have played in American history, and hopes to restore incredible richness as a "positive aspect of American life."
>
> [*Off the Wall Street Journal*]

Temporal Groups

Although "temporal groups" are not usually considered a sociological category, comedy blurs their identities as much as those of the more standard sociological categories (most of which were originally distinguished *spatially*). Each temporal group comprises the typical inhabitants of an historical period. Just as comedy collapses the identities of other social groups by injecting an *incongruous* element, it collapses the identities of temporal groups by injecting an *anachronistic* element. Unlike other social incongruities, however, humor grounds most temporal incongruities in a single source: the present.[16]

Temporal humor may shift present appearances (including postures and gestures) and accouterments back to the past, but more commonly it retrojects language, especially trendy speech. Although usually historicizing modern expressions, it sometimes shifts only modern meanings to outdated expressions, entangling them in comic incongruities retrospectively. Once respectable words that have recently acquired sexual connotations, for instance, now clash with their originally innocent contexts:

> And Jim Blewer, browsing a 1945 *Saturday Evening Post*, ran across an ad for Ovaltine, headlined "Wake up GAY!"
>
> [Herb Caen]

(So that's what causes it!)

To hear typical members of temporal groups spout current clichés breaks the wall our schooling has constructed between ourselves and our forefathers. Moreover, temporal humor also dissolves the patina of greatness that has come to surround the best-known historical figures, (down)transforming them into "regular guys" by attributing to them modern motives:

Alas the advent of singles want ads came a little too late for some of the great all-time classified catches, both past and present:
SLIM SELF-RELIANT WOODSY GUY seeks similar self-sufficient woman for walks in the wilderness, long talks. Must have contemplative nature, ability to subsist on little and love of outdoors, backpacking, nuts and berries. P.O. Box 837, Walden Pond, Mass.
[Gerald Nachman, *San Francisco Chronicle*, 17 Jan. 1985, p. 24]

Nearly all temporal humor reminds us that our ancestors did not inhabit a different (especially more noble) realm of being than ourselves, and that their character was essentially the same as ours—no worse and (especially) no better.

Ahistorical time.—Like historical periods, timeless myths and legends and fairy tales are realms removed from the present, which comedy can incongruously reconnect by slipping current life-styles into their enchanted "once upon a time" worlds. A William Hamilton cartoon (1983) portrays a mother reading a modern fairy tale book to her young daughter:

"Then she got single and lived happily ever after."

Current technology is used in a *Bizarro* (1989) cartoon showing a witch reading a cookbook of evil potions in front of a microwave oven:

". . . add one bat wing and a dash of cobwebs, microwave on high 3–4 minutes, rotate 1/2 turn once during heating. Remove from oven, leave covered for 2 minutes. Hexes six."

Primitive societies.—It is as amusing to hear the Flintstones and other cave men and women talk like moderns as to hear children talk like adults. Their contemporary speech implies that even members of the seemingly incomparable paleolithic society had the same concerns as ourselves. In an Unger cartoon (1983) a cavewoman is speaking to a cave man who is drawing hunters shooting arrows at deer:

"People are beginning to complain about too much violence on cave walls."

By portraying natives who talk and act like moderns, humor can undermine our romantic conception of them as more successful than ourselves in avoiding the corruptions of modern civilization (fig. 8). Primitive temporal humor also contrasts scale. The sophisticated social forms of the present become ludicrous when projected back onto the primitive technology of the past. A 1982 cartoon by W. Jole, for example, has soldiers besieging a castle. One soldier operating a very small stone catapult says to another:

"You used to hunt, fish and dance. Now all you
do is call your gallery in New York."

Figure 8

"I wish we'd never signed that strategic-arms-limitation treaty!"

The opposite form of primitive temporal humor treats modern society the way anthropologists treat native societies: It posits denigrating primitive meanings for our most esteemed technologies and folkways—for example, shopping has replaced hunting in the modern world, with marked-down items as "wounded prey," according to Elayne Boosler—and elevating sacred meanings for our most trivial objects and activities, as in David Macaulay's *Motel of the Mysteries:*

> A 41st-century schlemiel stumbles upon an American motel, buried since that tragic event in 1985, and proceeds to misinterpret the function of everything he finds. For instance, the Sacred Urn and its Sacred Collar and Sacred Headband with the holy chant inscribed on the front, "Sanitized for your protection".[17]

Past civilizations.—Filmgoers sometimes find it funny to see historical personages with present physiognomies:

> A Frenchman, to whose eyes American faces still have something exotic, finds comical the combination of the morphologies of these gangster-sheriffs with the little Roman fringe; [Mankiewicz's film *Julius Caesar*] rather looks like an excellent music-hall gag.
> [Barthes 1972:26]

Most historical humor, however, projects into the past contemporary speech and the situations that generate it. The Roman section of Mel Brooks's film *History of the World: Part 1* includes a "Vsed Chariot Salesman," a "V & X Cent Store," and the following conversation in an "Vnemployment Insvrance Office":

> "Occupation"
> "Gladiator"
> "Did you kill last week?"
> "No."
> "Did you try to kill last week?"
> "Yes."
> "This is your last week of Unemployment insurance. Either you kill somebody next week or we'll have to change your status."

Humorists retroject the catchwords of contemporary culture to historical periods to show that the form of human aspirations has remained the same even though the content may have changed. In a 1988 Reilly cartoon in *The New Yorker,* for example, an architect is explaining plans for remodeling a villa to a toga-clad yuppish Roman couple:

> "What I'm trying to achieve for you is an eclectic mix of classic B.C. and a touch or two of A.D. glitz."

Future civilizations.—Comedy treats even the inhabitants of the future like a temporal group, juxtaposing their imagined more sophisticated technology with our current modes of social communication and interaction. The Jetsons, for instance, are the Flintstones of the future: the similar contemporary speech and behavior of each set of cartoon characters is incongruous with vastly different temporal locales. In his preview of the *History of the World: Part 2*, Mel Brooks exaggerates even this kind of temporal incongruity by juxtaposing to future technology not merely present but past (though persistent) life-styles and languages. An episode entitled "Jews in Space" depicts yarmulked Hasidic Jews piloting a spacecraft—a backward-looking people in a forward-looking role.

5

Atypical Actions

Transferring Characteristics between Roles

Like humorous actors, humorous actions play off generally recognized patterns. If nothing is expected, nothing can be unexpected; consequently, nothing will be funny. Sociologists have termed these generally recognized patterns of actions *roles*. Roles are clearest in occupations, for which people are both hired and trained to perform specific patterned actions (for example, manager, worker), but also occur in other institutions whose hiring and training is less defined, such as the family (husband, wife). Humor aborts expectations about a role, like those about an individual or a collectivity, by extracting traits from one role and implanting them in another. The conjoined traits that explode into laughter expectations about a social role, like those about a social actor, reveal its essential components.

When humorists withdraw a feature from a role, how much their audience laughs determines how fundamental the feature is to their conception of this role:

> I just got married, but it's not going to work out. My wife expected to
> move in with me. Hey, lady, this is the 1980s.

This comic has discovered by negation what sociologists have found more directly (Davis 1973: chaps. 2, 6): that spousal cohabitation (or at least the mutual desire for it) is essential to the married role. Another elementary feature of an intimate relation has been so central to its definition that it has gone almost without noting by sociologists (but see Davis 1973:10):

> I went with this woman for four months. But she was so insecure. She kept wanting to know my name.
>
> [Monty Hoffman]

Different traits, of course, are essential to different kinds of roles. Certain roles may require role partners to be performed properly; for instance, parents cannot parent without children. Those who try to engage in these reciprocal role activities without role partners seem ludicrous:

> Then, there was a time, Mr. [Monrad] Paulsen [dean of the law school at Yeshiva University] related, that he was a visiting professor in England, and he was told this tale by a professor of jurisprudence at Oxford. The Oxford professor invited a Belgian professor to give a guest lecture in French. No one showed up, and the Oxford professor invited his guest outside for a beer. But the Belgian visitor resisted, and presented his lecture to empty seats. "The audience may be missing, but the problem remains."
>
> [New York Times, 30 Oct. 1977, 30]

The following joke manifests this role requirement by presenting a role, like psychiatrist, without its role partner, patient:

> "I will see you Mondays, Wednesdays, Fridays at three," says the psychotherapist to his new patient, "and I advise you to be on time because, if you're not, I start without you."

A role can be made ludicrous not only by deleting its essential traits but also by adding incongruous ones from other roles. By shifting a role element from one profession to another, for instance, humor can confuse the customary division of labor:

> A marquis of the court of Louis XV unexpectedly returned from a journey and, on entering his wife's boudoir, found her in the arms of a bishop. After a moment's hesitation, the marquis walked calmly to the window, leaned out, and began going through the motions of blessing the people in the street.
> "What are you doing?" cried the anguished wife.
> "Monseigneur is performing my functions, so I am performing his."

(This anecdote is funny not only because adultery is especially incongruous with the other elements of the bishop's role but also because the copulating component of the marquis's conjugal role is equated with the seemingly dissimilar blessing component of the bishop's role, which more abstractly equates the biological and spiritual aspects of the cosmos).

Comics can intensify this kind of humor by attaching to a role novel elements from not just any other role but from its partner's role, as in this domestic role reversal:

> I don't get no respect. . . . At home my kid sends me to my room for talking back.
>
> [Rodney Dangerfield]

A more complicated example of professional role reversal depicts a plumber who employs on a doctor the same placebo technique the doctor would employ on the plumber:

> A doctor calls a plumber at 3 a.m. about a drip in the toilet that is keeping his wife awake. The plumber is furious, and he tells the doctor he won't come in the middle of the night. But the doctor asks, "Wouldn't you call me if your child was sick?" "Okay," the plumber relents. "Throw two aspirin in the bowl, and call me in the morning."

Even more humor can be generated by attaching to a role an element from not merely its role partner but its "role antagonist" (negative role partner), as in Noel Ford's 1984 cartoon of a man returning home to his waiting wife:

> "My bartender doesn't understand me."

This complex cartoon exchanges traits between wife and bartender, traditional role antagonists vis-à-vis her husband. Although ideally a wife is supposed to "understand" her husband better than his (mere) bartender, actually—according to popular culture—a husband often complains to his understanding bartender that his wife doesn't understand him. This cartoon contradicts popular culture's transference of "relative misunderstanding" from bartender to wife by returning the trait to its original owner. Role occupants (for example, a bank guard) may also have difficulty distinguishing between the role's neutral partners (ordinary bank customers) and its negative partners (bank robbers) when a trivial trait is congruent with both:

> I think the hardest job in the world is to be a bank guard in Alaska. All the customers wear ski masks.
>
> [Dennis Miller]

Beside these two-sided exchanges, humor depicts one-sided acquisitions of the reciprocal role partner's qualities, especially where their statuses are discrepant. The lower status role partner may seize properties of the higher status:

> I had to move this month. It was my own fault, though. I put my house up for sale . . . and my landlord found out about it.
>
> [A. Whitney Brown]

Or the higher status role partner may appropriate attributes of the lower status, intentionally in this German Jewish joke:

> Plunder is raging in the streets during the 1918 German revolution. A middle-aged Jew is among the looters. "For God's sake, Herr Rubin, you too, looting?" "Shhh, it's my own store."

or unintentionally in this American radio (commercial) blooper:

> Remember, if you are going a'partying on New Year's Eve, it might be easier and wiser to take the bus than to drive after imbibing. . . . So remember, "Go by bus and leave the drinking to us!"

Finally, some role behaviors performed *reciprocally* cannot be performed *reflexively* without comically shifting meaning. You can do unto others what you logically or normatively cannot do unto yourself—without provoking laughter at what such reflexive behavior implies about you. Sometimes, it implies shrewdness, as in the self-looting joke. Usually, it implies stupidity. The comic bumper sticker—"Honk if I'm Polish"—plays off a familiar form of bumper stickers—"Honk if you're [a member of some collectivity: ethnic group, profession, whatever]." But whereas the latter creates fellow feeling among the driver's collectivity, the former calls into question the driver's intelligence by implying self-ignorance about something so basic as one's own collectivity membership. Inadvertent self-aggrandizement, conversely, amuses us as much as inadvertent self-denigration, as when President Ronald Reagan spoke to the Miami Hispanic Chamber of Commerce in 1983:

> When I was Governor [of California], I was speaking in Mexico City. And I sat down to a rather unenthusiastic and not very impressive applause, and I was a little embarrassed. It was worse when a gentleman followed me and started speaking in Spanish, which I didn't understand, but he was being applauded about every paragraph. So to hide my embarrassment, I started clapping before everyone else until our ambassador leaned over to me and said: "I wouldn't do that if I were you. He's interpreting your speech."

Transferring Characteristics within Categories of Institutions

Sociologists call an integrated complex of these roles an *institution*, especially when the stable and standardized role behaviors are governed by common values about socially central issues. An institutionalized role complex usually circumscribes the behavior of its members more than their uninstitutionalized roles do. In her famous line, "Marriage is a great institution, but who wants to live in an institution,"

Mae West expresses her preference for relatively free uninstitutional-ized role behavior over relatively constrained role behavior controlled by an institution—no matter how "great" (and moreover implicitly equates the institution of marriage with the most restrictive custodial institutions, such as mental hospitals).

Humor shifts attributes from one institution to another across their conventional social boundary; for instance, by transferring the discursive style of the courts to medicine.

> In a 1984 Rodrigues cartoon, for example, a doctor is reading from a lab report to his patient: Lab technicians Lopresti and Shaw say tests show you to be in perfect health. In a sharply worded dissenting opinion, lab technician Marcus takes a somewhat alarming view of your condition and accuses his two colleagues of gross. . . .

Most introductory sociology textbooks classify the institutions of our (or any) society into the four major categories: economic, political, familial, and cultural. I will describe how humor transplants the attributes of institutions *within* each of these categories in this section and *between* all of them in the next.

Economic Institutions

Although some institutional humor switches attributes between institutions that are merely different, most switch them between those *stratified* by various criteria. Economic institutions, for instance, are stratified by their size, assets, products, or prestige. Consequently, economic humorists have downshifted features of higher status businesses to lower status ones, such as their distinctive nomenclature,

> as in a Bill Hoest cartoon (1982) in which an adult is looking at a lemonade stand manned by two children, one in diapers. The older child says, "I'm the senior partner."

or their distinctive gratuities:

> My wife, the way she throws money around, it's ridiculous. I mean, who tips at toll booths?
> [Rodney Dangerfield]

Conversely, other economic humorists have upshifted features from lower status businesses to higher status ones, such as from garages to restaurants:

> Ever pick up your car and discover it was $100 more than the mechanic said it would be? . . . You don't walk into a restaurant for a steak dinner

and, after you're done, have the cook come out and say, "Well, it was a lot harder to make than we thought so it'll be $5 more."

[Bill Kirkenbauer]

or from restaurants to hospitals,

as in a 1987 *Bizarro* cartoon set in an operating room. A surgeon is walking by a patient who, though strapped to an operating table, is trying to tell him something. The surgeon says, smugly, "Sorry. This isn't my table." [1]

Political Institutions

Many political institutions are likewise not merely different but stratified, which allows political humorists to shift attributes between them vertically. The status of a government official's label, they observe, depends on whether his or her role partners are external or internal:

When you're abroad, you're a statesman; when you're at home, you're just a politician.

[Harold Macmillan]

The following anecdote undermines the expectation that members of higher status political institutions possess more privileges than equivalent members of lower status ones:

When Cal Coolidge was Vice-President, he lived in the Willard Hotel in Washington. A fire alarm in the middle of the night brought every guest into the lobby, in a variety of negligees and fancy pajamas. Mr. Coolidge speedily surmised that there was no danger and started to trudge back to his room. "Nothing doing," said the fire marshall, "get back in that lobby."

"You are speaking to the Vice-President," said Coolidge with some dignity.

"O.K., then," said the marshal. "Go ahead."

A moment later he called suspiciously. "What are you Vice-President of?"

"The United States," said Coolidge.

"Come right back down here," ordered the marshal. "I thought you were Vice-President of the hotel."

Familial Institutions

The dominant humor of a historical period centers on the most problematic institutional category, moving on to another institutional category when the first becomes either relatively less problematic or so problematic that such humor can no longer be tolerated by the authorities or its audience. In classical Greece, the focus of theatrical comedy shifted from politics to the family after authorities banned Old Comedy's caricatures of contemporary political figures (Levin 1987:158–59). During the late eighteenth and early nineteenth century in Europe, its focus shifted from economics to the family as audiences became more bourgeois (Levin 1987:174). Today in America, familial and quasi-familial relationships remain the primary focus of institutional humor.[2]

These relationships are stratified by their "closeness": from spouses at the top, descending through lovers, friends, acquaintances, and strangers—with various inlaw, ex-, and step- relations confusing this hierarchy's clarity (Davis 1973:xviii–xx). Relationship humorists often exchange one dimension of this closeness—physical, social, emotional—between higher and lower relationships while implicitly keeping the others. Thus they trade traits between spouses and lovers:

> The amount of women in London who flirt with their own husbands is perfectly scandalous. It looks so bad. It is simply washing one's clean linen in public.
>
> [Oscar Wilde]

between spouses and acquaintances:

> I'm dating again. And it's very exciting . . . because I'm married.
>
> [Mike Dugan]

and even between spouses and strangers:

> Do know what it means to come home at night to a woman who'll give you a little love, a little affection, a little tenderness? It means you're in the wrong house, that's what it means.
>
> [Henny Youngman]

Cultural Institutions

Since each cultural institution is stratified internally, humorists can switch attributes between its strata. Commingling features of high- and low-status sports, for instance, can produce incongruous hybrids like "cross-country bowling." Art too has lower and higher aspects, which jokes can reverse.

> The hostess at a large party, rather proud of her voice, rendered "Carry Me Back to Old Virginee" in a rich and throaty tremolo. She was touched to notice a distinguished, white-haired man bow his head and weep quietly as the last notes floated over the room.
>
> As soon as she could, she went over to him and said: "Pardon me, but are you a Virginian?"
>
> "No, madam," said the elderly man, brushing away a tear, "I am a musician."

This joke pivots our interpretation of a character's response to art from his apparent appreciation of high-status artistic content to his actual depreciation of low-status artistic form. Finally, it can be amusing to mix media. The cartoon in figure 9 illustrates the incongruity of using on the respected literary medium the newer technology of the less respectable television medium. And columnist Alice Kahn's "development" of the "Great Books" into "high-concept" film projects for Eddie Murphy translates the higher literary medium incongruously into this lower film format:

Hamlet: New Age wimp tries to avenge death of dad. Drives girlfriend nuts. Cuts self on poisoned blade. Can't do anything right.

Catcher in the Rye: Disturbed teenager launches anti-graffiti campaign.

Paradise Lost: Hell-raiser rebels against Big Guy. As a result, couple get evicted from property.

Don Quixote: Guy attacks alternative energy development.

The Great Gatsby: Guy overinvests in real estate to impress Jodie Foster look-alike.

Pride and Prejudice: Bitchy woman goes after clever guy, ends up with rich guy. Decides that's clever.

Crime and Punishment: Student kills neighbor. Gets caught by detective with hemorrhoids. Has religious experience.

Figure 9

King Lear: Dad asks kids if they love him. One puts him on a high-sodium diet.

Odyssey: Bummed out by war, hero sails around the world. Wife sets new Guinness record for fidelity.

Oedipus Rex: Man falls for older woman. Freaks when she turns out to be his mom.

[*San Francisco Chronicle,* "Sunday Punch,"2. Sept. 1990, 2]

Compressing their form, of course, squeezes the greatness out of their content while modernizing their language trivializes their theme.

Cultural institutions are also stratified externally by the importance of their prime value. Spiritual values are supposed to dominate the more prestigious ones—religion, philosophy, art—material values the less—leisure, mass media, sports.

Consequently, cultural humorists continually try to break down this hierarchy by transferring attributes from lower to higher cultural institutions. Iconoclastic humorists, for instance, have debased religion with leisure characteristics:

I came from a typical middle-class Jewish home: we were very wealthy. We belonged to the Beth Israel Temple & Yacht Club.

[Rita Rudner]

philosophy with mass media properties:

I was a DJ at an all-philosophy radio station: WYMI.

[Mike Dugan]

and art with sports features:

Now that it looks as if the [San Francisco] Giants are leaving, it behooves supporters of the fine arts to go after those disfranchised blue-collar crowds, a vital source of passion and, to be sure, income.

Likewise, many Giants supporters will be looking for something else to root for, eager for an opportunity to cheer "Go, Opera!" and "Humm, baby, Blomstedt!" or to boast, "Hey, how about those Post-Modernists!"

. . .

There's no reason why the same intensity that goes into pulling for the Giants can't be channeled into radio call-in shows where audiences might vent their feelings about culture as they do now about sports. . . .

"This is Artsphone '68. You're on the air."

"Hey, Ralph, that Herb Blomstedt's gotta be out of his cotton-pickin' *mind* playin' Phillip Glass ahead of Dvorak and Brahms!" . . .

Sportscaster Bill King, an avid balletomane, is the obvious choice to do the play-by-play on "Swan Lake." I can hear him now, leaning into the mike, screaming:

"I can't believe it! Cisneros must have jumped five feet! Holy cow, I haven't seen height like that on a cygnet since Margot Fonteyn! And willya look at that crazy Baryshnikov! It's hard to conceive that Mischa can still get off a series of entrechats at his age, but they don't call him 'Dr. B' for nothing."

[Gerald Nachman, *San Francisco Chronicle*, 15 Nov. 1989, B3]

Conversely, other humorists have elevated lower status cultural institutions, like popular music, by attaching to them attributes from higher status ones, like education.

I used to be in a rock group. They were very intellectual. They called themselves "The Whom."

[Jimmy Brogan]

So far, I have focused on the differences between institutions that make any transferred attribute inappropriate. But there must also be enough similarities between institutions to make transferring attributes possible. Like key-and-lock biological processes, an attribute can be transferred effectively from one social institution to another only if its new slot resembles its old one. For such a shift to be humorous, the transferred attribute must be similar enough to the one it replaces to fit in the new slot, but different enough to fit in only imperfectly—its incongruous aspects standing out against the background of its congruent ones.[3] If most of the differences between institutions humor exploits are *hierarchical*, most of their similarities are *systemic*.

Transferring Characteristics between Categories of Institutions

Midcentury American sociologist Talcott Parsons developed the conceptual scheme that allows us to understand the humorous exchange of characteristics between categories of institutions. (His unintentional contribution to humor theory is so ironic because his own social theory is so humorless.) Parsons theorized (1953) that systems can operate properly only by fulfilling four "functional prerequisites": *adapting* to their environment, pursuing their *goals, integrating* their subsystems, and *maintaining* their *pattern* by relieving internal tensions. Each major category of institution attempts to accomplish one of these functional prerequisites for the larger society (1955, 1957). Thus *economic institutions* try to solve their society's problems of "adaptation," *political institutions* try to solve its problems of "goal attainment," *cultural institutions* try to solve its problems of "integration," and *familial institutions* try to solve its problems of "pattern maintenance" and "tension management." Because the problem-solving output of one category of institutions is the input of another, all of them fit together into a "social system."

Moreover, Parsons adds (1953:192ff.), each system contains a nested set of similar subsystems that also solve system problems on lower levels—each "macrocosm" is constituted by a "microcosm." Each institution, then, not only specializes in one functional prerequisite to solve a problem for the entire society, but also contains features that fulfill all four functional prerequisites to solve its own systemic problems. In other words, every institution has adaptive, goal attainment, integrative, and pattern maintenance/tension management features. However different the primary processes of institutions, then, their secondary processes are similar.

Comedians take advantage of this latent similarity of all institutions to shift the seemingly unique characteristics of one institution to another. Every characteristic they transfer is similar enough to the feature of the new institution it replaces to function there conceivably, but different enough from the remaining features to function there incongruously.

For Parsons, in short, every institution exchanges its unique *products* to solve their society's systemic problems. For humorists, every institution has the potential to exchange similar *processes*. (Actually doing so, of course, would aggravate their society's systemic problems, throwing into question the organization of the whole social system—the ultimate goal of this kind of comedy). Let us examine some humorous examples of the six possible exchanges of processes between the four major categories of institutions.

Economic and Cultural Institutions

Our society ostensibly values its cultural institutions, concerned with the spiritual world, more than its economic institutions, concerned merely with money and the material world. Cultural institutions, consequently, can be debased by attaching economic attributes that highlight their "adaptive" rather than "integrative" functions. Thus humorists have ascribed commercial characteristics to religion, which profane its sanctity,

> as in the 1985 Callahan cartoon showing several doors to Catholic confessional booths. One door is labeled *eight items or less*.

Humorists have also employed business metaphors to puncture the sublimity of art, such as industrial machinery:

Jane Anderson offers a rather touching account of a Russian ballet corps dancer sadly reduced to giving dance lessons to little klutzes in Dallas. "Keep it light!" she admonishes them. "You're doing plies, not pumping for oil."

[*Los Angeles Times*, Sunday Calendar, 10 Oct. 1982, 48]

or corporate manipulations:

Yeats-Shelley Merger Stuns Wall Street

The chairman of the board of the William Butler Yeats Corporation, Makers of Fine Literature, . . . announced yesterday that the company had acquired controlling interest of the Percy Bysshe Shelley Communications empire.

As soon as the takeover was made public, stock in the Yeats Corporation soared from 43 a share to 76—despite the fact that in recent years the price of lyric poems has been at an all-time low. . . .

A few scholars and a handful of English teachers who have actually read the Shelley poems expressed dissatisfaction with the takeover, but the feeling on Wall Street is that the new arrangement will provide a more coherent approach to the study of literature. It is easier to deal with one poet than with two, and enormous savings are predicted by indexers who now can list all of Shelley's poems under the letter Y.

[Louis Phillips, *New York Times*, 15 Nov. 1988, A19]

Humorists have even observed how the most modern means of economic support for artists can embed itself into the very center of their art (fig. 10). Conversely, describing economic institutions in artistic terms may not elevate, but at least distorts, our conception of them. The straighter the business and the wilder the art, the more extreme our disorientation, as in the 1985 Mankoff street scene cartoon in which one very straight-looking man is saying to another,

"Have to run, Al—I've got an accounting gig at two."

Familial and Political Institutions

Humorists can depreciate political institutions by grafting them with family features. This kind of humor is *possible* because politicians often deal with family (pattern maintenance/tension management) issues, both as persons and as politicians. The following joke pivots around a common term between the grand generality of the political and the humiliating specificity of the familial:

"Senator," an aide called from the next room, "there's someone on the phone who wants to know what you plan to do about the abortion bill." Flushing, the politician sputtered, "Er . . . tell them I'll have a check in the mail by morning."

This kind of humor is *effective* because political institutions are supposed to be as stately as family ones are humble. The joke below in-

"In the final movement, the mood abruptly changes
from despair to joy as the composer is awarded a grant
from the National Endowment for the Arts."

Figure 10

verts their relative status by making the most prestigious political personnel subservient to the most trivial family activity:

> Mr. and Mrs. Knopf were leaving the White House after a tour when they bumped into the president. "Mr. President," said Mr. Knopf, "I know this is a great imposition, but—would you mind?" "Of course not," said the commander in chief. So they handed him the camera and posed in front of the White House."

Conversely, as in a Bill Hoest cartoon from 1985, someone who elevates the family beyond its station may be portrayed trying to exit its institutional framework with a political procedure. The cartoon has a bureaucrat talking to a man at the state department:

> "I'm afraid you'll have to get a regular divorce, sir. You can't defect from a marriage."

Economic and Political Institutions

Our society would like to believe that politicians are more noble than businessmen. The less reputable "adaptive" or economic orientation, the prime concern of businessmen, is supposed to be only a secondary concern of politicians, who should be concerned primarily with society's lofty goals. Political humorists, however, have long observed that politicians, far from being unconcerned with their personal finances, are as obsessed with money as businessmen—enough to steal it blatantly from their constituents:

> *Politician:* The other party has been robbing you for ten years, now give us a chance.

or even from criminals:

> Eugene Field once told how a large group of Illinois legislators were vacation-bound on a train that was held up by bandits. "After relieving the bandits of their cash and watches," concluded Field, "the legislators proceeded on their journey with increased enthusiasm and *joie de vivre.*"

If voting resolves political institutions' pattern maintenance or tension management problems, political humorists can subordinate this function as well to their adaptive function by depicting politicians who exchange money for votes:

> How did the election come out in your district?
> Oh, crooked politics beat us. We were fixing to offer one dollar for votes and the other side came along and offered two dollars. It was certainly a terrible blow to reform.

Economic humorists, however, rarely transfer these characteristics in the other direction to portray businessmen who act like politicians. Unless excessive or situationally inappropriate, attributing relatively positive traits is unfunny.

Political and Cultural Institutions

The following witticism suggests the superiority of Catholicism to the U.S. government by comparing the seemingly dissimilar "integrative" functions of their respective spiritual and corporeal symbolic rites:

"Sometimes," complained the presidential aide, "I wish we had a pope instead of a president. Then we'd only have to kiss his ring."

But since not every religious institution is more reputable than every political one, a humorist can also bring down a high status political institution by comparing it to a low status religious one. The following anecdote subordinates government's supposedly dominant goal and adaptive functions ("task-orientation" and "instrumental activity") to a disreputable cult's pattern maintenance/tension management and integrative functions ("social-emotional orientation" and "expressive activity"):

Less celebrated was the spirit-seeking seance that Abraham Lincoln once tolerated in the Red Room at the request of his wife. Lincoln later said the seance "sounded very much like the talk of my Cabinet."
[Francis X. Clines, New York Times, 23 Mar. 1983, 12]

Contact between the presidency and another disreputable cult in the 1980s produced a spate of jokes linking quasi-rational politics and pseudorational astrology. The following ironic letter to the editor in the New York Times, for instance, reversed their relative rank:

The report that important decisions in the White House were based on astrological advice is most disturbing. The results could undermine faith in astrology.

[Mel Mandell]

Although some artistic institutions are likewise more respectable than some political institutions, others are less so. The following well-known anecdote undermines a movie star's commitment to the role of a politician by reminding everyone that, before his institutional crossover, he merely "played" such roles—and supporting ones at that:

At a gala for Ford's Theatre in Washington last week, President Reagan told the time-honored story of what movie mogul Jack Warner had said

when he heard that Reagan was running for governor of California. "No,"
said Warner. "Jimmy Stewart for governor. Reagan for best friend."
[*San Francisco Chronicle*, 28 June 1988, A10]

(The subsequent extent of Reagan's crossover has weakened the
boundary between cultural [especially mass-media] and political institutions, which this conservative humorous anecdote tried to maintain.
Being less farfetched, crossovers between these institutions would be
less funny today.)

Finally, humorists have frequently exchanged features between politics and sports:

> Being in politics is like being a football coach. You have to be smart
> enough to understand the game and stupid enough to think it's important.
> [Eugene McCarthy]

Although this witticism begins by elevating sports into politics
through approving their common adaptive approach ("understand
[how] the game [is played]"), it ends by demoting politics into sports
through disapproving their common goal orientation ("think it is important").

Cultural and Familial Institutions

Marriage humorists, like Louis Safian (1967), contrast familial institutions with religious ones to show that the family's spiritual aspect is
unable to sustain its "integration" unless its worldly aspect functions
effectively to "maintain its pattern by managing its tension":

> Marriage: an institution that may be made in heaven, but is getting some
> gosh-awful maintenance work on earth.

If spiritual integration fails and the family fissions, its material resources must be reallocated among its members:

> Marriage: a knot tied by a preacher and untied by a lawyer.

Humorists may also imply that supposedly permanent family relations
are merely temporary, especially in some subgroups, by attributing to
them the tenuous integrative activity of another cultural institution
like tourism:

> A Hollywood star introduced her latest husband to her little daughter. "Dar-
> ling, this is your new daddy." "Oh, really?" said the perceptive child.
> "Will you please write something in my visitors' book?"

Conversely, it can be just as funny to link the family to the parts of
popular culture especially disjunctive with it, like rock music:

I once belonged to a punk rock group. We wanted to call the group by the most outlandish name we could think of so people would notice us. We rejected the usual punk names like "Scumbag" and "Razor" but eventually adopted the grossest name we came up with: "Your Parents!" And, sure enough, on our first gig, when the announcer introduced us by saying, "And now, let's listen to 'Your Parents,'" we emptied the auditorium.

Another cultural institution whose features humorists often fasten to the family is education. They can transfer merely common terms with different meaning in each institution:

Marriage: An institution in which a man loses his bachelor's degree, and a woman gets her master's.

But they can also transfer more substantial processes. Schools are not only repositories of integrative values; they also perform the same pattern maintenance function of socializing the young as families. Consequently, humorists can easily commingle their different socialization techniques into an incongruous hybrid. The hero of Peter de Vries's *Slouching toward Kalamazoo* fantasizes marrying his junior high school teacher, whom he has just gotten pregnant:

If I had to marry Miss Doubloon, would I be allowed to whisper and chew gum in the house? Or be required to take out the garbage if I did? Would home, in other words, be something like class? Would we have regular fire drills and recite the pledge of allegiance every morning? Would my comic books be confiscated? And until what age?

[1983:32]

The academic characteristic that seems to have spread to families most pervasively (and perversely) today is the language of social science. Social science, especially psychology and sociology, may have little effect on the way people actually live, but it has great effect on the way they *talk about* how they live. This abstract and stilted professional jargon is especially out-of-place in the family—as both humor theorists and humorists have frequently observed.[4]

For example, a 1985 *Guindon* cartoon portrays a yuppie-looking father brushing his teeth in the morning and saying to his son, "Ask your mother. She's *parenting* today."

Familial and Economic Institutions

Sociologists have long contrasted the organic, emotional, and diffuse social relations of the family (Gemeinschaft) with the mechanical, cognitive, and specific social relations of business (Gesellschaft). Humorists, however, have long tried to overcome their differences by smuggling traits across their borders—triggering laughter when caught.

Because our society professes to revere families more than businesses, our humor is more likely to attribute "lower" mechanical business characteristics to "higher" organic family relationships—as Bergson was the first to point out:

> Equally comic is the extension of business phraseology to the social relations of life—for instance, the phrase of one of Labiche's characters in allusion to an invitation he has received, "Your kindness of the third ult," thus transposing the commercial formula, "Your favour of the third instant." This class of the comic, moreover, may attain a special profundity of its own when it discloses not merely a professional practice, but a fault in character. Recall to mind the scenes in the *Faux Bonhommes* and the *Famille Benoiton*, where marriage is dealt with as a business affair, and matters of sentiment are set down in strictly commercial language. [1956:143–44]

A 1987 series of Mankoff's "Dollar\$ and Non\$en\$e" cartoons illustrates the humorous effect of describing various stages of intimate relations in business terminology (or, as Parsons would have put it had he had a sense of humor, describing pattern maintenance/tension management functions in adaptive phrases).

> In the first one a man is proposing to a woman who is using a hand calculator. She says, "Be patient. I'm calculating the risk-benefit ratio."
>
> In the second, a man and woman are talking over dinner. The man says, "Is there anyone else, Louise?" "Let's just say you've lost market share."
>
> And in the third a woman is saying goodnight to a man outside her door: "What do you say we just call it a failed joint venture?"

But Bergson did not notice (perhaps because it would have weakened his general theory) that some humor applies family characteristics to business organizations:

> Rita Rudner talked about life on the road living in Howard Johnsons, whose motto is "The next best thing to mother": "When I checked out, the desk clerk said, 'Go ahead, *leave*—I'll be dead in a few weeks anyway.'"
>
> [*San Francisco Chronicle*, 21 May 1990, F1]

And in a 1986 Bacau cartoon in the *Wall Street Journal* the chairman of a board of directors says to the rest of the board,

> "In a complex court settlement, our parent company gets custody of us on weekends."

The professions, particularly medicine, possess characteristics of both business and family (Parsons 1951: esp. chap. 4, 55ff.). Professionals like to claim that they and their clients form a gemeinschaft, based on collectivity-interest like a family. Cynical humorists, however, commonly point out that professional-client relations are actually a gesellschaft, based on pecuniary self-interest like a business:

> "He's a family doctor," Simpson told a friend. "He treats mine and I support his."

> Then there was the patient whose doctor told him he had three months to live. When the patient informed him that he couldn't afford to pay the bill, the physician gave him another three months.

Medicine is distinguished in the other direction from the family by its emotional distance from its activities. Consequently, humorists can overstep the medical/domestic frontier by suggesting that the family perform surgical activities from which even doctors have difficulty keeping their distance, as in this parody of late night television commercials which advertised the following products:

> Home Transplant Kit ("Donor not included")
> Home Autopsy Kit ("Why waste money with expensive coroners?")
> Family Pet Experiment Set ("Coming Soon")

Transferring Characteristics between Realities

Typical social units—individuals, collectivities, roles, institutions—exist in "ordinary" reality, the mundane world taken for granted. We have examined humor that confuses one typical social unit with another within this ordinary reality. But another form of humor, "transmundane," confuses typical social units with something outside it.

Beyond its normal bandwidth, ordinary reality is surrounded by (at least) two extraordinary realities: above its top boundary is the sacred, below its bottom boundary the perverse (Davis 1983). Those whose reality seems ordinary orient themselves by their location in their social system; those whose reality begins to seem extraordinary—either sacred or perverse—reorient themselves by their location in their anthropological system.

Transmundane humor shifts its audience's sense of reality between the ordinary and the sacred or the perverse. Because each extraordinary reality is incongruous with ordinary reality, phenomenologist Alfred Schutz observed (1973:23–24; Davis 1983:3–5), a person experiences each of these reality shifts as a "shock"—to which a common response is laughter. Transmundane humor tries to generate these

laughter-inducing experiential shocks by replacing an ordinary definition of a situation with a sacred or perverse one, and vice versa.

Transcending the Mundane

Centrifugal transmundane humor exploits the shock produced by
spinning its audience out of ordinary reality and into extraordinary
realities, both sacred and perverse.

Employing both ascending incongruities (see chapter 2) and
uptransformations (see chapter 3), the uplifting form of humor that
transforms objects and animals into humans and humans into gods
anthropologically induces its audience to transcend ordinary reality *phenomenologically*. Like poetry, this form of transmundane humor invites
its audience to wonder at the commonplace, drawing them into sacred
reality while eliciting less a loud laugh than a quiet smile (of beati-
tude). The rationalist Freud, who never understood this sense of the
sacred, called jokes based on it "stupid":

> A joke of Lichtenberg's takes a quite special place among these
> "stupid" jokes:
> "He wondered how it is that cats have two holes cut in their
> skin precisely at the place where their eyes are." To wonder
> about something that is in fact only the statement of an iden-
> tity is undoubtedly a piece of stupidity. It reminds one of Mi-
> chelet's exclamation which was meant to be taken seriously,
> and which to the best of my recollection runs: "How beauti-
> fully nature has arranged it that as soon as a child comes into
> the world it finds a mother ready to take care of it!"
> (1963:59–60).

Perverse—"negative sacred"—reality creates the opposite reaction,
for it violates all religious prohibitions, legal statutes, sexual norms,
and even physical laws. Those who experience this antinomian, seemingly chaotic, "gnostic" world (Davis 1983:173–83), call it macabre,
wicked, evil, decadent, unholy, vile, degenerate, scandalous. If sacred
reality is the realm of hyperorder, perverse reality is the realm of hy-
perdisorder.

This form of centrifugal transmundane humor depicts those,
pushed over the boundary of ordinary reality, who fall into perverse
reality to various depths. Like Dante's *Inferno*, perverse reality is hierarchical: ordinary experience is increasingly disorganized at each level.

Its shallowest level is *crime*, which undermines the ordinary reality of business especially. Many jokes show the line between business and crime to be easily crossed:

> I don't trust him. Before he gave me his business cards, he shuffled them.
> [Red Buttons]

Comics can degrade business into crime by describing legitimate business in terms not only of gambling but of drug dealing:

> An armored car was held up and robbed of $2 million worth of securities, with a *street value* of $29,000.
> [Mort Sahl, after the stock market crash of October 1987]

Below crime is the *mind-altering substance* scene. Parodists can descend to this level of perverse reality by treating their ordinary activities like addictions:

> I hadn't meant to go to the library. But a nagging question goaded me into wanting to look something up. That's how the cruel habit starts. First it's a dictionary that you're dipping into, next it's an encyclopedia, and, before you know it, books on travel, health, science and careers find their way into your hands. Inevitably you get a library card and check out several volumes at once. Suddenly you have an insatiable craving for the deeper stuff: fiction. You have become a "bookaholic."
>
> Fortunately, we live in a community that is doing its best to curtail the opportunity for bookaholics to indulge themselves. Due to budget cutbacks, many area libraries are able to open for only a few hours a day.
> [Russell Myers, *Los Angeles Times*, 13 Aug. 1982, pt. 2, 9]

Delving still deeper into perverse reality, as humorists portray it, uncovers *sexual deviations*, which they juxtapose not only to ordinary reality but to sacred reality—for perverse sexuality especially explodes the Christianized sacred that excludes it.

> *Naturally:* The San Francisco Music Box Co. just rec'd a complaint from a visitor who bought a musical nativity set from its store on Pier 39 and had it shipped to her home in the Midwest. "Look, I know you folks are the *San Francisco* Music Box Company," she wrote, but really—my creche has no Mary and two Josephs!"
>
> [Herb Caen]

Those who fall off the deep end of ordinary reality may descend all the way to *madness*, through whose distorted lens centrifugal transmundane humorists sometimes view ordinary concerns. After reading both Dostoyevsky's *Notes from Underground* and *Weight Watchers* magazine on the same plane trip, Woody Allen contemplates his corpulence—a common problem—hyperneurotically:

I am fat. I am disgustingly fat. I am the fattest human being I know. I have nothing but excess poundage all over my body. My wrists are fat. My fingers are fat. My eyes are fat. (Can you imagine fat eyes?) Flesh drips from me like hot fudge from a sundae.

[1972:65]

Comics sometimes push their characters over the border between sanity and madness:

A: Did you hear the results of the latest sociological research on the causes of wife battering?
B: No.
A: [suddenly shouting, slamming fist into palm repeatedly] They never fuckin' listen!

This joke first presents sanity in its extreme form as dispassionate scientific rationality, then suddenly shifts linguistic register to the speech style of passionate psychosis.

The deepest level of perverse reality is *death*, a favorite topic of the transmundane cartoonist Charles Addams. Addams is famous for oscillating his audience between ordinary and perverse realities by applying an innocent form to a macabre content. Many of his cartoons depict ordinary people unexpectedly encountering portents of death,

one of the best-known being a cartoon in which two innocent motorists who made a wrong turn in heavy rain stop at a river. The husband gets out, holding a map, and turns his flashlight on the ominous signpost: *Styx*.

Mundanizing the Transcendent

Centripetal transmundane humor exploits the shock produced by pulling its audience out of sacred or perverse realities and into ordinary reality. Robert Alter, who analyzes theological writings from a literary perspective, finds mundanizing the transcendent to be the predominant pattern of Jewish humor:

Jewish humor typically drains the charge of cosmic significance from suffering by grounding it in a world of homey practical realities. "If you want to forget all your troubles," runs another Yiddish proverb, "put on a shoe that's too tight." . . . *Weltschmerz* begins to seem preposterous when one is wincing over crushed bunions. . . . Against this general drift of literary modernism [which consciously remythologizes literature], writers significantly touched by the Yiddish heritage have often been de-mythologizers, using the wryness and homey realism of Jewish humor to suggest that a less melodramatic, less apocalyptic, perspective than that of myth might be appropriate for viewing even the disquieting state of affairs of the modern world. [1972:256–57][5]

Woody Allen, for instance, derives much of his humor from mundanizing the transcendent:

> The universe is merely a fleeting idea in God's mind—a pretty uncomfortable thought, particularly if you've just made a downpayment on a house.
>
> Eternal nothingness is O.K., if you're dressed for it.
>
> Not only is there no God, but try getting a plumber on weekends. [1972:31]

Centripetal transmundane humor secularizes sacred situations in many ways, like placing profane people in sacred scenes,

> such as when an astronaut in a 1957 Whitney Darrow cartoon who has just landed on Mars encounters a snake, a naked man, and a naked woman reaching for an apple on a tree. Caption (astronaut calling to the woman): "Miss! Oh, Miss! For God's sake, stop!"

or depicting sacred subjects who employ profane means:

> Three rowboats moved along the totally flooded streets, and the water was still rising as the torrent from heaven raged unabated. The rescuers spied a strange figure on the roof of a small building: a tall, bearded man, wearing a wide, flat black hat, his arms crossed.
>
> "Come down!" shouted the rowers. "Get into the boat!"
>
> The tall figure gestured calmly. "Save others. Do not worry about me. I am Rabbi Gershon Rosenbloom. The *Lord* will save me!"
>
> An hour later, another boat—this one with an outboard motor—approached. "Hey! You on the roof! Come down! The waters are still rising!"
>
> The rabbi, standing cross-armed despite water up to his waist, called out, "Go on! Save others. I am a rabbi. I have complete faith in my Lord!"
>
> And an hour after that, the rains still pouring down, a helicopter, searching for survivors of the flood, hovered above the rabbi on the roof, lowers its ladder, the pilot's voice bellowing out of a bullhorn: "Grab that ladder, man! The water's up to your *chin!* This is your last—"
>
> "Fear not!" sang the rabbi. "I am a man of God! And—He—will— *glub, glub, kmpf. . . .*" And Rabbi Gershon Rosenbloom, that good and faithful servant of the Lord, sank beneath the rising waters.
>
> Being a soul of the utmost virtue, without stain throughout his life, the rabbi, within an instant after drowning, found himself among the Heavenly Throng, gazing at the effulgent radiance of God Himself.
>
> "Oh, Lord!" cried the rabbi. "How *could* You? I had absolute faith in You, and You let me drown! How could You let me down—"
>
> "Let you *down?*" bridled the Lord. "I sent two boats and a helicopter to take you off that roof, you idiot!"

Besides sacred realms that are strictly religious, humor desanctifies other quasi-sacred realms like *art*. Our society has not only transferred religious emotion (awe) to art, but resanctified as "art!" many older religious objects that had lost their religious value. Since the bubble of an otherworldly orientation to art can be burst by thisworldly activity, a petty argument can comically profane an artistically sacred setting, as in the 1981 Hoest cartoon portraying a middle-aged husband and wife touring the parthenon:

"We're so lucky, Roger. How many couples get to bicker in the shadow of the Acropolis?"

The New Yorker has printed many cartoons that undercut great art's sacred aura with secular concerns, like the one by Barney Tobey from 1956 in which a couple rushes into a museum and asks the guard:

"Which way to the Mona Lisa? We're double-parked!"

Humorous also are quasi-sacred institutions like *marriage* that lose their romance to reality:

Marriage: definition: A romantic story that begins by a splashing waterfall and ends up over a leaky kitchen faucet.

When couples lament that the magic has gone out of their marriage, it may be that they have caught on to each other's tricks.

and quasi-sacred institution-destroying activities like *revolution* that dissipate their romantic spirit in practical minutiae:

In perpetuating a revolution, there are two requirements: someone or something to revolt against and someone to actually show up and do the revolting. Dress is usually casual, but if either faction fails to attend the whole enterprise is likely to come off badly. In the Chinese Revolution of 1650, neither party showed up and the deposit on the hall was forfeited.

[Woody Allen]

In a study of "commercial expression in humor," Monroe Friedman elaborates (though doesn't acknowledge) Bergson's insight (1956:143–44) about creating humor by extending "business phraseology to . . . social relations." Friedman points out (though in literary rather than phenomenological terms) that humor frequently mentions commercial products, one of ordinary reality's most pervasive hallmarks.

Code switching and code mixing . . . commercial terms and expressions . . . reveal amusing incongruities between the language of the marketplace and its linguistic counterpart in the less commercial spheres of American life. . . . [The most frequent type] of humorous commercial metaphors . . . found in our sample . . . represent those qualities of life we usually associate with the plain, the ordinary, or the pedestrian. . . . [For example,] simple household goods such as Ajax, S.O.S. pads, Saran Wrap, Liquid Prell, and Diet Shasta. . . . These "metaphors for the mundane" . . . were contrasted with various positively valued opposites of the mundane, such as the monumental, the profound, the sacred, the exciting, or the sophisticated. [Friedman 1989:281, 273, 279]

Comedians who induce their audience to have high-flown expectations can bring them back to earth with brand names:

Two examples are from *The Two-Thousand-Year-Old Man* by Mel Brooks and Carl Reiner, in which a man is interviewed who claims to have lived for 2,000 years. At one point in the dialogue the interviewer asks the man, "Sir, what do you consider to be the greatest medical discovery in the two thousand years that you've lived? Would it be the advent of transplants of organs? The use of antibiotics? The heart-lung machine?" The simple answer from the two-thousand-year-old man is "Liquid Prell." Elsewhere in the same interview a similar question is asked relating to the "biggest change" the two-thousand-year-old man has seen. He responds as follows: "In two thousand years, the greatest thing mankind ever devised, I think, in my humble opinion, is Saran Wrap."

[Friedman 1989:273–74]

More generally, humorists can employ commercial products to shift their audience from extraordinary realities (usually sacred, but also perverse) into ordinary reality—especially by putting them in the end or punch-line position (280). To exemplify this descending incongruity Friedman (274) quotes columnist Alice Kahn, who deflates yuppie romanticism about food by describing a restaurant's specialty dessert called "Chocolate Adolescence":

This is a cake made from five pounds of Venezuelan chocolate and equal parts of Amaretto, Grand Marnier and—a nouvelle touch—Diet Shasta.

The complementary form of centripetal transmundane humor elevates perverse reality into ordinary reality. If the line between business and crime is so fine that parodists can perversify business by describing it in criminal terms, they can ordinarize *crime* by describing it in business terms. The *Official MBA Handbook*

ranges over a broad class of material, from an annual report for a neighborhood lemonade-stand company to a marketing analysis of the Don Vito Corleone group. "Of most concern to the don, however, was the intense competition provided in the last year to Recreational Substances Ltd., the family's largest division. Recreational Substances historically had enjoyed a 95% share of the greater New York market. In the last year, however, the rival Solozzo group had backward-integrated into poppy fields in Afghanistan and was about to enter the market by under-pricing the Corleones by 50%. . . . The don was wondering whether to adopt the classical solution of asking the president of the Solozzo group to take an early retirement. Alternatively, perhaps the Corleones should backward-integrate as well. In recent months the don had priced land in several locations throughout Asia and had considered a hostile takeover of the Burpee Seed Corp. of Warminister, Pa.

[*Wall Street Journal,* 28 Sept. 1982, 26]

Although most people try to sustain their experience of sacred reality as long as possible, they try to normalize their experience of perverse reality as soon as it develops. A common form of centripetal transmundane humor depicts the disproportion between the relatively weak power of a normalizing technique (for example, psychological denial) and the awesome power of the perverse reality it is supposed to neutralize (like the mugging in figure 11). Social science jargon, de-

Pepper . . . and Salt

THE WALL STREET JOURNAL

"No, no. I'm not in the mood."

Figure 11

signed to normalize deviance, is likewise too bland to justify crime as it occurs,

as in the cartoon in which an old man and woman are shown holding up a middle-aged man. As they take his wallet and watch, the old woman explains, "This way, you see, we can supplement our social security payments and also retain a sense of participation in society."

[Handelman]

Literary terms, too elevated to capture the full range of experience, also fail to fully normalize the perverse reality generated by *mind-altering substances*. Take the cartoon drunk who says to the person sitting next to him at a bar,

"Sometimes I drink to assuage the vagaries of a stressful and hectic life, but mostly I drink to get crocked."

[Hoest]

The perverse reality of *sexual deviations* can be humorously normalized by treating them as mundane human activities. Men's magazines, like *Playboy, Penthouse,* and *Hustler,* whose ideological agenda has been to transfer sexual deviations from perverse to ordinary reality (Davis 1983:183–94), frequently exhibit this kind of centripetal transmundane humor, as in the Scotty cartoon depicting a naked woman talking on the phone while sitting on shoulders of naked man:

"Oh, not much, Marge, I'm peeing on George. What are you doing?"

Madness too is an extreme form of perverse reality not easily neutralized. Although the normalizing technique of providing compensation may work for everyday problems in ordinary reality, it is woefully inadequate to mundanize the mutilations of those who inhabit perverse reality:

The performance artist slowly and painfully castrated himself while photographing the action for his art show. When he drove into Fotomat to pick up his developed film, the girl in the kiosk told him they lost his film. "What! You lost my film!" "It's ok," said the girl, "We'll give you a free roll."

[Bob Goldthwait]

Somewhere between crime and madness lies the perverse reality of the torture chamber, which one cartoonist has mundanized by revealing the torturer's ordinary background.

A 1989 *The Far Side* cartoon portrays a dungeon with haggard prisoners chained to walls and tables. The hooded torturer giving a tour to his middle-class-looking parents says, "Now over here, Mom and Dad, is what we call The Rack and I'll show you how it works."

Finally, *death,* the deepest level of perverse reality, can never be totally transformed into an ordinary event. The ultimate agony of our existence, cartoonist Norman Dog knows, cannot be fully obscured by turning death into a game. He shows (1985) a page from the catalog of a scientific novelty company:

> Cancer Gum
> Amaze and embarrass your friends! Latest scientific research makes this carcinogenic caper possible! Then, the Fun begins . . . As you search for a cure! 5 packs. $99.

Woody Allen, who derives much of his humor from pulling into the ordinary the extremes of the extraordinary, shifts perverse as well as sacred realities into everyday reality. His method of mundanizing even perverse reality's terminus can be seen in these excerpts from his short play, *Death Knocks:*

> *The play takes place in the bedroom of Nat Ackerman's two-story house, somewhere in Kew Gardens. . . . The time is near midnight. Suddenly we hear a noise, and Nat sits up and looks at the window.*
> Nat: What the hell is that? . . . (*Climbing awkwardly through the window is a somber, caped figure. . . .*)
> Death (*for it is no one else*): Jesus Christ. I nearly broke my neck.
> Nat (*watching with bewilderment*): Who are you?
> Death: Death.
> Nat: Who?
> Death: Death, listen—can I sit down? I nearly broke my neck. I'm shaking like a leaf.
> Nat: Who are you?
> Death: Death. You got a glass of water? . . . or a Fresca? . . .
> Nat: I don't want to go yet.
> Death: You don't want to go? Please don't start in. I'm nauseous from the climb . . . up the drainpipe. . . . Look, let's just go. It's been a rough night. . . .
> Nat: Go where?
> Death: Death. It. The Thing. The Happy Hunting Ground. . . .
> Nat: Now, wait a minute. I need time. I'm not ready to go. . . .
> [*Since Death does not play chess, Nat offers to play him gin rummy for some extra time. Nat eventually wins.*]
> Death (exiting): I couldn't just take him and go. I had to get involved in rummy.
> Nat (*calling after him*): And be careful going downstairs. On one of the steps the rug is loose.

(And, on cue, we hear a terrible crash. Nat sighs, then crosses to the bedside
  table to make a phone call.)
Nat: Hello, Moe? Me. Listen, I don't know if somebody's playing a joke
  on me, or what, but Death was just here. We played a little gin. . . .
  No, *Death.* In person. Or somebody who claims to be death. But,
  Moe, he's such a *schlep!*

[1972:37–46]

Sociologists have distinguished typical individuals, groups, roles, institutions, and even "realities" as the major units of the social world; and have been trying to determine their essential characteristics. By continually switching features between typical social units on each level, however, comics seem to be trying to confuse what sociologists have been trying to clarify. But comics may actually be circuitously articulating subtler essential characteristics by refuting extrinsic ones than sociologists have done straightforwardly by affirming intrinsic ones.

Comics try to discover whether it provokes a laugh to contradict what they hypothesize to be an essential characteristic of a typical social unit. Specifically, they replace this hypothesized essential characteristic with another feature (from a different social unit) they believe so uncharacteristic that imagining it together with the first social unit's other features will be laughable.

Consequently, comics confirm their hypothesis that a particular feature is an essential characteristic of a typical social unit by their audience's laughter that rejects (negates) the opposite feature. Comics, in short, are also social scientists whose methods are merely indirect:

Comic (jokes): Is non-X an essential characteristic of typical social unit A?
Audience (laughs): No!
Comic (sotto voce): Therefore X must be an essential characteristic of typi-
  cal social unit A—Q.E.D.

6

Incompetent Functioning

Chapter 2 noted that comedy can undermine our "ideal" conception of the world by contrasting it with the actual world. The following three chapters will describe the most important application of this logical comic form: debunking social units that have become idealized in various ways.

Chapters 4 and 5 examined humor that blurs the horizontal distinctions between typical social units; chapters 6, 7, and 8 will examine humor that highlights the vertical distinctions between ideal and actual social units. Most idealist philosophic traditions—classical (for example, Plato), Christian (Augustine), German (Hegel)—focus on the difference between ideal and actual social worlds. The German idealist tradition, particularly its Marxist derivative, has tried to resolve this incongruity by *raising* the actual world to the ideal. The mischievous comic tradition, in contrast, has tried to resolve it by *lowering* the ideal to the actual, employing the sociological equivalent of the anthropological downtransformations described in chapter 3. Comedy, like sociology, brings conceptions of social units that have drifted into the ideal realm back to earth (to "reality").[1]

The comic mode that manifests the discrepancy between actual and ideal individuals, collectivities, roles, institutions—even whole societies—is satire.[2] Like "jujitsu, using the impetus of the opponent to defeat him" (Dwight Macdonald, quoted in Redfern 1986:94), satire exaggerates a social unit's claims to emphasize its failure to live up to them, widening the gap between its ideal and its actuality to expose these claims as mere "pretense." Satire, in short, focuses on social units that fall short of their ideal.

The foremost contemporary theorist to expose the discrepancy between our ideals and our actuality, to unmask our current vanities, was the late sociologist Erving Goffman. Although seldom mentioning humor, and jargonizing vanities as "self-presentations" and "fronts," Goffman's sociological studies clearly parallel humor theories and practices—like those of Pirandello (1974)—that unmask the ideal self to reveal the actual self. No other social scientist's work has produced as much amusement as Goffman's, especially through the particular examples by which he illustrates his general insights. In his first major work, *The Presentation of Self in Everyday Life* (1959), Goffman specifies how an individual creates an ideal self, why it sometimes collapses, and how he or she tries to save it. In his collected early essays *Interaction Ritual* (1967), and later works *Encounters* (1961b) and *Frame Analysis* (1974), he elaborates this model for other social units. The following chapters are heavily indebted to Goffman's conceptualizations, although stressing their usefulness for understanding how humor undermines, and consequently reveals, social ideals.

The jokes in the rest of this book indicate that our society has three major ideals for social units: their functioning should be competent, their presentations authentic, and their associated selves compatible. This chapter will examine the first.

Inept Individuals

Most people present themselves to others (and to themselves) as *more* competent than they really are. (Those who present themselves as *less* competent will be discussed at the end of the next chapter.) Competence may be ordinary or extraordinary, claims to it implicit or explicit.

Someone makes implicit claims to ordinary competence merely by being a member of society. Even without ever having pledged to perform most social actions competently, he or she is still expected to do so. Others will uphold the ideal that a person possesses ordinary competence even if he himself or she herself does not. Consequently, someone may be chagrined to discover humorists making fun of an incompetent action even though he or she has never overtly claimed to perform that particular action competently. Moreover, since ordinary competence is expected of everyone, the social status of those who fail to exhibit it drops drastically. The scent of failure spreads from one of their behaviors to all of them. Physical incontinence, for instance, implies more general functional incompetence. Amusement that stems from any particular failure, consequently, is augmented by amusement that stems from incipient total failure.

Someone may display ordinary incompetence for temporary reasons—being tired, absent-minded, drunk, drugged, or simply having a bad day—or for more permanent reasons—being stupid, senile, clumsy, or belonging to certain collectivities (see next section). Humor catches and freezes the natural occurrences of this ordinary incompetence:

> The human brain starts working the moment you are born and never stops until you stand up to speak in public.
>
> [Sir George Jessel]

The funniest forms of ineptitude, of course, are the most extreme, those creating the widest gap between ideal claims and actual performance. The actual performance of whoever implicitly claims only ordinary competence, then, must be abysmal to generate much amusement, such as wetting oneself in public.

Since failure of ordinary competence extreme enough to be funny rarely occurs naturally, practical jokers sometimes contrive artificial situations more likely to induce it. The television programs "Candid Camera" and more recently "Totally Hidden Video" allow their audience to observe how an unsuspecting person responds to an impossible situation; for instance, being required to perform a repetitive task—like answering a bank of ringing telephones or taking pies off a conveyer belt—faster than humanly possible. The victim's reaction to the breakdown of competence claims is presumably unpremeditated, revealing a naked self unshielded by the usual pretensions of personality. Such a breakdown provides its audience with a brief window not only on the dupe's nature but more generally on human nature itself, including their own. As Steve Allen (1987:60) put it, Candid Camera and similar shows reveal "real people being themselves"; that is, without their usual affected presentation of self in which they are "being someone else."

People's spontaneous reactions to the breakdown of competence claims reveals the neutralizing techniques they use to try to recover their precipitated status (Goffman 1959, 1961, 1967). The classic movie comedians—especially Charley Chaplin, Buster Keaton, and Laurel and Hardy—have remained popular not for their inane antics but for their perceptive displays of the neutralizing techniques we all use to maintain our dignity in the many mundane situations that continually threaten our competence claims: the paradigmatic human endeavor.

The gap between ideal claims and actual performance can be widened not only by degrading the performance but also by elevating the claims. If someone claims ordinary competence implicitly, he or she must claim extraordinary competence explicitly. But because others normally supply the praise that confirms extraordinary competence, whoever attempts to raise his or her image of competence through self-praise becomes vulnerable to the humorous put-downs that disconfirm it. Martin Mull and Dabney Coleman are perhaps the best known contemporary comic actors whose humor arises from the continual deflations of their pretensions. Collapse of explicit claims to extraordinary competence are both likelier and funnier than collapse of implicit claims to ordinary competence. Because exaggerated claims to competence expand the distance between ideal and actual farther than ordinary claims, the actual performances that undercut these expanded claims need be less abysmal to be amusing. Braggarts need not pee their pants to call their competence into question but only bungle their boast. Many jokes describe the failure of such explicit and exaggerated claims to extraordinary competence—traditionally called "human folly": "The world's collective wisdom, we may fairly contend, is compressed into its jokes, which are teeming granaries of human folly and conceit, credulity and presumption" (Louis Kronenberger, quoted in Hertzler 1970:18).

Foolish Collectivities

Collectivities, like individuals, also try to appear more competent than many of their members actually are. If the most important social categories—age, gender, race or ethnicity or religion, and class—consist of two complementary subcategories, our society has traditionally regarded one as being more competent, and consequently having more status and power, than the other. Thus it has ranked adults over children; men over women; whites over blacks, assimilated Americans over ethnic Americans, Christians over Jews; Protestants over Catholics (WASP being the summary term for the higher racial, ethnic, and religious subcategories); and the rich over the poor. Each subcategory's relative level of stratification determines the particular kind of incompetence attributed to it by humor.[3]

All "superior" groups—adults, males, WASPS, rich people—and all "inferior" groups—children, women, blacks, ethnics, Jews, poor people—are related on their respective levels. Since many features of one superior (or inferior) group are also features of the other superior (or inferior) groups, a stratificational joke enhances its humor by implicitly applying to all the groups on the same stratum. (The logical ascending and descending incongruities of chapter 2 and the anthropological up- and downtransformations of chapter 3 add their own comic resonance to this sociological stratificational humor.)

The recently popular light bulb jokes depict the behavioral incompetence of these collectivities through their characteristic way of performing a common trivial task. Jokes that portray members of the superior subcategories, such as the upper class, who perform it conceitedly suggest their claims to competence are exaggerated:

> How many Harvard Business School graduates does it take to screw in a light bulb? One. He stands still and the world revolves around him.

Jokes about members of the inferior subcategories, such as lower class ethnic groups, who perform it inefficiently suggest their actual competence is minimal:

> How many Polacks does it take to screw in a light bulb? Five—one to hold the bulb and four to turn the ceiling (chair, ladder, house).

The kind of behavioral incompetence most frequently targeted by humor is sexual (Cameron 1963:90). Jokes about sexual inadequacy focus on virgins and newlyweds who fail to live up to the sexual ideals of their own gender, on homosexuals and transvestites who fail to live up to the sexual ideals of either gender, on racial and ethnic groups whose sexual equipment is (relatively) deficient—

> Did you hear about the Jew with the erection who walked into a plate glass window? He broke his nose.
>
> [Alice Kahn]

—and on braggarts whose claims to sexual hypercompetence are deflated:

> What's a computer nerd? A guy who knows 147 technically possible ways to have sex but doesn't know any women.
>
> [Steven Wozniak and Larry Wilde]

Competence may be mental as well as behavioral. Steve Allen (1987:11) lists intellectual deficiency first among the many kinds of amusing shortcomings: "After all, what are jokes about? They are about how dumb people are, how drunk or stoned they were last night, how broke they are, how poor, how bowlegged, sexually frustrated, greedy or lazy." Jokes frequently make fun of the unintelligent:

> I have a twin brother. Yeah. But he's not too smart. Last year, he forgot my birthday.
>
> [Rodney Dangerfield]

Comedy commonly attributes feeble-mindedness to all the inferior subcategories, but seldom to the superior ones.

Comic members of inferior collectivities display several types of cognitive incompetence. First, they may be mentally slow:

> Do you know why they don't give Polacks a coffee break? It takes too
> long to retrain them.

The social world's complexities must be spelled out to the dim-witted, as though they were actually members of the paradigm inferior collectivity—children:

> Recently heard over the London airport loudspeakers:
> Air France—Flight 106, departing 2:30 p.m., Gate 12.
> British Air—Flight 22, departing 3:15 p.m., Gate 9.
> Polish Air—Flight 157, departing when the little hand is on the four and
> the big hand is on the twelve, Gate 5.

Second, they may make the logical mistakes described in chapter 2. Children frequently follow these erroneous rationalities, such as reversing causation:

> *Johnny (age 8):* How did Princess Diana *know* she was going to have a
> baby?
> *Connie (age 9):* She can *read,* can't she? My goodness, Johnny, it was in
> *all* the papers!

Likewise "dumb" ("scatterbrained," "dizzy") women, like Lucille Ball or Gracie Allen, fail to distinguish what's logically additive from what's not:

> Gracie would ask me, "Where do you keep your money?"
> "In a bank," I'd respond.
> "What interest do you get?"
> "Four percent."
> "Ha. I get eight."
> "You get eight?"
> "Yep—I keep mine in two banks."
>
> [George Burns]

or what's logically relevant from what's not:

> Gracie didn't think she was dumb—the whole world thought she was
> dumb. . . . For instance, once I said to Gracie, "Did the nurse ever drop
> you when you were a baby?" And Gracie said, "Don't be ridiculous. We
> were too poor to have a nurse. My mother had to do it."
>
> [George Burns]

This kind of humor also depicts members of the inferior ethnic groups who misapprehend the direction of physical sequences:

> Antonio Montero, fresh from Chile, at the Staten Island end of the ferry, raced at breakneck speed and hurled himself across the patch of water. He landed on the ferry boat with a tremendous crash—but picked himself up proudly, dusting his corduroy trousers, glancing around, grinning, for recognition of his feat.
>
> The only recognition came from a passenger of Colombian descent. "What ess you horry? We coming een! "

or social sequences:

> Wykowski was arrested for rape. "Don't worry," said the cop, "We'll treat you fair, we'll put you in a line-up with un-uniformed policemen." They did. They brought the victim in. Wykowski saw the woman, pointed to her and said, "Yeah, that's her."

Third, they may be illiterate. Many jokes depict children and ethnics, in particular, who make not only logical but cultural errors. For instance, they may misunderstand multiple, idiomatic, or figurative meanings:

> A detective, investigating the fall of a Black skytop construction worker, questions two Polish American coworkers, who cannot give a reason for the accident. Perhaps it wasn't an accident. Maybe, the investigator asks, it was a suicide? No, the coworkers cudgel their brains, he did not seem particularly depressed. There was nothing wrong in his life? No—wait a minute, one finally remembers. There *was* something.
>
> "He had two assholes."
>
> "What?! Did you ever see—?"
>
> "No, no—not on the job or anywhere. But we know."
>
> "How come?"
>
> "Well, we used to go to this bar sometimes and have a drink together. Every time we went in, the bartender would look at him and say, 'Oh, it's you, with the two assholes.' "

Beyond linguistic mistakes, lower strata groups may exhibit higher forms of cultural illiteracy;[4] for instance, by misunderstanding basic biology:

> Did you hear about the Polish woman who tried to get an abortion because she didn't think the baby was hers?

or relative values:

> Did you hear about the Pole who won a gold medal? He had it bronzed.
>
> [Henny Youngman]

In short, what humorists portray as slow, dumb, or ignorant can reveal what passes for sharp-wittedness, intelligence, or sophistication in their society. The "sociology of knowledge" should be complemented with a "sociology of stupidity" that derives a society's assumptions about cognitive processing, logical forms, and cultural knowledge—as well as the collectivities supposedly deficient in them—from their violation by "dumb" jokes, such as this one:

> Zoo keepers have failed to mate gorillas in the San Diego Zoo, especially because of the female's reluctance. They have a brainstorm and invite a big Polish football player, Grunowski, down to the zoo and ask him, for $5000, if he would consider substituting as a partner for the gorilla. Grunowski walks earnestly around the compound some minutes and returns, saying, "Three things. One: no kissing on the lips! Two: if there's a baby, he's got to be raised a Catholic. And three: can you give me about a month to raise the money?"

Comedy attacks not only those who belong to the inferior collectivities. If anything, it puts down members of the superior ones more frequently (especially in America today) by showing their competence does not justify their status. (Thus focusing *only* on the inferior or the superior collectivities skewered by the rapier of wit obscures its political ambiguity. Comedy is neither conservative nor radical, but both.)

Since Aristophanes, comedy has portrayed the conflicts within the major sociological categories: between age groups, genders, and classes (Levin 1987:33, 137, 159); as well as, in modern society, between racial, ethnic, and religious groups. Inferior subcategory members (whose comic motto seems to be: "If you can't join them, beat them!") usually win these conflicts by *outwitting* superior ones, reversing their relative status in the denouement of most comedies.[5]

Consider *age* groups or generations. Most of the classical comedies—Greek New Comedy, Roman Comedy, even Restoration Comedy—centered on the conflict between the son and the father (or someone of the father's generation), the *senex iratus* (Frye 1971:164–65, 172). The sons (or juniors) performed the expansive role of playboys, the fathers (or elders) the contractive role of killjoys (Levin 1987:36, 68, 95–96). Their conflict usually revolved around the son's sexuality and the father's money. "In Roman comedy the old father is jealous of his son for his sexual attraction and prowess, and the aged P may secretly be pursuing the same girl as the son. . . . The old father's money gives him a natural advantage in the struggle, in which the son is deliberately impoverished and therefore powerless" (Charney 1978:56–57). Viewing the girl pursued by both as a mother-surrogate completes the classic Oedipus situation. In the "comic Oedipus situation," however, the son triumphs over his father and gets the girl (Frye 1964:450–51;

1971:180–81).[6] Many modern jokes also reverse the statuses of the children and the parents:

> I have a house, but I'm still a kid. When my folks come over I make them play softball in the living room and put their feet up on the coffee table.
>
> [Garry Shandling]

Comedy overturns the traditional *gender* hierarchy by portraying men as incompetent, at least relative to women. Recent jokes have focused on their arrested emotional and even intellectual development:

> Q: What is the difference between government bonds and men?
> A: Government bonds mature.
>
> Q: Why are all dumb-blond jokes one-liners?
> A: So men can understand them.

Or they have depicted women who suddenly capsize men's claims to dominance:

> Following a whirlwind romance and marriage, Beverly and Sid came back to reality . . . and a sobering reality it was for them.
>   After making love one night, Sid threw Beverly his pants. "Here," he said, "try them on."
>   The woman did so and, standing beside the bed, said, "They're much too big."
>   "You got it," Sid replied. "I never want you to forget who wears the pants in this house."
>   Scowling, Beverly reached down, plucked her panties from the bed, and tossed them at her husband. "Try them on," she ordered.
>   Studying the garment, Sid snickered, "Forget it! I'll never get into these!"
>   Beverly headed for the bathroom. "Until your attitude changes," she said over her shoulder, "that's absolutely right."

Humor also inverts the stratification of *racial* groups:

> Football's a fair sport for my people. It's the only sport in the world where a Negro can chase a white man and 40,000 people stand up and cheer.
>
> [Dick Gregory]

and *religious* groups:

> The nun welcomed her new fourth-grade class to the Catholic school, and, as was her custom on the first day of school, she went around asking each of the children what they'd like to be when they grew up.
>   "I want to be a fire fighter!" said Barbara Emard.
>   "I want to be a nurse!" replied Jason Scott.

"I want to be a prostitute!" answered Jamie Van.

The nun fainted dead on the floor, and when she came to she found the children gathered around her.

"I—I'm sorry," she floundered, "but . . . Jamie, what did you say you wanted to be?"

"A prostitute," she repeated. Sitting up, the nun sighed, "Praise Jesus, I thought you said 'Protestant.'"

(This last joke pivots Protestants from higher status than Catholics to lower status than even prostitutes.) American humor in particular has portrayed many *ethnic* immigrants who prove superior to long-term natives. In the movie *The Cocoanuts*, for example, the hyperethnic Marx Brothers continually got the better of stuffy pompous DAR-ish Margaret Dumont.[7]

Marx Brothers movies exemplify American humor's tendency to combine ethnic or racial groups with class groups. Most traditional American jokes about the incompetence of the poor (unlike the rich) also implicitly deprecated ethnic or racial minorities (Stephenson 1951:572); most current jokes about the incompetence of ethnics (especially Poles, Italians, and Puerto Ricans) and blacks also implicitly deprecate the poor (Dundes 1987: 133, 137). The 1983 movie *Trading Places*, in which ghetto hustler Eddie Murphy switches life-styles with white preppie Dan Ackroyd, comically reverses the status of both classes and races. The 1980 movie *9 to 5*, in which female workers (Jane Fonda, Lily Tomlin, and Dolly Parton) continually turn the tables on their obnoxious male chauvinist boss (Dabney Coleman), comically reverses the status of both classes and genders. Dual category humor amplifies its comic effect by putting down or pulling up two inferior collectivities—class and ethnic or racial or gender groups—simultaneously.

Class reversals have been common in Western comedy, especially in antielitist America. Jokes that comically reverse economic statuses fall roughly into three main groups.

In the first, rich people suddenly lose the money that supports their status:

"They are a very prominent family. Their furniture goes back to Louis XIV, their silverware to Henry VIII."

"Yes, and their automobile goes back to the finance company tomorrow."

What do they call a Yuppie Broker on Wall Street [after the crash of 1987]? "Hey, waiter!"

Impoverished, they may even find themselves in underclass circumstances; for example, the 1991 movie *Life Stinks* (Mel Brooks). Like all comedies about one subcategory in the opposite one's milieu, established tastes and skills render the formerly rich comically incompetent to deal with the conditions of poverty.

In the second, members of the upper class become controlled by members of the lower class:

> Moreover, in modern comedies the characters who contrive and pursue such essentially prosaic intrigues are usually—like the slaves of Roman comedy—male servants or chambermaids who have no respect for the aims of their masters; these they advance or frustrate according to their own advantage, and what we have, finally, is therefore simply the familiar laughable spectacle of servants who are really masters and masters who are really servants. [Hegel 1979:198]

From the eighteenth to the midtwentieth century, theatrical and literary comedy portrayed the increasing power of the servant class vis-à-vis their masters, culminating in the omnicompetent servants and incompetent masters of P. G. Wodehouse, Evelyn Waugh, and J. M. Barrie (Levin 1987:87–91).

> It's all very well to have hired help, but they require special handling, as Mrs. Ronald Greville discovered when she was London's leading hostess in the 1920's. In the middle of a dinner party it became obvious her butler was tipsy, so she slipped him a note. "You are drunk. Leave the room at once." The butler read the note, put it on a silver tray, walked sedately around the table, and placed it in front of the guest of honor, British foreign secretary Austen Chamberlain.
>
> [John Berendt, *Esquire*, April 1993, 34, 37]

Although seemingly no longer a source of comedy [Levin 1987:88], master-servant inversions continue today in movie comedies about Beverly Hills, which portray the superiority of earnest Latin American maids and gardeners to their dissipated American employers.

In a third group of stratification inversion jokes, the affluent lose at least a conversational exchange with the indigent, such as beggars, tramps, or (today) the homeless:

> A [beggar] came to the back door of the Winkel house on his biweekly rounds. "I haven't a penny in the house," apologized Mrs. Winkel. "Come back tomorrow." "Tomorrow?" The mendicant studied her sharply. "Lady, I hope you don't let this happen again. A man can lose a *fortune*, extending credit."

Freud was one of the first to collect the Jewish version of jokes that (at least temporarily) reversed the statuses of those at opposite ends of the economic strata: the beggar [*Schnorrer*] and the baron.

The *Schnorrer* begged the Baron for some money for a journey to Ostend; his doctor had recommended sea-bathing for his troubles. The Baron thought Ostend was a particularly expensive resort; a cheaper one would do equally well. The *Schnorrer*, however, rejected the proposal with the words: "Herr Baron, I consider nothing too expensive for my health."

[1963:112]

Freud traced these status reversal jokes to the conflict between the ideal egalitarianism of Jewish Law and the actual economic hierarchy of society. Thus:

There is really no advantage in being a rich man if one is a Jew. Other people's misery make it impossible to enjoy one's own happiness.

[1963:113][8]

The same conflict between the ideal of egalitarianism and the actuality of class stratification occurs in American economic jokes. "There is a general propensity to ridicule the top and bottom of the status hierarchy in a kind of leveling offensive consistent with American values. . . . At the top of the hierarchy, the new-rich and the old aristocracy are the target of special ridicule. At the bottom, the servant or unskilled laborer of ethnic or racial origin foreign to the 'American type' is the focus" (Stephenson 1951:571). Both Jewish and American humor, then, are based on an egalitarian ideal that motivates their humorists to ridicule both economic deviants: the upper class and the lower class. Furthermore, since egalitarianism is an expansive ideology (as Tocqueville pointed out), it encourages the spread of ridicule to both the upper and the lower subcategories of *all* the major sociological categories.

This discussion of egalitarianism should alert us to the importance of ideology in humor. If the comically incompetent "fall short," they must fall short of some standard determined by the values of a particular ideology. The logically elegant and socially insightful work of British sociologist Christie Davies examines the relation between particular ideological values and incompetence jokes.

Davies (1982) first explains why so many jokes belittle the abilities of either the rich or the poor in terms of cognitive anthropology. These jokes articulate a society's social boundaries and moral ambiguities by employing marginal groups to highlight the conflicts between its core values. Societies that try to maintain two opposing values simultaneously produce jokes about those extremely successful at achieving one value (usually a marginal group) who are extremely unsuccessful at achieving the other. In our society, many jokes depict groups whose stupidity (or laziness) causes their failure at work, and groups whose craftiness or stinginess causes their failure at leisure—the very attributes that cause their success at the opposite endeavor (1982:384–93). In the U.S., the "stupid[-lazy] group" has been the Poles:

> There has been a temporary slowdown in Poland's space program. Their astronauts keep falling off the kite.

and the "crafty-stingy" groups have been the New England Yankees, Scots, and Jews:

> A Jewish coat-manufacturer who suffered from insomnia was advised by a friend to count sheep to help himself sleep. The next morning he looked more weary and exhausted than ever. "What's wrong with you?" asked the friend. "I've been counting sheep," said the manufacturer. "Last night I counted up to twenty thousand. Then I sheared the sheep, had the wool made into cloth and made twenty thousand overcoats. Then I spent the rest of the night worrying about where I could get twenty thousand linings."[9]

These jokes legitimate both the middle class's economic success relative to poorer groups (who are too stupid [or lazy] to succeed) and their economic failure relative to richer groups (who have cheated or obsessed their way to wealth).

Later, Davies (1988) explains incompetence jokes in terms of historical sociology. Their increasing frequency has paralleled the rise of industrial society whose ideology is "rationality." These jokes exert social control over irrational outsiders while reaffirming the rationality of the insiders who tell the jokes (1988:4). More important, these jokes also allay the fears of insiders that even *they* may be unable to function in rational industrial society. Drawing (implicitly) on Durkheim, who equated industrial society with specialization and the division of labor, Davies considers their negative impact on the individual. The top group of highly skilled specialists are aware of their potential incompetence outside their own specialty. Consequently, they enjoy jokes about the excessive comic destruction wrought by the introduction of a stupid outsider into a technologically artificial environment (submarine, airplane, etc.), which serves as a metaphor for the entire society:

> Pokorski got a job as a test pilot. He took a helicopter up to 5000 feet, 10,000 feet, 15,000 feet. All of a sudden it crashed. Pokorski woke up in the hospital ward. His boss was there asking him what had happened, "It got too cold," said the Polish pilot, "so I turned off the fan."

The bottom group of lowly skilled workers are also aware of their potential incompetence outside their own repetitive tasks. Consequently, they enjoy jokes about those (usually immigrants) too stupid for employment even in the lowest lines of work:

Did you hear about the Polack who lost his elevator operator's job because he couldn't learn the route?[10]

These jokes may express qualms about rationality itself, revealing the fear that the rational world is actually irrational. Drawing (explicitly) on Weber, who portrayed rationality as an "iron cage" that stifles the individual, Davies cites jokes that mock those excessively subordinate to its derivatives, such as work (Americans):

An American businessman visiting in Mexico watched an Indian making pottery vases. He asked the price. Twenty centavos each. And for 100? The native thought it over and then answered: "That will be 40 centavos each." The American thought the Indian was making a mistake in his quotation of the price so he tried again: "And if I bought 1000 all alike?" "All alike?" he said. "One thousand? Well, Senor, then they would cost you 60 centavos apiece." "Impossible! Why you must be insane!" "It could be," replied the Indian, "But I'd have to make so many and all alike and I wouldn't like that. So you see you would have to pay me for my boredom as well as for my work."

or money (Scotch):

Wee Willie Deegan loved his game of golf but one bright sunny day his friends saw him sitting disconsolately in the club house, his clubs nowhere in sight.
    "Why aren't you out playing, Willie?" asked the friend.
    "Ach, I nae can play agin'," sighed Willie.
    "Why not?" asked his friend.
    "Ach," said Willie, "I lost me ball."[11]

These jokes, Davies (1988:17–18) concludes, are the "mirror image" of jokes about those poor and stupid, for they treat those rich and smart as "irrationally rational."

Inadequate Role Performance

Shifting our attention from actors to actions allows us to examine the way humor dramatizes incompetent behavior not only in general but also in specific roles. As Joyce Hertzler puts it:

It is often not realized that considerable laughter, whether of individuals or collectivities, occurs when role performance upsets expectations. We laugh when persons in some way depart from the standard behavior set for them as friends, parents, children, husbands and wives, followers of vocations, members of particular types of social groups, members of social classes or ethnic or nationality groups, occupants of other hierarchical strata, or in almost any other activity characteristic of or essential to a social system. The lapse or irregularity of role performance may be that noted in the actual observed behavior of persons or groups or as presented in a joke, cartoon, comedy, comic strip, caricature, or satirical piece. [1970:86–87]

I prefer to distinguish the two meanings of *nonstandard* Hertzler conflates: unusual ("irregular") role performance, which I treated last chapter; and faulty ("lapsed") role performance, which I will treat here.

Because the presidency is the most difficult role in the United States, its potential or actual players do not always perform it proficiently. Because it is also the most important and visible role, humorists can freeze and magnify their every mistake. Furthermore, once their pattern of errors become well established, humorists can place them in situations that reveal their characteristic blunders:

> Pablo Picasso dies and goes to Heaven, and God says, "To get into Heaven, you must prove to Me you are who you say you are." So Picasso draws a picture, and God lets him in. Next Martin Luther King Jr. dies, and God says, "Prove that you're Dr. King." So he makes a long speech about civil rights, and God lets him in. Then Dan Quayle dies, and God says: "Prove you're Dan Quayle." Mr. Quayle asks why, and God says: "Because Pablo Picasso and Martin Luther King had to." And Dan Quayle says, "Who are they?" And God lets him in.

Jokes about the inadequacy of recent presidents have been especially frequent. Of the many ways to bungle the presidential role, humor about each office holder tends to focus on one overriding weakness. Thus Reagan humor has centered around his *senility*, and its associated confusion, forgetfulness, and torpor:

> "Ronald Reagan vetoed the Clean Water Act!" [Will] Durst exclaimed in his stage act. Cocking his head and furrowing his brow, Durst assumes the Gipper's befuddled persona: "Clean Water? Well, I dunno." "No matter what you think of Reagan's policies, you have to admire his ability not to get involved in them."
> [*San Francisco Examiner*, 30 Oct. 1988, E7]

> Ronald Reagan was never lazy. He was energy-efficient.
> [Senator Lloyd Bentsen]

And Bush humor has centered around his speech—especially its *incoherence*, which Dana Carvey mimicked, and its *slips:*

> George Bush is undoubtedly the gold medalists of gaffes. He is to slips of the tongue what Gerald Ford was to slips of the rest of the body. After [he]

was accused of insensitivity toward Jews because he did not take firmer action against campaign aides with alleged anti-Semitic backgrounds, this is what Bush said: "I hope I stand for anti-bigotry, anti-Semitism, anti-racism." Another Bush blunder sounds only slightly more plausible in its intended form. Instead of saying that "everyone who wants a job has a job," he proclaimed that "everybody who has a job wants a job." Perhaps this describes the [then] vice president's own desire to change jobs. And what about the speech in which Bush promised that he would reveal "my own drug problem," only to disappoint the media by producing his detailed drug *program*. But even these [slips] were nothing compared with his admission that he and President Reagan had had "sex," rather than "setbacks." (I'd love to hear him explain that one to Freud!)
[Alan Dershowitz, *San Francisco Chronicle*, *This World Magazine*, 16 Oct. 1988, 6]

Political leaders must make so many speeches that linguistic lapses are likely, especially when their attention wanders away from the speech at hand (probably written by someone else). Unfortunately for them, modern recording media preserves for posterity the blunders caused by undisciplined attention—a negative qualification for high political office.

Humorists in other countries have likewise called into question the competence of their own heads of state, especially in Eastern Europe before the downfall of their dense geriatric communist leaders:

Todor I. Zhivkov, Bulgaria's recently ousted Communist leader, went to a plastic surgeon and asked if it would be possible to graft a prominent birth-mark onto his head just like the one Gorbachev has.
"Certainly," the surgeon says. "But why would you want it, Comrade Zhivkov?"
"Because I just saw Gorbachev," is the reply, "and he kept tapping his head and saying, 'The problem with you, Comrade Zhivkov is that you have nothing up here.'"

Media critics have complained about the decline of political satire because it has recently focused on political figures' extraneous appearance, mannerisms, or personality (Dukakis's size, Bush's whiny voice, Clinton's sleaze, etc.), rather than on their more consequential programs.[12] But audiences seem to feel that those who mishandle minor matters—like language, kinesics, and relationships—will mismanage major matters like the fate of the nation: an implication that makes the chuckles normally evoked by their minor faux pas resound with anxious overtones.

Whenever we *personally observe* an inadequate role performance, we usually laugh at the *individual* who flubbed the role. But, except for a few famous role performers like the government officials mentioned above, whenever we *hear a joke* about an inadequate role performance, we usually laugh at the *collectivity* the individual who flubbed the role represents.

Humorists often imagine ethnic groups who perform roles for which their stereotypically dominant trait unsuits them:

> Did you ever notice that there are no major Jewish newscasters?
> They'd make the news sound worse than it is.
>
> [Dick Shawn]

More generally, the comic version of hell is where all collectivities (especially ethnic groups) are forced to perform the roles for which they are least qualified:

> Hell is a place where the French are the engineers, the British are the cooks, the Germans are the policemen, the Russians are the historians, and the Americans are the lovers.

Or in a more contemporary, more Asian version:

> You can always tell if the manager of an Asian subsidiary of a U.S. company is successful. If he is, he'll live in a British house, have an American salary, a Chinese cook and run things with Japanese ingenuity. If he's not, he'll live in a Japanese house, have an American cook flipping hamburgers, a Chinese salary, and run things with British ingenuity.

Humorists also play off our assumption that aptitude for one role implies aptitude for another. But roles may differ so greatly that success in one (like leisure) actually implies failure in the other (like religious):

> Rabbi Beckman, the young, new rabbi in a Connecticut temple, greatly loved to play golf.
> One sunny Saturday morning, after services, Rabbi Beckman felt so powerful a craving to play a few holes, that he begged God to forgive him for breaking the Sabbath, tossed his golf bag into the back of the car, and sped off to a course where he was certain no one would recognize him. With an apology to his Maker, the Rabbi teed off.
> Up in heaven, Moses suddenly bolted upright. "Lord! Lord!" he cried. "Do my eyes deceive me? There, Holy One—do you *see*?"
> "Y-yes," said the Lord.
> "That's Rabbi Sylvan Beckman!" said Moses. "Playing golf on Your Holy Sabbath!"
> "Dear Me," sighed the Lord.
> "Such a transgression!" said Moses. "How will You punish him?"
> "We must teach him a lesson." God cupped His hands over His mouth

and—just as Rabbi Beckman teed off for the second hole, the Almighty King of the Universe, let out His breath in a mighty, cosmic "Whoooosh!"

The powerful sound caught the rabbi's golf ball in midair, lifted it two hundred yards, flipped it around a tree, over a stream, and into the cup— for a remarkable hole in one!

Moses stared at God. "*That* You call a punishment, Lord?"

The Lord winked. "Whom can he *tell?*"

The role player's time and energy may be so limited that the more devoted to succeeding in one role, like occupational, the less left over to satisfy the demands of another role, like conjugal. Many comedies concern business successes who become family failures, such as the rich cuckold. "What some of these attacks reflected was a traditional aristocratic bias against the merchant class. 'If an alderman appears upon the stage,' wrote Joseph Addison, 'you may be sure it is in order to be cuckolded.' His financial success were duly paid for by his marital humiliations" (Levin 1987:46–47).

Those most likely to botch particular roles are those just learning their distinctive activities: *neophytes*.[13] Traditionally, comical neophytes have been developmentally immature individuals (the young) and historically dated collectivities—like migrants from less modern areas, domestic (rustics) or foreign (immigrants).

So laughable have been the mistakes of newcomers that historians of humor have even implicated incompetent rural neophytes in the origins of comedy itself. In book 3 of the *Poetics*, Aristotle derived the Greek term for comedy from both rustic roots and incompetent imagery. He credited the Dorian claim (discredited by modern scholars [Levin 1987:156–57]) that comedy comes from *comae*, "outlying villages"—"thus assuming that comedians got their name . . . from their strolling from hamlet to hamlet, lack of appreciation [because of their incompetence?] keeping them out of the city" (1984:2317–18). Since the Greeks, the *agroikoi* (rustics) have been one of the stock characters of comedy, whose sophisticated urban settings highlight rural naiveté (Frye 1971:172, 175–76). For example, the country squires and squiresses of Restoration Comedy: "Congreve and his fellow sophisticates often made a point of bringing in some awkward homespun booby as a foil for the polished urbanity of the beautiful people. 'Ah, rustic, ruder than Gothic,' scoffs Mistress Millamant, who abominates the countryside" (Levin 1987:110–11). "Wycherley's country wife (in *The Country Wife*) wants to know what the harm is in kissing, and all the London gallants rush in to instruct her" (Charney 1978:73). Although less common today, rural newcomers to urban roles and settings continue to appear in such TV sitcoms as *Cheers*, most of whose viewers are unaware of the ancient roots of the comic banter between the naive rustic assistant bartender (Woody) and the (pseudo)sophisticated habitues of the urban bar.[14]

(Since the early part of the twentieth century, immigrants from foreign lands have largely replaced migrants from rural areas as the main comic neophytes. Today, too, amusingly awkward newcomers to urban life come more from the suburbs than the provinces [Levin 1987:157].) The young and the rustic may be the paradigm neophytes whose faulty role performance is funny, but the accelerating swirl of modern society has made neophytes of us all; for it has flung the members of most major sociological subcategories into many roles for which they have been unprepared. The *vertical* circulation of American society has compelled those who belong to historically inferior subcategories to perform roles traditionally associated with the superior ones and vice versa.

Humor about low collectivity members suddenly thrust into high-status occupational roles frequently shows how their newly exalted position merely magnifies their characteristic incompetence. A few years ago many ethnic jokes concerned how Poles made inept popes:

> Did you hear about the new pope's first miracle? He made a lame man blind. He turned wine into water. He cured a ham.[15]

Lately, humorists have begun to assail the abilities of less-standard collectivities recently elevated with increased legal rights, such as the disabled, whose defining attributes have become incongruous with some of the newer roles and settings to which they now have access:

> Did you notice that they now have handicapped parking spaces in front of the Racket Club?

Humor that focuses on this "life-style lag" (the individual or collectivity version of "cultural lag") dramatizes the incongruity generated by a new performer of a high-status role, such as a black surgeon, who retains some low collectivity attributes, such as ghetto speech style:

> Can you imagine lying on the surgery table and some black doctor walking up and saying "Hey man, I be cuttin' yo appendix out!"
>
> [Eugene Broadnax]

Life-style lag threatens to disintegrate the image of those who must try to figure out how to overcome the comic incongruency between important new attributes and trivial old ones, between the contradictory attributes valued by modern and traditional ideologies, such as the woman in a Lynda Barry cartoon who says:

"These are very confusing times. For the first time in history a woman is expected to combine intelligence with a sharp hairdo, a raised consciousness with high heels, and an open, nonsexist relationship with a tan guy who has a great bod."

We laugh not only when members of low collectivities fail in high-status roles but also when they succeed exceedingly. Compare, for instance, the TV sitcom *The Beverly Hillbillies,* which portrayed the awkwardness of erstwhile lower-class rural whites who move to Beverly Hills, with the 1984 film *Beverly Hills Cop,* which portrayed an adroit black cop from the Detroit ghetto (Eddie Murphy) who solves a major crime in Beverly Hills more effectively than its own relatively inadequate police force could. (The first major film comedy to portray a member of a low-status racial group who performs a prestigious role more competently than members of the high-status racial group who usually perform it was Mel Brook's 1974 *Blazing Saddles,* a Western featuring a black sheriff.) Even the very disabilities of the disabled may suit them for certain roles and settings with which able-bodied people cannot cope:

Why don't they give houses out by the airport to deaf people?

[Gallagher]

Rustics, too, have navigated urban life more capably than cosmopolitans in some comedies (though the difficulty of finding true rustics in modern American society has prompted at least one recent comedy, the 1986 Australian film *Crocodile Dundee,* to combine ruralness with foreignness). Rural wise men, moreover, have become almost as common in comedy as rural fools. Rustics (like children, foreigners, and other neophytes) continually cross the fine line between *naïveté* that misunderstands urban ways and *perspicacity* that points out their incongruities. The avatar of the humorous American rural wise man first appeared in Mark Twain, passed through Will Rogers, and finds its current embodiment in Garrison Keillor:

Eating is a perfectly natural activity, we all have natural urges to eat, and we should be able to satisfy those urges simply and naturally without shame and anxiety and numbing self-consciousness. . . . It should be a joyous life-affirming experience, not (as I'm afraid it is for so many) *A Problem.*

When I was a boy, away out on the open prairie of the American heartland, we were happy eaters and weren't ashamed to have big appetites. Out there in Breughel, N.D., surrounded by an ocean of durum wheat, we got three squares a day, piled our plates and cried "Yes!" to seconds. . . .

All that has changed in Breughel and everywhere else, thanks to a tiny flock of puritanical food writers who have nagged and bullied and made us a picky people who take small bites and mull the food over in our mouths: Is it excellent? Are we having a truly unique dining experience? No, probably not, for once you pick food apart and hold it up to the light and examine it, you don't feel like eating the stuff. For one thing, it's probably cold.

So church suppers at Breughel Lutheran now are dismal affairs to which people bring elegant casseroles and sip dry wines and talk dry talk and exchange nervous glances. In the fall, the threshing crews sit down at plank tables under the cottonwood trees and eat stir-fried shrimp and pea pods, and each man talks about another meal he had at this absolutely marvelous little out-of-the-way farm that nobody ever heard of before. And Mom's Cafe has changed hands and is now a nouvelle Bulgarian restaurant but nobody goes there, they all know a better one in Bismarck.

Where are the great meals of my youth when we were loose and happy and loved the chow? Gone! Scared off by food authorities, ridiculed, made to seem cheap and coarse and not in good taste.

[*New York Times*, 2 Feb. 1983, 15]

Since rural life is not only spatially distant from urban life but historically delayed, rural humorists are able to criticize modern urban fads from the perspective of the near past—the golden age.

Humor about inferior collectivity members who succeed in reputable roles contrasts with humor about superior ones who fail in them. Those performing a role for a long time may become as comically incompetent in it as neophytes, having failed to keep up with changes in its required activities. "Laughter," observes Hertzler (1970:163) "criticizes and ridicules ineptness and archaisms in the behavior of the individual and shakes him out of bad habits, outmoded attitudes, obsolescent roles." These "paleophytes," who have lingered in a role too long, are most commonly the old, such as that staple of the academic novel, the comically senescent tenured college professor. Physical or mental deterioration may incapacitate the old from continuing to perform adequately even a role's unchanged activities. "Many 'old' jokes," notes historian and gerontologist Page Smith, "involve failure of memory":

An old man sees a friend sitting on a park bench weeping. "How have things been with you, Bob" he asks his old friend.
"Great. I just married a beautiful young woman."
"Wonderful! But then why are you crying?"
"I can't remember where I live."

Bittersweet humor often occurs at the point when neophytes and paleophytes reverse their relative power, when those on the way up, like maturing children, cross those on the way down, like aging parents:

> I went driving out to the ball game with my father yesterday. As we were almost there, he said, "If you see a gas station, pull over. I have to take a leak." "Well," I shouted mockingly at him, "Why didn't you go before we left home?"

Conversely, humor about *elevated* members of *low collectivities* who botch sophisticated roles contrasts with humor about *downcast* members of *high collectivities* who botch unsophisticated ones: (1) *urbanites* may behave awkwardly in *rural* environments, like the yuppies on the cattle drive in the 1991 film *City Slickers;*[16] (2) *civilians* may be too chic for the *military*, like the Jewish princess who enlists in the army in the 1980 film *Private Benjamin*. Since both rural life (derived from agrarian societies) and military life (derived from hunter societies) are more primitive than urban life, both kinds of humor portray urban civilians who find their cosmopolitan knowledge more hinderance than help in these relatively uncivilized settings; (3) members of the *higher class* sometimes sink to performing roles associated with the *lower class*. In the 1987 film *Maid to Order*, a formerly wealthy young woman is reduced to being a maid—a role for which she is entirely ill suited; (4) *whites* who try to perform roles commonly ascribed to *blacks* usually bungle them:

> I was mugged by a white guy yesterday. He didn't know how to do it. He put the gun to *his* head.
>
> [unknown black comic]

> I'm originally from Chicago . . . The only thing I miss about Chicago is the blues . . . It's not as good here [Los Angeles]. I went into a blues club here the other night, and there's four black guys and a white guy up on stage, and they're up there with their eyes closed, getting down, and I noticed the white guy *peeking* . . . I got my money back.
>
> [Margaret Smith]

Perhaps the ultimate race, status, and role reversal joke is the following:

> Just because blacks couldn't make slavery work, that's no reason to throw out the whole institution. What we need are new, better slaves. I nominate Canadians.

The humor of this joke depends both on its content, enhancing its race switching theme by giving an historically black role to Canadians—"ultrawhites" who are black's "polar" opposite—and on its form, complicating its double negative logic by asserting that blacks botched even the disreputable social role of slave, which whites could perform better—and therefore should! (5) Modern society has also required many *men* to perform the low status roles traditionally performed by *women*, such as doing housework or nurturing infants, which—as comedy depicts it—these men are barely able to muddle through. Like women, men today also suffer life-style lag as they try to synthesize incongruous personality attributes valued differently by current and traditional ideologies, as in the cartoon from Feirstein's 1982 book in which a woman says to a man seeing her off at her apartment:

> "Well, goodnight Ralph. It was nice meeting someone so sensitive, aware, and vulnerable. Too bad you're such a wimp."

Actors comically misperform roles either because the actors are inept or because the roles themselves are difficult to perform no matter how adept their actors. Because professionals need their role partners to believe in their competency, most doctors, lawyers, and academics try to appear more competent than they actually are—frequently by claiming arcane knowledge. ("All professions," said George Bernard Shaw in *The Doctor's Dilemma*, "are conspiracies against the laity.") Undermining their mystique through humor, consequently, has a long tradition, from theatrical comedies to modern jokes. The doctors, lawyers, and academics in the plays of Machiavelli, Ben Jonson, Shakespeare, and Molière (to name just the most famous comic dramatists) all speak in a pretentious quasi-Latinate jargon, designed to convince their patients, clients, and students that they know what they're talking about; the plays usually conclude with everyone's discovery that they don't (Charney 1978:65–68; Levin 1987:58–61, 91–93). Most modern jokes about the inadequacy of professional role performance stress the incompetence of the performers:

> Dr. Roche was such a busy man that at the hospital he only had time to scribble abbreviations on the patients' charts. *T* stood for tonsillectomy, *OH* was open heart surgery, *BS* meant brain surgery, and so on.
> As was his habit, Dr. Roche also greeted new interns as soon as they arrived. Unfortunately, he was a little late in getting to Dr. Cohen. Greeting the intern in the corridor after surgery, he asked, "So, Dr. Cohen, how did Mrs. Gaines's appendectomy go?"
> Cohen paled. "Appendectomy? I thought you wanted an autopsy."

> After a heated exchange during a trial, the judge asked both counselors to approach the bench.
> "Your Honor," said lawyer Cox, "I objected because my distinguished colleague was badgering the witness. It's obvious he's never heard of the Bill of Rights."
> "Rubbish!" snapped attorney Updike. "I happen to know them by heart."
> Cox cocked a disbelieving brow. "Do you, now? Well, Updike, I have a hundred dollars that says you can't even tell me the first few words."

Bristling, Updike accepted the challenge and began, "I pledge allegiance to the flag. . . ."

"Damn," Cox interrupted, fishing the money from his pocket, "I didn't think you'd know it."

The more profound ones stress the rigors of the role:

A lawyer listened very attentively while the prospective client gave details of the case. "You can't lose," said the lawyer finally. "If that case is presented properly, any jury in the land will deliver a verdict inside of ten minutes. Hand over a $100 retainer and I will handle the case for you."

"No, thanks," said the client. "I don't think I'll pursue the matter further. I was giving you the other fellow's side."

R.O. White, president of the Altoona Bank, went back to college for his class reunion. He dropped in on his old economics professor. And as they were chatting, the professor said, "Here's something that will interest you— this year's final exam."

White scanned the exam, then said, "I could swear these are the identical questions you asked my class twenty years ago!"

"Quite so," said the professor with a smile.

"But if you always ask the same questions, don't you think the students will get wise?"

"They do."

"Don't they pass the questions on to next year's class?"

"Sure."

"Then doesn't everyone get an A on every exam?"

"Not at all," said the professor. "In economics, the questions stay the same, year after year—but we keep changing the answers." [17]

Like those who produce theory, those who produce culture—artists, writers, etc.—become sanctified with success. Naturally, humorists regard such sanctification as a challenge to point out the human failings of those "who can do no wrong," as in the cartoon title of an exhibition at the New York Metropolitan Museum of Art:

"Bloopers and Boo-Boos of the Old Masters."

[Loneur]

Although humorists usually widen the gap between ideal and actual by exaggerating the lowness of the actual, they can also widen it by raising the ideal:

"I don't know," the world-famous novelist said to his editor. "I just don't think my newer books are as good as my earlier works."

"Rubbish," the understanding editor replied, "your writing is the same as it ever was. It's your taste that's improved."

Politicians too are frequently subjected to satire for a similar reason. They talk in terms of the country's sacred symbols (like patriotism) but work in ways exceedingly mundane (like trading votes), creating a comic incongruity between the ideal (the principle) and its actual embodiment (the man), as Emerson observed: "Politics also furnish the same mark for satire. What is nobler than the expansive sentiment of patriotism, which would find brothers in a whole nation? But when this enthusiasm is perceived to end in the very intelligible maxims of trade, so much for so much, the intellect feels again the half-man. Or what is fitter than that we should espouse and carry a principle against all opposition? But when the men appear who ask our votes as representatives of this ideal, we are sadly out of countenance" (1946:215). Since political rhetoric is so far removed from reality, continually realigning them is the central political skill:

> Political ability is the ability to foretell what is going to happen tomorrow, next week, next month and next year. And to have the ability afterward to explain why it didn't happen.
>
> [Winston Churchill]

Political success, this aphorism suggests, depends on the talent to justify one's own incompetence competently.

The military is another profession given to pretense, in part because the appearance of military prowess itself helps to demoralize the enemy and in part because the exploits claimed by military men occur so far from where they are boasted about that civilians cannot easily check their accuracy. Comedy has undermined military pretenders almost since the genre began. "The military pretender to heroic feats (who is actually a coward) is one of the most permanent of comic types. Plautus's *Miles Gloriosus* displays the character in fully developed form: Pyrgopolynices is a ferocious figure; he has the stature and the manner of a soldier, with all the appropriate phrases and gestures; he dresses magnificently and plays the part with distinction; he is inordinately boastful, with a circumstantial detail hard to resist, and, in fact, the *miles gloriosus* (or glorified soldier) is usually called the 'braggart'" (Charney 1978:63). Ben Jonson's Captain Bobadill, Shakespeare's Falstaff, and W. S. Gilbert's "modern major general" are later examples of this professional type (Charney 1978:63–65; Levin 1987:58). (Since Vietnam, the dearth of American wars has diminished attacks on military braggadocio.) Comedy exposes his bragging as sham by exaggerating it or by portraying his cowardly reaction to a minor incident in civilian society.

Finally, comedians portray those who fail in occupational roles whose standards of success have been raised by legendary performers. After countless novels and movies had romanticized the competence of *spies*, Maxwell Smart in the TV sitcom "Get Smart" continually blundered through situations that, say, James Bond would have handled with savoir faire. The *police* must take social norms seriously to perform adequately the highly technical, ritualized, and circumscribed behavior necessary to enforce them. Conversely, inadequate police performance calls into question the sanctity of the very norms they are supposed to be preserving—a repercussion frequently exploited in films from the 1914 Keystone Cops series to the 1984 *Police Academy* and the 1987 *The Naked Gun*. If it is difficult to defend society's mores, it is even more difficult to attack them—considering all the social sanctions brought to bear on lawbreakers. Thus *criminals* must also appear adept to convince their victims to go along with their unauthorized definitions of situations: "Do what I say and you won't get hurt!" Comically incompetent robbers run into difficulty whenever they try to say precisely what their victims are supposed to do. In Woody Allen's 1969 movie *Take the Money and Run*, a bank robber's criminal career suffered from the poor penmanship and spelling of the robbery note he handed to the teller: "Please put $50,000 into this bag and ak natural. I am pointing a gum at you." The low quality of robbers today prompted one humorist to advise them, like remedial English students, how to accomplish their stickups more effectively—generating a comic incongruity by employing a positive social means (education) for a negative social end (criminality):

It has become commonplace to read in our newspapers of a crime somewhere in America amusingly bungled by the criminal's ineptitude.

Droll though these news items may be they reflect an overlooked cost of our current national crisis in education. The basic learning skills of criminals have deteriorated to a shocking degree. Consider the following:

Item. A bank robber in Bumpus, Tenn., handed a teller the following note: "Watch out. This a rubbery. I hav an oozy traned on your but. Dump the in a sack, this one. No die pakkets or other triks or I will tare you a new naval. No kwarter with red stuff on them too."

Dr. Creon V. B. Smyk of the Ohio Valley Educational Council says such notes are, lamentably, the rule.

Smyk believes that the quality of robbery notes could be improved if criminals could be taught to plan before writing.

"We have to stress organization: Make an outline of your robbery note before you write it," he said.

A brochure being developed by the council offers the following example:

I . Stickup.
  A. Gun.
  B. Hands where can see.
    1. Except as needed to reach $.
II. No funny business.
  A. (Don't elaborate.)
  B. (Why put ideas in their heads?)
  C. Willingness to shoot.
    1. Human life means nothing to me.
III. Money
  A. $20 bills or better.
  B. Unless they don't have many.
    1. We'll take $10's and $5's then.
    [Colin McEnroe, *San Francisco Chronicle, This World Magazine*, 14
                                   Dec. 1988, 4]

Ineffectual Institutions

Although institutions that fail to live up to our ideals for them appear ineffectual, they may be effectively accomplishing different ends. Georg Simmel (1950:40–43; 1968:27–47) applied his core social theory, described in the introduction to part 2, most extensively and successfully to institutions. The institutions that people originally created in a human image have reshaped people in an institutional image. Human beings, to better serve their needs, routinized their interaction patterns into institutional forms; but these solidifying institutions have taken on a life of their own—increasingly free from human control and unconcerned with human benefit. Comedy points out how far from serving human needs an institution has drifted by (implicitly) contrasting its original ideal with its current actuality. In the early nineteenth century, Madame de Staël was the first to apply the conventional Enlightenment opposition between the institutional and the natural specifically to humor. "Swift, in *Gulliver* and *The Tale of a Tub*, like Voltaire in his philosophical writings, draws the happiest jokes from the opposition which exists between received error and proscribed truth, between institutions and the nature of things" (de Staël 1964:185). Later, Emerson described how humorists contrast the ideal operation of social institutions with the actual. "There is no joke so true and deep in actual life as when some pure idealist goes up and down among the institutions of society, attended by a man who knows the world, and who, sympathizing with the philosopher's scrutiny, sympathizes also with the confusion and indignation of the detected, skulking institutions. His perception of disparity, his eye wandering perpetually from the rule to the crooked, lying, thieving fact, makes the eyes run over with laughter" (1946:206). Freud (1963:108–15) also treated institutional humor under "cynical jokes"—though less extensively than his better-known discussions of sexual and aggressive jokes. (Not being a sociologist, Freud included under this type of joke a mixed bag of social units: morality, religious dogma, groups ["nation"—particularly the Jews], and one institution, marriage.)

The family, we saw, is the paradigm of a gemeinschaft institution with its affective, diffuse, particular, qualitative, and collectivity-oriented bonds. Cynical humor frequently undermines this gemeinschaft ideal of family life by portraying marriage as failing to fulfill the ideals that originally led the partners to matrimony: *sex* ("A wife is like an umbrella—sooner or later one takes a cab," which means that "marriage is not an arrangement calculated to satisfy a man's sexuality." [Freud 1963:110–11]), *love* ("One should always be in love. That is the reason one should never marry." [Oscar Wilde]), or *happiness* ("I never knew what real happiness was until I got married. And by then it was too late." [Max Kauffmann]). Worse, humor directs attention to how marriage itself debilitates gemeinschaft relationships ("Marriage: An arrangement that begins as a duet and ends up in a duel" [Louis Safian]).

Cynical humorists also portray how the nuclear family falls short of its gemeinschaft ideal. Sometimes their target is *affected* family members who pretend to be more gemeinschaft-minded than they actually are (fig. 12). More frequently their target is *antagonistic* family members who exchange insults (of the form "You live down to a negative ideal.") instead of compliments (of the form "You live up to a positive ideal."). For example:

> Mom's a real ego booster. We took some family photos. I looked at one and said, "That's a terrible picture of me." Mom said, "No, it's a great picture. You're just ugly."
>
> [Larry "Bubbles" Brown]

Occasionally, their target is *malevolent* family members who wish actual harm to befall one another:

> My mother told me never to take candy from a stranger unless he offered me a ride.
>
> [Harry Anderson][18]

The gemeinschaft institution of the family stands apart from the business, government, and cultural institutions of gesellschaft society. In sharp contrast to the family, gesellschaft institutions are characterized mainly by a *bureaucratic* structure: a formalized institutional process that transforms inputs into outputs. Many humorists have ridi-

LAUGH PARADE

by Bill Hoest

"Your father is home, children. Simulate enthusiasm."

Figure 12

culed bureaucracy's paramount problem in all gesellschaft institutions: its inflexibility. Unable to handle deviant inputs, bureaucracy often produces ineffectual outputs. A cartoon by MacNelly illustrates how sometimes human beings can accomplish their institution's own goals effectively only by circumventing its formalized bureaucratic means. The professor is talking to Shoe in an office situation:

> "We need more paper and pencils."
> "Well fill out this voucher and I'll initial it, then you can take it up to Supply and get a requisition form 93C. Either that or go downstairs and steal some from the advertising department."

Health care, for instance, was ostensibly institutionalized to serve the needs of patients. But humor indicates that hospitals have become increasingly bureaucratic gesellschaft institutions staffed by self-interested and incompetent personnel. "The jocular talk, cartoons, jokes, and get-well cards reflect society's decreasing confidence in the competency of the health professions, frustration over the increased bureaucracy of the system, and anger and concern about the skyrocketing costs of health care. . . . 'The doctor stops in to see me everyday and feels my purse.' One patient gave his surgeon a cartoon of two 'angels' sitting on a cloud. One says to the other: 'The last thing I heard was my doctor saying "Oops!"'" (Robinson 1983:115).

Although we citizens of Western societies experience difficulties with our bureaucracies, the citizens of Eastern European societies have had much greater trouble with theirs. Until very recently, far more Eastern European than Western humor concerned bureaucratic inflexibility and incompetence. Again the most astute analyst of Eastern European bureaucratic comedy has been Christie Davies, who extended his thesis—that jokes concern both "stupid" and "crafty" groups—from Western capitalist societies to Eastern socialist societies. There the "stupid" groups were not the lower classes but the bureaucrats, from political leaders through apparatchiks to militia (police). A Czech example:

> A policeman asked two citizens to show their identity cards. He opened one of them and began to read with difficulty: "I-den-tity ca-rd." He then examined the second man's I.D. card and said "I-den-tity . . . You are brothers?"
>
> [1982:394]

These jokes, Davies (1982:395) explained, "undermine the legitimacy of the elite members' success by ascribing to them the quality of stupidity, the hall-mark of failure in a rational social order. Success in politics, the higher bureaucracy and the militia is thus differentiated from the normal mode of success though competence that characterizes the world of work. Hence the paradox that the *apparatchik* of eastern Europe is given the same comic label as an Irish navvy or a Polish-American hard hat." Although Jews are one of the "crafty" groups in both Western and Eastern jokes, "craftiness now tends to be exercised in, through, or against the bureaucracy rather than in the marketplace." An Eastern European (Ukraine) example:

> Applicants for a position were being interviewed. Each was asked: "How much is two and two?" The answer was always: "Four." One candidate asked: "How much do you want it to be?" He was appointed.
>
> [1982:395]

Later, Davies added that jokes about "stupid" groups, which focus on weak minorities at the periphery of Western societies, focus on powerful authorities at the center of Eastern European societies (1988:18, 21). (Their incompetent and hence illegitimate center, which humor presciently exposed, explains their precipitous collapse after their external props were removed.) Eastern European humor's most telling criticism of socialist societies concerned their endeavor "to extend rational forms of bureaucratic planning and control beyond what is possible and beyond what is rational to attempt" (1988:22). Many jokes held their central economic planning bureaucracies responsible for institutional incompetence on a vast scale, especially in agriculture and consumer goods (1988:25–26):

> *Ukrainian joke:* When will the Cubans be certain that they have achieved socialism? When they begin importing sugar.

> *Polish joke:* Why do the Poles build their meat shops two miles apart? So that the queues won't get mixed up.

> *Russian joke:* The Russians have absolute proof that the Bible is wrong. According to the Holy Book originally there was chaos and then there was order. The Russians know from experience that this is not so. *First* there was planning and then there was chaos.

Davies concluded that Eastern European jokes regarded everyone as "caged twice—first in the familiar iron cage of rationality and secondly in an independent iron curtain cage whose bars are political, ideological, irrational" (1988:26).

Western humor rarely implies the ineffectual functioning of an entire society, though such jokes were heard in Britain during the 1970s and America during the 1980s:

> One of the biggest laughs [at the Alfalfa Club's annual dinner] came when Senator Bentsen told of the reaction of his wife, Beryl Ann, when he said he was going to be spending the evening with the great political and corporate powers who hold America's future in their hands. She commented, "Oh, you're going to Tokyo."
> [New York Times, 30 Jan. 1989, A6]

Eastern European humor, however, indicted entire societies far more frequently because the contradiction between their overidealistic ideology and undercompetent bureaucracy created extreme social and individual stress.[19] No other countries have had greater discrepancy between ideal and actual, whose enormous gap the collapse of communist ideology recently revealed. The *New York Times* of 7 April 1990 reproduced a cartoon from a Soviet magazine showing Marx, Engels, and Lenin as beggars (fig. 13). One says to the others, "But the theory was right." It is perhaps no accident that the only joke I've been able to find that seems to castigate *all* societies for failing to live up to their ideals was formulated by an Eastern European:

Figure 13

When asked to define the "Spirit of Prague," Milan Kundera defines it as "Humor with infinite pessimism. For instance, a Czech requests a visa to emigrate. The official asks him, 'Where do you want to go?' 'It doesn't matter,' the man replies. He is given a globe. 'Please, choose.' The man looks at the globe, turns it slowly and says: 'Don't you have another globe?' "

[*New York Times Magazine,* 19 May 1974, 80]

7

Inauthentic Presentations

Social humor ridicules those who lack authenticity as well as those who lack competence. We assess the competence of actors' behavior by evaluating their *external aspects,* by judging whether their output functions optimally: "*doing* what they claim to do." We assess the authenticity of actors' identity by evaluating the *relation between* their *external and internal aspects,* by judging whether their presented outer identity reflects their inner self accurately: "*being* what they claim to be." Humor reveals the discrepancy between essence and appearance, between inner self and outer identity claims—in short, inauthenticity.[1]

Self-aggrandizing Humor: Unmasking Others

We can imitate, Bergson observed (1956:156), not only others but ourselves. Ironically, we often do it poorly. (On his performance in *The Band Wagon* Oscar Levant once commented, "I played myself. I was miscast.") For we usually try to imitate our ideal—rather than our typical—selves. Erving Goffman (1959:35ff.), who examined the ways people idealize both "doing" and "being,"[2] assumed that most people, most of the time, try to present themselves to others, and even to themselves, as *nobler* (purer, finer, higher status) than they really are. (At the end of this chapter I will supplement Goffman's model by discussing those who present themselves as *baser* than they really are.) Perhaps the best-known example of human pretensions in all of Western literature is Cervantes's Don Quixote, who tries to live up to a heroic ideal in an unheroic age. "Cervantes' Don Quixote is utterly ridiculous. The ridiculous incongruities are many and diverse—between his phantasy and the reality, his ideal and his bodily shape, his speech and appearance, between the role of his lady, his horse, his servant and their actual nature" (Riezler 1950:179).[3]

Don Quixote, of course, tried to convince others that he was an authentic knight not to deceive them but because he deceived himself, being self-deluded into believing he was nobler than he actually was. Consequently, he falsely claimed nobility only *implicitly*, for he was unaware that his own characteristics were ordinary. Don Quixote exemplifies Plato's view in the *Philebus* (1961:1129–31) that humor reveals a person's "self ignorance" about his own characteristics: "The ridiculous . . . is . . . the opposite of the inscription at Delphi . . . : 'By no means know thyself.'" Plato specifies three characteristics that self-ignorance permits people to idealize, which comedy commonly mocks: imaginary wisdom, good looks, and virtue (corresponding to more general Platonic and Greek ideals: truth, beauty, and goodness.) A fourth, imaginary wealth, seems out of place in his list, though comedy also derides its consequent extravagance.

Today more people falsely claim nobility *explicitly* for self-aggrandizement than implicitly from self-ignorance, because the potential for social mobility is greater in modern society. Even those aware of their own qualities' quality still try to present them to their audience as better than they know they are. (Since people are self-conscious to various degrees, the self-ignorance and self-aggrandizement sources of false identity claims are continuous rather than dichotomous. Those fully aware of the falseness of their identity claims initially, moreover, may gradually forget the discrepancy over time.)

It is the humorist who points out the artificial coupling between an actual self and the idealized identity presented to others. We call the essential inauthenticity of those whose social-psychological seams are showing "pretense," "phoniness," or "affectation." Henry Fielding derived comedy itself primarily from inauthenticity and its species. "The only source of the true Ridiculous . . . is affectation. . . . Now, affectation proceeds from one of these two causes, vanity or hypocrisy: for as vanity puts us on affecting false characters, in order to purchase applause; so hypocrisy sets us on an endeavor to avoid censure, by concealing our vices under an appearance of their opposite virtues. . . . Ugliness, infirmity, or poverty [are not] ridiculous in themselves, . . . but when ugliness aims at the applause of beauty, or lameness endeavors to display agility, it is then that these unfortunate circumstances, which at first moved our compassion, tend only to raise our mirth" (1964:249–51). Both the vain and the hypocrite pretend to be more noble than they are, but, Fielding argues, we are more amused to discover hypocrisy than vanity. "From the discovery of this affectation arises the Ridiculous, which always strikes the reader with surprise and pleasure; and that in a higher and stronger degree when the affectation arises from hypocrisy, than when from vanity; for to discover anyone to be the exact reverse of what he affects, is more surprising, and consequently more ridiculous, than to find him a little deficient in the quality he desires the reputation of" (250).[4] Fielding's contemporary, Samuel Johnson, provides a comic example of both vanity and hypocrisy (as well as logical self-negation) in his depiction of "the moral philosopher discoursing to his audience, and 'swelling with the applause which he has gained by proving that applause is no value'" (Bate 1977:492).

The "masks" a person wears, then, comprise the false nobilities that disguise one's true aspects. Because their connection is only tenuous, however, masks are readily removed—which suddenly reveals the "truth" about a person. The humorist's central task, Pirandello asserts, is to strip away people's masks—both those they show to others and, more profoundly, those they show to themselves:

> Let us begin with . . . the construction that each of us makes of himself through the work of illusion. Do we see ourselves in our true and genuine reality, as we really are, or rather as what we should like to be? . . . Do we not in good faith believe ourselves to be different from what we essentially are? And we think, act, and live according to this fictitious, and yet sincere, interpretation of ourselves. Unwillingly, unknowingly, [man] is always wearing the mask of whatever it is that he, in good faith, fancies himself to be: *handsome, good, courteous, generous, unhappy,* etc. etc. To think of it, all this is so ludicrous . . . yet we lie psychologically just as we lie socially. Everybody straightens up his mask the best he can—that is, the external mask, for we also have the inner mask, which often is at variance with the outer one.
>
> The humorist readily perceives the various simulations used in the struggle for life; he amuses himself by unmasking them, but he does not become indignant: it's the truth! We, as individuals, experience something inherent and essential to social living, the vanity of seeming different from what we really are, and we avoid any analysis which, unveiling our vanity, would prompt our remorse and humiliate us before ourselves. But it is the humorist who does this analysis for us and

who can also take up the task of unmasking all vanities and of depicting society, as Thackeray himself did, as a *Vanity Fair.* [1974:132, 134, 139]

Pirandello referred to his later, largely comic plays as "naked masks" (Levin 1987:74).

The Catskills, Broadway, and television monologist Jackie Mason provides a modern model for this endeavor to unmask inauthenticity: the comedian as private eye:

> When he began doing stand-up in the late 1950's, [Jackie Mason] "always tried to puncture hypocrisy and sham," he said. "The standard at the time was Danny Kaye, Milton Berle— there was nothing profound or original. I was so new to comedy I didn't even know who Lenny Bruce was. But I realized that Lenny Bruce was doing with filthy words what I did with clean words."
>
> Mr. Mason thinks of himself as an investigator, not a gadfly. "I feel I'm a detective researching new things endlessly, every day of my life," he said. "I have the detective's inquisitive attitude toward people—their ethnicity, their religion, how much money they have, their racial and family status. All my comedy is social and psychological commentary. I do it instinctively."[*New York Times,* 24 July 1988, 14]

Comedians unmask an actor (individual or collectivity) by revealing a low-status attribute concealed behind a pretended high-status one. To do so, they must violate the norm of tact that prevents most people from prying behind other people's masks. The comedian is prepared to take up Alice Roosevelt Longworth's famous invitation, "If you can't say anything good about someone, sit right here by me!"

Since characterizing someone overnicely idealizes them, a common comic technique is *diseuphemization.* Today, it is easy to get a laugh by diseuphemizing "politically correct" speech, a terminology that obscures the dark side of human existence, for replacing its nice—and therefore inauthentic—characterizations with more straightforward terms creates a (con)descending incongruity.

> In a recent "Saturday Night Live" skit about a parent-teacher conference, the teacher (Dennis Hopper) says to the parents, "No, your child doesn't have a learning disability. He's just stupid! In fact, he's the stupidest kid I've ever taught."

Individuals try to appear "higher" than they are by constructing inauthentic masks out of specific linguistic, physical, psychological, and sociological attributes. Let us examine how comedians strip each of them away.

Since speech indicates social status, those from lower social backgrounds often try to speak like those from higher ones. To the amusement of their audience, however, they usually don't know how to go about it—producing malaprops or bloopers that make them sound ridiculous. Their stereotype of educated speech is incorrect, mainly because they believe it requires complicated grammar and rarely used "big" words; though, in fact, the truly educated speak more plainly. "Grandiose and grandiloquent language" usually brings a laugh:

> The copious outpouring of hifalutin language on the part of a person is laughable for many when it is used in all seriousness, not to be funny but to be impressive. It consists in some extravagance or exaggeration for the particular person of vocabulary or rhetoric or style or enunciation. This is the "big words" and other show-off language of children, the language affectations of the inadequately tutored but zealous social climber, the flamboyant verbiage of the young M.D. trying to be imposingly scientific with his *auricular appendage* for "ear." [Hertzler 1970:183]

Another aspect of identity that people falsely try to improve is their physical appearance. Comedians enumerate the many situations in which one's actual physical appearance fails to live up to one's ideal:

> Have you gone through this—have you woken up in the middle of the night and looked like your driver's license picture?
>
> [Garry Shandling]

So too one's body doesn't always live up to one's preferred body image. Humorists make much of our attempt to conceal its unwanted features, like fat, through clothing.

Being the chief means for concealing the body, clothing is the physical paradigm of what humor is trying to "strip away." Pirandello describes the humorist as divesting our formal dress to disclose our disheveled dishabille: "The humorist sees the world, not exactly in the nude but, so to speak, in shirt sleeves. He sees a king in his shirt sleeves, a king who makes such a fine impression when we see him composed in the majesty of his throne, with his crown, scepter, and mantle of purple and ermine. . . . In his *Sartor Resartus*, Carlyle says that 'man is a dressed animal' and that 'society is founded upon cloth.' And cloth is also something that *composes* and *conceals*, two things which humor cannot stand" (1974:143–44). Sartorial humor, more literally, commonly depicts the removal of overwear and the revelation of underwear. For instance, zipper jokes, which broadcast inadvertent openings between them (and hint at what is beneath), appeal to those becoming aware that their presentation of self is layered. The following jokes were collected from ninth graders:

> Are you modest?
> Yes, I am.
> Your zipper ain't.

> Did the president die today?
> No.
> Then how come your fly is at half mast?

In the 1986 play *Social Security,* directed by Mike Nichols, a married couple is forced to take care of a senile parent who, at an inopportune moment, strips to her underwear. A critic describes the long theatrical tradition of such scenes:

> For what might be called the Comedy of Undress is one of the theater's longest-running gags, going back through Mack Sennett's two-reelers, burlesque and vaudeville, to the great nineteenth-century French farceurs and on through Shakespeare to Plautus, the bad boy of classical theater who was the first to dramatize a character getting caught with his pants down.
>
> The fact is that underwear (traditionally red flannel) is as vital to farce as ketchup is to tragedy. . . .
>
> The farceur's making a fetish of underwear is understandable. Strip a cruel king or cardinal, or a puffed-up captain of the guard, down to his long johns, or reduce a haughty dowager or an evil-tempered prima donna to her bra and panties, and—presto!—you create instant democracy. In fact, the Comedy of Undress deserves a place of honor alongside the Magna Carta and the Declaration of Independence as one of the world's great levelers, and it is not surprising that so many dramatists have availed themselves of its power of impeachment. [William H. Honan, *New York Times,* 8 June 1986, sec. 2, 5]

Humorists, we saw, unmask hypocrisy—the psychological intentions a person claims to be more noble than they are—by disclosing actual lower motives behind apparent higher ones. Those who pretend to be rational are actually irrational (see chapter 2) and those who pretend to be spiritual are actually driven by corporeal and materialistic desires (see chapter 3). To these comic exposés we can now add those who pretend to have social (altruistic or moral) motives who actually have selfish (egoistic or immoral) motives:

> The spirit of humor demands that we acknowledge, in spite of our need for love, our undeniable lust, and in spite of our ca-

pacity for caring, our inclination to not give a good goddamn. We are reluctant to make these acknowledgments because they clash with our image of ourselves as good people. A good person, we rightly believe, is characterized by unselfishness, concern for others, and a real ability to love. Humor, however, is not allied to goodness; it is allied to nature and to wholeness. [Mindess 1971:73][6]

One of the best examples of humor that unmasks this kind of hypocrisy, that reveals the secret egoism behind the displayed altruism, is the famous Steinberg cartoon in which a man is saying to a woman "I-Thou" while thinking to himself "I-It."

Professions are plagued by this kind of hypocrisy because, we saw in chapter 5, they are supposed to value their clients' interest as much as their own. It is usually funnier to unmask hypocrisy in the professions than in an individual because of the greater discrepancy between their well-known ideal of communal interest and their suspected actuality of self-interest. The legal profession, for instance, appears to uphold the communal norm of justice whereas in fact they are concerned only about their side winning:

> An attorney journeyed to California to try an important case, promising to wire his partner the moment a decision was announced. At long last, the wire came and it read, "Justice has triumphed." The partner in New York wired back, "Appeal at once."

Politicians, too, are supposed to be altruistically concerned with the common good. Political humor, however, points out that the claimed communal orientation merely disguises their actual self-orientation:

> Politics—the gentle art of getting votes from the poor and campaign funds from the rich, by promising to protect each from the other.
>
> [Oscar Ameringer]

All professions implicitly claim to be "honest"—to manifest their intentions in their expressions sincerely—and none more so than the legal profession, whose raison d'être is to uphold the law. Consequently, one of the funnier hypocrisies humorists can expose is a lawyer's dishonesty:

> "Tell me," said the personnel director of a large corporation, "are you an *honest* attorney?"
> "Honest?" the lawyer replied. "Let me tell you something. My father lent me ten thousand dollars for my education, and I paid him back in full after my very first case."
> "I'm impressed," he said. "And what case was that?"
> The attorney squirmed slightly. "He sued me for the money."

Politicians who *make* the law are also supposed to be especially honest; although they usually fall far short of this ideal in the political humor of most societies. A Soviet example:

> An Eskimo kills a lot of fur seals, sells the furs, makes a bundle, goes to Moscow and buys a car. There aren't too many cars on the streets but no-parking signs are everywhere. Finally, he gets to the Red Square, which is conveniently empty and has no signs. He parks the car and starts to walk away when a policeman stops him: "Comrade, you cannot park your car here." "Why?" asks the Eskimo. "There are no signs." "That's true," says the policeman, "but this is the Red Square, a very special place. Look, Lenin's mausoleum is right behind there, and people are standing in line." "All right." answers the Eskimo. "They are over there, the car is over here. It's not in the way." "You still don't understand, Comrade, this the Red Square, a very important place. Members of the government, of the Central Committee, of the Supreme Soviet, they all pass here." "So what?" asks the Eskimo. "I'll lock up the car."

An American example is the well-known picture of Richard Nixon with the caption, "Would you buy a used-car from this man?"

Religious professions, which have the "highest" moral standards, are therefore most devastated by revealed hypocrisy. External religious ceremony without internal religious sentiment has been a traditional butt of jokes:

> And as the religious sentiment is the most real and earnest thing in nature, being a mere rapture, and excluding, when it appears, all other considerations, the vitiating this is the greatest lie. Therefore, the oldest gibe of literature is the ridicule of false religion. This is the joke of jokes. In religion, the sentiment is all; the ritual or ceremony indifferent. But the inertia of men inclines them, when the sentiment sleeps, to imitate that thing it did; it goes through the ceremony omitting only the will, makes the mistake of the wig for the head, the clothes for the man. [Emerson 1946:209]

Even more amusing is unmasking pretended sanctity as hypocritical sanctimoniousness, revealing not merely religious indifference but base (usually sexual or economic) motives. Molière defends his play *Tartuffe* from accusations of sacrilege by maintaining it unmasked pretended rather than true religiosity:

> If they will take the trouble to examine my comedy in good faith, they will perceive doubtless . . . that it is not intended to hold sacred things up to ridicule; . . . and that I have employed every possible art and care plainly to show the difference be-

tween the character of the hypocrite and that of the truly devout . . . . Now, not only does [Tartuffe's] politeness not suit his
manifest baseness and not produce the effect which he claims
(which makes him ridiculous . . .), but that politeness, as well
as that baseness, is extreme and produces the most evil result
it could, which makes him extremely ridiculous. [1964b:156;
1964a:147–48]

Sometimes, all it takes is a single word to unmask idealized spirituality
as earthly corporeality, "such as an expletive by the clergyman in the
pulpit" (Hertzler 1970:183).

Along with these linguistic, physical, and psychological attributes,
humor unmasks sociological ones. Since each sociological attribute locates an individual in a collectivity, this kind of humor ridicules collectivities, as well as individuals, who lack authenticity. In what Goffman
might have called "the presentation of group in everyday life," some
collectivities fail to live up to their own and others' images of themselves. People idealize a collectivity's image by believing all its components are more positive and congruous than they really are. Comedy
undermines the membership claims of those who pretend to belong to
these idealized collectivities. The poet's idealizations of social groups
are continually torn down by the comic's cynicismo, endlessly recapitu-
lating their ancient war.

When people *romanticize* their membership in one of their own collectivities, humor contrasts its actual with its idealized attributes. Consider age groups. Cynical humor undermines people's nostalgic tendency to idealize their own childhood, and by extension childhood in
general, by exaggerating its actual negative characteristics. For instance, if teachers wrote honest report cards, they might read:

> Your child has absolutely no potential. We'd hold him back a year, but,
> frankly, it'd just be a waste of milk.
>
> [Mike Dugan]

Such cynical humor also undermines the tendency to romanticize the
other end of the life cycle, old age. If we normally regard old women
as kind and fragile creatures, comedy portrays them with cruel and
aggressive traits incongruous with their imagined serenity: the machine gun on the lap of Whistler's *Mother*, the sweet old landlady who
regularly poisons her gentlemen lodgers with elderberry wine in *Arse-
nic and Old Lace*, the gangs of "senile delinquents" with "Hell's Gran-
nies" on their leather jackets who attack defenseless young men in a
Monty Python pseudodocumentary (Charney 1978:57–58).

People romanticize their society's history as well as their own. Consequently, humorists attack social as well as individual nostalgia by observing that the actual past fell short of its remembered ideal.

> I always liked what Helen McConnell, the big band singer, had to say about the swing era, when she was with Jimmy Dorsey. "If I'd known it was an *era*, I'd have paid more attention," she said. "All I remember is sleeping in the back of the bus."
>
> [Herb Caen]

During periods of rapid social change, some sociological subcategories rise in status while complementary ones sink. Many members of sinking subcategories (for example, men today) try to adopt the traits of rising ones (for example, women today), creating an unstable mixture primed for comic detonation.[7] Bruce Feirstein, in his best-selling comic essay *Real Men Don't Eat Quiche,* assumed a conservative persona which romanticized a subcategory's "indigenous" traits before its contamination by "exogenous" ones from its complement:

> There was a time when this was a nation of Ernest Hemingways. *Real Men*. The kind of men who could defoliate an entire forest to make a breakfast fire—and then wipe out an endangered species while hunting for lunch. But not anymore. We've become a nation of wimps. Pansies. Quiche eaters. Alan Alda types—who cook and clean and *relate* to their wives. Phil Donahue clones—who are *warm* and *sensitive* and *vulnerable* . . . .
>
> And where's it gotten us? I'll tell you where. Just look around the world today. The Japanese make better cars. The Israelis, better soldiers. The Irish better violence. And everybody else is using our embassies for target practice.
>
> [1982:9–10]

Feirstein's humor comes from exaggerating traditional male traits while trivializing newly acquired female ones, which supposedly weaken the ideal man.

Some witty blacks and gays "ritually insult" others for identifying with their group too much:

> Blackness is [another] theme of black ritual insults. Early work emphasized self-hatred and rejection of blackness both in the sense of skin color and in the sense of "country" or "low-down nigger" behavior. Insults such as "You so black you sweat Super Permalube oil" seem to denigrate blackness.
>
> The classic [gay] queens accepted feminine labels, seizing thereby the advantage of being able to denigrate others' masculinity without defending their own. Being penetrable is one

thing, but being too penetrable is and was an attribute that can be targeted, as in the following: "We can't afford to lose another sofa" (disappearing up your distended anus). . . . "Cross your legs, your hemorrhoids are showing." . . . "Peeking under the door in the washroom again?" . . . [These examples] include recurrent charges of being too overtly homosexual (a "flaming queen"). [Murray 1987:121, 125–26, 129]

Likewise some jocular Jews reproach others for being "too Jewish" (Murray 1987:131), as in the classic Jewish joke:

Three women were discussing their sons, with customary pride. "My boy," said the first, "is a famous surgeon, and president of his medical association!" "My son," said the second, "is a professor in the law school." "My son," said the third, "is a rabbi." "A *rabbi!* What kind of career is that for a Jewish boy?"

But, "just as it is possible to be too black or not black enough in appearance and behavior, or too overtly gay or too 'closeted,' it is possible to be judged too assimilated—'denying your heritage'—or too stereotypically Jewish" (Murray 1987:131). Comedy, then, attacks not only those who overidealize and consequently overidentify with their own groups but also those who underidealize and consequently underidentify with them.

In *In the Heat of the Night*, Rod Steiger played a bigot, and Sidney Poitier played a Negro to the best of his ability.

[Mort Sahl]

To underidealize and underidentify with one's own subcategory is to overidealize and overidentify with its complement, against which one's own is defined. Those who disclaim membership in their own subcategory try to alter their own sociological attributes, "passing" as a member of the complementary subcategory by *imitating* their traits. Comedy can unmask these imitators because imitation is inauthentic by definition.[8]

Just as humor reveals "formational" inauthenticity by exposing the reality of one's own reconstructed and romanticized subcategory, it also reveals "transformational" inauthenticity by exposing a person's failed attempts both to *deny* membership in his *own*—usually "inferior"—*subcategory* and to *claim* membership in the *opposite* —usually "superior"—*subcategory*. Comics have combed all the sociological categories for instances where those who appear to belong to a superior subcategory actually belong to an inferior one: children who try to mimic adults in language and conceptualization, women who try to act like men in their new employment opportunities, gays who try to comport themselves like straights:

> There is *no* level of overtness which cannot be faulted by someone as either "flaunting it" or as "trying to hide it." Still, it is the latter that occasions the "bitchiest" comment. "Closet queens" are said to wear "crystal veils," i.e., disguises transparent to other gay men. Closetry is an acceptable topic for insult among queens, clones, and even the most politically-correct politicos . . . : "You're 'bout as straight as a fever chart in a malaria ward." "You're about as straight as a rattlesnake ready to strike." "You straight? Yeah, like Highway One curving up the California coast." [Murray 1987:128]

and blacks who try to look like whites:

> Kochman argued that whiteness—again, either shade or culture—may also be a target [of ritual insult]. Abrahams similarly suggested that "aping" or "selling out to" white culture are weighty charges. . . . Labov reported the following whiteness insult: "Your mother's so white she have to use Mighty White." [Murray 1987:121–22][9]

Jews who try to pass as gentiles deserve special mention because there have been so many jokes about them[10]—perhaps reflecting the large number of Jewish joke-tellers and/or both their need and opportunity to pass. These jokes imply that some Jews pass unintentionally because of their ambiguous *appearance*:

> Mr. Lurie, a resident of Los Angeles for fifty years, approached a young man waiting for a bus on Wilshire Boulevard. "Young man, excuse me. Can I ask a personal question? Are you Jewish?"
> "No. I'm not."
> "Are you sure?"
> "Of course I'm sure!" The young man laughed.
> "You're not just teasing me?"
> "No. Why should I tease you?"
> Mr. Lurie sighed. "Well, excuse my question. I didn't mean to embarrass you."
> "Wait, mister," the young man glanced around and, lowering his voice, said, "can you keep a secret?"
> "Absolutely!"
> "Well, not a soul in the world knows it—except you. The truth is: I am a Jew."
> "My, my," clucked Mr. Lurie. "You don't *look* Jewish."

that some Jews pass intentionally by changing their *name:*

> When Messrs. Motzner and Krupnick opened their new store, they decided, for tactical reasons, to call it "Donahue and Donahue."
>
> On their first day, a customer asked one of the salesmen, "I want to talk to Mr. Donahue."
>
> "Which Mr. Donahue do you want?" replied the salesman. "Motzner or Krupnick?"

but that even Jews of ambiguous appearance who change their name can still be unmasked as inauthentic by their spontaneous *speech:*

> Abner Gormitsky, having made a good deal of money in his leather works, was considering his wife's suggestion that they move from Central Park West to one of the tonier parts of Long Island. "—and Abner, if we do that, I think we ought to change our name."
>
> After some weeks, the Abner Gormitskys became the Alexander Gormans, and they bought a fine mansion in Oyster Bay and furnished it with antiques. Their friendliness made friends for them easily, and their hospitality was so gracious, their cuisine so excellent, that the Gormans soon shone on the social scene. Indeed, they were invited to become members of the emphatically non-Jewish St. Andrew's Country Club.
>
> The trustees gave a huge welcoming dinner at the club for the newly elected St. Andrewians four couples: the Townsend Fillmores, the Clyde Watson-Setons, the Harley Hammonds, and the Alexander Gormans.
>
> And there, at the head table, the liveried servant serving Mrs. Gorman spilled an entire bowl of St. Germain soup in her lap.
>
> "Oy!" cried Mrs. Gorman—but swiftly added, "—whatever *that* means!"

In short, Jewish passing humor—like all subgroup passing humor — expresses the dilemma of trying to live up to majority ideals while retaining minority ones, by depicting the failures of taking either alternative to the extreme (Davies 1991:191–92).

Note that those who *pass* try to mundanize rather than aggrandize themselves, exhibiting a "false ordinariness" rather than the more common "false extraordinariness." Many criminals, for instance, try to pass as ordinary "respectable" citizens—a tendency to which the following riddle gives a sartorial and racial twist:

> What do you say to a black man in a three-piece suit?
> "Will the defendant please rise."
>
> [Don Irreria]

Comedy also unmasks neophytes who claim to be paleophytes, especially ethnic immigrants who try to appear true Americans (as well as pass economically or religiously). Jewish immigrants, in particular, had to choose between two opposite strategies of assimilation, displayed in exaggerated form by Charlie Chaplin and Groucho Marx. Chaplin's tramp strove to appear an American upper-class WASP through his clothes (especially his hat) and his obsequious but cunning demeanor. But most of his movies ended with his pretensions exposed and his accumulated gains (money and [WASP] girlfriend) stripped away. Groucho's con man also strove to appear various upper-class American types, but he always cynically let his ethnic attributes (especially his looks and speech) show through. Most of his movies—unlike Chaplin's—ended with Groucho conning the true American upper-class WASPs (like Margaret Dumont) successfully— although his brothers Chico and Harpo, who remain more "authentically" ethnic than Groucho, also con *him* out of his gains (see Altman 1971:187–89).

Because most of those discontented with their own identity have idealized, and consequently imitated, higher economic strata, most comic exposés have unmasked those who claim to be higher class than they are. Ever since Roman times, comic dramatists have depicted slaves and servants who try to imitate their masters, though less elegantly, in parallel scenes (Bergson 1956:120). Our comic term *zany* ("silly, foolish, crazy") is derived from the dramatic tradition in which slaves and servants imitated their masters grossly:

> Doubling had its histrionic basis in imitation, which has been the prime mover of drama and of art itself. Its primary exponent has been the *zany*, or *zanni*, whose sobriquet was a nickname for Giovanni. . . . He was the clownish underling who, with heavy-handed ineptitude, aped the airs and went through the motions of some more respectable and competent exemplar. . . . Servants being the principal zanies, it is worth recalling that actors were *servi* in ancient Rome, which meant that they were enslaved. In both Old and New Comedy, the exposition was often entrusted to a dialogue between a pair of slaves, prefiguring the butler and chambermaid of a later day. . . .
>
> Now a manservant, accompanying his master on adventures, which are amorous more often than not, sooner or later finds himself zanily courting a maidservant. Harlequin takes up his perennial flirtation with Columbine . . . Accomplice as well as imitator, he acted as liaison between the upper and lower levels of the plot. . . . [The underplot] follows the conventional practice of parodying the main plot at a lower level. In a normative situation, we would have two couples at two levels in four relationships. [Levin 1987:84–85][11]

Through the Great Depression, the main vehicles to make fun of those who strove to imitate the rich were tramp jokes. "Although [tramp] jokes are no longer popular, the tramp used to be a principal object for jokes and comic situations. It is significant, however, that the tramp was usually a medium for laughing at the pretensions and strivings of people of high status rather than the butt of the joke" (Stephenson 1951:572). The dialectical humor of tramp jokes suggested that those at both extremes of the class hierarchy are surprisingly similar.

If the lower class imitates the upper class awkwardly in traditional comedy,[12] the middle class does so in modern comedy. No matter how much money the bourgeois accumulate, their concern with money itself will prevent them from ever being accepted as a full member of the aristocratic class. A bourgeois is forever doomed to be a comic character because his focus is too narrow and his imitation of aristocrats too imperfect. "The protagonist of tragedy is an aristocrat. . . . The bourgeois . . . is always the subject of comedy; even the gods in comedy are bourgeois—Dionysus in *The Frogs*, Heracles in the *Birds*, Hermes in the *Plutus* " (Cook 1964:492–93).

Bourgeois mundanity seemed especially comic against the standard of aristocratic ideals during their historical transitions. "In great comedy—Aristophanes, Molière, Shakespeare—there is tension between the normative past as the ideals of the aristocracy, and the norms of present life as the life of the bourgeois" (Cook 1964:493). The temporal incongruity between aristocratic and bourgeois historical periods, together with the descending incongruity between higher and lower significance, lend force to Marx's well-known generalization at the beginning of *The Eighteenth Brumaire of Louis Bonaparte:* "Hegel remarks somewhere that all facts and personages of great importance in world history occur, as it were, twice. He forgot to add: the first time as tragedy, the second as farce." Marx proceeds to specify this generalization by ridiculing the ("zany") French revolutionists of 1848 for trying to imitate those of 1789.

Twentieth-century American humor has frequently focused on those who want to appear upper class but fail: upstarts, parvenus, nouveaux riches, social climbers, status seekers, title hunters, etc. "To affect the style of one's occupational or social betters," observes Goffman, "is to make claims that may well be discredited by one's lack of familiarity with the role" (1967:107). Humor points out the aspects of "high class" our society deems essential, which social climbers don't possess:

What people laugh at regarding the behavior of aspirants to higher status indicates . . . what is essential or valid in the status allocation. The hopefully upwardly mobile who seek acceptance in a higher stratum thus are confronted with the possibility of laughter . . . as a sharp device for challenging and checking upon their suitability and their competence to fulfill the demands of the higher status and its roles. . . . Among the aspirants there always are the upstarts, the fourflushers, the phonies, the too-eager beavers, the braggarts, the bunk shooters, the glad-handers, and the apple polishers. By means of the laughter at them . . . their claims and qualifications are scrutinized and kept in check. . . . The false and/or incompetent claimants are thus deflated (cut down to size), scared out, and quite likely, kept out. Laughter also may be a device for pruning the status structure of deceitful climbers and ambitious small-timers. [Hertzler 1970:127–28]

The essential aspect of "high class" revealed by humor turns out to be personal cultivation, refinement, and taste, which—the social climber learns—money can't buy.[13] Thus much American humor has ridiculed the upwardly mobile who have money without culture:

A significant and somewhat ambivalent attitude toward [culture and refinement] is demonstrated in jokes which ridicule the new-rich in their attempts to assume the style of life characteristic of the upper class. In such situations, Mrs. Newrich is prepared to buy "a Van Gogh, that new French car," hires a tutor to teach her son the "most foreign" language, and exchanges a Louis XIV bed for a Louis XVI because the former is too short for her husband. The humor in such situations is seen in the attempt to be something one is not or in trying to assume characteristics which one cannot have by virtue of his previous experience. These jokes function to express the value of being one's self . . . despite differences in wealth. [Stephenson 1951:572–73]

More subtle class and cultural distinctions may be seen in *New Yorker* cartoons, which display the contempt of the intellectual, artistic, and professional classes for the cultural aspirations and pretensions of the high bourgeois.

One by M. Twoby in 1989 shows a husband and wife in an art gallery. The saleswoman who is showing them an abstract picture on the wall says, "You rarely see this kind of joy for under ten thousand."

Yuppie offspring of the high bourgeois are also frequently targets.

In another cartoon from that year, one trendy woman is discussing her boyfriend with another: "Julian attended Columbia and Zabar's."

Some American humor has also ridiculed the downwardly mobile who have culture without money. Today, however, most of those who have culture without money are *upwardly* mobile. Amusing incongruities in life-style result when lack of money forces those who aspire to create high culture must take low-class jobs at the beginning of their careers (fig. 14).

Recent satirists of the bourgeoisie outside New York include Erma Bombeck on their suburban variant and Alice Kahn on their urban variant. Both achieve their comic effect largely by describing how the upper middle class's amorphous spirituality bogs down in their trivial material possessions and life-style—updating traditional Jewish humor's central theological incongruity between the sacred and the profane worlds. Thus Alice Kahn (1985:83–91), who coined the term in

Figure 14

1983, originally described "yuppies" in religious terms, contrasting their "worship" of the "gods" of occupational "obedience" with "severe agoraphilia, love of the marketplace"—an incongruous life-style of ascetic work ethic and hedonistic consumptive practices that produces existential alienation and psychological instability. "Being *into* something is an essential part of Yupritude . . . [ranging] from Yoga to jogging to practicing law to snorting cocaine to eating vegetarian to living with Fred (or Mary). The underlying assumption is that one goes in and out of things, that there is no constancy or stability but an endless series of flirtations with life, a deep cultural promiscuity" (1985:86).

Finally, humor shows how inauthenticity can infect not only certain roles (for example, lawyer) or institutions (religion) but whole societies. Inauthenticity, as well as incompetence, was a special problem for Eastern European societies. Since their communist ideology inflated their ideal far beyond their actuality, pretense permeated the lives of all their citizens—which their best-known witticism expressed: "We pretend to work and they pretend to pay us." (With the recent collapse of their repressive governments, their most common kind of joke incongruity should shift from the actual to the atypical, for their rapid but uneven modernization will juxtapose contemporary Western products, ideas, and behaviors with their established ones.)

The comedy of inauthenticity requires not only a "vertical" dichotomy between higher and lower selves but also a "horizontal" one between public and private selves. Public and private selves began to uncouple when society began to differentiate social appearances from psychological actuality. "The greatest vice in comedy is hypocrisy, especially the preoccupation of polite society with appearances, which must be maintained at all costs. For the hypocrite, so long as the letter of the law is satisfied, it doesn't matter what consenting (and lecherous) adults do in private. This looks like an old-fashioned moral stance, but in practice the emphasis falls on pretense rather than full-flavored hypocrisy—on social rather than moral foibles. The pretended gentleman becomes the equivalent of the villain, and his labored and fatuous efforts to achieve distinction are automatically doomed to failure" (Charney 1978:60).[14] Molière explicitly designed his comedies to reveal nefarious private selves behind seemingly benign public identities. Characters whose idealized external identities are shown to be discrepant from their actual inner selves, Molière argues, appear "ridiculous." "Now if disproportion or incongruity is the essence of the ridiculous, it is easy to see why the gallantry of [Tartuffe] appears ridiculous, and also hypocrisy in general: . . . because the secret actions of bigots do not fit the public image that their pious affectation and the austerity of their language has formed of them. . . . If the ridiculous consists in some incongruity, [then] all lies, all concealment, deceit, dissimulation, all outward appearance different from reality, all contrariety between actions which stem from the same principle, [are] essentially ridiculous" (1964a:147, 151; see also 1964b).

Artificial identities in comedy have a spatial aspect, for characters require a *boundary* between private and public spheres to be able to transform their true selves on one side into false selves on the other. Goffman (1959:106–41) described the social-psychological consequences of this experiential boundary in theatrical terms by analyzing the secret selves and manifest identities of those who oscillate between "backstage" and "frontstage." Harry Levin describes the various concrete blocking devices provided by these physical boundaries that allow theatrical characters to sever their private selves from their public identities: "Dupery is sustained by the shady devices of masking, disguise and concealment. A lover's part would be monotonously straight, if he did not frequently need to gain access to his well-guarded lady. It is not enough for Count Almaviva to pose incognito as Lindor in *Le Barbier de Seville;* he must disguise himself as a drunken soldier to be billeted into Don Bartolo's house, and as a music teacher to teach Rosine her lessons" (1987:75–76). Physical boundaries also help characters sustain this separation. "When an interloper is threatened with exposure, he must seek a place to hide—the cruder the funnier, if it happens to be a cask or a chest or a basket or the underside of a bed" (1987:76).

But the difficulty of sustaining social appearances different from psychological actuality leads to revelations of inauthenticity. Most theatrical comedies conclude with the sudden disclosure of a character's backstage self, especially one contradicting the frontstage self constructed and maintained for the other characters throughout the play. This revelation occurs when the boundary between private and public, between backstage and frontstage, is breached or collapses. The same strategy of concealment that helps create this boundary may also undermine it. Those who conceal their bodies behind furniture may see or hear the secret identities of those who conceal their selves behind masks (Levin 1987:76). Moreover, walls or pants may fall down, revealing the temporarily undisguised character's shortcomings. Doors are a common stage device in theatrical comedies; performers frequently walk through them into backstage areas, suddenly catching disguised characters without their customary masks in place or trysting couples in compromising positions (even inadvertently)—disclosing disreputable identities. British playwright Joe Orton frequently used this comic device in *What the Butler Saw,* a reviewer observed:

> "Why are there so many doors?" asks Dr. Rance upon arrival. "Was this house designed by a lunatic?" At the lunatic farcical level, "What the Butler Saw" is ingeniously conceived. Characters constantly tear through swinging doors to catch one another in compromising states of undress, until finally Dr. Prentice, an utter nonentity, stands circumstantially accused of being "a transvestite, fetishist, bisexual murderer." [*New York Times,* 9 Mar. 1989, B1]

A comedy, then, traditionally ends with the public revelation of its characters' secret selves—specifically, their true physical attributes, psychological motives, or sociological subcategories. "More traditional are those recognition scenes which open all eyes, unmask the disguised, reveal what has heretofore been concealed, and dispel the murky shadows with bedazzling illumination. The complications of New Comedy—the Aegean shipwrecks and mercantile adventures, the long-lost foundlings and cast-off mistresses, the broken families suddenly reunited—built up to such an *anagnórisis*" (Levin 1987:79–80). In chapter 4 I noted that comedy usually proceeds by correcting an early false recognition scene, in which one (or more) characters misinterpret another character's identity, with a later true recognition scene, in which they reinterpret it correctly. The true recognition scenes that usually conclude comedies, I will now add, reveal that the correct identity is either "superior" or "inferior" to the mistaken identity. The characters in a comedy may come to recognize not only the hero's or heroine's "good" attributes—those that seemed lower than they are: family relationship, siblingship, twinship, etc.—but also the villain's or villainess's "bad" attributes—those that seemed higher than they are: motivewise, classwise, etc.[15]

Comedy reveals an inauthentic identity with amusing swiftness (in contrast to tragedy, which reveals it with agonizing slowness). A false identity collapses in comedy both rapidly and repercussively because the deceptions necessary to construct and maintain it become increasingly complex, and consequently increasingly precarious. One misstep and the whole edifice rapidly comes tumbling down—with shock waves spreading from the character's collapsing false identity to the identities of all the other characters it supported.

Self-depreciating Humor: Revealing Oneself

In chapter 6 and so far in chapter 7, I have analyzed humor about the inadequacy and inauthenticity of individuals and collectivities who present themselves as *more* competent and noble than they actually are. Humor about those who present themselves as *less* so is more complex.

Ever since the seventeenth century when Hobbes postulated that the prime motivation of human beings is to increase their power, observers of Western society have described the ways people try to appear better (more competent and noble) than they really are. This motivational premise undergirds Goffman's well-known study of modern mores, *The Presentation of Self in Everyday Life* (1959), which analyzed how we play up our high-status aspects while playing down our low-status ones. "Perhaps because of the orientation upward found in major societies today, we tend to assume that the expressive stresses in a performance necessarily claim for the performer a higher class status than might otherwise be accorded him" (1959:37). In this Hobbesian self-aggrandizing view of human nature, people laugh who feel "sudden glory" from discovering in themselves some new superiority over others (and weep when feeling "sudden dejection" from discovering some new inferiority to them). Unable to find this superiority in themselves directly, they may still find it indirectly by revealing the falseness of other people's self-aggrandizements—as Hobbes himself states clearly in the *Leviathan* (part I, chapter 6): "Sudden glory is the passion which makes those grimaces called *laughter;* and is caused either by some sudden act of their own that pleases them; or by the apprehension of some deformed thing in another, by comparison whereof they suddenly applaud themselves" (1987b:19). Few observations support the Hobbesian view of human nature so blatantly as this comment about the Hollywood moguls:

> It was not enough that they should succeed; they needed their friends to fail. [derived from La Rochefoucauld]

But some people intentionally profane their own selves rather than others'. Hobbes could easily explain why such self-profaners induce laughter in their audience—who feel superior to them—but not why they would want to be laughed at. Self-mockery also contradicts the Goffmanian assumption that people always hold their selves as sacred. "The concept of self-mockery is intended to provide a counterpoint to the dominant view of the self and of self-presentational practices. . . . In contrast with the view which holds that the self is a sacred object that needs to be handled with care, it suggests that the self can be profaned—and that this can occur without creating problematic incidents. To the view that the self is presented in an idealized or impressive fashion, it juxtaposes the presentation of the self as a ridiculous character" (Ungar 1984:131).[16] Self-depreciating humor goes against the grain of our normal tendency to strive at least for self-respect if not for self-aggrandizement. Indeed, reflexive incongruities enhance the humor of those who profane their own supposedly sacred selves by revealing their base elements. In *The Speakers Handbook of Humor*, Maxwell Droke (1956:30) advises that the more successful jokes portray the speaker as inept ("succeeding only by dumb luck") than as heroic (a "wise guy").

Other-depreciating comedians try to *elevate* their own status relative to the butt's by pointing out the discrepancy between the butt's pretended superior identity and normal authentic self ("Your hair piece is on backwards!") or between the butt's expected normal identity and inferior authentic self ("Boy, your date looks old. Are you dating your mom?"); Don Rickles, who integrates disreputable elements into other people's self-images, could preface his profanations with: "You don't get no respect!" Self-depreciating comedians, in contrast, try to *depress* their own status relative to normal people by pointing out similar discrepancies between their own pretended or expected identities and "authentic" selves; Rodney Dangerfield, who integrates disreputable elements into his own self-image, does preface his self-profanations with: "I don't get no respect." (Don Rickles, who insults others, and Rodney Dangerfield, who insults himself, would make an effective comedy team, self-contained but unbalanced.)

Self-depreciating comedians try to depress their own status by flaunting the same types of base physical, psychological, and social attributes, mentioned above, that others try to conceal:

> I know I'm ugly. How ugly? Last Halloween a kid tried to rip my face off!
> . . . I get no respect. Called Suicide Prevention. They put me on hold!
> [Rodney Dangerfield]

> Catching a glimpse of himself naked in a mirror, [Richard Lewis] has to confess that "I looked like Flipper." Masturbation is suspect because "I'm afraid I might give myself something, quite frankly." Fortunately for himself and his act, Mr. Lewis notes, "low self-esteem is very popular right now."
> [*New York Times*, 20 June 1988, B3]

Those unaware of depreciating themselves add the psychological insult of ignorance to the sociological injury of indignity:

> My mother told me there's always one weirdo on every bus. But whenever
> I get on a bus, I look around and never see one.
>
> [Guichy Guy]

People can also debase themselves by debasing their physical environment:

> We held our high school prom in the Waldorf Astoria, and I was in
> charge of the decorations so I decorated it to look like our high school
> gym.
>
> [Elaine May]

Thus objects as well as people can present themselves as less than they are. Martin Mull once advertised a furniture store with the inverted motto, "Expensive furniture need not look expensive."

Laughing at oneself has always posed a problem for humor theorists who assume the individual is an integral being that naturally desires to express aggressive desires outwardly by attacking others. Even Hobbes had to confront the problem of self-depreciating humor, which he did in *Human Nature* by splitting the aggressive individual between a *present* (attacker) *self* and a *past* (attacked) *self:* "I may therefore conclude that the passion of laughter is nothing else but sudden glory arising from some sudden conception of some eminency in ourselves, by comparison with the infirmity of others, *or with our own formerly;* for men laugh at the follies of themselves past, when they come suddenly to remembrance, except they bring with them any present dishonor" (Hobbes 1987a:20; emphasis added).[17] An example:

> When I was a kid, I was so weak I got beaten up by my imaginary
> friends.
>
> [Jimmy Brogan]

The self-splits and fragmentations of the romantic period brought more attention to the problem of self-depreciating humor. In 1808, August Wilhelm von Schlegel tried to explain it by splitting the individual between a criticized lower *animal self* and a (mildly) critical higher *intellectual self:*

> There are other moral defects, which are beheld by their possessor with [some] satisfaction, and which he even makes it a principle not to get rid of, but to cherish and preserve. Of this kind is all that, without selfish pretensions, or hostile inclinations, merely originates [mostly] in ... the animal being. This may, without doubt, be united to a high degree of intellect, and when such a person [considers] his own character, laughs at himself, confesses his failings, or endeavors to reconcile oth-

ers to them by setting them in a droll light, we have then an instance of the *Self-Conscious* Comic. This species always supposes a certain inward duality of character, and the superior half, which rallies and laughs at the other, [is similar] in its tone and occupation . . . to the comic poet himself. [1964:345]

Humor theorists in the British empiricist (specifically Hobbesian) tradition, like Freud, explain self-depreciation humor as natural aggressiveness toward others "turned inward." In contrast, humor theorists in the continental idealist tradition, who locate the source of the ludicrous in the self rather than in the external world, consider self-depreciating humor primary and other-depreciating humor secondary. Jean Paul Richter, for instance, viewed humorists as splitting their ego into a *finite self* and an *infinite self*, comparing the former unfavorably with the latter, and projecting the conflict into the external world. "I divide my ego into two factors, the finite and the infinite, and I make the latter confront the former. People laugh at that, for they say, 'Impossible! That is much too absurd!' To be sure! Hence in the humorist the ego plays the lead; wherever possible he brings upon his comic stage his personal conditions, but only to annihilate them poetically. For he is himself his own fool and the comic quartet of Italian masks, himself the manager and the director" (quoted in Winston 1972:271). Recent "Richterites" are more succinct:

> A satirist is a man who discovers unpleasant things about himself and then says them about other people.
>
> [Peter McArthur]
>
> If you can't laugh at yourself, laugh at other people.
>
> [Bobby Slayton]

A more modern analysis splits the self of the self-depreciating humorist into two more general parts: a criticized inessential *objective self* ("me") and a criticizing essential *subjective self* ("I"). "By switching to the humorous realm, individuals are seeking to effect a split between their true selves (the real) and their debased selves (the unreal) and gain absolution for the latter through laughter or ridicule" (Ungar 1984:130). This conception of the dual self, especially in its modern form, helps explain why humorists would want to depreciate themselves, for they are depreciating only their inessential surface self not their essential core self. Although lowering the status of their attacked objective "me," self-depreciating comedians raise the status of their attacking subjective "I," which acquires the virtues of detachment and perceptiveness.

The desire to raise one's own status, in fact, may motivate self-depreciating humor as much as other-depreciating humor. Other-depreciating humorists raise their own status *relatively* by attempting to lower another's status. Self-depreciating humorists raise their own status *paradoxically* by attempting to lower their own status. If other-depreciating humorists reveal other people's core selves to be *inferior* to their aggrandized surface selves, self-depreciating humorists imply their own core selves to be *superior* to their own depreciated surface selves by exhibiting the inner strength necessary to reveal outer failure.[18] Even self-depreciating humor may become a form of self-aggrandizing vanity, however, if humorists believe they gain more status by appearing able to articulate self-depreciating truths about themselves than they lose by the self-depreciating truths themselves.

Self-depreciating comedians who present themselves as less competent and authentic than they really are may speak not only for themselves but also for their collectivities. All marginal groups, by definition, feel they fall short of their society's ideals: they are especially unsure how the larger society evaluates their competence or authenticity.

Even more than most marginal groups, Jews have been insecure about both their social competence and authenticity. Consequently, Jews have been given to much self-critical humor, which Freud (we saw in chapter 6) was one of the first to note. "A particularly favorable occasion for tendentious jokes is presented when the intended rebellious criticism is directed against the subject himself, or, to put it more cautiously, against someone in whom the subject has a share—a collective person, that is (the subject's own nation, for instance). The occurrence of self-criticism as a determinant may explain how it is that a number of the most apt jokes . . . have grown up on the soil of Jewish popular life. They are stories created by Jews and directed against Jewish characteristics. . . . Incidently, I do not know whether there are many other instances of a people making fun to such a degree of their own character" (1963:111–12).[19] For instance, humor about their low self-esteem:

> Remembering a boyhood sports contest between two Jewish schools, he says "Both teams claimed defeat."
>
> [Richard Lewis]

or their high blameworthiness:

> My mother got excused from jury duty—she insisted *she* was guilty.
>
> [Cathy Ladman]

Like the humor of self-depreciating individuals, however, the humor of group-depreciating Jews may actually be group-enhancing. "Though much Jewish humor appears to diminish and ridicule Jews, in its brilliant word-play and hidden meanings the joking displays an intellectual superiority that in itself laughs (however bitterly) at the potential oppressors. Thus Jewish ethnic humor is . . . apparently deprecatory but ironically aggressive" (Schutz 1989:174). For instance,

Q: How do you know Jesus was Jewish?
A: He lived at home till he was thirty; he went into his father's business; he thought his mother was a virgin; and she thought he was God.

Jewish humor questions identity as much as behavior. In *The Comic Image of the Jew*, Sig Altman examines the historical sources of self-depreciating "Jewish self-irony":

It is the frame of mind of an "uncomfortable" minority that results in the Jewish joke, and that discomfort can emerge both out of a strained sense of being in "exile," as was the case in Russia, as well as out of a strained sense of being "at home," as was the case in Germany. But the Russian exile involved at most a questioning only of Jewish "chosenness" in view of day-to-day indignities and deprivations; the German home involved the question of Jewish identity itself. Thus Jewish Humor, growing in the gap between the ideal and the real, was a staple of Eastern Europe, but the Jewish Comic Image, bearing the notion that being Jewish is absurd, was typical only of Central Europe. [1971:198]

Although these European social causes of the "inauthentic" Jewish comic image no longer operate in America, Altman continues, the image has endured from "cultural lag." "On one side, the American mechanisms of immigrant absorption provoke the transformation of all members of ethnic groups into Americans of specific religious denominations; on the other side, the Jew proves incapable of fitting perfectly into this American pattern. He holds on, for one thing, to an ironic self-image that militates ultimately both against the "respectability" of Judaism and against the perfect Americanization of the Jew" (1971:200). Thus one Jewish trait, self-irony, which developed in nineteenth-century Europe, has become the *essential* Jewish trait in America that allows Jews to maintain a sense of being Jewish (a drinking does for the Irish). "Herberg shows that of all religious groups in America, Jews *believe* the least. And the deadly earnest of old is no longer present even in the synagogue. In those mountain retreats, on the other hand, where vacationing American Jews may be said to have been most 'genuinely' themselves, it is not the rabbi but the comedian who officiates, and the daily liturgy is not the Hebrew prayer but the comic monologue" (1971:202).[20] The Jewish comedian, in short, has been the paradigm of the self-ironic, self-depreciating comedian; for modern Jews have been so uncertain of their competence and authenticity that they suspect—and try to depreciate—*any* identity that could conceivably characterize them. It is no accident that a Jewish comedian has articulated the social-psychological contradictions experienced by those who feel their inner selves are so superior to their external identities that they desire membership only in groups that likewise reject the latter. Or so goes one interpretation of Groucho Marx's famous paradox, "I wouldn't want to belong to any club that would have me."

All the racial (especially blacks and Asians), ethnic (especially Hispanics), and gender (women and homosexuals) collectivities that have been assimilating into American society in the late twentieth century have experienced similar competence or authenticity concerns, which the humor of their new comedians reflects.

8

Incompatible Selves

The incompetent functioning of comic figures may lead not only to inauthentic self-presentations but to incompatible actual selves. Those whose behavior is inadequate may be forced to split their selves between the outward appearance of adequacy and the inward awareness of its illusion, which in turn can disintegrate their selves even further. Emerson, we saw in the introduction to part 1, traced the core of comedy to these "non-performances," which split the self. "The essence of all jokes, of all comedy, seems to be an honest or well-intended halfness; a non-performance of what is pretended to be performed, at the same time that one is giving loud pledges of performance" (1946:205). Emerson's theory of humor contrasts the (ideal) world of "being," intuitively experienced as a whole (gestalt), with the (actual) world of "seeming," experienced as incomplete ("halfness") because it splits consciousness into incompatible parts—what one pledges to be doing and what one is actually doing—much like Goffman's more recent theory of self presentation. All humor, for Emerson, results from the phenomenological bifurcation between claims and achievements.

Emerson's elliptical humor theory adumbrates Pirandello's elaborated one. The humorist, for Pirandello, points out that our ideally unified self is actually composed of many contradictory and contending partial selves. "There lives in our soul the soul of the race or of the community of which we are a part. We unconsciously feel the pressure of other people's way of judging, feeling, and acting; and as simulation and dissimulation dominate in the social world—the more habitual they become, the less they are noticed—we too simulate and dissimulate with ourselves, doubling and often even multiplying ourselves" (1974:134). In a later passage, Pirandello emphasizes that our actual self, which humorists describe, is not only incoherent but discontinuous—disunified not only at each moment but also over time:

> And precisely the various tendencies that mark the personality lead us seriously to think that the individual soul is not *one.* How can we claim that it is *one,* in fact, if passion and reason, instinct and will, tendencies and ideals constitute as many separate and mobile systems functioning in such a way that the individual—living now one of them, now another, and now some compromise between two or more psychic tendencies— appears as if he really has within himself several different and even opposed souls, several different and conflicting personalities? Pascal observed that there is no man who differs from another man more than he differs, with the passing of time, from himself.
>
> The oneness of the soul contradicts the historical concept of the human soul. Its life is a changing equilibrium; it is a continual awakening and obliterating of emotions, tendencies, and ideas; an incessant fluctuating between contradictory terms, and an oscillating between such extremes as hope and fear, truth and falsehood, beauty and ugliness, right and wrong, etc. . . . This conflict of memories, hopes, forebodings, perceptions, and ideals, can be seen as a struggle of various souls which are all fighting among themselves for the exclusive and final power over our personality. [1974:136]

The Comically Discordant: Characteristics

We expect people's physical *appearance,* even more than their other self aspects, to be coherent and continuous. The paradigm of those who violate the coherence of appearance are clowns (so much so we call whoever else violates it a "clown"):

> Self-contradiction, indeed, is the clown's most significant feature. Whatever predicate we use to describe him, the opposite can also be said, and with equal right. . . . He is . . . ugly and repulsive, yet not without elegance and attractive charm. His chalk-white face, in which the eyes almost disappear while the mouth is enlarged to a ghoulish bigness, looks like the mask of death; but the children in the audience greet him with laughter and delight as a well-known friend. . . . His ill-fitting rags, his baggy sagging pants, loose waist coats, and battered

hats, mark him as a bum and disorderly person; . . . yet he is considered good fun for the whole family. [Zucker 1969:77][1]

Charlie Chaplin, the best-known film clown, once described the incongruities of his tramp costume: "I thought I would dress in baggy pants, big shoes, a cane and a derby hat. I wanted everything a contradiction: the pants baggy, the coat tight, the hat small, and the shoes large" (*New York Times*, 2 Apr. 1972). The most recent major comedian to appear as a visual oxymoron is Steve Martin: "a meticulously coifed, almost annoyingly earnest gray-haired young man in a three-piece white suit with an arrow through his head." (*New York Times Magazine*, 31 May 1992, 44). Besides the coherence of appearance, it can be comic to violate its continuity:

> I loaned a friend $8000 for plastic surgery. Now I don't know what he looks like.
>
> [Emo Phillips]

We may also be amused when we don't get the coherence and continuity we expect in *kinesics* (body motions and gestures). The clown is "clumsy and inept, but, simultaneously, incredibly agile and endowed with astonishing skills" (Zucker 1969:77). We smile at pedestrians who suddenly stop in the middle of a street and turn around, unless they also snap their fingers to indicate that their break in kinesic continuity was at least motivated. Steve Martin also contrasts his very straight looks with very "crazy" kinesics, suddenly carried away dancing by his "happy feet" (apparently no longer controlling, but controlled by, a body part).

Humor also undercuts our expectation of coherent and continuous *speech*. Speech can be incongruous internally, or externally relative to kinesics (or appearance). Comedian Emo Phillips augments his words' humor by misaligning them with his speech's fluctuating meter and pitch, and with his gestures' mismatched rhythms. The characters of comic playwright Ionesco are funny in part because "what they say is often at grotesque variance with what they do" (Hoy 1974:965).

Besides these sensory self aspects, we expect coherence and continuity in psychological ones like *cognition*—"Two Jews: three opinions"—*temperament*—The clown is "crude and mean, but also gentle and magnanimous" (Zucker 1969:77)—and overall *personality*. An article on how Americans have carried litigation to extremes today facetiously describes the ultimate plaintiff a dissociated defendant is likely to face in court:

In an interesting Oregon case, a man sued himself, claiming he was responsible for all his own troubles—that he had, through omission and commission, caused himself not to become rich and generally conducted a vendetta against himself.

The plaintiff argued that this vendetta was the proximate cause of substantial financial losses, oppression, pain and suffering. He asks for $500,000 in damages, citing a paid-up homeowner's policy that would cover the judgement.

You be the judge. What's your verdict?

[Jon Alan Carroll, *San Francisco Chronicle*, 16 Dec. 1989, 2]

The funny stories of successful public speakers first delineate a character to set up audience expectations about his or her typical behavior, before suddenly breaking them by describing an incongruous act (Droke 1956:28). The term *humor*, in fact, originally connoted the "temporary mood" in which a person (for physiological reasons) behaved incongruously to the typical character his acquaintances or audience had grown to expect.[2] More complex comedy shifts the baseline by redefining the seemingly incongruous behavior as normal and the characteristic behavior as exceptional:

My brother was always drinking. But for 17 years I never knew he drank. Then one day I saw him sober.

[Ray Pasquin]

Finally, we may find funny *interaction* that doesn't exhibit its expected coherence and continuity. Comedienne Sandra Bernhard has "a quicksilver temperament that [rapidly] changes from free-floating hostility to melting tenderness" (*New York Times*, 28 Feb. 1988, sec. 2, 38) because she rapidly switches her interaction with her audience between erotic and aggressive:

"I like you, Dick. See, I like you. I feel good about you. I think you're neat. . . . I'd like. . . ." She abruptly changes tone. "I'd like to smack your [expletive] face off, Dick. Like to give you a hair transplant tonight, Dick." She switches her tone again. "No, I like you. I do. I feel very open with all of you tonight. I feel vulnerable. I want to share things. I want to show you things. I want to show you my breasts. And yet I'm frightened."

Again, a more sophisticated form of humor will maintain the stylistic consistency of the interaction while switching the interactants, say from adult-adult to adult-child:

I had a relationship that lasted 13 years, and ended just like that. She said, "Let's just be friends." I said, "OK Mom."

[Judy Carter]

I noted in chapter 7 that tragedy paints the self's slow evolution whereas comedy sketches its sudden conversion. Thus the final laughs of many theatrical comedies come not only from the incongruity between the characters' unconverted and converted selves but also from the quickness of the change, which undercuts the audience's ideal of self stability.

Our society must idealize self-coherence and self-continuity very much for humorists to bother to point out so many inharmonious characteristics of dissonant selves.

The Comically Discordant: Causes

If divided and discontinuous selves are the crux of comedy (at least this form of it), how do they come about? The actuality of modern Western society must somehow contradict its ideology, which presumes the selves of its citizens to be unified and stable. To specify how our society undermines its members' selves we must synthesize both social-structural and symbolic-interactional explanations of humor, for comically discordant selves are produced in social interactions distorted by inconsistent social structure. Humor brings out the discrepancy between the clearly articulated social structure ideally presumed by social norms and the ambiguous incongruous social structure empirically encountered in social interaction.

A particular social interaction may force an individual to simultaneously manifest incompatible selves derived from antithetical larger divisions of social structure. Comedy points out and heightens the contradiction between the ideal *unified* self and the actual *disunified* self, pulled apart by anomalous combinations of collectivities, roles, or institutions.[3]

Distinctions between the Individual and Supraindividual Social Units

In the previous section I described how people express their disintegrating selves through disintegrating behavior (in the largest sense—including their appearance, kinesics, speech, cognition, temperament, personality, and interaction). But causation can flow both ways: not only can selves determine behavior, behavior can determine selves. Indeed, the main conceptual revolution of recent sociology has been the shift in ontological priority from entities to processes, from beings who behave to behaviors that merely *imply* beings. Incompetent behaviors, we saw, imply incompetent beings.

How accurately behavior implies being, however, is problematic.

Most people realize their outer behavior sometimes reflects their inner selves incorrectly. Kierkegaard's comic theory focuses on the contradiction between outer behavior and inner being, especially of the religious person at prayer:

> Prayer expresses the highest pathos of the infinite, and yet it is comical, precisely because it is, in its inwardness, incommensurable for every external expression; especially when one conforms to the scriptural injunction to anoint the head and wash the face while fasting. The comic is here present in a twofold manner. The obnoxious form of it would be illustrated if a robust fellow stepped forward to pray, and to signify the inwardness of his prayer proceeded to writhe in a series of athletic contortions instructive for an artist studying the musculature of the arm, especially if the speaker obliged by rolling up his sleeves. The inwardness of prayer, and its inexpressible sighs, are not commensurable for the muscular. The true form of the comic is that the infinite may move within a man, and no one, no one be able to discover it through anything appearing outwardly. [1968:83–84]

More generally, for Kierkegaard, this boundary between being and behavior makes the religious person imprisoned in human existence comical:

> Now when we take a religious individual, as a knight of the secret inwardness, and set him down in the medium of existence, in relating himself to the environment there will emerge for him a contradiction, of which he must needs become conscious. . . . The contradiction is, that with all this inwardness hidden within him, . . . his appearance is precisely like that of other men. . . . Something comical is here present, for there is a contradiction here, and where there is a contradiction, there the comical is also present. This comical aspect, however, does not exist for others, who know nothing about it; but it exists for the religious individual himself. [1968:446–47]

But just because behavior doesn't always imply being correctly does not mean that it doesn't imply being at all. Those who resent its implication must take steps to disassociate their being from their behavior ("behavior distance")—both the preventive and corrective steps Erving Goffman excelled at observing (1959:208–37; 1967:47–96, 113–36; 1961b:17–81). Unsuccessful attempts to disassociate behavior from being may add the humor of incompetence to the original source of humor.

Goffman (1959) and others have noted that, just as people's selves determine their appearance, people's appearance determine their selves. Whenever the latter flow of influence is greater than the former, humor is potentially present, for the usual relation between people and their possessions is reversed—as Emerson pointed out:

> The lie is in the surrender of the man to his appearance; as if a man should neglect himself and treat his shadow on the wall with marks of infinite respect. It affects us oddly, as to see things turned upside down, or to see a man in a high wind run after his hat, which is always droll. The relation of the parties is inverted—hat being for the moment master, the by-standers cheering the hat. The multiplication of artificial wants and expenses in civilized life, and the exaggeration of all tri-fling forms, present innumerable occasions for this discrepancy to expose itself. . . . The same astonishment of the intellect at the disappearance of the man . . . is the secret of all the [laughter at] eminent fops and fashionists. . . . So among the women in the street, you shall see one whose bonnet and dress are one thing, and the lady herself quite another, wearing withal an expression of meek submission to her bonnet and dress. [1946:212–14]

Sartorial satirists depict those subservient to their clothing, especially slaves to fashion.

Besides behavior and appearance, beings are determined by their attributes. An individual dominated by one attribute becomes a member of the social types or collectivities discussed in chapter 4. Types, too, have self implications. It is funny, Bergson noted, when the type determines the individual completely, when the individual is *only* a type:

> Every comic character is a *type*. Inversely, every resemblance to a type has something comic in it. Though we may long have associated with an individual without discovering anything about him to laugh at, still, if advantage is taken of some accidental analogy to dub him with the name of a famous hero of romance or drama, he will in our eyes border upon the ridiculous, if only for a moment. And yet this hero of romance may not be a comic character at all. But then it is comic to be like him. It is comic to wander out of one's own self. It is comic to fall into a ready-made category. And what is most comic of all is to become a category oneself into which others will fall, as into a ready-made frame; it is to crystalize into a stock character. [1956:156–57]

Kurt Riezler extends Bergson's theory of comic types from literary archetypes to more mundane social types: "The comic poet creates the comic 'type' for the sake of the comic—the braggart, the miser, the lover, the bawd, the whore, the professor, the bureaucrat, or the politician—man as a product of his profession. Each of these types corresponds to some part of the social reality and is ridiculous in its mannerisms" (1950:175–76). This kind of humor targets especially those who *intentionally* submerge themselves in one of their collectivities (for example, the childish or the born middle-aged, the "feminine" [*in itself*] or the "feminist" [*for itself*], the black nationalist or the Klansman, etc.). Although Riezler agrees that comedy dissolves individuals into types, he adds that individuals are more than merely comic types: "Yet the comic poet, by doing so, sets limits to his own art. He makes us laugh, but the type as type does not yield humor. No concrete man, seen in his totality, is merely a type. Not even the most soldierly soldier is nothing but a soldier; no mother-in-law only a mother-in-law. Yet, whenever the comic poet reaches beyond the type for the individual in his totality, he oversteps the boundary of a mere comedy that aims at nothing but laughter. The concrete individual is never only ridiculous" (1950:176). Comedy is funny in part because its abstracting and generalizing nature actually *reduces* individuals to only one of their attributes. The two Jews who go into a bar—as many jokes begin—are more than merely two Jews. Just as beings must sometimes manifest behavior distance to show that their selves are more than their behavior indicates, so individuals must sometimes manifest "type distance" or "collectivity distance" to show that they are more than their social type or collectivity indicates.

If particular behaviors imply simple aspects of the self, more complex role behaviors imply its more complex aspects. These implications may be powerful enough to override the phenomenological boundary not only between the behaver and the behavior—for example, the dancer and the dance—but also between the person and the role. But whereas many philosophers and social scientists distinguish them only with great difficulty, ordinary people must distinguish them relatively easily because they laugh at humor that denies this boundary exists. They make fun of those, like the martinet or the bureaucrat, whose self-concerns are too subservient to their role demands. Much of Pirandello's concrete humor comes from his portrayal of people as merely role players, especially in his later plays: *Rules of the Game; Six Characters in Search of an Author; Henry IV;* and *Thus It Is, If It Seems So* (Levin 1987:26, 120–21). Two modern anecdotes illustrate the humor that results from denying the normative distinction between person and role, actor and character:

> I've made so many movies playing a hooker that they don't pay me in the regular way any more. They leave it on the dresser.
>
> [Shirley MacLaine]
>
> Awful conversation backstage at the opry house a few nights earlier. Supernumerary Susan Weiss to makeup artist James Geier before *La Bohème:* "I'm a drunken slut." James: "And what are you in this opera?"
>
> [Herb Caen]

Yet if roles are supposed to be distinct from their performers, they nevertheless strongly imply something about the kind of person who performs them—which Goffman (1961b:102–5) has analyzed better than anyone else. To neutralize this self-implication, people often resort to "role distance": the "'effectively' expressed pointed separation between the individual and his putative role" (1961b:108). The techniques that create role distance by driving "a wedge between the individual and his role, between being and doing" (1961b:108) are frequently, if not usually, humorous (Coser 1966:179). For example, "by introducing an unserious style, the individual can project the claim that nothing happening at the moment to him or through him should be taken as a direct reflection of him, but rather of the person-in-situation that he is mimicking. Thus, there is in our society a special tone of voice and facial posture through which 'baby talk' is conveyed at strategic moments, for example when a second helping is requested by an individual who does not want to appear to be intemperate" (Goffman 1961b:105). Role distance is not unique to modern society, for performers of theatrical comedy have traditionally disengaged themselves from their performances:

> There must be a certain inner tension whenever anyone tries to convince others that he or she is really—for a stated interval—someone else. And there may remain some gap in that attempt, some degree of disparity between the person who does the acting and the personage that he or she enacts. This would be perceived as an imperfection in serious drama, which requires implicit acceptance for its psychic involvements. In comedy there is plenty of room for the actor to revert to himself or else to exaggerate his portrayal, to step out of his part or to overdo it. He can be disengaged from dramatic contexts much more easily than the tragic protagonist. [Levin 1987:62]

Ironically, one way to create role distance from an occupational role is to become so famous for it that our society begins to subordinate the generic role to the unique individual:

The most embarrassing thing about me: I want to be famous. . . . It's not enough for me to die as some unknown stand-up comedian. That's what would happen if somebody broke into my house and stabbed me to death and they bothered to even print some little snippet about me. The headline would be something like *Comedian Found in Pool of Blood*.
Ever notice how the media will always relegate you to your occupation? You never find a headline like: *Snappy Dresser Found in Pool of Blood*. The only exception to this rule is if you're famous. If I had done anything, anything substantial with my life, and you guys knew who I was, then they would print: *Rick Reynolds Found in Pool of Blood*.
I'd like that.

Humorous self-implications can issue not only from the discrepancies *between* people and their collectivities or roles, but also from the inconsistencies *within* their collectivities or roles (as well as institutions), to which we now turn.

Collectivity Combinations

If membership in a collectivity has self-implications, membership in contradictory collectivities may lead to contradictions within the self. Much comedy concerns split selves, which can result not only from *in*authenticity but also from what might be called "*bi*authenticity." Comedy frequently depicts those who belong to two (or sometimes more) collectivities—the relation between which determines the type of humor. If both collectivities are antithetical, dual membership paralyzes the self. Or if both are "inferior," dual membership reinforces their negative traits. Humorists have mined each of the major sociological categories for plausible depictions of individuals who intermingle its incompatible subcategories.

Although humor about those who combine two age groups ("biageists") is relatively rare, the late 1980s saw a cluster of comic movies that portrayed members of different generations who switched their bodies but retained their minds. *Big* depicted a boy suddenly transformed into a man, but only physically not psychologically; *Like Father, Like Son* and *Vice Versa* depicted this intergenerational transference between fathers and sons; *18 Again* depicted it between a grandfather and his college age grandson. All these movies derive from the 1977 movie *Freaky Friday*, in which a mother and a daughter exchanged bodies. (It would take an intensive sociological analysis of the gender-cultural currents of the times to determine why the masculine transference occurred in the 1980s whereas the feminine transference occurred in the 1970s.) These movies enhanced their humor beyond their basic premise of hybrid identities by portraying how incompetently the wrong age-collectivities play age-associated roles.

Those who combine incompatible traits from the opposite sexes might best be termed "bigenderists" (because the term *bisexuals* is already taken). A comic suggested anatomical bigenderism as a cure for loneliness: "shave one of your legs and pretend you're sleeping with someone." The 1984 film *All of Me* depicts behavioral bigenderism: Steve Martin portrays both his own character and Lily Tomlin's, whose "soul" has transmigrated into one side of him. With both genders squeezed together in the same body, Steve Martin can articulate the difference between male and female mannerisms literally side by side. (The humor generated by two selves in one body undermines the self's unity; the humor generated by one self in two bodies, as in identical twins, undermines its uniqueness.) Comics have also dealt with the specifically sexual bigenderists, for instance, by finding a virtue in their vice:

> The nice thing about being bisexual is that it doubles your chance for a date on Saturday night.
>
> [Woody Allen]

The largest number of bicollectivity jokes concern those who are biracial, biethnic, or bireligional—perhaps because this era of intermarriage makes such combinations more plausible than biageism or bigenderism. Usually a comic simply juxtaposes the different cultural traits of two groups:

> I'm half-Spanish and half-Irish. In my house, they served corned beef enchiladas and Jameson sangrias.
>
> [D. J. Hanard]

Occasionally they mix together more than two, enhancing incongruity with excess:

> This lack of a clear national identity [in Argentina] is illustrated by a joke that describes an Argentine as an Italian who speaks Spanish with a French accent and dresses like an Englishman.
>
> [*San Francisco Examiner*, 28 Sept. 1986, A22]

Since the large number of stereotypically Jewish traits—wealthy, greedy, cheap, hard-working, obsessed, religious, uncouth, ugly, urban, intelligent, expressive, cowardly, guilty—makes Jews partially incompatible with just about any other group (not to mention their own), comics (usually Jewish themselves) often crossbreed them for humorous effect. Joan Rivers intermingles the innocent restrained Swiss and the urbane expressive Jew at least in the title of her humor book, *The*

Life and Hard Times of Heidi Abromowitz. Comics also combine urban religious Jews with rural secular types:

> I'm Jewish, and from West Virginia. Sort of a hillbilly Jew. My rabbi didn't circumcise me, he sort of whittled it down.
>
> [Bob Rubin]

> The image of a Jewish cowboy—a gun-toting, bowlegged fellow sporting a yarmulke and drawling, "Hitch up de veggons, podneh, ve gonna titch dem fellas vots vot"—strikes us as ludicrous because of its incongruity.
>
> [Mindess 1971:227]

Even funnier are racial, ethnic, or religious hybrids who mingle characteristics from different cultural levels:

> I had a black father and a white mother. I didn't know whether to go to my room and play basketball or go outside and study. I dreamed of having a Cadillac with a gun rack.
>
> [D'Alan Moss]

> What's the right career for the son of a Polish-Jewish marriage? Janitor in a medical school.

> I had a friend what was half Iranian and half Mexican. He grew up to own and vandalize his own gas station.
>
> [Paul Rodriguez]

Juxtaposing two ethnic groups' negative traits is funnier if they reinforce each other:

> I'm half-Spanish, half-Irish. That means I drink a lot and I drink a lot.
>
> [D. J. Hanard]

> My best friend is half-Jewish, half-Italian. When he can't buy it wholesale, he steals it.
>
> [Jackie Mason]

Funnier still if they negate each other:

> Did you hear about the man who was half Italian and half Polish? He made himself an offer he couldn't understand.

> Why didn't the black man marry a Mexican? He didn't want the kids to grow up too lazy to steal.

Combinations of negative traits are comic because each cancels out the other's negativity—creating "a negation of a negation," as the Hegelians would put it.

Comedians have also combined economic classes in the same person. Much of the incongruity of clowns stems from their appearance, which jumbles the physical attributes of various economic classes:

The clown is not simply a pauper who clothes himself with the worn-out garments cast away by more fortunate members of society. . . . On the contrary, his incongruent dress is deliberately chosen with a kind of laughing contempt for all status. When he adds to his attire some foppish accessory, as a stiff top hat, a useless flexible cane, or the attaché case of an office clerk, he does it not in a futile attempt to improve his appearance. Rather he demonstrates with such additions his disregard for all status symbols. . . . Holding himself outside of the social stratification, he arbitrarily mixes and confuses the symbols of status by which the special order, the "nomos" of society, simultaneously manifests and reinforces itself. The art of debunking, practiced by the clown with superb skill, is not a weapon of the person who is [merely] excluded from the higher ranks. . . . Only the one who stands outside of all order can make the symbols of the order ridiculous. [Zucker 1969:78]

Charlie Chaplin's tramp character managed to combine in one person both higher- and lower-class clothing, accouterments, demeanor, and circumstances. "The most exemplary of modern comedians, Charlie Chaplin, managed to incorporate an agon—nay, virtually a class-struggle—within his fragile, shabby-genteel figure: the threadbare little tramp with the minute moustache and the mincing manners, crowned by a bowler hat and armed with a walking-stick, politely smiling, fastidiously tipping his hat, and waddling away into the sunset" (Levin 1987:57). Chaplin deserves to be called a *classic* comedian because his amalgam of "rags and riches" embodied the larger sociological contradictions and clashes of his society during his time.

Finally, humor often occurs at the points of "status transition" when someone's self is temporally between two incongruous collectivities— particularly when switching age statuses (especially during birthdays that signal the movement between significant age groups) or class statuses (especially during celebrations of lottery winning, awards, or major job promotion).[4]

Institutional Incongruities

Since roles have self-implications, incongruous combinations of the aspects of a role, or the roles of an institution, cause self-contradictions. If role incompetence leads to inauthentic selves, role incongruence leads to incompatible selves.

Anthropologist Mary Douglas suggested that role incongruence on the social level leads to joking on the symbolic level, which (I will add) expresses the self-contradictions of the psychological level. "My hypothesis is that a joke is seen and allowed when it offers a symbolic pattern of a social pattern occurring at the same time. As I see it, all jokes are expressive of the social situations in which they occur. The one social condition necessary for a joke to be enjoyed is that the social group in which it is received should develop the formal characteristics of a 'told' joke: that is, a dominant pattern of relations is challenged by another. If there is no joke in the social structure, no other joking can appear" (1979:98). Thus someone may joke as long as—and only as long as—his role is incongruous to the web of other roles that constitute the dominant institutional structure:

> Take as an example Fredrik Barth's analysis of the social situation on board a Norwegian fishing boat. Here the skipper is in full charge of the crew until the boats are lowered into the water. Then the net boss takes over. Before that point the net boss is not subject to the skipper as are other crew members. He is there on the boat, nominally under the skipper, but potentially a source of authority which will supplant the skipper for a brief period. There is in this social pattern the perfect joke form. All the time that the skipper and the other members of the crew are busily expressing superordination and subordination within the frame of common commitment to the enterprise, the net boss expresses his detachment and individuality by witty sallies. As soon as he takes over responsibility, however, his joking stops short. The essential point is that the joking by the net boss expresses a pattern of authority which arises out of the technicalities of fishing: it does nothing to create the situation, it merely expresses it. [Douglas 1979:98–99]

Let us examine the potential incongruities within and between the roles of two major institutions, family and work, to see how they split the selves of family members and workers—making these institutions common motivations for, and topics of, humor.

Family.—Many recent anthropological and sociological theories explain humor as a response to the psychological disintegration caused by opposing social forces. Most of these theories can be traced back to A. R. Radcliffe-Brown's discussion of the contradictory pressures in primitive societies that motivate certain kinship categories to joke with each other.

In the two chapters on "joking relationships" in his book *Structure and Function in Primitive Society,* Radcliffe-Brown (1965:90–116) described the humor that develops between those who belong to formerly distinct groups—families or clans—that have become related to each other. These two recently related groups experience both the *conjunctive force* of their newly formed intermarriage (91) or alliance (either economic or symbolic; 94–95, 102) and the *disjunctive force* of their traditional desire for separateness, wariness of outsiders, and mutual hostility (94–95, 108)—a combination that strains the relationships between their members. For instance, "the relation [between a husband and his wife's family involves] both attachment and separation, both social conjunction and social disjunction" (91). Those who belong to these partially connected, partially disconnected kinship categories either avoid each other or joke with each other. Radcliffe-Brown defined the "joking relationship," which may be symmetrical or asymmetrical, as "a relation between two persons in which one is by custom permitted, and in some instances required, to tease or make fun of the other, who in turn is required to take no offense" (90). The joking relationship allows members of a hybrid group to express both the conjunctive and disjunctive social forces they feel.[5] Joking relationships are most common between a husband and his wife's brothers and sisters, but they are also found "between cross-cousins, between mother's brother and sister's son, and in a somewhat milder form between grandparents and grandchildren" (106).

Radcliffe-Brown's theory of joking relationships has one major drawback that prevents it from being readily applied today. None of the specific joking relationships of the extended family Radcliffe-Brown mentioned exist in modern society (Fine 1983:165), except perhaps that between grandparents and grandchildren, especially in Europe (Zijdervelt 1968:296). To salvage Radcliffe-Brown's potentially fruitful concept of joking relationships, modern humor theorists have been forced either to broaden their definition or to seek them in institutions other than the family.

The apparent dearth of joking relationships in the modern family disappears if we shift their specification from "joking with" to "joking about." Like joking *with* or teasing[6] relationship partners, joking *about* them also indicates relationships strained by opposing social forces. Such a definitional shift reveals at least one common joking relationship in the modern kinship system:

> This Russian goes to the wake for his friend's mother-in-law, extends his condolences and asks, "What did she die from?"

"Poisoning," the bereaved man answers solemnly.
"Poisoning?" the friend says perplexedly. "Then why is the body so bruised and battered?"
"She didn't want to take the poison," the son-in-law says.

Since there are many mother-in-law jokes in both Russia and America, the conjunctive and disjunctive forces that strain spouse/mother-in-law relationships in modern societies must be similar to those that strain other kinship relationships in primitive societies. Similar but not identical, for the more mothers-in-law are joked *about*, the less they are joked *with*. Actual relations with mothers-in-law in our society are more "avoidance" than "joking."

Another difference between primitive and modern kinship humor is that marriage itself has become a joking relationship, at least in the "joking about" sense. Max Eastman used matrimony as the paradigm example of his generalization that "any subject matter upon which we have two contrasted or conflicting attitudes of feeling becomes . . . a prevailing topic of laughter" (1939:224). Eastman didn't say what these "two contrasted or conflicting attitudes of feeling" are, but the opposing social forces operating on marriage in modern society differ from those operating on it in primitive society reported by Radcliffe-Brown. Although the conjunctive force may still be similar, the disjunctive force has shifted from the opposing extended families to the opposing spouses themselves. Each marriage partner's conjunctive desire for security and sexual satisfaction is now countered by a disjunctive desire for freedom and independence:

> Married life is a job just the same as like a telegraph operator or a embalmer and every employ is entitled to 2 wks. vacation per annum and if the husband takes a 2 wks. vacation trip every summer and vice versa, why they will get so as they won't miss their regular jobs ½ as much as if they was on it all the wile. For inst. I knew a couple where the husband used to go South for a mo. every Winter and one time she didn't know he was still missing till one night in August when a bat got in the house and she screamed and nobody told her to shut up.
>
> [Ring Lardner]

Marriage partners are tied together by many different connections, which can get out of alignment when some communicate distance while others communicate closeness (Davis 1973). Those on lower levels of intimate relations devote much of their energy to switching each connection from distant to close. These premarriage or, if stabilized, quasi-marriage relations contain more conjunctive and disjunctive contradictions than marriage because they combine both close and distant connections, falling short of the ideal marriage in which all connections are close. Their easily misaligned connections make them an even more popular target for comedy than marriage:

> I just broke up with my girlfriend. She moved in with another guy and I drew the line. She said, "Let's be friends." "Fine," I said. "We'll go out and have a few drinks and pick up chicks."
>
> [Garry Shandling]

The contradictions between the biological (sexual), psychological (romantic), and social (institutional) connections of unraveling marriages also frequently evoke humor.

> The ideal of marriage is a relationship in which both these elements are synthesized; husband and wife are simultaneously involved in relations of physical love and the love of personal friendship. . . .
> From the personal point of view . . . sexual desire, because of its impersonal and unchanging character, is a comic contradiction. The relation between every pair of lovers is unique, but in bed they can only do what all mammals do. . . .
> Marriage is not only a relation between two individuals; it is also a social institution, involving social emotions concerned with class status and prestige among one's fellows. This is not in itself comic; it only becomes comic if social emotion is the only motive for a marriage, so that the essential motives for marriage, sexual intercourse, procreation and personal affection, are lacking. [Auden 1962:374–77][7]

Love and marriage, for example, may cease to be correlated:

> Holtzman: I've been married twenty-eight years today, and I'm still in love with the same woman.
> Glazier: That's wonderful.
> Holtzman: And if my wife ever finds out, she'll kill me!

In modern Western society, most jokes about structural incongruities in the kinship institution focus not on the extended but on the nuclear family. Comedy frequently depicts nuclear families strained by forbidden sexual conjunctions that clash with required social disjunctions. Many jokes concern the paradoxical—biologically desired but normatively forbidden—Oedipal relation. One variation transposes it to adults:

I'm very loyal in relationships. Even when it's my mom. When I go out with my mom, I don't look at other moms. I don't ask, "I wonder what her macaroni and cheese tastes like?"

[Garry Shandling]

Another variation transposes it to the professional relationship that *treats* Oedipal problems (fig. 15). Almost from its beginning, Western comedy has depicted those who *almost* violate Oedipal and incest taboos.

> The possibilities of incestuous combinations form one of the minor themes of comedy. The repellent older woman offered to Figaro in marriage turns out to be his mother, and the fear of violating a mother also occurs in *Tom Jones*. . . . The *cognito* in comedy, in which the characters find out who their relatives are, and who is left of the opposite sex not a relative, and hence available for marriage, is one of the features of comedy that have never changed much. . . . We have noted that the *cognito* of comedy is much concerned with straightening out the details of the new society, with distinguishing brides from sisters and parents from foster-parents. The fact that the son and fa-

Keeping Up

© Chronicle Features, 1988

Willard, I am not talking to you as your analyst now. I am talking as your mother.

Figure 15

ther are so often in conflict means that they are frequently rivals for the same girl, and the psychological alliance of the hero's bride and the mother is often expressed or implied. The occasional "naughtiness" of comedy, as in the Restoration period, has much to do, not only with marital infidelity, but with a kind of comic Oedipus situation in which the hero replaces his father as a lover. [Frye 1971:170, 180–81]

Modern jokes differ from traditional comedy by depicting not merely potential but actual violations of Oedipal and incest taboos:

> The 14-year-old backwoods boy was making love to his 12-year-old sister. "Sis," he wheezes, "You're almost as good as Maw!" "Yeh," she gasps back, "That's what Paw says."

> A liberal father, anxious that his sixteen-year-old son should be painlessly initiated in the way of sex, gives the boy $50 and dispatches him in pursuit of a prostitute. Later, the son returns and proudly tells his father that he has been doubly successful in losing his virginity while saving the $50.
> "I told Granny where I was going," explained the boy, "and she said she'd do it for free."
> "What?" screamed the father, "You screwed my mother?"
> "Why not?" asked the son, "You screwed mine."

The social humor of Oedipal and incestuous jokes is augmented by "anthropological" repercussions, for short-circuiting kinship structure also shocks cosmological structure.

Work.—Whereas Radcliffe-Brown focused on joking relationships in the *family* institutions of primitive societies, sociologists (and some anthropologists) have sought them in the *economic* institutions of modern society:

> Joking relationships are also found in work environments. . . . Although joking on the job probably occurred as soon as there were workers and tedious jobs, the first discussion of this phenomenon was in the context of the Hawthorne studies, the now classic study of industrial sociology. In the bank wiring room, workers joked with each other, played tricks on each other, and otherwise had a good time in the course of the workday. . . . Perhaps the most influential study of joking in a factory was the participant observation conducted by Roy. Roy found that one set of machine operators had developed a quite intricate set of joking norms and procedures by which they structured the workday and dealt with potential personal conflict and strains. These joking occasions came to be ritualized, such as "banana time" (the memorable title of Roy's article), which consisted of one worker stealing another worker's ba-

nana—an event that occurred each day at nearly the same time. While the ritualized quality of the joking day is surprising and is due to the isolated conditions in which these men worked, joking relationships are found among peers in all occupations. Studies of department store clerks, coal miners, mental hospital employees, and printing press workers have yielded similar findings showing that workers kid and joke with each other to relieve the tedium of the work. [Fine 1983:165–66]

Why is there so much on-the-job joking in modern society? If joking relationships result from opposing social forces, what conjunctive and disjunctive forces motivate coworkers to joke with each other? The conjunctive social force seems to be group *unification,* through which long-term associates become friends. "No one should be greatly surprised that much joking is found among groups of friends, particularly friends who are together for extended periods of time or in isolated areas. These joking relationships seem (or at least seemed) particularly characteristic of all-male groups.... In an ethnography of life in a working class tavern, LeMasters found that banter and kidding were almost continuous among certain members of the group. Some of the remarks [there] might have provoked fights if they had been made by strangers" (Fine 1983:165).

Sociologists (and some anthropologists) have noted two disjunctive social forces in modern economic institutions. The first, as in primitive families, is *differentiation.* The various styles of joking relationships express the conflict between the conjunctive force of group unification and the disjunctive forces of several kinds of differentiation. Individual differentiation motivates teasing or joking about one's peculiarities: fatness, baldness, hoarseness, etc. Social differentiation motivates teasing or joking about one's social categories: age (boy, old man), gender (potential homosexuality), ethnicity (stupidity), class (pretentious, slob). Self-interest (as opposed to group-interest) is a hyperdifferentiating force that leads to joking relationships between competitors and rivals. "Joke-induced laughter is widely resorted to as a means of easing strain in many other forms of relationships between individuals. Its use between competitors and rivals is well known; for example, sales representatives of competing companies joking at luncheon or when they meet on the street; clerks in offices, tellers in banks, sales assistants in retail establishments, using it to avoid clash and strain as they vie with each other for positional favors or sales" (Hertzler 1970:141). Humor can diminish a group's internal differentiations by increasing its external differentiation from its institutional environment. In a study of hospital patients, Rose Coser described how humor unifies even short-term associates into a group by demarcating patients from their hospital: "These jokes . . . imply rebellion against the routine, against the 'mechanical encrusted upon the living,' and against the staff who on the basis of their authority may intrude any time they wish on the privacy of the patient. . . . The jocular gripe is the collective expression of an individual complaint. . . . It strengthens the boundaries between the group of laughers and the outsiders, between the patients and those who are in authority, doctors and nurses. . . . This type of behavior . . . strengthens group identification among persons whose relationships are only transitory" (Coser 1959:176, 177, 179).

The second disjunctive force in economic institutions (as well as in traditional families and modern marriages) is *hierarchy,* which opposes the conjunctive force of *equality.* Humor also facilitates group formation by confirming its members equality (Fine 1983:165); for instance, by contrasting the egalitarianism of patients with the hierarchies of hospitals: "Unlike the complainer, the patient who invites others to laugh with him creates or strengthens the feeling of equality in the participants. . . . [Jocular griping] stresses the equality of all patients within a social structure otherwise characterized by its rigid hierarchy" (Coser 1959:178–79). In another study of a (mental) hospital's staff, Coser noted that humor can also flatten a group's own stratification: "In laughter, all are equal; social barriers, such as those of status, temporarily are lowered, because to laugh with others presupposes some degree of common definition of the situation" (1960:81). The senior staff, she found (1960:86–88), makes fun of the junior staff, but not vice versa. The junior staff can make fun of only (the even lower) patients or themselves (through self-depreciating humor). She concludes: "At the meetings . . . observed, [humor relaxed] the rigidity of the social structure without, however, upsetting it. Those . . . of higher status position more frequently took the initiative to use humor; more significant still, the target of a witticism, if . . . present, was never in a higher authority position than the initiator. To Radcliffe-Brown's proposition, that humor . . . reconcile[s] tendencies of association and dissociation within a group, it may be added that in a *hierarchically* ordered social structure [humor] tends to be directed downward" (1960:95).[8]

Theatrical comedy, Harry Levin (following Northrop Frye) observes, combines differentiating and hierarchical forces with unifying and egalitarian forces *sequentially* rather than simultaneously. "Aristophanic comedy moves toward a celebration, but along the way it engages in recrimination; it castigates behavior by laughing at it, with the feasting to offset the fighting" (1987:30). Levin, in effect, temporalized Coser's conception of comedy by noting how theatrical comedy begins by accentuating the differentiation and stratification systems, and concludes by minimizing them.

Mary Douglas raised the opposing social forces that underlie this form of humor to the most abstract level by equating unity and equality with "community," and differentiation and hierarchy with social "structure." For Douglas, then, humor subordinates the disjunctive forces of social structure (both differentiation and hierarchy) to the conjunctive forces of community (both dedifferentiation and dehierarchicalization):

> John Barnes used the term *network* to indicate an undifferentiated field of friendship and acquaintance. In his Morgan Lectures, Victor Turner has suggested that the word *community* could be applied to this part of social life. In "community" the personal relations of men and women . . . form part of the ongoing process which is only partly organized in the wider social "structure." Whereas "structure" is differentiated and channels authority through the system, in the context of "community," roles are ambiguous, lacking hierarchy, disorganized. "Community" in this sense has positive values associated with it; good fellowship, spontaneity, warm contact. Turner sees some Dionysian ritual as expressing the value of "community" as against "structure." This analysis gives a better name to, and clarifies, what I have elsewhere crudely called the experience of the nonstructure in contrast to the structure. Laughter and jokes, since they attack classification and hierarchy, are obviously apt symbols for expressing community in this sense of unhierarchised, undifferentiated social relations. [1979:104]

In summary, then, Radcliffe-Brown spawned research into the conjunctive and disjunctive institutional forces that motivate individuals to joke with each other to accommodate these contradictory pressures. He himself focused on the marriage *relationship*, strained between the spouses' unification and their families' differentiation. Sociologists, who studied businesses rather than families, focused on the *group*, strained between its integrative equality and its disintegrative hierarchy. Finally, anthropologists focused on *whole societies*, strained between their associative community and their dissociative structure.

Interactional Bifurcation.

Just as British anthropologist Radcliffe-Brown's chapters on joking relations developed the paradigmatic concepts for research into the opposing *macroinstitutional* sources of humor, British sociologist Tom Burns's article "Friends, Enemies, and the Polite Fiction" (1953) developed them for research into its opposing *microinteractional* sources. If the large-scale Radcliffe-Brown tradition has located humor's conjunctive forces in homeostatic relationships, groups, or communities and its disjunctive forces in differentiation, hierarchy, or structure, the small-scale Burns tradition has located humor's conjunctive force in the homeostatic "encounter" and its disjunctive force in the "alternative selves" an interacting individual must manifest simultaneously. As Burns himself put it, "the roles an individual plays [that is, the selves an individual possesses] in different social situations may sometimes be present as possible alternatives in the same situation" (1953:654). These macro and micro traditions of humor research are related through the *social-psychological* nature of the alternative selves, for the individual *psychologically* internalizes a self from each of his or her many supraindividual *social* units—collectivities, roles, and institutions.

If unresolved, this self-conflict leads to "embarrassment," which "arises through the failure to establish or maintain consensus about the range of social norms affecting behavior in an interaction. It is potential typically in situations in which two statuses are presented simultaneously" (1953:662). Embarrassment is a painful psychological state that rapidly brings social interaction to a halt. (*Embarrass* stems from the Italian *imbarrare*: "to bar, impede.") Burns's best-known successor, Erving Goffman, starting from a similar model,[9] elaborates the way embarrassment blocks behavior: "A completely flustered individual is one who cannot for the time being mobilize his muscular and intellectual resources for the task at hand, although he would like to; he cannot volunteer a response to those around him that will allow them to sustain the conversation smoothly. He and his flustered actions block the line of activity the others have been pursuing" (1967:100–101).

Because the self-conflict of embarrassment is so psychologically painful and sociologically disastrous, people go to great lengths to avoid it. Either they try to maintain the separation between the incompatible alternative selves by segregating the roles or other social units that produce them (Burns 1953:659–60; Goffman 1967:108). Or, if this segregation breaks down, they try to resolve the potential self-conflict humorously by affirming one self while rejecting the other (and by extension the social units that produce each self). "When the ambiguities in such situations become stressed, the fictive character of roles emerges into obviousness and a false social position has to be resolved by some declaration pointing to association with one of the groups—an affirmation of one status—and rejection of the other. But since such declarations carry with them a threat to a status in which the individual is involved, and which therefore constitutes a value to him, they are with rare exceptions covered by entry into a form of joking relationship and emerge as banter" (Burns 1953:654–55).

Burns distinguishes two kinds of humor that defend the primary self and relationship against the secondary in different ways (1953:657): *banter* ("to play at being hostile, distant, unfriendly, while intimating friendliness" [655]) and *irony* ("to play at being friendly . . . while intimating enmity, rejection" [657]). Banter overtly rejects the secondary self but safeguards it for the future (662) whereas irony covertly rejects the secondary self while not obviously threatening it in the present. Banter maintains the secondary relation by sharing the joke with it (conjunctive force), as well as with the primary relation; irony rejects the secondary relation by sharing the joke only with the primary relation (conjunctive force) while pointedly excluding the secondary relation from getting the joke (disjunctive force) (657).

Humor, in short, resolves the social psychological conflict of individuals forced to present incompatible selves in an encounter at the same time. Burns, Goffman, and others have elaborated this humor theory in two directions: they have specified the various social sources of the alternative selves (disjunctive forces) and the various aspects and kinds of encounters that bring these alternative selves together (conjunctive forces).

Since membership in a supraindividual social unit has self-implications, we saw, membership in contradictory ones will produce the incompatible selves best reconciled by humor. Burns's examples include selves derived from contradictory collectivities, like age—"Banter, then, becomes a style for managing children taken by parents or teachers when other adults are present and forbid the adoption of a role attaching exclusively to their status as teacher or parent"—gender—"It is frequent among adolescent boys and girls when they are together and there is a desire both to retain the security of the individual's status in his own peer-group and to assume a sexually attractive role towards the opposite sex" [10]—and class—"It is used by married people and intimate friends in argument, when each is concerned to maintain both the status of an intimate and the status of membership in a larger group whose prestige— . . . as educationally, socially or economically powerful—weighs in the argument" (1953:655). Banter also occurs when selves derived from the whole group meet those derived from its subgroups. "Situations are therefore constantly arising in which a clique-membership status is presented in interaction situations which also involve the status of membership in the organization as a whole. In certain areas of interaction, when clique and subcommunity statuses come near to equivalence in importance, banter becomes the prevailing style—it is almost impossible to behave in any other way in messrooms and canteens" (1953:655).

Incompatible selves also come from contradictory roles and institutions. Different institutions sometimes force individuals to perform their disparate roles simultaneously, leading to self-contradictions likely to be resolved comically (Duncan 1953:53). Family and work, we saw, produce the interinstitutional role conflict most likely to motivate humor. Much kidding occurs at the intersections of these two institutions. "A man may invite workmates or colleagues into his home and meet them in the same situation as that in which he enacts the role of husband and parent. . . . At work, the member of a staff of a factory who is in a clique [family type] relationship with some other members may find a similar overlapping, or juxtaposition, of the two roles" (Burns 1953:654). Even a single institution sometimes forces an individual to perform its disparate roles simultaneously, like husband and parent in the family.[11]

Encounters themselves form the conjunctive arenas that hold together these disjunctive institutional roles and consequently incompatible selves—opposing social forces that transform many meetings into battlefields of banter.

Encounters are conjunctive, Goffman observes, especially because "physical closeness easily implies social closeness" (1967:107). Large work institutions contain many locations where all members are regarded as equals. "An illustration may be taken from the social life of large establishments—office buildings, schools, hospitals, etc. Here, in elevators, halls, and cafeterias, at newsstands, vending machines, snack counters, and entrances, all members are often formally on an equal if distant footing" (1967:109). These egalitarian locations bring together those of different statuses in the institutional hierarchy:

> The democratic orientation of some of our newer establishments, however, tends to throw differently placed members of the same work team together at places such as the cafeteria, causing them uneasiness. There is no way for them to act that does not disturb one of the two basic sets of relations in which they stand to each other. These difficulties are especially likely to occur in elevators, for there individuals who are not quite on chatting terms must remain for a time too close together to ignore the opportunity for informal talk—a problem solved,

of course, for some, by special executive elevators. Embarrassment, then, is built into the establishment ecologically. [1967:110]

The conflict between hierarchical institutional roles and egalitarian encounters creates another set of incompatible selves that members have difficulty manifesting simultaneously. "Behind the conflict in identity lies a more fundamental conflict, one of organizational principle. . . . Behind the apprentice's claim for a full share in the use of certain plant facilities there is the organization principle: all members of the establishment are equal in certain ways *qua* members. Behind the specialist's demand for suitable financial recognition there is the principle that the type of work, not mere work, determines status. The fumblings of the apprentice and the specialist when they reach the Coca-Cola machine at the same time express an incompatibility of organizational principles" (1967:111–12). Those who experience this self-conflict, Goffman (foot)notes, may resolve it through *either* embarrassment or banter. Unlike Burns (unmentioned but obviously in mind), Goffman believes *both* minimize the self-conflict by dramatizing it:

At such moments "joshing" sometimes occurs. It is said [by Burns] to be a means of releasing the tension caused either by embarrassment or by whatever caused embarrassment. But in many cases this kind of banter is a way of saying that what occurs now is not serious or real. The exaggeration, the mock insult, the mock claims—all these reduce the seriousness of conflict by denying reality to the situation. And this, of course, in another way, is what embarrassment does. It is natural, then, to find embarrassment and joking together, for both help in denying the same reality. [1967:112n.]

The hierarchical and egalitarian relations that produce incompatible selves are clapped together not only in the ordinary encounters caused by *chance*, which Goffman discusses, but more intensely in the extraordinary encounters caused by *crises*. A chance meeting in an elevator that forces different statuses to ride a few floors together as equal passengers generates a tension left unresolved by embarrassment or resolved by banter. Since everyone in a crisis, however, becomes "more equal," an elevator breakdown that forces them to spend an indefinite period of time together in a potentially dangerous situation generates much greater tension—increasing pressure toward humorous resolution. The greater egalitarianism of the second situation, Mary Douglas observes, affects its social and cultural dynamics:

I hope that I have established that a joke cannot be perceived unless it corresponds to the form of the social experience: but I would go a step further and even suggest that the experience of a joke form in the social structure calls imperatively for an explicit joke to express it. Hence the disproportionate joy which a feeble joke often releases. In the case of a bishop being stuck in the lift, a group of people are related together in a newly relevant pattern which overthrows the normal one: when one of them makes the smallest jest, something pertinent has been said about the social structure. Hence the enthusiasm with which a joke at the right time is always hailed. Whatever happens next will be seen to be funny; whether the lowliest in the no longer relevant hierarchy discover the right switch and become savior of the mighty, or whether the bishop himself turns out to be the best mechanic, the atmosphere will become heady with joy, unless the bishop has made the mistake of imposing the external hierarchy. [1979:100]

The contradiction between *hierarchical* and *egalitarian* roles, suddenly conjoined during a crisis, may be heightened by the contradiction between *technical* and *intimate* ones. Generalizing Joan Emerson's classic description of the gynecological exam, Vera Robinson describes how professionals and patients, thrown together during an illness, often resolve their contradictory relations—vertical and horizontal, narrow and broad—through humor:

In times of illness, crisis, and stress, strangers (patient and professional) are suddenly thrust into intimate and somber contacts. There is not time to build a relationship, yet there is an expectation of trust and cooperation. The patient must submit to invasive, foreboding procedures and is expected to reveal intimate personal information and his innermost thoughts and feelings, all without question. Emerson found that a form of interaction that quickly provides this sense of familiarity, does not offend, and is easily facilitated was needed. Humor met these criteria and, because of its "joke-frame," provided the flexibility for easily terminating the interaction or moving into a serious discussion. The humor usually took the form of bantering, pleasantries, and jocular talk. [1983:114]

Incompatible selves can be consecutive as well as concurrent. Goffman specifies the major transition points in family and work that force those who cross them to manifest past and present selves simultaneously, if only briefly, for their social circle. "To experience a sudden change in status, as by marriage or promotion, is to acquire a self that other individuals will not fully admit because of their lingering attachment to the old self" (Goffman 1967:106). Self-transitional, like self-bifurcating, situations are embarrassing, motivating much humor in or about them:

> "Well, son, let me congratulate you. You're going to look back on this day as the happiest of your whole life!"
> "But, Dad, I'm not getting married today. I'm getting married tomorrow."
> "That's right, son."

Like the individual who combines collectivities in himself, whom we saw above, the individual who performs reciprocal institutional roles by himself may counteract himself. An institution's roles are reciprocal whenever one role's output is the other's input (for example, personnel gatekeeper and job seeker). If a quirk of fate causes the same person to perform both roles, the reflexive role conflict that may result leads to ludicrous self-negations:

> Wonderful are the ways of Washington bureaucracy! Here's a story about a Californian who applied through regular channels for a job in Washington he knew he was qualified to fill. While cooling his heels awaiting a reply, he happened to meet, in person in San Francisco, the head of the very agency to which he had applied, and was given the position on the spot.
> The scene now shifts to Washington. Our Californian had been doing a fine job there for three months when a letter was forwarded to him from his old address telling him that, unfortunately, his application for the job he was now holding down had been denied because he lacked the necessary qualifications.
> And here's the kicker. The letter had been signed by himself.

Ironically, the hypercompetent—"renaissance"—men and women who play multiple roles within an institution are most likely to get themselves into these absurd self-contradictory situations. Steve Allen faced this problem when he had to host a television show during an actor's strike:

> I myself had mixed emotions when they called me [to host this show]. . . . But that's because I'm in a sort of odd position personally, in that I'm a writer and an actor but also a producer. In fact all last week, I was picketing my own office. . . . But that was all right because I had myself thrown off the premises, ladies and gentlemen, and I intend to sue myself for unfair labor practices and collect a pretty penny too.
> [1987:233]

I have tried to specify in this chapter the opposing social forces that kindle the comic by splitting the self. *The conjunctive force* of a monolithic abstract social unit conflicts with *the disjunctive force* of its disparate concrete subunits: the collectivity versus its contrary subgroups, the role versus its discrepant required behaviors, the institution versus its antithetical alternative roles, and the society versus its irreconcilable institutions. Besides the opposition between each social unit and its subunits, there are also oppositions between the social subunits themselves. *The conjunctive forces* of unifying, egalitarian, and broad ones conflict with *the disjunctive forces* of differentiating, hierarchical, and narrow ones: collectivization versus individualization, intimate versus utilitarian relationships, family versus business institutions, and Gemeinschaft (community) versus Gesellschaft (society). These opposing forces on the *social* level are transformed through the *encounter* into opposing forces on the *individual* level. *The conjunctive force* of "individualization" (disjunctive on the social level but conjunctive on the individual level) that organizes identity components—appearance, kinesics, speech, cognition, temperament, personality, interaction style— into a unique individual conflicts with *the two disjunctive forces* that disorganize them—both "socialization" that reorganizes them upward around supraindividual social units or "psychologicalization" that reduces them downward to disconnected identity fragments. All these opposing social forces that disintegrate an individual's integrity motivate humor—which allows us to tolerate, even enjoy, the dissolution of our very selves by denying that its consequences are serious.

Novelty shops exist in nearly every American major metropolitan area—usually on the sleazy side of its urban core, which suggests they threaten almost the same conceptual underpinnings of our society as adult book stores and theaters (see Davis 1983). To my knowledge, there have been no sociological studies of this widespread enterprise.[1] A pity, for the "novelty" content of these shops can illuminate many taken-for-granted aspects of our cultural and social worlds. A first pass at sorting these novelties discloses their attack on each of the expectation systems considered in this book—substantiating evidence that they are the true targets of humor.

Like "theoretical" or abstract jokes, all the "practical" or *objectified jokes* sold in novelty shops are designed to annihilate expectation systems. All are "deceptive objects," which visually set up an expectation about their nature that they unexpectedly explode—sometimes with a bang. If we are surprised by joy buzzers and squirting flowers, which suddenly tickle or splash us with unexpected sensory stimuli, we are shocked by exploding matches, chocolates, and golf tees, as well as by spring snakes erupting from peanut or jam jars, which blast us with them percussively.

Beside "ambiguous verbalisms," such as the puns embossed on bumper stickers, buttons, and T-shirts, that contradict our *linguistic systems*, are more concrete "ambiguous objects," such as the visual puns of optical illusions, that contradict our *semiotic (nonverbal) commu-*

nication systems—like the image of a woman whose clothing continually appears to disappear and reappear.

But most novelties are various kinds of "incongruous objects." A few are "illogical objects" that confound our *logical systems*, such as "Lichtenberg's knife without a blade, which has no handle" (Freud 1963:61n.), which lacks the very criteria that defines it. Related to these, but much more common, are "unnatural objects," which deny *natural systems*: card, coin, or rope tricks, stunt rocks that look heavier than they are, and spigots seemingly supported in the air solely by the very streams of water that flow down from them—all seem to violate the laws of nature (one reason humor is closely connected to magic).

Novelties that undermine *anthropological systems* transfer either human or biological features to objects. "Humanized objects" include talking toilets or laughing boxes. "Biologized objects" include edibles or excrementals that cross the boundaries of the body. Edible novelties are worse than they appear: hot pepper or garlic-flavored chewing gum, rubber bon bons, candy whose center tastes like rotten mackerel. Excremental novelties appear worse than they are: fake vomit, blood, or snot; soft plastic dog doo or human excrement, whoopee cushions, fart powder, or stink bombs. (Some potentially edible novelties, like plastic bugs in ice cubes or foods, also appear worse than they are.) "Fragmented objects" disintegrate the organic unity of the body, and hence of the human being. Thus novelty stores sell recognizable (though obviously fake) body parts amputated from the human whole, such as wind-up walking shoes or feet, simulated fingers or ears or eyes, and plastic skeletons or skulls.

Novelties also assault *social systems*. "Unusual objects" deny the social world's *typicality;* for instance, by mismatching form and function: phones shaped like shoes contradict their social usage; phones shaped like lips overly reinforce theirs. "Deromanticizing objects" undermine the social world's *ideality.* For instance, "dysfunctional objects," which don't do what they're designed to do, make their victims appear *incompetent.* Thus a dribble glass, relighting birthday candle, or disappearing ink draws attention to their inability to accomplish a seemingly easy task. "Humiliating objects," which weaken the authenticity of respectable self-presentations, make their victims appear *undignified.* Thus sneezing or itching powder calls into question their (usually implicit) health claims, and sucker soap (which dirties its user) or inked telescopes (which leave black circles around the eye) make them seem careless about their appearance. "Pseudo-transformative objects" graft onto people new, usually romanticized, identities, *incompatible* with their original identities. Thus masks, costumes, and props seem to

transform their owners into heros (including supermen and su-
perwomen) or villains (including monsters), such as sweatshirts
stamped with "Property of Alcatraz Prison" or transparent film bullet
holes that create criminal identities. These transformations are merely
pseudo-, however, because they are so obviously fake. Both the compatibility and incompatibility between original and transformed identity
make these masquerades amusing, for their compatibility degrades the
extraordinary persona while their incompatibility emphasizes its incongruity with the ordinary person who dons this disguise.

All these deceptive novelties—ambiguous or incongruous, illogical
or unnatural, humanized or biologized or fragmented, unusual or deromanticizing (dysfunctional or humiliating or pseudotransforma-
tive)—display the set of trajectories along which humor can suddenly
hurl us out of the monotony of everyday life.

Having summarized comedy's assault on our assumptions by analyzing its most concrete examples, I can now synthesize its most abstract implications: on structure, on system, on society, and on self. I
will conclude by describing the kind of sociology appropriate for a
society that can be decomposed by comedy.

One of the themes of this book—and therefore one of the reasons
its topic has been so difficult to pin down—is that comedy negates
organization, structure, form, even clarity itself. Comedy attacks not
merely the conception of social structure, Mary Douglas observed (see
chapter 8), but the more general conception of structure itself. "A joke
confronts one relevant structure by another less clearly relevant, one
well-differentiated view by a less coherent one" (1979:105). In rejecting
conceptual structure (for instance, by searching out the basic similarities that underlie apparently different social units [see chapter 5]), comics resemble mystics.

> Perhaps the joker should be classed as a kind of minor mystic.
> Though only a mundane and border-line type, he is one of
> those people who pass beyond the bounds of reason and soci-
> ety and give glimpses of a truth which escapes through the
> mesh of structured concepts. Naturally he is only a humble,
> poor brother of the true mystic, for his insights are given by
> accident. They do not combine to form a whole new vision of
> life, but remain disorganized as a result of the technique which
> produces them. [1979:108].

In particular, comics weaken the legitimacy of the *dominant* conceptual
structure (1979:95–96), which permits other potential ways to organize

the world. The joker's "jokes expose the inadequacy of realist structuring of experience and so release the pent-up power of the imagination. The joker . . . promises a wealth of new, unforeseeable kinds of interpretation. He exploits the symbol of creativity which is contained in a joke, for a joke implies that anything is possible." [1979:108][2]

Thus comedians challenge those who presume the world has a particular organization, structure, or form, such as social structuralist Talcott Parsons. They also challenge those who presume its processes have priority. Social antistructuralists like Hobbes reduce social structure to the *process* of social conflict (controllable only by a strong sovereign).[3] Comedians, however, reject the basically unorganized worldview as much as the rigidly organized one. Comedy, which disorganizes organization through incongruity and ambiguity, requires some organization to disorganize.

Comedians, in short, view the world from the middle ground between structuralists and antistructuralists. Unlike antistructuralists, comedians assume that the world hangs together coherently and predictably. But unlike structuralists, comedians also assume that its coherence and predictability are neither rigid nor eternal. Therefore, those who possess a sense of humor must see the world as clearly organized, but also as capable of being temporarily disorganized, easily and safely. If either the extreme structuralist conception of a completely coherent and predictable world or the extreme antistructuralist conception of a wholly incoherent and unpredictable world were correct, no one would ever truly laugh.[4]

The humorist, then, is a humanist—sustaining a precariously balanced worldview between pairs of extreme philosophical positions that give precedence to extrahuman structures and processes. Unlike these nonhumanistic structuralist and antistructuralist schools, which either take for granted or disbelieve in the current organization of the world, comedy denies its necessity while affirming its presence. Like the humanistic constructionist schools (Marxism, Simmelianism, symbolic interactionism, and dramaturgical sociology), comedy assumes that *human beings construct* their organizations of the world, though henceforth experience its *structure* as preexisting naturally. Unlike even these constructionist schools, however, comedy focuses not on how the world is constructed but on how it can be *deconstructed*.[5]

Comedy deconstructs these humanly constructed organizations back to their elements through negation. It discovers the elements from which a system has been constructed by positing a second (alternative) system that differs from the first (original) system by only one element.

If the implied comparison between these two systems results in laugh-ter, the *novel element* of the second (alternative) system stands out as incongruous with its other elements—revealing the *traditional element* of the first (original) system it replaced to be congruous with its other elements, and therefore necessary to that system.

But one person's incongruity is another person's insight. Laughter also implies that the entire first (original) system itself is arbitrary, for around the incongruous novel element excluded by the first (original) system could be created a third (comic) system in which that novel element would be congruous. Thus comedy can pivot us away from our enervating familiar world into an energizing strange *parallel uni-verse* in which elements incongruous to our original universe are con-gruous (like the "toontown" segment of the 1990 film *Who Framed Roger Rabbit*).

Comedy's political implications, consequently, are paradoxical, for it makes both conservative statements—"A system's traditional ele-ments are *necessary* to this system"—and radical statements—"The traditional system as a whole is *arbitrary*"—simultaneously.

Since people have organized the elements of their world into sepa-rate (though interacting) *gestalts*, comedians take apart each of its *sys-tems:* cultural (linguistic, logical, and anthropological) and social (typi-cal and ideal). But people must organize these systems continually because their previous organizations continually break down.

Social systems, in particular, are less able to maintain their elements in place than all other major gestalts (except linguistic). Characteristics occasionally leak between sharply defined collectivities, roles, or insti-tutions—blurring their boundaries. By speeding up this slow natural diffusion of features with intentional and forceful transpositions, com-edy implies that social units can gain or lose properties even more readily than they do. Thus comedy, like sociology, undermines the ap-parent solidity of the social world by disclosing and accentuating its fluidity (Berger 1963; Zijderveld 1968:287).

By suddenly dismantling our social systems—seemingly so perva-sive, massive, and immutable—comedy, like sociology, reminds us that they are not given but created by ourselves. After organizing elements into the larger systems of our social world, we forget we have done so. Jokes jolt us into remembering (at least momentarily) that we are responsible for their organizations—and, consequently, can change them.

In *modern* society, the migration of qualities between collectivities, roles, or institutions has greatly accelerated. Consequently, comics who willfully violate their integrity by smuggling exogenous traits across their borders are even more in step with this modern movement than sociologists. By accentuating its current drift, modern comedy reveals a rapidly changing society whose components have lost their previous distinctness. For instance, the declining correlation between a collectivity and its traditional traits (such as race and education) or roles (such as gender and occupation) has increasingly confused the conventional image of our society, which comics repeatedly point out.

More precisely, comics are the spokespersons for the highest virtue of *postmodernism*—ambiguity—which helps account for their recent surge in popularity. As the first postmodern hero, the stand-up comic reconciles the contradictions of the age symbolically through ambiguity. (While out of their spotlight, in the darkness at the back of the auditorium, notebook in hand, sits the comic theorist, faithful— though wistfully—to the credo of passé modernism: "where ambiguity is, let clarity be.")

For humanists, humorists can be peculiarly self-destructive. Comedy can suddenly shift from taking apart larger social units to reducing even the supposedly irreducible self of the individual—the terminus of most humanisms—into its components. And not merely the selves of others. Renaissance comedies, particularly their fools, were supposed to *mirror* their audience (Levin 1987:22, 24, 54), to insinuate: "So's yourself! The comically decomposed selves you have seen on stage—incompetent, inauthentic, incompatible—are the same as yours." Those who can accept the fact that larger social units, or even the selves of others, have been socially constructed are usually disconcerted to discover that their own self has also been socially constructed—and not very coherently at that.

Yet if the lowest form of humor points out how arbitrary and tenuous our linguistic system is—which everyone already knows—the highest form of humor points out how arbitrary and tenuous our own self system is—which everyone tries to ignore. For those who possess a sense of humor differ from those who don't by their willingness to tolerate a disunified identity for the benefit it bestows: more insight into the world from the multiple interpretations of its multiple perspectives.

Humor theorists who started from various viewpoints—practice like Steve Allen (1987:14), linguistics like Victor Raskin (1985:115), psychology like Jerry Suls (1972:84–85)—have converged to describe the dual interpretations that characterize humor: one for the system and another for a second system—irreconcilable with the first when connected by an incongruity ("unresolved incongruity humor"), super-seding the first when connected by an ambiguity ("resolved incongru-ity humor"). Despite social and psychological pressures to simplify, the humorist possesses the ability to *sustain* multiple, even contradictory, interpretations of phenomena[6]—unlike the ideologist who accepts one and rejects the others or the nihilist who rejects them all. Just as the binocular and binaural senses of sight and hearing allow *perception* of the world in stereo, the bisociative sense of humor allows *conception* of it in 3-D. And being able to conceive of a multidimensional objective world in turn makes for a more substantial subject. Since contemplat-ing the implications of each side in a multiple interpretation expands the psyche, the humorist develops more *breadth* of character than the one-eyed ideologist or the sightless cynic. Since withstanding the psy-chic reverberations from accepting all sides in a multiple interpretation requires "psychic distance," the humorist develops more *depth* of char-acter as well.

If sociologists initially articulated the ordinary person's inchoate conceptions of social phenomena into collectivities, roles, and institu-tions, they now need to take into account humorists' denial of the very social units they established. A *comically informed social theory*, then, would be the "negative synthesis" of all current social theory: derived from all the social negations comics can devise.

But it would be more than merely the opposite of current social theory. True, the social incongruities revealed by humorists stand out against the background of the social congruities of the "serious" world revealed by sociologists. But just as social norms articulate comic devi-ance, comic deviance articulates social norms—which comedians have perceived as long ago as Molière: "To recognize the ridiculous we must know the reasonable whose lack it shows" (1964a:144, 147). By annihi-lating social phenomena, comedy proves their (original) existence; by provoking laughter at deviations from standard social actors and ac-tions, comedy proves the (heuristic) value of the sociological worldview that formalizes them. In short, sociologists can acquire a more sophisticated view of the social world *indirectly* by studying the social discontinuities humorists disclose than *directly* by studying so-cial continuities themselves.

In the introduction I quoted Peter Berger (1963:165), who asserted (in effect) that a sociologist without a sense of humor will never be able to understand the workings of the world. We can now understand why: humor separates the joints of the seemingly seamless social structure, making them visible. Sociologists can use the way humor deconstructs the social world to comprehend more precisely how people have constructed it.

Moreover, this *humorizing sociology* I propose would differ from both sociology's accepting positivist and critical constructionist schools by bringing out the amusing absurdities and deficiencies of *both* the status quo *and* its alternatives. Its rhetorical goal would be to undermine the self-righteousness which increasingly blinds the proponents of *any* social system to its flaws. Its political goal would be to destabilize *all* social systems enough to prevent their flaws from ossifying, maintaining their potential for beneficial change.

And of course the time may come when this humorizing sociology—grown old and orthodox—must be directed, reflexively, at itself.

Introduction

1. Although *humor* is the broadest term for what causes laughter, it has so wimpish a sound that stylistic reasons frequently moved me to substitute more vigorous, if less encompassing, synonyms: "comedy," "comic," "joke," "wit," "ridiculous," "ludicrous," "laughable," "amusement," and "what's funny." There are dozens of partial synonyms for humorous phenomena—see the lists in Keith-Spiegel (1972:14) and Koller (1988:5) and of course *Roget's Thesaurus*— roughly grouped into nouns and adjectives for people (for example, jokers) or objects (jokes) that produce amusement or verbs and adverbs for the acts of amusing others (joking) or expressing amusement (jokingly). I don't distinguish these synonyms, as for instance the philosopher John Morreall (1987:5) does, for several reasons: they overlap; few remember a theorist's distinctions between various kinds of humor: "Comedy is so rich and various that it is trivial to classify it descriptively as Aristotle, Freud, and Bergson do. The point is to probe its depths, not to chop it into portions. We remember Freud's theory of wit as the dispelling of hostility by cathexis, not his classes of jest, displacement, substitution; Bergson's theory of comedy as machine, not his 'comedy of forms,' or 'comedy of movements'" (Albert Cook [1964:475]); and all of them are merely aspects of the larger comic complex that is my topic. I distinguish them only when necessary to articulate the various edges of this totality. (Although I consider the entire realm of humor to be my topic, I have had to omit some of its forms—especially its longer or visual ones—that were too extensive or expensive to present in this book.)

2. The Greek philosophers also inhibited future humor research by attributing ignoble motives to the comic subject. Professors Harry Levin (1987:50) and John Morreall (1987:3) find the seeds of "superiority theory" in the way both

Plato (1961:1129–31) and Aristotle (1984:2318–19) discuss humor: comic subjects (comedians and their audience) produce or consume comedy to feel superior to comic objects. Because the scorn or malice inherent in such feelings of superiority stems from the "base" part of human nature, many later philosophers have disdained to study any human activity derived from these "lower" motives—like comedy.

3. Following the shift in focus from laughter's objects to its subjects at the beginning of the nineteenth century, major thinkers began to note laughter's potential for self-revelation:

> Goethe: There is nothing in which people more betray their character than in what they laugh at.
> Schopenhauer: Persons whose laughter is always affected and forced are intellectually and morally of little worth, just as generally the way of laughing and ... the occasion of it are very characteristic of the person.
> Emerson: A human being should beware how he laughs, for then he shows all his faults.
> Dostoyevsky: One can know a man from his laugh, and if you like a man's laugh before you know anything about him, you may confidently say that he is a good man.

4. Kronenberger's and Hertzler's unacknowledged source for seeing humor as symptomatic of a society is that European traveler and protosociologist of culture, Madame de Staël, who observed in 1800: "One can discern different kinds of joking in the literature of all countries, and nothing better serves to reveal the customs of a nation than the character of the mirth generally adopted by its writers. Alone, one is serious; one is merry for others—above all in one's writing. And laughter can be produced only by notions that are so familiar to those hearing them that they strike them instantly and do not require their careful attention" (1964:182).

5. "None yet have satisfactorily expressed what laughter is, though many have tried it" (Quintilian, quoted in Eastman 1921:132); "Now . . . the essential nature of laughter, the way it is occasioned, where it is seated, and how it comes into being, and bursts out so unexpectedly that, strive as we may we cannot restrain it, and how at the same instant it takes possession of the lungs, voice, pulse, countenance and eyes—all this I leave to Democritus: for . . . I should still not be ashamed to show ignorance of something which even its professed expositors do not understand" (Cicero 1942:373).

6. Presumably, the opposite of the humor agnostic would be the much rarer "humor gnostic." No one epitomizes their outlandishly brazen certainty better than Schopenhauer: "In volume one I regarded it as superfluous to illustrate [my] theory by examples. . . . However, to come to the aid of the mental inertness of those readers who always prefer to remain in a passive state, I will meet their wishes here. . . . so that there will be no question that here, after so many fruitless attempts, the true theory of the ludicrous is given, and the problem propounded but given up by Cicero definitely solved" (1969; 2:92).

7. From Aristotle until recently, critics believed aesthetic and intellectual forms should be appropriate to their content. In 1750, for instance, Francis

Hutcheson noted the prevailing view that humor should not be discussed non-humorously: "To treat this subject of laughter gravely may subject the author to a censure . . . because [he] wrote in a manner very unsuitable to the subject" (Morreall 1987:35). The ideal compatibility between form and content has also hindered attempts to treat "lower status" contents, like humor, with "higher status" forms, like science.

8. This is not to say that the history of humor theories is unimportant, but that it tells us less about humor than about theorists and their time. The aspect of humor that interests a theorist usually reflects contemporary concerns. Thus the concern with self-knowledge and social control in classical Greece influenced Plato to specify the objects of laughter as those "self-ignorant" of their limitations; the concern with personal salvation in early Protestantism influenced Hobbes to specify the subjects of laughter as those who feel "sudden glory" relative to others; the concern with subjectivity in the late Enlightenment influenced Kant to describe the subjective experience of laughter as the sudden annihilation of a "strained expectation." Even twentieth-century discussions of humor have followed the more rapid shift in larger relevances: in the early years, industrialization's increasing controls over social behavior led Bergson to find humor in human beings who behaved "mechanically," while lingering Victorian controls over moral behavior led Freud to focus on how humor circumvented "psychic censorship"; in the middle years, ideological conflict led Arthur Koestler to derive humor from the collision of conflicting "frames of reference"; and in the later years, the rise of both the quantitative sciences and the threat of nuclear war led John Allen Paulos to describe the structure of jokes in terms of mathematical logic's newly developed "catastrophe" concepts.

9. Marvin Koller (1988:33) reprints a chart by Richard Alford that lists the number of humor studies (a total of 1119) by discipline from approximately 1900 to 1980. Psychology produced more studies of humor (578) than sociology (75), anthropology (90), philosophy (19), and "other" (357) combined. The number of humor studies in all disciplines (with some minor exceptions) has increased in part because researchers throughout the academy have proliferated.

10. But research on the sociology of humor has still had little effect on sociology as a whole. Even Gary Alan Fine (1983:159–60), who denied that sociological studies of humor were rare, conceded that most of them did not appear in the major sociology journals. Nor has any "Introduction to Sociology" textbook taken much notice of the topic (unlike gender or ethnomethodological studies, to cite some recent inclusions in their canon). The sociology of humor has been ignored, I believe, because it has merely analyzed comic phenomena in terms of standard sociological concepts rather than using comedy to generate new theories of culture and society, which I will try to do here.

11. Note that my approach to humor would be the opposite of Karl Popper's. He believes science should proceed by looking for what is wrong with a theory; I believe it should proceed by looking for what is right with it. His small-minded conception of science seems to stem from assuming that human

existence is finite, so only one truth about it can be correct; my more expansive conception of science stems from assuming that human existence is fecund, so many truths about it can be correct. Since I believe it is more important to generate these multiple verities than to criticize them, I intend to show the kernels of truth in humor theories that are inadequate on the whole. In this way, no insight into human life, however small, need be lost.

12. I will be merely organizing already accepted ideas and propositions about humor, or more generally merely locating (in an architectonic) traditional schools of humor previously thought to be competitive. Thus I will be using the same method as Freud: "The criteria and characteristics of jokes brought up by these authors . . . seems to us at first sight so very much to the point and so easily confirmed by instances that we cannot be in any danger of underrating such views. But they are *disjecta membra*, which we should like to see combined into an organic whole. When all is said and done, they contribute to our knowledge of jokes no more than would a series of anecdotes to the description of some personality of whom we have a right to ask for a biography. We are entirely without insight into the connection that presumably exists between the separate determinants" (1963:14). I too will be connecting the isolated insights of others, though examining different others and finding different connections. I hope no critic will accuse me of originality for the particular insights into humor presented in these pages, though I will protest less the same accusation about their connections.

13. This schema of humor theories was first adumbrated by Sully (1902), who distinguished *incongruity* and *superiority* theories, augmented by Monro (1963:83), who added *release from restraint* and *ambivalence* theories, and elaborated by Keith-Spiegel (1972), who further distinguished *biological, surprise, configurational,* and *psychoanalytic* theories. I will collapse Keith-Spiegel's complex classification back into a tripartite division by subordinating ambivalence, surprise, and configurational theories under incongruity theories; psychoanalytic theory under release from restraint (tension relief) theories; and biological theories under superiority theories.

Introduction to Part One

1. Keith-Spiegel (1972:8) notes some pre-Kantian precursors of the incongruity theory of humor. So does Morreall (1987:130), who mentions Aristotle and quotes Pascal: "Nothing produces laughter more than a surprising disproportion between that which one expects and that which one sees."

2. The conception of comedy elaborated here also holds in a purely subjectivist scheme in which neither system nor incongruity exist in the world, but only in the mind. In this purely subjectivist scheme, the comic contradiction is not between the subjective expectation system and the objective real system, but between two sides of the subjective expectation system: not between what we *expect* to be going on in the objective world and what is *really* going on there, but between what we *expect* to be going on in the objective world and what we *believe* is really going on there.

3. Joyce Hertzler lists the various synonyms for "incongruity" that have appeared in the literature on humor: "Human beings tend to respond with laughter when they are confronted with the incongruous, the contradictory, the inharmonious, the unfitting, the inappropriate, the imperfect or crude; the accidental, the disorderly, or unusual; the unexpected, unaccustomed, or unconventional; the startling, the mischievous, the awkward; the ironical, the ludicrous, the ridiculous, or absurd; the pretentious, inflated, humbug, or masquerading; the eccentric or queer; the clever and exceptional; the exaggerated, the miscarried, or misshaped; the logically incoherent or implausible; the irrational, the nonsensical, the stupid, or idiotic; the monstrous, the indecent, the deformed, the deviate, the grotesque" (1970:13–14). I will explore the nuances that distinguish some of these terms in the text.

4. This statement needs two qualifications. First, not every incongruity is funny. Incongruities that collapse expectation systems cause laughter *only under the extrasystem conditions* I hope to specify elsewhere. Second, some congruities are funny, especially hypercongruities. Summarizing previous humor theorists, Joyce Hertzler concludes that "much laughter is a response to some breach of the usual or regular or expected order of events," but he goes on to note that "we also laugh occasionally because of the surprise or satisfaction afforded, not by the unexpected but rather by the expected, as when some person suspected of cockiness or stupidity does perform in a cocky or stupid manner" (1970:13–14). Freud explained the laughter that results from this "rediscovery of what is familiar" in terms of the "economy of psychic expenditure" it creates (1960:120–21). But if we laugh whenever something confirms rather than denies our expectation, our psychic savings account would grow so large that we would be laughing almost all the time. A better explanation is that we sometimes expect human variability but encounter inhuman invariance instead.

5. We should not forget D. H. Monro's *Argument of Laughter,* the first modern synthesis of the history of humor theories (written mostly during World War II—a not irrelevant circumstance). Before Koestler, Monro described the production of humor by the intersection of systems or frames, which he called "universes":

> In discussing the stories of Kimmins' schoolchildren, we have seen that they often depend on the intrusion into one sphere of an incident or attitude of mind which is appropriate only to an utterly different sphere. The Indian rajah spreads his costly silks before the king with all the courtly ceremony that accompanies Oriental gifts. And the king, instead of responding with similar courtliness, is represented as exclaiming: "Ow much for the lot?" . . .
> But the story of the rajah does not depend merely on contrast. There is here the mental shock of being jolted out of a whole frame of mind, a whole universe of discourse, with all sorts of rich associations, all sorts of stock responses leaping to the forefront of consciousness. . . . We put kings in one mental compartment, and costers [cart sellers of fruits or vegetables] in another. We surround each of them with different associations, and we respond to each with a particular attitude. . . .
> The point is merely that a particular atmosphere has been built up, an atmo-

sphere that does depend largely on stock responses. And this atmosphere is suddenly destroyed by a single inappropriate remark. It is this which gives the sensation of being suddenly hurled from one universe into another. . . .

Universe-changing is a very important element in humour; we may even find it is the key to all humour. [1951:45–46; see also 62–67]

6. Cameron also notes that some jokes emphasize the reality of the new frame by deemphasizing the reality of the old frame: "The shift of frame of reference in which what we thought was true is suddenly shown to be false is a basic element in jokes, at least in our culture. Many jokes end on a tag line in which one of the characters says to the other, 'Oh, thank Heaven, I thought you said. . . .' . . . An example is the man who hears a speaker predict the end of the world and says in fright: 'When did you say?' 'One hundred million years.' 'Oh, thank heaven, I thought you said a million!' . . . We have many jokes about deafness, in which the deficiency confuses frames of reference" (Cameron 1963:89).

7. Raskin also gives a more technical formulation of his theory: "The *Main Hypothesis* on which this approach is based can be formulated as: *A text can be characterized as a single-joke-carrying text if both of the [following] conditions are satisfied: (1) The text is compatible, fully or in part, with two different scripts [and] (2) The two scripts with which the text is compatible are opposite. . . . The two scripts with which some text is compatible* are said to *overlap fully or in part on this text*" (1985:99).

8. It is surprising that Raskin, at least in his main work (1985), does not acknowledge the influence of Koestler. Some contributors to Raskin's journal *Humor*, however, have pointed out the connection. Salvatore Attardo (1988:358ff.) finds commonalities between European humor research derived from Koestler's "bisociation" theory and Raskin's semantic "script overlap" theory. Neal Norrick (1989:119) compares Raskin's "opposition between semantic scripts" with Koestler's "bisociation" and with his own "schema conflict." The Workshop on Humor and Cognition, held at Indiana University in February 1989 and synopsized in *Humor* (1989:417–40), also compares Raskin's semantic "script opposition" theory of humor with Douglas Hofstadter's cognitive psychological "frame blend" theory.

9. Hazlitt criticized Locke's definition of wit for being too broad because other mental functions that reveal unexpected similarities are not funny: "On this definition Harris . . . has very well observed that the demonstrating the equality of the three angles of a right-angled triangle to two right ones, would, upon the principle here stated, be a piece of wit instead of an act of the judgment, or understanding, and Euclid's *Elements* a collection of epigrams" (1930; 6:19).

10. Humor theorists have often described wit's ability to find similarities between apparently opposing frames in terms of those paradigms of the union of opposites—sex: "Wit, you know, is the expected copulation of ideas, the discovery of some occult relation between images in appearance remote from each other" (Johnson 1969:251); and marriage: "A favorite definition of joking has long been the ability to find similarity between dissimilar things—that is,

hidden similarities. Jean Paul [Richter] has expressed this thought itself in a joking form: 'Joking is the disguised priest who weds every couple.' Vischer carries this further: 'He likes to wed couples whose union their relatives frown upon'" (Freud 1963:11).

11. Although humor increases as the comic begins to sustain a comparison between seemingly different realms, beyond a certain point the humor changes to absurdity as the comparison becomes more farfetched (see Davis 1971). For instance, a comic may point out that advocacy groups have shifted from "human rights" to "animal rights," and then proceed to reduce their views to amusing absurdity by imagining them shifting still further to "fish rights," "insect rights," and even "vegetable rights."

12. Thus comics can amuse their audience merely by pointing out that ordinary things do not make sense (that is, cannot be located in any coherent system):

> "In a nutshell, I would say that I spot absurdities," [Jim Samuels] said after [winning the 1982 San Francisco Comedy Competition]. "The world makes no sense, and we don't have to take it."
>
> He would joke about Jack in the Box serving croissants ("Whenever I'm in the mood for French food, I head for Le Box") and describe his cure for San Francisco's parking problems ("Drive a forklift"). [obituary for San Francisco comedian Jim Samuels]

Of course, not everything that does not make sense is amusing. Few find funny such extraordinary existential absurdities as a comic's premature death: Samuels died of AIDS at age 41.

13. The main psychological tradition of humor research—see Deckers and Buttram (1990) and McGhee, Ruch, and Hehl (1990) for references—has distinguished an "incongruity" model of humor from an "incongruity-resolution" model of humor, which parallels my own distinction between an "annihilated single system" model of humor that centers on "incongruity," and the "transposed double system" model of humor that centers on "ambiguity." The psychological models of humor focus on its audience's cognitive equilibrium whereas my system models of humor focus on the abstract properties of systems that create it. This psychological tradition of humor research (see especially McGhee 1990) has expended much effort to confirm that most people find "incongruity-resolution" humor funnier than pure "incongruity" (nonsense) humor, and that appreciation for "incongruity" humor decreases with age whereas appreciation for "incongruity-resolution" humor increases with age.

14. Burke derives this concept from the writings of Nietzsche and his followers, which accounts in part for their witty style:

> These are historical perspectives, which Spengler acquires by taking a word usually applied to one setting and transferring its use to another setting. It is a "perspective by incongruity," since he established it by violating the "properties" of the work in its previous linkages. The device as used by Spengler is, in a blunter way, precisely the same as it is used in Nietzsche. . . . Nietzsche establishes his perspectives by a constant juxtaposition of incongruous words,

attaching to some name a qualifying epithet which had heretofore gone with a different order of names. He writes by the same constant reordering of categories that we find in the Shakespearean metaphor. . . . Nietzsche knew that probably every linkage was open to destruction by the perspectives of a planned incongruity. Throughout his life he "undermined," carefully qualifying his nouns by the juxtaposition of modifying matter that had the "wrong" moral inclination. The humorists, the satirists, the writers of the grotesque, all contributed to this work with varying degrees of systematization, giving us new insights by such deliberate misfits. [1965:90–91]

His "perspective by incongruity" is especially appropriate for describing linguistic oxymorons like Veblen's term *trained incapacity:* "Our notions of what goes with training naturally suggest capacity rather than incapacity" (91). Rather unsystematically, Burke lists seven ways to apply his perspective by incongruity, which (I will add) humorists also employ: (1) see the large in the small, (2) see the small in the large, (3) see the good in the bad and vice versa, (4) omit the background knowledge customarily used to interpret a phenomenon, (5) adopt a false premise, (6) apply the jargon of one field to another, (7) see what is usually distant from close and what is usually close *sub specie aeternitatis* (119–24).

15. Comics need not crack human creations deliberately. Sometimes they crack on their own:

There constantly exists, for a certain sort of person of high emotional content, at work creatively, the danger of coming to a point where something cracks within himself or within the paragraph under construction—cracks and turns into a snicker. Here, then, is the very nub of the conflict: the careful form of art, and the careless shape of life itself. What a man does with this uninvited snicker (which may closely resemble a sob, at that) decides his destiny. If he resists it, conceals it, destroys it, he may keep his architectural scheme intact and save his building, and the world will never know. If he gives in to it, he becomes a humorist, and the sharp brim of the fool's cap leaves a mark forever on his brow. [White 1941:xix]

16. For more detail, see the classic studies of the history of American humor by Constance Rourke (1953) and Walter Blair (1960).

17. Those who connect to a topic, such as a role, all such laughter-inducing incongruities, all its anti-essences, will have cataloged a complete set of the phenomenon's essential attributes, thus *exhausting its comic possibilities*. The long running TV sitcom "One Day at a Time" was ultimately canceled because its writers complained they had "exhausted the comic possibilities of the single mother's role," the incongruous situations in which to put her. The later TV sitcom "Kate and Allie" added a new set of comic possibilities to this role by pairing *two* single mothers.

18. Since these larger orders threatened by humor are arguably only in the mind, humor theorists can contribute to the "science of the subjective," an intellectual tradition running from Kant to Goffman. This science has tried to determine our subjective views of the natural (Kant) and social (Goffman) worlds—the external boundaries and internal organization of these mental phenomena—by observing what happens when they are contradicted.

19. The Workshop on Humor and Cognition (1989) developed a similar dis-

tinction. In this important workshop, Douglas Hofstadter developed the notion of "ur-jokes":

> The idea . . . of an abstract skeleton shared by many different jokes, was the next major topic that Hofstadter addressed. He pointed out that in humor there are certain recurrent themes, or joke skeletons, upon which many jokes are built, much as in mathematics, certain abstract structures crop up over and over in the proofs of theorems. He terms such a skeleton as an *ur-joke*. . . .
> To exemplify the ur-joke notion, Hofstadter chose the theme of *role reversal*, in which there is a switching of normal or default roles or concepts. . . . Here is a typical joke based on the "role reversal" ur-joke:
> *Question:* What did Mickey Mouse get for Christmas?
> *Answer:* A Dan Quayle watch. [430–31]

20. This organization of the systems disintegrated by comedy synthesizes those adumbrated by critic William Hazlitt (1930; 6:7–8), psychologist Harvey Mindess (1971:21–23), and sociologist Anton Zijderveld (1968:299ff.).

Chapter One

1. I will draw much of my material from Walter Redfern's provocative book *Puns* (1986), a compendious but chaotic collection of humanistic conceptions of linguistic humor. Redfern's own conception of linguistic humor is deliberately ambiguous; since mine isn't, I will deliberately disambiguate his. For the more scientific literature on linguistic humor, see Hertzler (1970:175–88), who summarizes the older more comprehensive sociolinguistic studies, and Pepicello and Weisberg (1983: 59–83), who summarize the more recent and more technical psycholinguistic research. The journal *Humor* emphasizes current linguistic studies of humor.

2. After summarizing European humor research, Salvatore Attardo concludes that a more complete account of linguistic humor would include both the rules of serious texts and the *additional rules that make these texts humorous:* "The descriptive models of humor that have been briefly examined usually contain two components: a linguistic component which insures the processing of normal, 'serious' texts and a 'humor' component which provides additional rules that enable the model to process the 'peculiar' humorous texts" (Attardo 1988:359). But we need not give priority to serious texts. Beyond the basic rules for making a text comprehensible, if there are additional rules that make it humorous, there must also be alternative *additional rules that make it serious.*

3. More recently, anthropologist Edmund Leach made the same point more technically: "A familiar type of purely linguistic taboo is the pun. A pun occurs when we make a joke by confusing two apparently different meanings of the same phonemic pattern. The pun seems funny or shocking because it challenges a taboo which ordinarily forbids us to recognize that the sound pattern is ambiguous. In many cases, such verbal taboos have social as well as linguistic aspects" (quoted in Redfern 1986:91).

4. Groups who must deal with amalgamated languages are the most prone to word play—particularly the British who had to learn that linguistic melting pot called English, and the Jews who had to handle at least three languages: Yiddish, Hebrew, and their native language (Leo Rosten, *New York Times*, 31

May 1986, 10). Moreover, the Jews and the British are surprisingly connected through the study of Hebrew, for many of the Elizabethan English punners were Hebrew scholars: "The study of Hebrew . . . and the existence of English Bibles with alternatives in the margin, may have had some influence on the capacity of English for ambiguity: Donne, Herbert, Jonson and Crashaw, for instance, were Hebrew scholars. . . . Hebrew, having very unreliable tenses, extraordinary idioms and a strong taste for puns, possesses all the practical advantages of a thoroughly primitive disorder" (William Empson, quoted in Redfern 1986:50).

5. Occasionally someone creates more complex acoustical knots that tie together more than two disparate strings of thought. The uncommon triple pun connects three rather than two, such as the political, financial, and sexual strings in the following:

> News item: "Gary Hart's quitting the presidential race may cost his campaign as much as $800,000 in federal funds." Karyn Hunt: "I knew there'd be a penalty for early withdrawal."
>
> [Herb Caen]

And a bumper sticker I once saw even achieved the very rare quadruple pun: "Poles do it the *hard* way"—which could mean (1) with the most unyielding mental or physical force, (2) with the least efficient method, (3) with an erection, (4) anal sex.

6. Actually, the form of pun that ties together the meanings of a word most tightly connects two intensities of a single meaning (for example, of *like*):

> A woman consults an analyst. She explains tearfully, "My family thinks I'm crazy. And why? Because I like pancakes. Tell me, what's wrong with liking pancakes?" The analyst reassures her: "Of course there's nothing wrong with liking pancakes. I like them myself." "You do!" cries the delighted patient. "I'll give you some of mine—I have a whole bureau full of them!"

Verbal humorists frequently use the word *like* because it conveys ambiguous intensity not only in its meaning of "affection for" but also in its meaning of "similar to":

> One [audience member] tells [comedienne Judy Tenuta], "I have a girl at home just like you." To which Tenuta jabs, "Oh, my father couldn't have been that drunk!"
>
> [*San Jose Mercury News*, 20 July 1989, 3F]

Puns based on two different intensities of one meaning, however, are difficult to distinguish from puns based on two different meanings, which are far more common.

7. Raskin uses the term *lexicon* for this dictionary list of a word's meanings (1985:76ff.). Although his model is a little unclear at this point, his better-known concept of "script" seems to comprise both a lexicon and a set of "combinational rules" on the appropriate way to select meanings. We select meanings from the lexicons of several words appropriately if we can combine them consistently.

8. Sometimes there is even a public dispute about which meaning of a word is primary. A Berkeley graffito I saw recently read:

Fuck the Rich!

But someone had crossed it out and substituted:

That's elitist! Why should the rich get all the pleasure?
Fuck the Poor!

Sometimes, both meanings are publicly compared, as in the following graffito:

Alimony: The screwing you get for the screwing you got.

9. Languages that do not distinguish figurative from literal make humor harder:

On paper, it seemed like a superhuman sales achievement. Someone from the Laff Stop, a comedy nightclub here, sold out one show to the Dayle McIntosh Center for the Disabled, many of whom are deaf.
Stand-up comedy for the deaf? Unheard of. . . .
Jeannine Harris, standing stage right and mugging, gesturing, miming and posturing, translated every bit of shtick—red, white, and mostly blue—into American Sign Language for the deaf. . . .
Communication by sign language requires a great deal of acting, because the signs give only the literal meaning of the word, she said. The connotation—whether it is said clinically or vulgarly, sweetly or angrily—has to be shown with facial expressions and body language. . . .
The humor of the deaf, she said, is different from that of hearing persons. "We hearing people think so much in abstract terms. Theirs is a more concrete language. It's very hard to pun or use slang in sign language, almost impossible. They take the language very literally. So if you ask a deaf person where he's 'coming from,' he'll probably say something like 'New Jersey.'" [Los Angeles Times, 19 May 1978, part 2, 6]

10. "Most words might be said to have a *physical* and a *moral* meaning, according as they are interpreted literally or figuratively. Every word, indeed, begins by denoting a concrete object or a material action; but by degrees the meaning of the word is refined into an abstract relation or a pure idea. If then the above law holds good here, it should be stated as follows: '*A comic effect is obtained whenever we pretend to take literally an expression which was used figuratively*'; or, '*Once our attention is fixed on the material aspect of a metaphor the idea expressed becomes comic*'" (Bergson 1956:135).

11. Words that rhyme usually entail rhythms that correspond. But Ogden Nash gained fame by parodying conventional poetry with partial rhymes and mismatched meters that override conventional patterns of stress and pronunciation:

And that is why I admire a suave prevarication
because I prevaricate so awkwardly and gauchely,
And that is why I can never amount to anything
politically or socially. [quoted in Charney 1978:24]

12. "The first of Spooner's spoonerisms, and one of the few that have been authenticated, was spoken by the great man in 1879, when he was conducting a service at the College and announced the hymn as '*K*inkering *K*ongs Their Titles Take.' Other switches attributed to Spooner (most of them spuriously)

include: 'Three cheers for our *q*ueer old *d*ean!' (referring to Queen Victoria); 'Is it *k*istomary to *c*uss the bride?'; 'Stop *h*issing all my *m*ystery lectures'; . . . and 'The Lord is a *Sh*oving *L*eopard'" (Christopher 1987a:26).

13. If the metathesis of meaning turns sexual, spoonerisms turn into what Richard Christopher (1987a:27) calls "poonerisms," whose appreciative audience are adolescents:

> What's the difference between a magician and a chorus line? A magician has a cunning array of *sl*u*n*ls. . . .
> What's the difference between an epileptic oysterman and a whore with diarrhea? One *sh*ucks between *f*its. . . .

14. Technically, Robin Williams here relates the paraphone (paranym) *mental/menstrual* with the monophone (polyseme) *period piece,* whose primary meaning in this case is a "movie about a historical period" and whose secondary meaning is a "movie about menstruation." This form of wit, then, exhibits the ability to discover "secondary synonyms"—words whose secondary meanings are related, though it's cleverer if their primary meanings also are.

15. Raskin (1985:114–17)) calls the ambiguous word (or more complex forms of linguistic ambiguity) where this trope occurs a "semantic script-switch trigger" because it is the point where the pun or joke changes the script that interprets its meaning.

16. For the record, here is the entire St. Louis team roster:

Position	Player	Grammatical Function
First base:	Who	Interrogative pronoun
Second base:	What	Interrogative pronoun
Third base:	I-Don't-Know	Interrogative response
Shortstop:	I-Don't-Care	Interrogative response
Pitcher:	Tomorrow	Temporal adverb
Catcher:	Today	Temporal adverb
Center field:	Because	Conjunction
Left field:	Why	Interrogative adverb

17. Because the semantic ambiguities of humor reach Zen-like complexity, I am unable to analyze any more of them here. In their review of linguistic humor research, however, Pepicello and Weisberg (1983:69–72) note that T. R. Shultz and his coworkers have distinguished humor based on *surface-structure ambiguity* in which a different bracketing of words expresses a different semantic interpretation ("'I saw a man eating shark in the aquarium.' 'That's nothing I saw a man eating herring in the restaurant.'") from humor based on *deep-structure ambiguity* in which different deep structures, specifying two different sets of structural relation between the key words in the sentence, are mapped onto a single surface structure ("'Call me a cab.' 'You're a cab.'"). But Pepicello and Weisberg, who criticize this distinction, prefer to distinguish humor based on *phrase structure ambiguity* in which a given surface sequence of words has more than one syntactic analysis ("How is a duck like an icicle? Both grow down.") from humor based on *transformational ambiguity* in which two different underlying structures have an identical surface form ("What do you call a man

who marries another man? A minister."). A dispute between linguists is one in which I prefer not to get involved. Although semantic ambiguities may eventually be sorted out into a single system, their linguistic organization itself is currently too *ambiguous* for me to proceed further. I will say only that all semantic ambiguities cause what Bergson calls "the *reciprocal interference* of two sets of ideas in the same sentence" (1956:138).

18. Recent sociolinguistic research has found that only mutual interference between equals induces both to switch from transmission to reception more or less simultaneously; mutual interference between unequals (in class, gender, age, or institutional position) induces the higher status to maintain or even increase transmission power until the transmissions of the lower status are overwhelmed and fade out.

19. Elizabeth Pretorius (1990:259–76) observes that linguistics, which has traditionally studied language structurally up to the sentence level, has been unable to analyze the processual interchange of actual communication at the suprasentential level ("discourse"). Theater and movie comedians, like Monty Python (and of course the Marx Brothers), often generate humor by violating the specific norms and expectations of discourse, such as cooperation and politeness. To launch the linguistics of humor in this provocative new direction she points out the misplaced elements in this Monty Python exchange that generate its humor.

20. Humor writers have also composed other TV programs out of comic crossovers (A) between education and action shows:

Sesame Emergency—Gage and Desoto respond to (1) a garbage-can fire that leaves its furry inhabitant with third-degree burns and (2) the letter "T," its limbs crushed by a collapsing condemned building, is in danger of becoming an "I";

(B) between fantasy and children shows:

Twilight Romper Room—Children, reciting their "Do Bees" and "Don't Bees," are turned into syrup;

(C) between family and crime shows:

Father Knows the Untouchables—Betty cries over being stood up while Jim puts out a contract for the culprit;

(D) between sitcoms and detective shows:

Laverne and Quincy—It's a race against the clock as Quincy, trying to prove poisoning, discovers Laverne has accidentally used the body for meatloaf.
[Kip Gordy, *Los Angeles Times*, 21 Sept. 1980, 101]

21. Before cemeteries were standardized and death solemnified, puns frequently appeared on tombstones, especially in England and New England. The epitaph usually centered around the ambiguity of the deceased's *name:*

An eminent barrister, Sir John Strange, has this epitaph on his final resting place:
Here lies an honest lawyer . . .
and that is Strange.

On the tombstone of one Doctor Potter, Archbishop of Canterbury, A.D 1736, we find:

Alack and well-a day,
Potter, himself, has turned to clay!

Another curious tombstone is to be found in Bath Abbey. It reads:
Here lies Ann Mann:
She lived an old maid, and died an old Mann;

or the deceased's *occupation:*

And there is a tribute to a lady named Oldfield, who was an actress in her day:
This we must own, in justice to her shade,
'Tis the first bad exit Oldfield ever made.

There lived a Music Master, whose name was Stephen. When he died, someone
put these words on his stone:
Stephen and Time are now both even;
Stephen beat time, but now Time's beat Stephen.
[collected or repoted by Larry Schieber, *San Francisco Chronicle,*
"Sunday Punch," 25 Nov. 1990, 6]

Perhaps epitaphs were frequently puns because of their economical form: their ability to say several things at once in a small space, to sum up an entire life in a brief sentence.

22. "In [puns], a familiar word acquires increased meaning. Instead of being confined to its usual connotations, it is made to suggest two different things at the same time. . . . Why is this amusing? Unbeknownst to our conscious judgement, it seems, we experience our language as a restrictive mode of expression. The trick of saying a new thought with old words, or a double thought with a single word, affords us a sense of mental expansion, for adherence to correct verbal usage inhibits the natural play of our minds. . . . A grammatically correct phrase makes one point at a time; it does not say several unrelated things simultaneously. But we experience unrelated things simultaneously" (Mindess 1971:86). Mindess, however, notes that wordplay is only mildly amusing because word controls are only mildly constricting: "If this is really the case, why are puns such a weak form of humor? . . . Plays on words are rarely very funny, because the restrictions imposed by words are rarely very frustrating. While it is true, as we have seen, that some mental operations cannot be expressed by following the rules of ordinary language, most of us suffer only minor inconvenience as a consequence" (1971:88).

23. If "concentration" is to focus on only one meaning, then to see many meanings must be a "distraction." "When we are concentrating we shut out all potential other meanings, but . . . when we relax, in dream or if illness upsets our normal control, puns come into their own" (Frédéric Paulhan, summarized in Redfern 1986:12). Redfern concludes this line of thought: "Do puns distract, or concentrate, the attention? No doubt the worst do the former, and the best do both" (1986:24).

24. At about the same time, Freud seemed to distinguish "good" from "bad" jokes according to whether their connections between incongruous circles of ideas were more than verbal: "If, by means of a word with two mean-

ings or a word that is only slightly modified, I take a short cut from one circle
of ideas to another, and if there is not at the same time a link between those
circles of ideas which has a significant sense, then I shall have made a 'bad'
joke. In a bad joke like this the only existing link between the two disparate
ideas is the one word—the 'point' of the joke. . . . A 'good' joke, on the other
hand, comes about when . . . the similarity between the words is shown to be
really accompanied by another, important similarity in their sense" (1963:120–
21n.). Yet, in some of his most obscure writing, Freud does not completely
characterize merely verbal jokes as bad or conceptual jokes as good, for he
continues, "we find that the 'bad' jokes are by no means bad as jokes—that is,
unsuitable for producing pleasure" (1963:121n.). He proceeds to distinguish
verbal and conceptual jokes not according to their badness or goodness but
according to their sources of pleasure: verbal jokes provide the pleasure of
"psychic relief" from our intellectual upbringing in general whereas conceptual jokes provide the pleasure of "psychic economizing" by protecting the
verbal pleasure of "psychic relief" from criticism and by lifting specific inhibi-
tions (1963:127–28, 138n.). One would think he would conclude that conceptual
jokes are "better" or "funnier" than verbal jokes because they include more
sources of pleasure, but I could find no actual statement to this effect.

Chapter Two

1. Some humor research in Europe, especially by the Hungarian Ivan Fò-
nagy (Attardo 1988:356–57), and in America, especially by John Allen Paulos
(1980), has recently begun to explore the types of logical contradictions found
in humor.

2. People employ the term *bullshit* literally for the excrement of male cows
far less frequently than figuratively for statements by a close friend or distant
political figure that seem to make sense (at least to the speaker) but in fact
don't (at least to them). Most people who use this term today are unaware that
their predecessors have called faulty logic "bull" since at least the seventeenth century.

The *Oxford English Dictionary* defines *bull* in this sense as "a self-
contradictory proposition; in modern use, an expression containing a manifest
contradiction in terms or involving a ludicrous inconsistency unperceived by
the speaker." In related senses *bull* means "bubble" and "ludicrous jest." Unable to specify its exact origin, the *OED* traces the term back to Old French
(*boul:* "fraud, deceit, trickery") and middle English (*bul:* "falsehood"). Along
the way, the *OED* dismisses theories that the term originated in "a contemptuous allusion to papal edicts," the repeated blunders of the London lawyer
Obadiah Bull, or Irish bombast. Today, *shit* is often appended to *bull* by those
who wish to call attention to the conceptual chaos such false logic could create
(see Douglas 1970).

In 1803 the Reverend Sydney Smith gave *bull* its best known definition: the
sudden discovery that apparently congruous ideas are really incongruous;
which he contrasted to *wit:* the sudden discovery that apparently incongruous
ideas are really congruous. A "bull is an apparent congruity and real incongru-

ity of ideas suddenly discovered. . . . [It is] the very reverse of wit; for as wit discovers real relations that are not apparent, bulls admit apparent relations that are not real. The pleasure arising from wit proceeds from our surprise at suddenly discovering two things to be similar in which we suspected no similarity. The pleasure arising from bulls proceeds from our discovering two things to be dissimilar in which a resemblance might have been suspected" (Smith 1869:76; see also Martin 1974:20 for problems with Smith's contrast, and Redfern 1986:121 for a more appreciative view of *bull*).

3. The logic is not only "feminine," of course, but can refer to the alleged mode of thinking of any disparaged group, for example, "Negro logic," "Jewish logic," "Polish logic." Imputing a different logic to an outgroup is one means to maintain ingroup boundaries. For who could take seriously those whose very mode of thinking is different from our own?

4. It is curious that the medical establishment hasn't diagnosed this aspect of the comic mind, which disadvantages its possessor in bureaucratic settings, as a mental disease. They could easily claim that those afflicted with the compulsion to reverse everything suffer from the cognitive problem of "dyslogia," by analogy with the syntactic and semantic problem of "dyslexia": "I'm sorry to have to tell you this, but your son has been diagnosed as a 'dyslogic.' We suspected it when he became the class clown, and now our cognition tests have confirmed it. Luckily, his 'humor problem' is not so severe that it can't be treated and controlled."

5. Molière (in an anonymous letter attributed to him) defended his play *Tartuffe* from charges of immorality by claiming to have designed it to educate the innocent about the unintended consequences of improper means:

> We judge ridiculous what altogether lacks good sense. Now, when certain means produce an end different from that for which they are employed, we suppose, with good cause, that one chose them with little good sense. . . . Thus, because we see that Panulphe [Tartuffe] does not persuade his lady, we conclude that the means of which he avails himself are in great discrepancy with his ends, and that consequently he is ridiculous in using them. . . . Panulphe's arguments—which are the contrivance he employs to achieve his goal—were stamped as ridiculous in the mind of whoever has seen that play . . . ; naturally, any woman against whom one would like to use them after that would render them vain. [Molière, 1964a:147, 149]

6. Most recently, the mathematician John Allen Paulos (1980:75–99) has described descending incongruities in the terms and graphs of "catastrophe theory." He diagrams the ways an anxiety-provoking reference (sex, authority, etc.) at the beginning of a joke elevates a person's physiological excitation—which suddenly shifts from a high to a low level when the punch line at the end of the joke releases the built-up nervous energy as laughter.

7. In keeping with his own theory of humor, however, Bergson claims that we laugh at these cause-effect examples not because of their disproportion or degradation but because their transpositions are *mechanical* (1956:116, 141).

8. To avoid digressing into an extended discussion of the differences between the conventional and the truly rational views of a topic, here I will sim-

ply define conventional views as "folk rationality." Though logic professors might disagree, most people regard their own view of a topic as rational. (Even when they don't, they must at least know what the folk-rational view of the topic is to willfully chose to ignore it in favor of their subjective opinion.)

9. Since the least alterable processes are natural, comic exaggerators may even claim that someone or something is inordinate enough to alter nature; for instance, by bending physical laws:

> And he's pretty clumsy. I once saw him spill Vaseline.
>
> [Red Buttons]

or by reversing biological behavior:

> One of the best jokes ever written was Fred Allen's line about a scarecrow that was so scary that the crows not only stopped stealing corn, they brought back corn they had stolen two years earlier.
>
> [Steve Allen 1987:36]

10. Hazlitt contrasts this minimizing understated kind of humor, which he calls "wit," with maximizing overstatement, which he calls "poetry":

> Wit, as distinguished from poetry, is the imagination or fancy inverted, and so applied to given objects, as to make the little look less, the mean more light and worthless; or to divert our admiration or wean our affections from that which is lofty and impressive, instead of producing a more intense admiration and exalted passion, as poetry does. . . . The favorite employment of wit is to add littleness to littleness, and heap contempt on insignificance by all the arts of petty and incessant warfare; or if it ever affects to aggrandize, and use the language of hyperbole, it is only to betray into derision by a fatal comparison, as in the mock-heroic; or if it treats of serious passion, it must do it so as to lower the tone of intense and high-wrought sentiment, by the introduction of burlesque and familiar circumstances. [1930; 6:15]

Although Hazlitt implies that poetry is similar to the humor of overstatement, they obviously differ. Both exaggerate, but the humor of overstatement exaggerates beyond the tipping point of ludicrousness. Extreme poetry, however, which approaches this perilous boundary, may sometimes trip over it— causing even its most sympathetic readers to laugh.

11. Related to the distinction between metalevel and object-level statements is the distinction between "mention" and "use." Paulos reports an anecdote that demonstrates the humor that results from suddenly switching between using an obscenity and merely mentioning it: "A colleague of mine, working on a paper at home in his study, was disturbed repeatedly by his five-year-old son's use of the expletive 'shit!' in the next room whenever his blocks collapsed. My colleague warned him not to use the word any more. Returning to his study he heard his son say it again whereupon he whirled around and barged into his son's room only to hear him continue defensively, ' . . . is a bad word. "Shit" is a bad word. Right, Daddy'" (1985:44).

12. If we expand the locus of "self" in self-reference to include its setting, positive self-referential humor reveals that internal propensities can be correlated with external settings too closely. Certain psychological states should be at odds with their environment:

I moved to New York for health reasons. I'm very paranoid, and New York is the only place where my fears are justified.

[Anita Wise]

And certain settings should try to counteract, rather than reinforce, the psychological states they produce:

My dentist is really sadistic. He has a picture of Munch's "The Silent Scream" in front of the patient's chair.

13. Erving Goffman's *Frame Analysis: An Essay on the Organization of Experience* (1974) analyzes these metalevel/object-level distinctions in great detail, focusing especially on the paradoxes inherent in negative self-reference. Although rarely analyzing humor per se, his book is humorous in part because it seems so profound. *Frame Analysis* seems profound or, more precisely, recondite because Goffman frequently extends his analysis of self-reference chains beyond what most readers can easily comprehend, at least on first reading. His introduction (1–20), for example, includes comments on introductions and comments on comments on introductions. His continual self-referencing of his analysis of self-reference adds further convolution and complexity, which both overstimulates and overtires the mind. When readers eventually give up following his increasingly abstruse analyses, they laugh—for their intellectual tension is suddenly released.

14. Parody operates by applying a standard form to an inappropriate content. The better the parody, the closer the match between the parodying and the parodied forms but the harder to decide whether the content is inappropriate. Since scientific forms are general enough to apply to almost any content, there are few internal cues of inappropriateness. Without an external cue, consequently, readers often mistake the spoof for the real thing, throwing both into question—as another review of the *Journal of Irreproducible Results* brings out:

The contrived articles are sometimes so convincing that, when the journal stopped labeling the spoofs, havoc erupted because some readers couldn't distinguish them from real research articles. A few gullible readers have tried to look up the authoritative—but faked—footnotes. One bogus article on statistical methods was reprinted without copyright permission in a college manual for students. . . .
Scholars whose serious articles are reprinted in the journal can get upset when they see years of diligent research turned into a joke. [*San Francisco Chronicle*, Scene/Arts, 29 Jan. 84, 4]

15. This distinction, and the humor that blurs it, is derived from Marshall McLuhan's more general dichotomy of message and medium, whose difference he denies in his well-known catch phrase, "The medium is the message."

16. Nachman goes on to give the radio roots of this TV form of frame-breaking humor:

On the Burns and Allen show, George speaks to us, but always in the guise of the character in the show (so much as Burns plays a "character") and usually he only discusses the plot or uses it as an excuse to deliver jokes. Shandling, however, backs *away* from the plot, acknowledges it is a "plot" with literary devices and takes us along on a journey through the script and the show itself. This is why it's like Jack Benny's radio show. Benny's show . . . was about the problems of getting the show on. Like Shandling's, it was a show about a show where funny things intruded on the progress of the show and the characters kept frustrating the story line and wouldn't behave like characters, sort of a "Six Characters in Search of a Show." . . . The fun of the show is pretending it isn't a show at all, a cagey device that both disarms and diverts us. [*San Francisco Chronicle*, "Datebook," 1 May 1988, 17]

17. W. H. Auden (1962:381) expresses the same idea in more modern logic by describing a form of wit that treats "members of overlapping classes as if they were members of the same class."

Neither Schopenhauer nor Auden, however, deals with the converse case, which is also amusing: when identical objects are erroneously subsumed under different concepts (or when members of the same class are erroneously treated as if they were members of different classes). For example:

> The minister was just hitting the high point of his sermon by exclaiming, "Every man in this parish must die!" when he noticed a man in the back row laugh and get up to leave. Later, in town, the minister ran into the man and asked him to explain his strange behavior, "Why were you laughing?" "I'm not from this parish," replied the man.

Although the sermon discussed the fate of all humanity, the man erroneously believed it did not apply to him because he did not belong to the subgroup of humanity to whom it was specifically directed. Bergson (1956:64) attributes the humor of an adumbrated version of this joke to social integration rather than cognitive misconception.

18. Schopenhauer joins those who prefer logical humor to linguistic humor by also contrasting wit with pun: "To complete the theory, we still have to mention a spurious kind of wit, the play upon words, the *calembour*, the pun, to which can be added the equivocation, *l'équivoque*, whose chief use is in the obscene (smut, filth). Just as wit forces two very different real objects under one concept, so the pun brings two different concepts under one word by the use of chance or accident. The same contrast again arises, but much more insipidly and superficially, because it springs not from the essential nature of things, but from the accident of nomenclature. In the case of wit, the identity is in the concept, the difference in the reality; but in the case of the pun, the difference is in the concepts, . . . the identity in the [word]" (1969; 1:61).

19. Schopenhauer defines two other species of the ludicrous in terms of his theory·"*irony:* intentionally subsuming 'something real and perceptible . . . directly under the concept of its opposite'; and *parody:* 'subsum[ing] the plain realities it sets forth under the lofty concepts given in the theme, under which in a certain respect they must now fit, whereas in other respects they are very incongruous therewith (1969; 2:95).

20. Despite their irrationality, emotions are expected to exhibit almost as much consistency as rationality does. Otherwise "emotional non sequiturs," such as despair suddenly reversing into anger, would not be funny:

Sometimes I can't take it no more. Last week I was so depressed I wanted to pack my suitcase and run away. Then I thought of my wife and kids—why should I make them happy.

[Rodney Dangerfield]

21. Although nonsense humor frees us from rationality for both Freud (1963:125–26) and Mindess (1971:75–83), it is only "a recess from reason" for Mindess (77) whereas it reveals our deeper subjection to unconsciousness processes for Freud (131, 215).

Both Freud and Mindess, however, sometimes blur the distinction between the meaningful and the rational. Since human communication can be meaningful without being bound by the further restrictions of pure logical rationality, we should distinguish nonsense humor that is *alogical* or more precisely *asemantical* (meaningless: not understandable at all), which undermines linguistic systems, from nonsense humor that is *illogical* (irrational: understandable but misleadingly based on faulty logic), which undermines logical systems.

22. Slightly earlier, however, Kant's Jewish disciple, Moses Mendelssohn (1729–1786), based laughter (as well as crying) "on a contrast between perfection and imperfection," although his specification of this moral contrast sounds closer to the merely ordinal contrast of Francis Hutcheson: "Every lack of harmony between means and ends, cause and effect, between thought[s] and manner of their expression, above all, *every contrast of the great, venerable, pompous and significant, with the valueless, contemptible and little*, whose consequences put us in no embarrassment, is laughable" (Bergler, 1956:12–13; emphasis added).

23. Comedy affirms the ideal logical order *indirectly* by denigrating actuality. Consequently, comedy is critical, mocking the final claims of finite things. Tragedy affirms the logical order *directly* by approving actuality, by finding the ideal in the actual. Consequently, tragedy is appreciative, demonstrating that no matter how limited and problematic finite things are, they are still part of the infinite (Feibleman 1949:93ff.).

24. Literary deconstructionism is the latest update of this leveling technique. Roland Champagne, for instance, notes "the importance of humor in revealing the stakes of dominant ideologies by reducing their lofty status of dominating a hierarchical system of values" (1990:179) and cites the examples of Bakhtin's discussion of carnivals that invert social hierarchies and Bataille's portrayal of deviant sex that inverts specifically gender hierarchies.

25. Those who subordinate supposedly more valuable sexual and marriage relations to alcohol, adds Christie Davies (1990:374), usually belong to certain ethnic groups:

An Aussie loves his beer, his mates and his wife—and in that order.

An Irishman has been defined as somebody who would trample over twelve naked women to reach a bottle of Guinness.

From a cross-cultural analysis of similar jokes, Davies concludes that ethnic groups vary in how much they value sexual and marriage relations, with Jews supporting them more than average whereas Australians, Irishmen, and Finns prefer an "all-male hard-drinking bachelor culture."

26. Contemporary philosopher John Morreall (1989:10ff.), who notes that the ancient Greek philosophers defined the human being as *both* "the rational animal" and "the laughing animal," emphasizes the similarities between rationality and risibility whereas I have emphasized their differences. Apparently, I view human nature, which contains both rationality and risibility, as more internally incongruous than he does.

27. A science of humor, of course, would bring them together. One way to maintain their separation while still allowing for the possibility of a science of humor is to reserve scientific rationality to metalevel formal statements and humor to object-level content statements, as Lawrence La Fave suggests: "Earlier, in discussing metatheory, logical consistency was indicated to be a sine qua non of an adequate scientific theory. Yet logical inconsistency, we have seen (such as confusing levels of analysis), is often employed to generate jokes. . . . Are we ourselves then not consistently inconsistent? . . . No! an adequate scientific theory of humour would need to be consistent at the metalinguistic level though it talks about and uses inconsistency at the object language level as so-called joke formulae" (1977:247). This procedure would generally work; but because humor can integrate the metalevel and object-level statements that science segregates, this kind of science of humor would be especially prone to a reflexive humor of science which would bring out its inconsistencies.

Chapter Three

1. Lacking a less misleading term, I will use *anthropological* in its older philosophic sense—popularized by Marx's precursor Ludwig Feuerbach—as the *hierarchical* differences *between* human and other kinds of beings, rather than in its newer, social science sense as the *cross-cultural* differences *within* the human species. The newer and older senses converge when anthropologists investigate "totems," visual representations of the ways tribes locate themselves within hierarchies of beings.

2. Lovejoy, the preeminent modern scholar of this traditional belief system, describes its influence and character:

> The result was the conception of the plan and structure of the world which, through the Middle Ages and down to the late eighteenth century, many philosophers, most men of science, and, indeed, most educated men, were to accept without question—the conception of the universe as a "Great Chain of Being," composed of an immense . . . number of links ranging in hierarchical order from the meagerest kind of existents, which barely escape nonexistence, through "every possible" grade up to the *ens perfectissimum*— . . . every one of them differing from that immediately above it and that immediately below it by the "least possible" degree of difference. [1960:59]

His paradigmatic intellectual history *The Great Chain of Being* (1960) traces the variants of this cosmic conception back to the timeless hierarchies by which Plato organized ideas and Aristotle organized animals, and forward to the temporal hierarchy of Darwin's theory of evolution. Lovejoy rarely describes the Chain's major links because he is concerned more with their analogies than distinctions. The divine, angelic, human, animate, and inanimate levels of the Great Chain of Being are delineated more clearly in E. M. W. Tillyard's *The Elizabethan World Picture* (esp. 26–28). Tillyard argued that British poetry flowered when the systematic medieval belief in the Great Chain of Being began to lose its coherence, for conceiving of the cosmos in loose vertical analogies makes it easier to do poetry—and, I will add, comedy.

3. This chapter contains numerous cartoons because a visual format is especially suited to crossing the subhuman/human boundary humorously. Unlike narrative comic forms, a cartoon can dramatize the incongruity between an object's or animal's appearance and its humanlike words by presenting them simultaneously.

4. Two logical humor forms reinforce these two anthropological humor forms, accentuating the different tones of their laughter. Ascending incongruities, which relax muscles and evoke the delicate emotion of wonder (Spencer 1910:464), amplify the uptransformations of anthropological apotheosis. Descending incongruities, which contract muscles and evoke the dynamic motions of laughter, deepen the downtransformations of anthropological degradation.

5. Note, however, that it is sometimes difficult to distinguish uptransformations from downtransformations. Since anthropological humor commingles attributes belonging to beings from different levels of the Great Chain of Being, we may be uncertain whether the defining characteristics of the new incongruous being that results come mostly from above or from below. If both physical appearance and speech are essential to the definition of human beings, are the talking animals discussed above human beings whose appearance has been downshifted or animals whose speech has been upshifted?

6. During this period, most aristocrats preferred downtransformative wit whereas most bourgeois preferred uptransformative humor. Perhaps the declining aristocratic class put others down to maintain their own status whereas the rising bourgeoisie raised others up to justify their own ascension by universalizing it.

7. "Heine is said to have made a definitely blasphemous joke on his deathbed. When a friendly priest reminded him of God's mercy and gave him hope that God would forgive him his sins, he is said to have replied: 'Bien sûr qu'il me pardonnera: c'est son métier.' This is a disparaging comparison . . . , since a *métier*, a trade or profession, is what a workman or a doctor has—and he has only a single *métier*. But the force of the joke lies in its purpose. What it means to say is nothing else than: 'Of course he'll forgive me. That's what he's there for, and that's the only reason I've taken him on (as one engages one's doctor or one's lawyer).' So in the dying man, as he lay there powerless, a consciousness stirred that he had created God and equipped him with power so as to make use of him when the occasion arose. What was supposed to be the created being revealed itself just before its annihilation as the creator" (Freud 1963:114–15).

8. Since extraterrestrials are the modern version of angels, it is also humorous to cripple their superhuman power with typical human problems, as in Bill Hoest's 1982 cartoon portraying an ET-like alien speaking to a puzzled couple in front of his spaceship:

> "I'm afraid this will be our last trip here for awhile. . . . We've had massive budget cuts."

9. Likewise, the more august the person, the more tripped-up by physicality. Francis Hutcheson applies his vertical incongruity theory of humor, described in chapter 2, to the person: "Again, any little accident to which we have joined the idea of meanness, befalling a person of great gravity, ability, dignity, is a matter of laughter, for the very same reason; thus the strange contortions of the body in a fall, the dirtying of a decent dress, the natural functions which we study to conceal from sight, are matters of laughter when they occur to observation in persons of whom we have high ideas. Nay, the very human form has the ideas of dignity so generally joined with it, that even in ordinary persons such mean accidents are matter of jest; but still the jest is increased by the dignity, gravity, or modesty of the person, which shows that it is this contrast, or opposition of ideas of dignity and meanness, which is the occasion of laughter" (quoted in Morreall 1987:33).

10. A historical perspective reveals that associating the "higher" human activities with the lower body has not always debased them. In the Middle Ages and in Rabelais, such downtransformations were merely neutral translations (Bakhtin 1984:108–9). Only after the conception of the body changed during the seventeenth and eighteenth centuries did these downtransformations become debasing.

11. The high status, however, can still retain their social distinction by denying the relevance of their biological similarity:

> "It is true," a great man once said, "that I also have to pee, but for quite different reasons."
>
> [Tommaso Landolfi, "Gogol's Wife"]

12. Another reason for criticizing sexual humor as too easy is the pervasiveness of sexual connotations throughout the English language. Sexual connotations that disrupt nonsexual denotations can be found for almost any English word if one is motivated—as adolescents often are—to look for them:

> Double entendres, some planned but most fortuitous, lurk everywhere in the English language, whose loss of declensions, conjugations, and exact syntax makes it vulnerable to sexual ambiguity. Any unsecured use of "it" in English is almost automatically sexual, and a vague "do" has similar connotations, as in the request associated with barbers, "May I do you now, sir?" or the suggestive Clairol hair-coloring ads: "Does she or doesn't she? Only her hairdresser knows for sure." Certain words like "fix" have such a multiplicity of meanings that they tend to spark off sexual suggestions unless they are specifically excluded by the context. In speech, of course, even innocent words like "come" and "put" can be instantly endowed with double entendre by a mere gesture or intonation (not to speak of a knowing leer). This gives the English language a quality of phonetic innuendo not present in other, more exactly inflected language systems. [Charney 1978:20]

13. Likewise, the 1974 cult film *Groove Tube* described sexual intercourse in the asexual linguistic style of sports announcing, humorously breaking the boundary between these two vastly different leisure activities.

> An announcer is reporting the 34th Annual Sex Games as though it were Olympic skating: "The West German couple is doing it free style. They begin with a classical frontal embrace, favored by most Europeans . . . He's bringing his left hand into play . . . A swerve, a curl, and a lovely probe . . . The strokes are long, controlled, and very even . . . A thrust, a thrust, a double thrust, a lift, a plunge . . ."

14. Besides copulation, comics can debase religion with bodily excretions:

> A drunk was staggering down the main street of the town. Somehow he managed to make it up the stairs to the cathedral and into the building where he crashed from pew to pew, finally making his way to a side aisle and into a confessional.
>   A priest had been observing the man's sorry progress and, figuring the fellow was in need of some assistance, proceeded to enter his side of the confessional. But his attention was rewarded only by a lengthy silence. Finally he asked. "May I help you, my son?"
>   "I dunno," came the drunk's voice from behind the partition. "You got any paper on your side?"

And by describing those who regurgitate in toilets as "worshipping at the old porcelain altar," Robin Williams points out that vomiting may be very different from praying in expression but surprisingly similar in posture.

15. More precisely, Bakhtin believes the body and comedy are bivalent, combining both negative (destructive) and positive (regenerative) features, although he clearly prefers to emphasize the latter (for instance, 1984:62, 435). Excrement is especially dual: both decaying and renewing, debasing and elevating (1984:335, 372; Douglas 1970:188ff.)—hence a popular pivot for puns. Humorists can easily segue from one meaning to the other to express our ambivalence about certain esteemed human activities:

> Introductory sociology is like a giant manure spreader—fertilizing all fields.
> [Bobbie Helling]

16. Sociologist Richard Brown stresses our lingering attachment to the humanness of those whom comedy has objectified. Asserting that its victims have become objects while implying that they could remain human is the irony of irony: "the ironist *objectifies* the persons under study, he makes them objects. This process of objectifying also contains its opposite; to see the irony of a person acting as an object is, at the same instant, to assume that he is capable of acting as subject. In this fashion *irony humanizes as it objectifies*" (1977:210).

17. The irony of human sexuality—what makes it so funny—is that sexual desire (a quintessential human trait) can transform human beings down not merely to the animal level but even farther to the object-level, if *object* is defined as something compelled to move by forces outside its autonomous control. Those obsessed with their sexual drive to the exclusion of all their other drives and social obligations increase the incongruity between their human and object aspects while decreasing the unity of their psychophysiological selves. No wonder we laugh at those "carried away" by sex: they are carried away from their humanness.

18. Erving Goffman (1974: esp. 38–39) distinguishes more clearly than Bergson "social frames," which attribute to people "human guidedness," from "natural frames," in which people seem to lack this self-control. We laugh, Goffman implies but never actually asserts, at those caught between natural and social frames. "Bergson approaches this argument in his fine essay 'Laughter.'" In Goffman's terminology, Bergson is saying "individuals often laugh when confronted by a person who does not sustain in every way an image of human guidedness." Goffman criticizes Bergson for not concluding that we continually monitor people's conformity to the social frame of human guidedness, "finding it to be no laughing matter."

Like Goffman, I am concerned with the way humor points out the usually unnoticed aspects of human life. Unlike Goffman, I am more concerned with *what* is unnoticed than *that* it is unnoticed.

19. We have already seen that ordinary anthropological humor calls attention to the body by distorting the anatomy or portraying those whose anatomy is distorted. Bodily distortions cease to be cute (as in fun-house mirrors or chubby comedians) and become grotesque, however, when exaggerated beyond a certain degree, and especially when they exaggerate not all the body's points but only its weak points.

20. Since the human body is the model for other organic unities, such as art, disintegrating them can also be amusing. "Other sources of innocent laughter are situations in which *the part and the whole* change roles, and attention becomes focused on a detail torn out of the functional context on which its meaning depended. When the phonograph needle gets stuck, the soprano's voice keeps repeating the same word on the same quaver, which suddenly assumes a grotesquely independent life" (Koestler 1974:9).

21. The opposite of stretching out or pulling apart the body is compressing it, a corporeal distorting process also subject to grotesque humor. In contemporary German humor, the Holocaust produced "condensed Jews":

A child plays with a bar of soap. . . . Granny says, "Keep your fingers off Anna Frank."

Do you know why there is a shortage of soap? Because the authorities are trying to turn the soap back into Jews.

22. The disabled need not be subject only to grotesque humor. They can also be the subject of uptransformative ("good") humor:

Three "unimpaired humorists" did stand-up comedy at San Francisco's Zephyr Theater on Friday night. The show began when Troy, the guide dog of the first performer, stuck his head out from behind the curtain to check out the audience.

Mike Lee, who is blind and was led up to the microphone by Troy, said that the evening was intended to demonstrate that the disabled "are no different from anyone else, except we do get those great parking places in front of the bank." . . .

Benjamin Stuart, who has a congenital bone disease, is 2 1/2 feet tall and uses a wheelchair, talked about being in Berkeley—"the wheelchair capital of the world"—one day, when someone rolled up next to him in a chair with a cellular phone and laptop computer. "He leaned over and said, 'Excuse me, do you have any Grey Poupon?'"

The uptransformations of the disabled, however, sometimes come at the expense of the downtransformation of the lower orders:

> Lee talked about the problems of air travel with a guide dog. It's bad enough finding enough space for yourself on a plane, he said, but he has an especially hard time "shoving Troy into the overhead compartment."
>
> [*San Francisco Chronicle*, 21 May 1990, A10]

23. Grotesque humor can transform into objects not only dead humans but also dead animals. The more revered the animal and the more mundane the object, the more effective the humor. The cover cartoon of the best-seller *101 Uses for a Dead Cat* shows two tennis players using dead cats as tennis rackets. Objectifying animal corpses, of course, has less extreme cosmic ramifications than objectifying human corpses. *101 Uses for a Dead Human* may be too macabre for bestsellerdom.

Introduction to Part Two

1. But comedians, at least modern ones like Woody Allen, *do* make fun of themselves. Bergson, however, could retort that they are actually making fun of only their oblivious acting self, which they have differentiated and externalized from their more essential observant perceiving self.

2. Humor researchers who read only Bergson's essay on comedy may fail to appreciate its significance, for his positivist views on this subject can be fully understood only in the context of his definitely nonpositivist overall philosophy. He reserved his positivism, which emphasizes external and general aspects, for the surface world of materialism and mechanism, conceived by the intellect and studied by science. Beyond this lies the deeper world of internal and individual human experience, apprehended directly by pure perception and intuition, and described by art and metaphysics (philosophy). He regarded comedy, however, less as an art or a philosophy than as a science, less "intuitive" than "cognitive" (1956:64, 170). Comedy, consequently, deals merely with the contradictions in the external and general surface world of materialism and mechanism, and therefore not with what is most real and important about human life. Only with this larger theme in mind can we interpret the otherwise obscure ending to Bergson's essay on comedy: "Such is also the truceless warfare of the waves on the surface of the sea, whilst profound peace reigns in the depths below. . . . Laughter comes into being in the selfsame fashion. It indicates a slight revolt on the surface of social life. . . . It, also, is a froth with a saline base. Like froth, it sparkles. It is gaiety itself. But the philosopher who gathers a handful to taste may find that the substance is scanty, and the aftertaste bitter" (1956:190).

3. Although the term *system* is out of fashion for describing society today, critics have attacked mainly its more particular meaning of "self-maintenance" or "equilibrium" rather than its more general meaning of "ordered."

4. I use *deconstruction* in its original sense without its recently acquired esoteric meanings. Mine is a social science definition, designed to counter the social constructionists, rather than a literary definition, designed to counter the literary structuralists. For me, *deconstruction* simply means taking apart a

social system into the components out of which it was originally constructed. Since my goal is only to describe these components not condemn them, my usage does without the political and ideological implications of literary deconstruction.

Note that *deconstruction* has the same double meaning as *cracking:* (1) humor deconstructs cultural and social phenomena; and (2) humor theorists deconstruct humor to recover the original phenomena.

5. Actually, Bergson's position is not as far from Pirandello's as this contrast implies, for he too advocated using humor to destroy our intellectual fictions. Bergson believed we should deliberately and systematically introduce contradictory concepts to make people realize that most problems discussed by philosophy are pseudoproblems, problems merely in the divisions of our artificial logic system, not problems in nature or human life, which are actually continuous (see Burke 1965:92–94, 99–100).

6. Indeed, Pirandello equated objectivism-positivism with sociology itself while reserving subjectivism-phenomenology for humor: "While the sociologist describes social life as it appears from external manifestations, the humorist, armed with his intuition, reveals how profoundly different the outer appearances are from what takes place in inner consciousness" (1974:134).

7. Mikhail Bakhtin describes how their dispute developed historically in comic theory, which parallels its historical development in social theory:

> The historic-allegorical method illustrates the disintegration of laughter that took place in the seventeenth century. The sphere of laughter became more and more narrowed and lost its universal character. On the one hand it became linked to all that was typical and common in everyday life. On the other hand it was related to personal invective; that is, it was directed at one single, private person. The historical universal individuality ceased to be the object of laughter. This quality of carnival humor gradually ceased to be understood. When there was no typical character, commentators began to look for a specific individual. . . .
>   In the seventeenth century an important process was started in all ideological spheres. Generalization, empirical abstraction, and typification acquired a leading role in the world picture.
>   This process was completed in the eighteenth century. The very pattern of the world was changed. Next to the general the singular remains, acquiring its meaning only as a specimen of the general, only so far as it is typical, average, and can be generalized. . . . The Enlighteners had . . . a tendency to abstract generalization and typification. . . . They were quite incapable of understanding and appreciating Rabelais. [1984:115–16]

8. The surface differences between social units, however, may not be very great, for the boundaries between many social units in our society are relatively weak. (In general, social systems are more malleable than logical or anthropological systems, though less malleable than linguistic systems.) Since jokes that break weak boundaries are "poor" (that is, they snap perception between gestalts less intensely), jokes that break these weak social boundaries produce smiles rather than laughs. Just as jokes that violate linguistic boundaries are generally poorer than those that violate logical boundaries, jokes that violate social boundaries are generally poorer than those that violate anthropo-

logical boundaries. Thus I may account for (if not apologize for) the jokes in this section, which make up in instructiveness whatever they lack in funniness.

Chapter Four

1. The prevalence of transferable language in humor may be an artifact of the medium that dominates its dissemination. Printed jokes can convey the flavor of speech better than appearance ("You had to be there") and printed cartoons allow the speech bubble or caption to be attached to persons or groups unlikely to have said it in the real world. Comic plays and films, on the other hand, can better display transferable aspects of physical appearance.

2. Bergson temporalized Pascal's static observation by equating the similar with the mechanical. "The truth is that a really living life should never repeat itself. Wherever there is repetition or complete similarity, we always suspect some mechanism at work behind the living. Analyze the impression you get from two faces that are too much alike, and you will find that you are thinking of two copies cast in the same mould, or two impressions of the same seal, or two reproductions of the same negative—in a word, of some manufacturing process or other. This deflection of life towards the mechanical is here the real cause of laughter" (1956:82). Thus Bergson grounds replicative social humor in the anthropological downtransformations discussed in chapter 3.

3. Although twin humor usually pivots around those similar physically while differing psychologically, it can also pivot around those similar psychologically while differing physically. In the latter case, humorists can exaggerate either the twins physical difference, such as by casting the dwarfish Danny DeVito with the muscular Arnold Schwarzenegger in the 1988 film *Twins*, or their psychological similarity, such as by sharing stigmatized opinions in the following cold war joke:

> Two East German sentries are on duty. One says to the other, "What do you think of our regime?" The other says, "I don't know. Same as you, I guess." The first sentry says, "Then it is my painful duty to arrest you."

4. Auden observes that clichés compromise the unique linguistic aspects of a person's identity:

> Banality is the illusion of identity, for, when people describe their experiences in clichés, it is impossible to distinguish the experience of one from the experience of another.
> The cliché user is comic because the illusion of being identical with others is created by his own choice. He is the megalomanic in reverse. Both have fantastic conceptions of themselves but, whereas the megalomanic thinks of himself as being somebody else—God, Napoleon, Shakespeare—the banal man thinks of himself as being everybody else, that is to say, nobody in particular. [1962:379]

Consequently, the parodist (the impressionist of linguistic style) can comically generalize a person's identity by putting clichés in his or her mouth. "The trick of the parodist is to take the unique style of the author, *how* he expresses his unique vision, and make it express utter banalities; *what* the parody expresses could be said by anyone. The effect is of a reversal in the relation between the author and his style. Instead of the style being the creation of the man, the man becomes the puppet of the style" (1962:382). He gives the example of Henry Reed's famous parody of T. S. Eliot:

> As we get older we do not get any younger.
> Seasons return, and to-day I am fifty-five,
> And this time last year I was fifty-four,
> And this time next year I shall be sixty-two.
> And I cannot say I should like (to speak for myself)
> To see my time over again—if you can call it time:
> Fidgeting uneasily under a draughty stair,
> Or counting sleepless nights in the crowded tube.

[1962:382]

But Auden fails to note that putting sparking original *bons mots* in the mouths of very ordinary people may also induce more laughter than the wit itself would warrant.

5. This cultural difference in comic styles has been attributed to ecological and sociological factors. "Pointing out the essential Englishness of the word [*humor*] and its vein, [Sir William] Temple [in 1690] attributes this favorable outgrowth to the native soil, the changeable climate, and above all a government which tolerates free opinion and free speech. The environment fosters an individualism which brings out eccentricities to a degree not paralleled elsewhere. Where the conformities of the Continent are expressed through the same old typical characters, England glories in its Originals, whose varieties are mirrored in the theater. 'We are not only more unlike one another than any nation I know, but we are more unlike ourselves too at several times'" (Levin 1987:186; see also Madame de Staël 1964).

6. Humanists (such as philosophers and literary critics) do not distinguish social types and sociological categories the way sociologists do. But this distinction helps us comprehend social comedy more clearly, for humanists often use the terminology of social types to discuss comic features more characteristic of sociological categories.

7. No one depends on costumes for their comic effect more than clowns. Most "character clowns" dress as tramps or policemen (Culhane 1973:19). Pairing these easily recognizable social types allows clowns to dramatize the extremely visual physical interaction between hyperdeviants who continually perform disallowed behavior and hypernormatives who continually attempt to punish it.

8. In the classical comedies, one character commonly learns another's identity by hiding and eavesdropping. In the *false* recognition scene early in the play, a concealed character may believe he has discovered a potentially duplicitous character's true backstage identity, but has actually attributed an erroneous identity by misinterpreting everything said by or about the latter. In the *true* recognition scene at the end of the play, this misperception is corrected as twinning is disclosed, disguises removed, and biographical information reinterpreted.

9. Dundes (1987:102, 96–97, 137), however, defends jokes that draw on stereotypes by pointing out their positive features: they may contain a kernel of

truth, may help us to interact with those who belong to groups whose members we have never met personally before, may secretly please those who discover that their group identity is vital enough to provoke such slurs, and may even reinforce the stereotyped group's value system.

10. Exaggeration also humorizes social types by contrasting their extreme to their typical version; for instance, juxtaposing the obsessed lover to the average suitor or the niggardly miser to the ordinary financial conservative. The classic cry of the archetypal Jewish Mother—"Help! Help! My son, the doctor, is drowning!"—humorously overstates her supposed obsession with her children's social status to the extent of equating it with their very lives.

11. Those who deplore stereotypes should applaud humor that explodes them. But their antipathy toward stereotypes, if not toward humor itself, is usually great enough for them to contend that even this kind of humor reinforces stereotypes, for its audience must recollect and consequently resurrect the stereotype to understand why something incongruous to it is funny.

12. Freud (1963:181–236) explains "naive humor" in terms of the different amounts of psychic energy expended by adults and children: the excess energy produced by reducing an adult to a child is expelled as laughter. But Freud has more difficulty using *psychological* energy reduction to explain "sophisticated humor," which elevates the child cognitively into an adult. Perhaps a *sociological* explanation would be better: both naive and sophisticated humor are funny because our society's conceptions of child and adult social categories, which exchange traits, are antithetical.

13. In *The Dark Voyage and the Golden Mean,* Cook applies his abnormality theory of comedy to the age dimension, noting the importance comedy (unlike tragedy) attaches to its protagonists' ages, and especially to their *age-inappropriate behavior:*

> In tragedy the age of the protagonist is an incidental part of the symbol. . . .
> In comedy social man's position is determined by his relation to generation and to family. . . .
> Comedy represents ideas not as eternal truths but as the probable clothing of a specific time of life. The radical younger generation becomes conservative as it grows older. . . . The young romantic lover becomes the prosaic middle-aged husband. What is normal for one generation is abnormal for another. Liberalism is expected for the young Pheidippides but abnormal and ridiculous in the middle-aged Socrates. Gilbert presents in many characters the slightly ridiculous figure of the middle-aged woman who plays the romantic lover, like Buttercup in *H.M.S. Pinafore,* and Katish in *The Mikado.* . . .
> In tragedy man is a soul before God; his history is a history of his sins and good acts. In comedy social man is a youth, a middle-aged father, or an old grandfather. All activities are normal for a certain age only. If you try to indulge in what is improbable for your age, you yourself become improbable and ridiculous. [1964:480–82]

14. "On the one hand, [Sambo] was childish and comical, given to outlandish gestures, physical gyrations and funny clothes. He could be clever but his cleverness was supposedly unknown to him, a kind of innocent quality. He might be folksmart, displaying little witticisms, but he was not regarded as

being wise. . . . Irresponsibility was a cardinal characteristic and buffoonery was an anticipated act on his part. On the other level was Sambo the natural slave and servant who displayed the qualities of patience, humbleness, nonviolence, and sharpness. Here responsibility was expected and smartness rewarded—though both virtues were carefully controlled" (Boskin 1987:252–53).

15. European humor, however, contrasts its national groups binarily on a broad array of traits, resulting in many jokes that explicitly or implicitly exchange stereotypical characteristics between French and Germans, Dutch and Belgians, Swedes and Norwegians, Poles and Russians, etc.

16. Many people may recognize a temporal incongruity in which neither side is the present, such as Romans engaging in medieval jousts, but only a professional historian may find it meaningful enough to be funny. On the other hand, even ordinary people may laugh when one side of a temporal incongruity is neither the present nor the distant past but the recent past. Since American films often maintained contemporary hair styles (especially for women) in biblical and Roman epics, later audiences found the anachronistic combination of dated hair and period clothing ludicrous. (But even here the humor may result from a three-cornered temporal incongruity between the present, the recent past, and the historical period.)

17. The other best-known humorous anthropological "studies" of modern society are Horace Miner's "Body Ritual among the Nacirema," which describes our cleanliness habits as primitive ritual and David Webster's "Journey to Fortran: A Yankee Way of Knowledge," which supposes that our society's most materialistic members possess the esoteric wisdom we attribute to primitive sorcerers (Adams 1982:21–22).

Chapter Five

1. The last two examples illustrate how humor can provide sociologists with insights into social life obscured by their traditional methods. The garage-restaurant transfer points out an important distinction between business institutions generally overlooked by economic sociologists: how payment for services is determined. The restaurant-hospital transfer points out an unsettling parallel between dining and surgery generally overlooked by ethnographic sociologists: the relative physical position between the participants, the knives, the bibs, the splatter, etc.

2. Familial institutions do not dominate the humor of all other countries. In a lecture to the Institute for Historical Study in 1988, Polish-American humor historian Bogna Lorence-Kot reported that, during her last visit to Poland to collect jokes, she encountered *no* jokes about personal relations, but *only* jokes about politics. In Poland, and in Eastern Europe generally, political institutions seemed to be far more problematic than familial ones, at least before the fall of Communism.

3. Of course, a humorist may transfer an attribute from one institution to a totally dissimilar slot in another institution. But if there is no congruity to articulate the incongruity, the result will be only nonsense or absurdist humor—to laugh at which sober adults must be in a silly mood.

4. "Certain professions have a technical vocabulary: what a wealth of laughable results have been obtained by transposing the ideas of everyday life into this professional jargon!" (Bergson 1956:143).

5. Jewish humor stems from a long tradition of integrating biblical citations and Talmudic styles into secular texts. Judith Stora-Sandor suggests it reflects a cosmic view in which there is no boundary between ordinary and sacred realities. "But even if, on a stylistic level, this mixture of sacred and secular texts does not always take place, the mixture of the sublime and the trivial is a phenomenon that is found throughout Jewish literature. It springs from the very spirit of Judaism as reflected in the Talmudic debates, where all aspects of life are taken into account. There is no duality between the mind and the body, between the miraculous and the prosaic. 'It *is* not in Heaven' (Deuteronomy 30:12), says the Bible, meaning that the Torah, given by God, has come down to Earth. On the literary plane, this amalgam of the most elevated with the most trivial, whether manifesting itself on the level of style or of ideas, is an excellent humoristic procedure, and Jews have practiced it willingly" (1991:217). On the other hand, Jews must believe that sacred reality transcends ordinary reality in fact if not in theory, for Jewish humorists continually juxtapose them to oscillate their audience between each incompatible gestalt.

Chapter Six

1. Although "comedians" seem to undermine morality, George Paton (1988:206–7) argues that they are actually "disguised moralists." Comedians juxtapose "legitimated [ideal] moral codes and actual moral behavior," pointing out sexual and other hypocrisies ("double standards"). Even more than avowed moralists, comedians insist that our moral logic be consistent by pointing out instances where it is not.

Comedians who seem to contrast "morality" and "reality," moreover, actually contrast an explicit moral code with an implicit one.

2. As noted in chapter 2, satire has been confused with parody often enough to make the terms almost interchangeable. Nevertheless, their distinction is worth maintaining: satire undermines *the social units* that present themselves as ideal whereas parody undermines *the cultural forms* that *re*present these social units idealistically as their content.

3. Of course, not all jokes about collectivity hierarchies are dichotomous. The following, for instance, is trichotomous:

> [During World War II] Mrs. Chauncey Ashley III telephoned the headquarters of the infantry base near Great Oaks, her ancestral home. "This is Mrs. Chauncey Ashley the Third, and with Thanksgiving coming up, I thought it would be nice for us to have ten of your fine enlisted men share our family feast."
> "That's very kind of you, Mrs. Ashley."
> "There's only one thing—I'm sure you understand: my husband and I prefer not to have any Jews."
> "Madam, I *quite* understand."
> When her front doorbell rang on Thanksgiving Day, Mrs. Ashley, dressed to the nines, hurried to the door herself. She flung it open. "*Wel*come to Great—" She stopped, aghast.
> Under the great portico stood ten smiling black soldiers.

"Omigod," gasped Mrs. Ashley. "There has been a terrible mistake!"
The black sergeant said, "Oh no, ma'am. Captain Finkelstein *never* makes a mistake."

4. Some jokes portray those ignorant of *sub*cultural knowledge:

When Marilyn Monroe was married to Arthur Miller [who was Jewish], his mother always made matzo ball soup. After the tenth time, Marilyn said, "Gee Arthur, these matzo balls are pretty nice, but isn't there any other part of the matzo you can eat?"
[Ann Barr and Paul Levy, *The Foodie Handbook*.]

5. "Topsyturvydom" is the inelegant term used by Bergson (or his anonymous translator) for the comic status inversion often portrayed by those who write comedies: "Picture to yourself certain characters in a certain situation: if you reverse the situation and invert the roles, you obtain a comic scene. . . . Thus, we laugh at the prisoner at the bar lecturing the magistrate; at the child presuming to teach its parents; in a word, everything that comes under the heading of 'topsyturvydom'" (1956:121).

6. Several psychologists—such as Ludwig Jekels (1964) and Charles Mauron (McFadden 1982:152ff.)—have analyzed comedy in terms of this Freudian model, pointing out the displacement of guilt from the son in tragedy onto the father in comedy, which degrades the father into the son. This convoluted psychological interpretation of comedy may be unnecessary, however, for the son may win simply because "the comic dramatist as a rule writes for the younger men in his audience, and the older members of almost any society are apt to feel that comedy has something subversive about it" (Frye 1971:164).

7. Other countries whose natives have treated Jews as a despised racial or ethnic, rather than purely religious, group are also subject to humor that inverts their indigenous hierarchies:

[Scene: Berlin, 1936. A Jew, crossing the street, accidentally bumped into a burly Storm Trooper.]
"*Schweinhunt!*" snapped the Nazi.
"Goldberg," bowed the Jew.

In Leningrad, two KGB agents saw old Boris Glatkoff on a park bench—reading a book.
The first KGB agent asked, "What is that book you are reading?"
"A book about grammar," said Glatkoff. "Hebrew grammar."
The second KGB agent sneered, "Why bother, Jew? We'll never let you go to Israel."
"Well," sighed Boris, "I think that in Heaven, they speak Hebrew."
"What makes you think you'll get to Heaven? Suppose you go to Hell?"
Boris shrugged. "I already know Russian."

8. The "*Schnorrer*, who in his thoughts treats the rich man's money as his own, has actually, according to the sacred ordinances of the Jews, almost a right to make this confusion. The indignation raised by this joke is of course directed against a Law which is highly oppressive even to pious people. . . . [The Baron] is obliged by the Law to give him alms and should, strictly speaking, be grateful to him for giving him an opportunity for beneficence. The ordinary, middle-class view of charity is in conflict here with the religious one;

it is in open rebellion against the religious one in the other story, of the Baron who, deeply moved by a *Schnorrer's* tale of woe, rang for his servants: 'Throw him out! he's breaking my heart!'" (Freud 1963:112–13).

9. Though less important in American humor than British, the Scottish examples Davies cites better illustrate what it means to fail at leisure roles. "The Scotsman's life is so rigidly controlled, so utterly devoted to the rational pursuit of gain for its own sake that he has lost sight of one of the basic utilitarian reasons for seeking material success—the enjoyment of its rewards" (1982:389).

> A Deeside wife listened for a whole evening to the jokes and patter of Billy Connolly without the hint of a smile. Next day she confided to a friend: "He's a great comic. It was all I could do tae keep from laughing."

> "It's terrible," said a Scotsman, "I never get to drink a cup of coffee the way I really like it. At home in order to save money I only take one spoonful of sugar. At friends' houses where it is free I take three. Now what I really like is a cup of coffee with two sugars."

10. To demonstrate that a rationalist ideology has spread to all industrial or industrializing societies Davies points to other countries' jokes about their own stupid marginal groups:

> *Canadian:* A Toronto woman called a firm which was renowned for its landscaping and interior decorating. A man from the company soon arrived and the lady showed him around the house. Every time she asked what colors he would recommend for a particular room, he went to the window, raised it and called out "Green sides up!" before answering her. This happened several times and the woman's curiosity got the better of her. "Is this some kind of a ritual?" she asked. "No," he replied, "it's simply that I've got two Newfies [Newfoundlanders] next door laying sod."

> *Indian:* A Sardarji [Sikh] working on a building site was trying to knock a nail into the wall head first. Another Sardarji seeing that his efforts were unavailing said to him, "You're using the wrong kind of nail. That nail is meant for the wall opposite."

11. Davies, like Weber, stretches the ideology of "rationality" by subsuming under it other values of Western industrial societies, such as work or money, that have been only historically *associated* with rationality, not logically *derived* from it.

12. The golden age of political satire has always been in the past, perhaps because it's cyclical: little appreciated when present, much lamented when absent. Among the few praised for satirizing issues more than personalities have been the club performances of Tom Lehrer, Lenny Bruce, and Mort Sahl; the newspaper comics and cartoons of Garry Trudeau and Jules Feiffer; and the television commentary of Jay Leno, Will Durst, and Dennis Miller (*San Francisco Examiner,* 30 Oct. 1988, E1, E7; *New York Times,* 19 Apr. 1992, H29). But Steve Allen (1987:138), whose historical perspective is longer, points out that there has never been much political satire in America, especially on television. (Nor in the theater; for, as George S. Kaufman said, "Satire is what closes on Saturday night.")

13. "Laughter is also important in the repeated resocialization of the indi-

vidual. For example, when new statuses and roles are assumed, as in the case of the newly married or the new incumbents of a job, or when newcomers are in the process of assimilation in a new community or society, the individuals try to avoid being laughed at because of their ignorance or clumsiness" (Hertzler 1970:162–63; see also 87, 102).

14. Urban audiences are also amused by rustics in rural settings, though less because of their incompetence than their quaintness. Since rural life is simpler and slower to change than urban life, their life-styles are incongruous both developmentally (childlike vs. adultlike) and historically (old-fashioned vs. newfangled) [Levin 1987:112]). Thus urban audiences find funny the simplicity of both rural language, with its localisms and provincialisms (Hertzler 1970:181), and rural customs:

> Remember "Bob's Bank," whose motto is "save at the sign of the sock."
> [Garrison Keillor]

A few years ago, urban sophisticates laughed at rural art, whose innocence they called "camp" or "kitsch." "Camp and kitch are a modern parody of pastoral innocence and naivety, expressed in a bucolic setting with (or without) sheep, shepherdesses, and camp counselors" (Charney 1978:18).

15. Jesse Bier (1988:140) argues that Polish jokes have become common not because Poles are the major lower class *white* ethnic group, as Dundes (1987:133) believes, but conversely because Poles have been *rising* in economic status.

16. The demographic flow that determines the dominance of urban or rural humor has reversed over the course of American history:

> In the early days of America we laughed at the city slicker, because we were an agrarian people. Soon after the Civil War, we began to laugh at the country rube; we were becoming an urban people. Characters once heroic became foolish, not because of changes in the character as such but in the social scene in which this character acted.
> In the struggle for power between rural and urban Americans from 1875 to 1925, each was laughing at the other, but, when rural economy changed to a money base, rural laughter about the "city slicker" in his daily character, the "drummer," was tinged with envy. [Duncan 1953:51–52]

17. Academics are more prone to obfuscate through the opposite technique—not too little conceptual rigidity but too much: "In science the jest at pedantry is analogous to that in religion which lies against superstition. A classification or nomenclature used by the scholar only as a memorandum of his last lesson in the laws of nature, and confessedly a makeshift, a bivouac for a night, and implying a march and a conquest tomorrow—becomes through indolence a barrack and a prison, in which the man sits down immovably, and wishes to detain others. . . . The pedantry of literature belongs to the same category. In both cases there is a lie, when the mind, seizing a classification to help it to a sincerer knowledge of the fact, stops in the classification; or learning languages and reading books to the end of a better acquaintance with man, stops in the languages and books; in both the learner seems to be wise, and is not" (Emerson 1946:211–12).

Comedians, of course, love to make fun of pedants. Sometimes, however, they hit the wrong target: "The endeavor to learn or teach life's lessons gets caught up at times in the mindless rote of hypothetical schemes or automatic systems, which encourage it to overlook the matter-of-fact and down-to-earth pragmatism of common sense. The quest for knowledge all too readily freezes into an *idée fixe*, which needs to be unfixed, unfrozen, or liberated. Hence schools can be the incubators of pedantry, and the pedant is the silliest of fools—the very opposite of Socrates—because he pretends to be truly wise, though such knowledge as he possesses is the most narrowly specialized kind. . . . Aristophanes' . . . *The Clouds* had reduced a school of thought, the philosophy of the Sophists, to the burlesque of an academy, the Phrontistérion or think-tank of the pseudo-Socrates" (Levin 1987:60).

18. If television comedy accurately reflects audience feeling, cynicism about American family life increased during the 1980s, especially in contrast to the 1950s. The idealized middle class families portrayed on television in the 1950s ("Father Knows Best" and "Ozzie and Harriet") featured strong authority figures and loving members who ultimately handled minor problems rationally and compassionately. The idealized upper middle class family sitcoms of the early 1980s ("Family Ties" and "The Cosby Show") also featured an intact, if occasionally challenged, authority structure. Although aggression between family members increased on the surface, they were still basically loving enough to temper their insults with compliments and encouragement (of the form: "Despite current shortcomings, you *will* eventually live up to a positive ideal."). The more realistic (in some instances, negatively idealized) lower middle class family sitcoms of the late 1980s and early 1990s ("Roseanne," "The Simpsons," "Married . . . with Children"), which depict much aggression and little love between family members as well as weak and continually defeated authority figures, seldom employ the traditional affectionate and altruistic rhetoric of family life.

19. "Since totalitarian regimes have trouble in living up to their own propaganda, they offer a standing incitement to satire, which of course they can ill afford. It broke out in Soviet Russia, while permitted, through such ironists as Mikhail Bulgakov, Valentin Kataev, and Ilf-and-Petrov; and, though now suppressed in the mother country, is exported by Andrei Siniavsky and Vladimir Voinovich. Yet their major theme, the bunglings of the bureaucracy, had deep roots in the Tsarist tradition, and could hark back to Gogol as its past master" (Levin 1987:203).

Chapter Seven

1. Lionel Trilling (1972) distinguishes "sincerity," which he defines as "a congruence between avowal and actual feeling" (2), from "authenticity," which emphasizes "the sentiment of being," "self-definition" [as opposed to being defined by others], and the "painful, ignoble, or socially unacceptable" (99–100). But his distinction is too fine for my purpose because comedy attacks both aspects of identity simultaneously. Therefore I will use "authenticity" in the broad sense that includes "sincerity."

2. Goffman does not clearly distinguish competence from authenticity, perhaps because he believes that "doing *is* being," that behavior determines self. Nevertheless, he emphasizes failures of competence claims in *The Presentation of Self in Everyday Life* (1959), "Facework" (1967:5–46), "Alienation from Interaction" (1967:113–36), and "Fun in Games" (1961b:17–84); and failures of authenticity claims in *Asylums* (1961a), *Stigma* (1963), and "Role Distance" (1961b:85–152)—to consider only his early writing.

Goffman's social psychological theories gained a wide audience mainly because his examples for them were so amusing. In contrast to Goffman, I will try to determine here why it is funny for idealized self claims to collapse, working back up from amusing examples to social psychological theory.

3. "*Don Quixote* . . . grew out of its author's simple intention of asserting the claims of quotidian practicality against those of the heroic ideal" (Trilling 1972:88). Trilling sees the comic potential of the heroic ideal but suggests that comedy, rather than merely responding adversely to it, actually helps to constitute it, for "at the moment at which men think of themselves as funny they have conceived the idea of their dignity. As soon as they joke about their natural functions, about the absurdity of defecation and copulation and the oddness of the shapes their bodies grow into, they are on the way to contriving to appear nobler than they really are. How else do men recognize their ignobility than by imagining their potential nobility?—a state of being which in time will come to burden and bore them and arouse their mockery" (1972:87). Trilling's view is generalizable to any ideal, for we find funny an attack on whatever we are drawn to but ambivalent about.

4. Fielding's distinction between the vain and the hypocrite parallels the Greek distinction between two comic types: the *alazon* (blusterer) "who bombastically claims more than he can fulfil" and the *eiron* (dissembler) "who knows more than he slyly admits" (Levin 1987:55, 65).

5. Pirandello (1974:132) distinguishes the different approaches to unmasking taken by the comic writer, the satirist, and the humorist. The comic writer is amused merely by the process itself; the satirist is disdainful of the illusions unmasked; the humorist is compassionate with those who must live by illusions. Pirandello clearly prefers the last approach.

6. The hierarchy of motives is not absolute but relative to the society. One can imagine a society where people pretended to be irrational, erotic, and materialistic, as well as egoistic and immoral; but their humorists revealed them to be actually rational, ascetic, and spiritual, as well as altruistic and moral. In fact, bohemian subgroups, such as the "flower children" of the 1960s, have already inverted Western society's dominant hierarchy of motives; and they have already been unmasked by satirists as actually reverting to normal.

7. Thus some members of traditionally "higher" subcategories imitate members of traditionally "lower" ones: older adults try to act like younger adults, men like women, whites like blacks, natives like ethnics, Christians like Jews, the upper class like the lower class. In a rare alliance, those who hold traditional and revisionary views of social stratification both ridicule this "radical chic" inauthenticity. Whoever believes traditionally lower subcategories

are still "lower" mocks those foolish enough to try to *descend* to them from traditionally higher ones. And whoever believes traditionally lower subcategories are now "higher" (or at least morally "purer") also mocks those presumptive enough to try to *ascend* to them from (originally higher but) now lower ones.

8. Whether the collectivity subject to such humor is typical or ideal depends on whether we focus on *how closely* an imitator replicates its traits or *how far short* an imitator falls from replicating them perfectly.

9. Occasionally, passing can be inadvertent. Jokes about unintentional passing are especially funny because the revelation of the incongruity between assumed and actual subcategories is news to the passer as well as the audience:

> The governor of a southern state goes for a long-overdue physical examination. Concerned about his health, he calls the doctor the next day and asks for a report. The doctor says he has good news and bad news.
> "Well," the governor says, "what's the good news?"
> "The good news is that you have six months to live."
> "The good news is I have six months to live? What's the bad news?"
> "The bad news is you have sickle-cell anemia."

10. There are also a few jokes about Jews who *don't* try to pass as gentiles when they should, who overtly claim membership in their persecuted collectivity at the worst possible time:

> One thing I learned in life: During an airplane hijack, never raise your hand to order a kosher meal.
>
> [Mike Binder]

11. Levin extends the traditional concept of zanic imitation to cover modern comedy, which reflects a society without servants. "But there could be no falling-off for zanyism in its arena, the theater. Servantless juvenile leads simply had to do their own legwork and dirty work. Lower-class types, such as tramps, received independent attention. The sense of inferiority was transferred from a social to a psychological attitude, and introverted accordingly, so that the modern zany tends to be an insecure little man—a Woody Allen—striving vainly and nervously to meet the demands or live up to the pretensions of a high-pressured lifestyle" (1987:91).

12. According to Hegel, lower-class characters are more appropriate for comedy than higher-class ones because pricking the balloon of their more illusionary aims is less consequential. "Comedy can indulge itself best with characters that do not have the responsibilities of princes or statesmen. . . . It is better for comic effect to bring lower-class characters into play—characters who can 'put on airs,' spread themselves transparently. When they negate themselves, together with their apparent interests and values, such characters reveal the requisite negation of a negation, which is the essence of comedy" (Paolucci 1978:106; see also Hegel 1979:198).

13. Jewish American Princess (JAP) jokes, for example, attack a collectivity whose stereotype combines inauthenticities of class, religion, ethnicity, and gender—additively augmenting the humor. These jokes portray JAPs as trying

to pass for high class ("princess") but betrayed by their crass nouveau riche tastes, their unearned wealth, and their general incompetence:

> How many JAPs does it take to change a light bulb? Two. One to get the JAP-juice [diet cola], and one to call Daddy.

trying to pass for WASPs ("Jewish-American") but betrayed by their appearance and behavior:

> Many of our synagogue gift shops carry Bunny Bagelman greeting cards. Bunny has a large hooked nose, kinky curly hair, and a figure that can only be described as zaftig. She shops for clothes and jewels . . . and a husband.

and trying to pass for female but betrayed by their asexuality and egoism:

> How do you know when a JAP has an orgasm? She drops her nail file.

See Alperin 1989, and Spencer 1989.

14. Although comedy has frequently focused on the split between private and public selves, the recent social histories that trace the emergence of "private life" in the West suggest that this social-psychological split we take for granted is not part of human nature but developed gradually from specific historical and sociological causes.

15. Scenes in which identity is mistaken and then recognized occur not only in comic plays but also (occasionally) in "real life." In *Asylums*, Goffman (1961a:112) observed that "identity joking" is common in mental hospitals where both staff and patients tell anecdotes about times when a member of one category was mistaken for a member of the other. Goffman implied that crucial parts of our social identity can suddenly become ambiguous, whether we like it or not—dragging us into situations we find increasingly humorous, if the mistaken social identity is higher status than our own, or increasingly horrifying, if lower (at least until a "recognition scene" allows us to "see the humor" in even the most nightmarish identity mistake).

16. To be fair to Goffman, he does recognize that many people are not always self-aggrandizing, at least not obviously so. "In fact, however, many classes of persons have had many different reasons for exercising systematic modesty and for underplaying any expression of wealth, capacity, spiritual strength, or self-respect" (1959:38). Nevertheless, most of his book examines the implications of "upward" rather than "downward" self-presentation. And his short discussion of downward self-presentation (1959:38–41) concerns restraining the self's upward tendencies rather than actually profaning it.

17. Hobbes's definition of laughter included self-depreciating humor in his relatively psychological *Human Nature* in 1640 but omitted it in his relatively sociological *Leviathan* in 1651, perhaps because this aspect of human nature undermined his competitive conception of society.

18. E. B. White, the paragon of the self-mocking traditional *New Yorker* humorist, may have had such motivation for his distinctive approach—"the comic story told on himself"—which exemplified James Thurber's dictum, "The proof of humor is the ability to put oneself on awkward public record" (Tanner 1989:52).

19. Several humor theorists have tried to specify which Jews are actually being criticized by seemingly generic Jewish humor. Christopher Wilson argues that Freud thought Jewish humor criticized not all Jews but only lower class ones. "The [beggar and Baron] jokes seem anti-semitic to the gentile for they depict two stereotypic Jewish traits—of greed and meanness—reflected in the behavior of beggar and Baron, respectively. However, Freud argued, the aim of the humor is not to disparage Jews *en masse*, but to criticize a sub-set which abuse the onerous charity law. The jokes were told by middle class Jews who used their right of ethnic membership to criticize 'beggars.'

"It appears that shared ridicule expresses conflict within an ethnic group. The evidence that I have examined indicates that it is generally directed downwards in the class structure, rather than being levelled at the whole ethnic group" (1979:219–20). Dan Ben Amos, among others, argues that "Jews ridicule only the Jews whom they consider inferior," according to a reviewer who concludes: "Jewish humor [is not] necessarily self-deprecating. . . . Self-deprecatory aspects of humor are characteristic specifically of Eastern European Jews in the diaspora. . . . Israelis . . . studiously refrain from ridiculing themselves. . . . In an illuminating experimental study, Ofra Nevo shows that although Israeli Arabs laugh mainly at themselves, Israeli Jews direct their disparaging humor at Arabs. . . . [Therefore, in general,] self-deprecatory humor characterizes low-status minorities, regardless of ethnic affiliation" (Brandes 1988:411–12).

20. Altman (1971:202–3) concludes by noting two relatively minor uniquely American sources of Jewish self-irony: the discrepancy between the "official" American definition of Jews (as a religion) and their self-perception (as something more), and the success of Jewish comedians has made it a self-perpetuating "show biz" device. The even more complex post–World War II American Jewish identity, I will add, includes the dialectic between comic self-irony and deadly serious (and hence unironic) contemplation of the specter of the Holocaust.

Chapter Eight

1. Zucker (1969:75ff.) contrasts the disintegrated self of the clown with the hyperintegrated self of the hero. The clown, self-contradictory on all dimensions, expresses the absurdity of human existence—for which he was banished from the stage during the Enlightenment.

2. "More casually, humor could be conceived as a person's state of mind at the moment: a mood, a caprice, a whim, an inclination to be indulged—or humored (Shakespeare was apparently the first to use the verbal form). Persons subject to such passing states—moody, capricious, whimsical—were said to be humorous" (Levin 1987:182). The opposite form of "humor" also stems from an incongruity between behavior and situation, but rather than changing people's behavior (capriciously) while holding constant their situation, it holds constant their behavior (inflexibly) while changing their situation.

3. These anomalous combinations produce humor either by undermining

the typicality of the supraindividual social units, as we saw in chapters 4 and 5, or by undermining the integrity of the individual involved in them, as we will explore here. Humorists undermine their audience's *typical conception of social units* by portraying participants in one social unit who possess a few traits from another, or their audience's *ideal conception of unified individuals* by portraying those who possess so *many* traits from another that it becomes unclear to which one he or she ultimately belongs. Both these typical and ideal forms of humor converge as the relative number of traits from two different social units an individual possesses approaches 50 percent.

4. Rose Coser distinguishes what I have called "collectivity distance," specifically the humor surrounding these status transitions, from what Goffman called "role distance," (though she inexplicably wants to reserve the latter term for the former concept). "I further propose that we distinguish between the case of taking distance from a *status one intends to abandon* or from a status one does not have a claim to and the case of temporarily relinquishing some prerogatives associated with status position, as when one lowers his claims for recognition *the better to maintain his status*. I suggest that the term 'role distance' be applied only to the former. The two acts differ in several respects. The first occurs in the transition from one status position to another and serves to resolve the sociological ambivalence derived from two roles, the old one and the new. It is typical in situations of social mobility, either with respect to age or to class, and is illustrated here by the clowning of the eight-year-old boys and the adolescent girls. The latter occurs in many established status relationships and serves to maintain them as defined by removing the threat posed by sociological ambivalence. It is illustrated by humor in the operating room" (1966:183). Interns, for instance, pretend to move themselves or others up or (more often) down age hierarchies:

> *Chief Surgeon Jones (in this case a senior resident):* A Small Richardson please.
> *Scrub Nurse:* Don't have one.
> *Dr. Jones:* O.K., then give me an Army and Navy.
> *Scrub Nurse:* It looks like we don't have one.
> *Dr. Jones (lightly joking):* No Army or Navy man here.
> *Intern (dryly):* No one in the armed forces, but Dr. Jones here is in the Boy Scouts.

or class hierarchies:

> *Intern (looking for towel clamps around body):* Where in the world . . . ?"
> *Scrub Nurse:* Underneath the towel.
> (Intern turns to the nurse and in slow measure makes a full cold bow to her.)
> [Goffman 1961b:118]

But distinguishing collectivity distance from role distance in humor may not be easy, for some of Goffman's illustrations of operating room humor, like the above, depict those who use collectivity distance to achieve role distance, and vice versa.

5. "The alternative to this [avoidance] relation of extreme mutual respect and restraint is the joking relationship, one, that is, of mutual disrespect and license. Any serious hostility is prevented by the playful antagonisms of teasing, and this in its regular repetition is a constant expression or reminder of

that social disjunction which is one of the essential components of the relation, while the social conjunction is maintained by the friendliness that takes no offence at insult" (Radcliffe-Brown 1965:92).

6. Marcel Griaule (Radcliffe-Brown 1965:105ff.; Douglas 1979:92), an early critic of Radcliffe-Brown, noted that the "joking relations" he discussed are more "teasing" than joking, for the participants don't tell jokes to each other but insult each other—albeit humorously.

7. Auden here follows Schopenhauer, though not his cognitive theory of humor (1969; 1:58–61; 2:91–101), which derives it from mistakenly subsuming a perceptive *particular* object under an abstract *general* concept, but his logically parallel biological theory of marriage, which derives it from mistakenly subsuming an *individual* desire to love a particular person under the *species* desire to have sex impersonally with almost any member of the opposite gender. Problems arise, according to Schopenhauer, if those whose individual and species desires are temporarily in phase choose to marry. For the ebbing of the species desire "leaves behind a detested partner for life" (see Davis 1983:270 n. 23).

8. Anton Zijderveld, who deals with hierarchical joking relationships in more explicitly economic institutions than Rose Coser, suggests that superiors "joke down" to subordinates for ideological rather than structural reasons. " 'Joking-down' and 'joking-up,' that is, joking with those in inferior and superior positions, is an important corroboration of the power relations in stratified societies, but in modern society is not as clearly institutionalized as the primitive ['joking-across'?] relationships discussed by Radcliffe-Brown and others. Though not as crystallized in the social structure, joking relationships nevertheless can be observed as regularly recurring behavior in industrial society. The director of a huge concern, chatting with employees, and suddenly treating one of them as his buddy, or even as an equally ranked official, is a common figure in many stratified structures. . . . The leader can prove his 'democratic spirit' by bridging, even momentarily, the gap between top and lower echelons on the social ladder—a gap that can become dysfunctional" (1968:297). Although such humor seems to shift the joking relationship—at least momentarily—to the relatively egalitarian family, Zijderveld emphasizes the family's own hierarchy:

> By doing so he can moreover provide his subordinates with a feeling of "belonging to the family." This hits then right at the heart of this matter: these joking relationships of the joking-down type are paternalistic devices to keep the lower ranks in their place. All joking with inferiors, from the nursing personnel in a hospital [Coser 1959], treating their patients as helpless children, to the director of an industrial concern, joking cordially with "his" workers, is of this paternalistic kind. Adults are treated as if they were children. Thus these joking relationships are part of a perverted kinship system. . . .
>
> Adults who themselves often are fathers of children, are gently transported to the world of children, joking being the means of transportation. But also the higher ranked, powerful joker is transported from his position of manager to that of "father." It is an over-all transition from the meaning of one life-sector (business, work) to that of another (family). [1968:297–98]

Zijderveld, then, comes to the Marxist conclusion that, by superimposing family hierarchies on top of business hierarchies, those who "joke down" are actually employing ideological egalitarianism to enhance economic stratification.

9. "Often important everyday occasions of embarrassment arise when the self projected is somehow confronted with another self which, though valid in other contexts, cannot be here sustained in harmony with the first" (Goffman 1967:108). Goffman's better style and more interesting examples have elevated his reputation far above Burns's. Goffman does not mention his intellectual debt to Burns in his 1956 article on embarrassment (1967:97–112), but repairs this omission in a note to his 1961 article on role distance (1961b:114 n. 29).

10. Goffman notes that gender identity is frequently incompatible with other selves, requiring much intergender humor to reconcile their conflict:

> Age-sex identifications during task performances typically express concerns that are felt in addition to the task, not in opposition to it. Sometimes, however, there is an "overdetermined" flavor to these expressions, suggesting that role distance is involved and requiring the individual to withdraw a little from the occupational game in order to be momentarily active in the older one:
>
> *Scrub Nurse (to intern):* Take one [hemostat] in each hand, he'll need 'em.
> *Intern:* Yes, Ma-ma.
> *Scrub Nurse (half apologetically):* I'm really interested in your learning.
> *Intern (with mock intrigue):* Well, how about teaching me?
> *Scrub Nurse:* I gave you a book, what else can I do?
> *Intern:* Oh there's lots else you can do. . . .
>
> I would like to add that it would be wrong indeed to overestimate the sexuality of these sexual references. They resemble a tickle much more than a caress. Sex here seems to be made a convenience of, seized upon not for itself but to demonstrate a little independence regarding one's situated role. If serious at all, these joking remarks allow the surgeon to stake a claim to roles he might want to be available to him at another time and in another setting. [1961b:138]

Fear of sexual harassment suits has begun to block this humorous technique for reconciling incompatible task and gender selves. Whatever its sexist origins, the nonsexist repercussions of its prohibition for mental health, interaction ease, and role performance remain unexplored.

11. Moreover, a single *role* itself may force the individual to perform its disparate aspects simultaneously. Humor-producing self-contradictions, Goffman pointed out, occur not only between but *within* particular roles. One source of the "simultaneous multiplicity of selves" that motivates the surgeon to express role distance, usually through humor, is the "conflict or discrepancy between the self generated in a situated circuit of vital hospital activity and the self associated with a formal status and identity: medical man. No doubt we have here an exaggeration of the kind of discrepancy that can exist between a broad social title and a particular activity system sustained while on duty. . . . Surgery requires acts unbecoming a surgeon, just as mothering requires acts that are unmaternal" (1961b:134).

Another instance of the internal role contradictions that may motivate humorous expressions of role distance is the discrepancy between the many activities required by the same role. "While an activity system situation in a social establishment may provide a fairly coherent, self-consistent bundle of tasks for a given participant, he will, at the same time, be *officially* involved in other, multi-situated matters that have a relevant claim on his time—a claim that he may be able to honor only by diverting some of the concern . . . owed the situated activity. For example, in the many cases where the surgery ward is carrying on some kind of training activity, the surgeon directing the operation will periodically halt or slow up the flow of action to instruct the residents and interns in what is happening. . . . In all these ways in which the individual may properly act as a hospital staff man, he may find that he must express some small distance from the specific operation at hand" (1961b:134–35).

Conclusion

1. I have found a journalistic interview with Bud Adams (Copetas 1989), whose family-run S. S. Adams company seems to have single-handedly invented and marketed 150 of the most popular novelties in America since the beginning of the twentieth century, grossing over $2 million a year. Although the Adams company has owned the rights to the joy buzzer (the world's best selling novelty) since the 1920s, they foolishly turned down the rights to the whoopee cushion (which became the world's second best selling novelty) in 1930. The Adams company is currently losing market share to Asian competition, who can make novelties more cheaply. A society that no longer produces its own humorous artifacts may suffer a spiritual decline ultimately worse than the economic decline brought on by no longer producing its more pedestrian manufactured goods.

2. But because humor merely *suggests* that the world could be different without—seriously—specifying how, Douglas regards its destructuring of the conventional world as frivolous: "The joke merely affords opportunity for realizing that an accepted pattern has no necessity. Its excitement lies in the suggestion that any particular ordering of experience may be arbitrary and subjective. It is frivolous in that it produced no real alternative, only an exhilarating sense of freedom from form in general" (1979:96).

3. The cognitive equivalent of the social antistructuralists are the ethnomethodologists, most notably professor Harold Garfinkle, who reduce cognitive structures to the *process* of sustaining them. Laughter, for ethnomethodologists, is a technique to maintain these illusionary structures by dismissing whatever would weaken them.

4. This is not to say that laughter has no place in structuralist and antistructuralist worldviews. Although Parsons is silent on the subject, he would probably regard laughter as a homeostatic technique to denigrate deviance and reinforce social structure. Hobbes actually does regard laughter as a disequilibrium technique to increase relative status in the social conflict of society. For Parsons and Hobbes, then, people may laugh—but only *for* its social structure- or individual status–enhancing functions rather than *from* its cosmic-disorganizing cause.

5. As noted (introduction to part 2, note 4), I use *deconstruction* in a sense different from the literary sense. Many of the newer sociologies, however, are derived from literary deconstructionism. Being antistructuralist, they also have difficulty dealing with humor. For humor needs stiff cultural and social structures to snap. No structure, no snap, no laugh. A purely deconstructed world in the literary sense, filled only with the flux of unattached attributes, would be void of mirth.

6. More than any other ethnic group, modern Jews have been noted for their sense of humor, which I suggest stems from their historic tendency to sustain multiple interpretations. During the last two centuries, the relation between Western society and its Jews has been the same as the relation between system and incongruity (and the alternative system implied by that incongruity). By accepting the dual validity of their larger society's culture and their subgroup's culture despite the contradictions, Jews have acquired the more general mindset that accepts the dual validity of any system and its incongruities.

References

Adams, David, ed. 1982. *Using Humor in Teaching Sociology: A Handbook*. Washington, D.C.: American Sociological Association.

Addison, Joseph. 1965. *The Spectator*. Vol. 1. 1711. Ed. Donald Bond. New York: Oxford University Press.

Allen, Steve. 1987. *How to be Funny: Discovering the Comic You*. New York: McGraw-Hill.

Allen, Woody. 1972. *Getting Even*. New York: Warner Books.

Alperin, Mimi. 1989. JAP jokes: hateful humor. Reprinted speech delivered to the Miami Chapter of the American Jewish Committee. *Humor* 2(4):411–16.

Alter, Robert. 1972. Jewish Humor and the Domestication of Myth. In *Veins of Humor*, ed. Harry Levin, 255–67. Cambridge: Harvard University Press.

Altman, Sig. 1971. *The Comic Image of the Jew: Explorations of a Pop Culture Phenomenon*. Rutherford, Madison, Teaneck, N.J.: Fairleigh Dickinson University Press.

Apte, Mahadev. 1988. Disciplinary boundaries in humorology: an anthropologist's ruminations. *Humor* 1(1):5–25.

Arieti, Silvano. 1976. *Creativity: The Magic Synthesis*. New York: Basic Books.

Aristotle. 1984. *Poetics*. Trans. I. Bywater. In *The Complete Works of Aristotle*, The Revised Oxford Translation, ed. Jonathan Barns, 2316ff. Princeton: Princeton University Press.

Attardo, Salvatore. 1988. Trends in European humor research: toward a text model. *Humor* 1(4): 349–69.

Auden, W. H. 1962. Notes on the comic. In *The Dyer's Hand and Other Essays*, 1952, ed. W. H. Auden. New York: Random House.

Bakhtin, Mikhail. 1984. *Rabelais and His World*. 1965. Trans. Hélène Iswolsky. Bloomington: Indiana University Press.

Barthes, Roland. 1972. *Mythologies*. Ed. and trans. Annette Lavers. New York: Hill and Wang.

Bate, W. Jackson. 1977. *Samuel Johnson*. New York: Harcourt Brace Jovanovich.

Bateson, Gregory. 1972. A theory of play and fantasy. In *Steps to an Ecology of Mind*, 1955, ed. Gregory Bateson, 177–193. New York: Ballantine Books.

Baudelaire, Charles. 1972. On the essence of laughter, and generally of the comic in the plastic arts. Trans. P. E. Charvet. In *Baudelaire, Selected Writings on Art and Artists*, 1855, ed. Charvet, 140–61. Cambridge: Cambridge University Press.

Beard, Henry, Michael O'Donaghue, and George W. S. Trow. 1985. Our white heritage. *National Lampoon* (Mar.):42. The Best of 15 years: 1970–1974.

Benchley, Robert. 1983. What does it mean? In *The Benchley Roundup*, ed. Nathaniel Benchley. Chicago: University of Chicago Press.

Berger, Peter. 1963. *Invitation to Sociology: A Humanistic Perspective*. Garden City New York: Doubleday Anchor.

Berger, Peter, and Thomas Luckmann. 1967. *The Social Construction of Reality: A Treatise in the Sociology of Knowledge*. Garden City: Doubleday Anchor.

Bergler, Edmund. 1956. *Laughter and the Sense of Humor*. New York: Intercontinental Medical Book Corp.

Bergson, Henri. 1956. Laughter. In *Comedy*, 1900, ed. Wylie Sypher, 61–190. Garden City: Doubleday Anchor.

Bier, Jesse. 1988. The problem of the Polish joke in derogatory American humor. *Humor* 1(2):135–41.

Blair, Walter. 1960. *Native American Humor*. 1937. San Francisco: Chandler Publishing Company.

Blalock, Hubert. 1960. *Social Statistics*. New York: McGraw-Hill.

Boskin, Joseph. 1987. The complicity of humor: the life and death of Sambo. In *The Philosophy of Laughter and Humor*, ed. John Morreall, 250–63. Albany: State University of New York Press.

Brandes, Stanley. 1988. Review of *Jewish Humor*, edited by Avner Ziv. *Humor* 1(4):411–13.

Brooks, Charles. 1957. On the difference between wit and humor. In *Composition: A Course in Writing and Rhetoric*, 1919, ed. Richard Weaver, 546–49.

Brown, Richard. 1977. *A Poetic for Sociology: Toward a Logic of Discovery for the Human Sciences*. Cambridge: Cambridge University Press.

Bruce, Lenny. *The Essential Lenny Bruce*. 1967. Ed. John Cohen. New York: Ballantine Books.

Burke, Kenneth. 1965. *Permanence and Change: An Anatomy of Purpose*. Indianapolis: Bobbs-Merrill.

Burns, Tom. 1953. Friends, enemies, and the polite fiction. *American Sociological Review* 18:654–62.

Cameron, William. 1963. *Informal Sociology: A Casual Introduction to Sociological Thinking*. New York: Random House.

Carlyle, Thomas. 1908. *Sartor Resartus and On Heros*. 1833–35. New York: Dutton.

Cerf, Bennett, ed. *Vest Pocket Book of Jokes for All Occasions.* 1956. New York: Random House.

———. *Laugh Day: A New Treasury of over 1,000 Humorous Stories and Anecdotes.* 1967. New York: Pocket Books.

Champagne, Roland. 1990. The engendered blow job: Bakhtin's comic dismemberment and the pornography of Georges Bataille's 'Story of the Eye'. *Humor* 3(2):177–91.

Charney, Maurice. 1978. *Comedy High and Low: An Introduction to the Experience of Comedy.* New York: Oxford University Press.

Christopher, Richard. 1987a. Poonerisms. In *The Best of Maledicta: The International Journal of Verbal Aggression,* ed. Reinhold Aman, 26–28. Philadelphia: Running Press.

———. 1987b. Ethiopian jokes. In *The Best of Maledicta: The International Journal of Verbal Aggression,* ed. Reinhold Aman, 188–93. Philadelphia: Running Press.

Cicero. 1942. *De oratore.* Ed. H. Rackham. Trans. E. W. Sutton. Loeb Classical Library, vol. 3, books 1–2. Cambridge: Harvard University Press.

Coleridge, Samuel Taylor. 1951. *Lectures on Shakespeare, etc.* 1836. New York: Dutton.

Cook, Albert. 1964. The Dark Voyage and the Golden Mean. In *Theories of Comedy.* 1949. Ed. Paul Lauter, 475–96. Garden City: Doubleday Anchor.

Copetas, A. Craig. 1989. The happy life of a joy buzzer baron. *San Francisco Chronicle,* Sunday Punch (26 Nov.): 3.

Cornog, Martha. 1987. Tom, Dick, and Hairy: notes on genital pet names. In *The Best of Maledicta: The International Journal of Verbal Aggression,* ed. Reinhold Aman, 108–17. Philadelphia: Running Press.

Coser, Rose. 1959. Some social functions of laughter: a study of humor in a hospital setting. *Human Relations* 12(2):171–82.

———. 1960. Laughter among colleagues: a study of the social functions of humor among the staff of a mental hospital. *Psychiatry* 23 (Feb.): 81–95.

———. 1966. Role distance, sociological ambivalence, and Transitional Status Systems. *American Journal of Sociology* 72(2): 173–87.

Culhane, John. 1973. School for clowns. *New York Times Magazine,* 12 Dec., 10ff.

Davies, Christie. 1982. Ethnic jokes, moral values and social boundaries. *The British Journal of Sociology* 33(3):383–403.

———. 1988. Stupidity and rationality: jokes from the iron cage. In *Humour in Society: Resistance and Control,* ed. Chris Powell and George E. C. Paton, 1–31. London: Macmillan.

———. 1990. An explanation of Jewish jokes about Jewish women. *Humor* 3(4):363–78.

———. 1991. Exploring the thesis of the self-depreciating Jewish sense of humor. *Humor* 4(2):189–209.

Davis, Fred. 1988. Gender, fashion and the dialectic of identity. In *Communication and Social Structure,* ed. Carl Couch and David Maines, 23–38. Springfield: Charles C. Thomas.

Davis, Murray S. 1971. That's interesting! Towards a phenomenology of sociology and a sociology of phenomenology. *Philosophy of the Social Sciences* 1(4):309–44.

———. 1973. *Intimate Relations*. New York: The Free Press.

Davis, Murray S., and Catherine J. Schmidt. 1977. The obnoxious and the nice: some sociological consequences of two psychological types. *Sociometry* 40(3):201–13.

Davis, Murray S. 1979. Sociology through humor. *Symbolic Interaction* 2(1):105–10.

———. 1983. *Smut: Erotic Reality/Obscene Ideology*. Chicago: University of Chicago Press.

de Staël, Madame. 1964. *Literature Considered in Its Relation to Social Institutions*. In *Theories of Comedy*. 1800. Ed. and trans. Paul Lauter, 182–87. Garden City: Doubleday.

de Vries, Peter. 1983. *Slouching towards Kalamazoo*. New York: Penguin Books.

Deckers, Lambert, and Robert Buttram. 1990. Humor as a response to incongruities within or between schema. *Humor* 3(1):53–64.

Donatus. 1964. A fragment on comedy and tragedy. Trans. George Miltz. In *Theories of Comedy*, ed. Paul Lauter, 27–32. Garden City: Doubleday Anchor.

Douglas, Mary. 1970. *Purity and Danger: An Analysis of Concepts of Pollution and Taboo*. Baltimore: Penguin Books.

———. 1979. Jokes. In *Implicit Meanings: Essays in Anthropology* , 90–114. London: Routledge & Kegan Paul.

Droke, Maxwell. 1956. *The Speakers Handbook of Humor*. New York: Harper & Row.

Duncan, Hugh Dalziel. 1953. *Language and Literature in Society*. Chicago: University of Chicago Press.

Dundes, Alan. 1987. *Cracking Jokes: Studies of Sick Humor Cycles and Stereotypes*. Berkeley: Ten Speed Press.

Eastman, Max. 1921. *The Sense of Humor*. New York: Scribners.

———. 1939. *Enjoyment of Laughter*. 1936. New York: Halcyon House.

Eco, Umberto. 1984. *The Name of the Rose*. Trans. William Weaver. New York: Warner Books.

Emerson, Ralph Waldo. 1946. The comic. In *The Portable Emerson*, 1843, ed. Mark Van Doren, 204–16. New York: Viking Press.

Feibleman, James. 1949. *Aesthetics: A Study of the Fine Arts in Theory and Practice*. New York: Duall, Sloan and Pearce.

Feirstein, Bruce. 1982. *Real Men Don't Eat Quiche: A Guidebook to all That Is Truly Masculine*. Illus. Lee Lorenz. New York: Pocket Books.

Fielding, Henry. 1964. Author's preface to *Joseph Andrews*. In *Theories of Comedy*, 1742, ed. Paul Lauter, 246–52. Garden City: Doubleday Anchor.

Fine, Gary Alan. 1983. Sociological approaches to the study of humor. In *Handbook of Humor Research*, vol. 1, ed. Paul McGhee and Jeffrey Goldstein, 159–81. New York: Springer-Verlag.

Frame, Donald. 1977. *François Rabelais: A Study*. New York: Harcourt Brace Jovanovich.

Freud, Sigmund. 1963. *Jokes and their Relation to the Unconscious.* 1905. Vol. 8 of *The Standard Edition of the Complete Psychological Works of Sigmund Freud.* Ed. and trans. James Strachey. New York: W. W. Norton & Co.

Friedman, Monroe. 1989. Commercial expressions in American humor: an analysis of selected popular-cultural works of the postwar era. *Humor* 2(3):265–83.

Fry, William F., Jr. 1963. *Sweet Madness: A Study of Humor.* Palo Alto: Pacific Books.

Frye, Northrop. 1964. The argument of comedy. In *Theories of Comedy,* 1948, ed. Paul Lauter, 450–60. Garden City: Doubleday Anchor.

———. 1971. *Anatomy of Criticism: Four Essays.* 1957. Princeton: Princeton University Press.

Geltrich-Ludgate, Brigitta. 1987. Teenage jokesters and riddlers: a profile in parody. In *The Best of Maledicta: The International Journal of Verbal Aggression,* ed. Reinhold Aman, 61–74. Phildelphia: Running Press.

Goffman, Erving. 1959. *The Presentation of Self in Everyday Life.* Garden City: Doubleday Anchor.

———. 1961a. *Asylums: Essays on the Social Situation of Mental Patients and Other Inmates.* Garden City: Doubleday Anchor.

———. 1961b. *Encounters.* Indianapolis: Bobbs-Merrill.

———. 1963. *Stigma: Notes on the Management of Spoiled Identity.* Englewood Cliffs: Prentice-Hall.

———. 1967. *Interaction Ritual: Essays on Face-to-Face Behavior.* Garden City: Doubleday Anchor.

———. 1974. *Frame Analysis: An Essay on the Organization of Experience.* New York: Harper & Row.

Goldstein, Laurence. 1990. The linguistic interest of verbal humor. *Humor* 3(1):37–52.

Graham, Harry. 1961. *Ruthless Rhymes for Heartless Homes, and More Ruthless Rhymes for Heartless Homes.* 1899. New York: Dover.

Griffiths, Trevor. 1976. *Comedians.* London: Faber and Faber.

Gruner, Charles. 1978. *Understanding Laughter: The Workings of Wit and Humor.* Chicago: Nelson-Hall.

Hazlitt, William. 1930. Lectures on the comic writers, etc. of Great Britain. In *The Complete Works of William Hazlitt,* vol. 6, 1819, ed. P. P. Howe, 5ff. London: J. M. Dent & Sons.

Hegel, G. W. F. 1979. *Hegel: On the Arts.* 1842–43. Ed. and trans. Henry Paolucci. New York: Frederick Ungar Publishing Co.

Hertzler, Joyce. 1970. *Laughter: A Socio-Scientific Analysis.* New York: Exposition Press.

Hetzron, Robert. 1991. On the structure of punchlines. *Humor* 4(1):61–108.

Hobbes, Thomas. 1987a. *Human Nature.* In *The Philosophy of Laughter and Humor.* 1640. Ed. John Morreall, 19–20. Albany: State University of New York Press.

———. 1987b. *Leviathan.* In *The Philosophy of Laughter and Humor.* 1651. Ed. John Morreall, 19. Albany: State University of New York.

Hoy, Cyrus. 1974. Comedy. In *Encyclopedia Britannica,* 15th ed., 958–67.

Hutcheson, Francis. 1987. *Reflections upon Laughter.* In *The Philosophy of Laughter and Humor.* 1750. Ed. John Morreall, 26–40. Albany: State University of New York Press.

Jekels, Ludwig. 1964. On the psychology of comedy. Trans. I. Jarosy. In *Theories of Comedy,* 1926, ed. Paul Lauter, 424–31. Garden City: Doubleday Anchor.

Johnson, Samuel. 1969. *The Rambler.* In *The Yale Edition of the Complete Works of Samuel Johnson.* 1750–52. Ed. W. Jackson Bate and Albracht Strauss. New Haven: Yale University Press.

Kahn, Alice. 1985. *Multiple Sarcasm.* Berkeley: Ten Speed Press.

Kant, Immanuel. 1951. *Critique of Judgement.* 1793. Trans. J. H. Berhard. New York: Hafner Press.

Keith-Spiegel, Patricia. 1972. Early conceptions of humor: varieties and issues. In *The Psychology of Humor,* ed. Jeffrey Goldstein and Paul McGhee, 3–39. New York: Academic Press.

Kierkegaard, Soren. 1968. *Concluding Unscientific Postscript.* 1846. Trans. David F. Swenson and Walter Lowrie. Princeton: Princeton University Press.

Knott, Blanche. 1982. *Truly Tasteless Jokes.* New York: Ballantine Books.

———. 1983. *Truly Tasteless Jokes Two.* New York: Ballantine Books.

Koestler, Arthur. 1974. Humour and wit. In *Encyclopedia Britannica,* 15th ed. 5–11.

Koller, Marvin. 1988. *Humor and Society: Explorations in the Sociology of Humor.* Houston: Cap and Gown Press.

Koziski, Stephanie. 1984. The standup comedian as anthropologist: intentional culture critic. *Journal of Popular Culture* 18(2):57–76.

Kronenberger, Louis. 1954. *Company Manners: A Cultural Inquiry into American Life.* Indianapolis: Bobbs-Merrill.

La Fave, Lawrence. 1977. Ethnic humour: from paradoxes towards principles. In *It's a Funny Thing, Humour,* ed. Antony Chapman and Hugh Foot, 237–49. Oxford: Pergamon Press.

Lamb, Charles. 1964. On the artificial comedy of the last century. In *Theories of Comedy,* 1822, ed. Paul Lauter, 295–302. Garden City: Doubleday Anchor.

Lauter, Paul, ed. *Theories of Comedy.* 1964. Garden City: Doubleday Anchor.

Legman, Gershon. 1971. *Rationale of the Dirty Joke: An Analysis of Sexual Humor.* New York: Grove Press.

Levin, Harry. 1987. *Playboys and Killjoys: An Essay on the Theory and Practice of Comedy.* New York: Oxford University Press.

Levine, Donald. 1985. *The Flight from Ambiguity: Essays in Social and Cultural Theory.* Chicago: University of Chicago Press.

Lipps, Theodor. 1964. *The Foundation of Aesthetics.* In *Theories of Comedy.* 1903. Ed. Paul Lauter. Trans. Lee Chadeayne, 393–97. Garden City: Doubleday Anchor.

Locke, John. 1939. An essay concerning human understanding. In *The English Philosophers from Bacon to Mill,* 1690, ed. Edwin A. Burtt, 238–402. New York: Modern Library.

Lovejoy, Arthur. 1960. *The Great Chain of Being: A Study of the History of an Idea.* 1936. New York: Harper Torchbooks.

Lynch, William. 1969. The humanity of comedy. In *Holy Laughter: Essays on Religion in the Comic Perspective,* ed. M. Conrad Hyers, 28–44. New York: Seabury Press.

Malcolm, Norman. 1958. *Ludwig Wittgenstein: A Memoir.* New York: Oxford University Press.

The Best of Maledicta: The International Journal of Verbal Aggression. 1987. Ed. Reinhold Aman. Philadelphia: Running Press.

Martin, Robert. 1974. *The Triumph of Wit: A Study of Victorian Comic Theory.* Oxford: Clarendon Press.

McFadden, George. 1982. *Discovering the Comic.* Princeton: Princeton University Press.

McGhee, Paul. 1979. *Humor: Its Origin and Development.* San Francisco: W. H. Freeman and Co.

McGhee, Paul, Willibald Ruch, and Franz-Josef Hehl. 1990. A personality-based model of humor development during adulthood. *Humor* 3(2):119–46.

Mead, George Herbert. 1934. *Mind, Self and Society: From the Standpoint of a Social Behaviorist.* Ed. Charles Morris. Chicago: University of Chicago Press.

Meiers, Mildred, and Jack Knapp, eds. *5600 Jokes for All Occasions.* 1980. New York: Avenel Books.

Metcalf, Fred, ed. *The Penguin Dictionary of Modern Humorous Quotations.* 1986. New York: Viking Penguin.

Mindess, Harvey. 1971. *Laughter and Liberation.* Los Angeles: Nash Publishing.

Mingo, Jack. 1983. *The Official Couch Potato Handbook.* Santa Barbara: Capra Press.

Molière. 1964a. Letter on *The Imposter [Tartuffe].* Trans. Mrs. George Calingaert and Paul Lauter. In *Theories of Comedy,* 1667, ed. Paul Lauter, 145–54. Garden City: Doubleday Anchor.

————. 1964b. Preface to *The Imposter [Tartuffe].* Trans. Henry Van Laun. In *Theories of Comedy,* 1669, ed. Paul Lauter, 155–61. Garden City: Doubleday Anchor.

Monro, D. H. 1963. *Argument of Laughter.* 1951. Notre Dame: University of Notre Dame Press.

Morreall, John, ed. *The Philosophy of Laughter and Humor.* 1987. Albany: State University of New York Press.

Morreall, John. 1989. Enjoying incongruity. *Humor* 2(1):1–18.

Moulton, Powers, ed. *Best Jokes for All Occasions.* 1948. New York: Permabooks.

Murray, Stephen O. 1987. Ritual and personal insults in stigmatized subcultures. In *The Best of Maledicta: The International Journal of Verbal Aggression ,* ed. Reinhold Aman, 118–40. Philadelphia: Running Press.

Nilsen, Don. 1987. Sigma Epsilon Xi: sex in the typical university classroom. In *The Best of Maledicta: The International Journal of Verbal Aggression,* ed. Reinhold Aman, 77–89. Philadelphia: Running Press.

————. 1989. Review of *On Puns: The Foundation of Letters,* by Jonathan Culler (ed.). *Humor* 2(4):397–400.

Norrick, Neal. 1989. Intertextuality in humor. *Humor* 2(2):117–39.

Palmer, Jerry. 1988. Theory of comic narrative: semantic and pragmatic elements. *Humor* 1(2):111–26.

Paolucci, Anne. 1978. Hegel's theory of comedy. In *Comedy: New Perspectives,* vol. 1, ed. Maurice Charney, 89–108. New York: New York Literary Forum.

Parsons, Talcott. 1951. *The Social System.* New York: The Free Press.

Parsons, Talcott, Robert Bales, and Edward Shills. 1953. *Working Papers in the Theory of Action.* New York: The Free Press.

Parsons, Talcott, Robert Bales, James Olds, Morris Zelditch, and Philip Slater. 1955. *Family, Socialization and Interaction Process.* New York: The Free Press.

Parsons, Talcott, and Neil Smelser. 1957. *Economy and Society: A Study of the Integration of Economic and Social Theory.* New York: The Free Press.

Paton, George E. C. 1988. The comedian as portrayer of social morality. In *Humor in Society: Resistance and Control,* ed. Chris Powell and Paton, 206–33. London: Macmillan.

Paulos, John Allen. 1980. *Mathematics and Humor.* Chicago: University of Chicago Press.

————. 1985. *I Think, Therefore I Laugh: An Alternative Approach to Philosophy.* New York: Columbia University Press.

Pepicello, William, and Robert Weisberg. 1983. Linguistics and humor. In *Handbook of Humor Research,* vol. 1, ed. Paul McGhee and Jeffrey Goldstein, 59–83. New York: Springer-Verlag.

Perret, Gene. 1982. *How to Write and Sell (Your Sense of) Humor.* Cincinnati: Writer's Digest Books.

Pirandello, Luigi. 1974. *On Humor.* 1908. Trans. Antonio Illiano and Daniel Testa. Chapel Hill: University of North Carolina Press.

Plato. 1961. *Philebus.* Trans. R. Hackforth. In *Plato: The Collected Dialogues,* ed. Edith Hamilton and Huntington Cairns, 1086–1150. New York: Bollingen Foundation.

Pretorius, Elizabeth. 1990. Humor as defeated discourse expectations: conversational exchange in a Monty Python text. *Humor* 3(3):259–76.

Rabelais, François. 1955. *Gargantua and Pantagruel.* 1564. Trans. J. M. Cohen. New York: Penguin Books.

Radcliffe-Brown, A. R. 1965. On joking relationships and a further note on joking relationships. In *Structure and Function in Primitive Society: Essays and Addresses,* 1940–49, 90–116. New York: Free Press.

Raskin, Victor. 1985. *Semantic Mechanisms of Humor.* Dordrecht, Holland: Reidel.

————. 1988. Editorial comment. *Humor* 1(1):1–4.

Redfern, Walter. 1986. *Puns.* New York: Basil Blackwell.

Rezwin, Max, ed. *The Best of Sick Jokes.* 1962. New York: Pocket Books.

Riezler, Kurt. 1950. *Man: Mutable and Immutable: The Fundamental Structure of Social Life.* Chicago: Henry Regnery Co.

Robinson, Vera. 1983. Humor and health. In *Handbook of Humor Research,* vol. 2, ed. Paul McGhee and Jeffrey Goldstein, 109–27. New York: Springer-Verlag.

Rosten, Leo, ed. *Leo Rosten's Giant Book of Laughter*. 1985. New York: Crown Publishers.

Rourke, Constance. 1953. *American Humor: A Study of National Character*. 1931. Garden City: Doubleday.

Rovin, Jeff, ed. *1,001 Great Jokes*. 1987. New York: Signet.

Safian, Louis, ed. *An Irreverent Dictionary of Love and Marriage*. 1967. New York: Belmont Books.

Schafer, Kermit, ed. *Best of Bloopers*. 1973. New York: Avenel Books.

Schiller, Friedrich. 1964. On simple and sentimental poetry. In *Theories of Comedy*, 1795, ed. Paul Lauter, 307–13. Garden City: Doubleday Anchor.

von Schlegel, August Wilhelm. 1964. *Lectures on Dramatic Art and Literature*. In *Theories of Comedy*. 1808. Ed. Paul Lauter. Trans. John Black, 324–49. Garden City: Doubleday Anchor.

Schneider, Louis. 1975. *The Sociological Way of Looking at the World*. New York: McGraw-Hill.

Schopenhauer, Arthur. 1969. *The World as Will and Representation*. 1819–44. Trans. E. F. J. Payne. New York: Dover.

Schutz, Alfred, and Thomas Luckmann. 1973. *The Structures of the Life-World*. Trans. Richard Zaner and H. Tristram Engelhardt, Jr. Evanston: Northwestern University Press.

Schutz, Charles. 1977. The psycho-logic of political humour. In *It's a Funny Thing, Humour*, ed. Antony Chapman and Hugh Foot, 65–69. Oxford: Pergamon Press.

———. 1989. The sociability of ethnic jokes. *Humor* 2(2):165–77.

Shalin, Dmitri. 1984. The romantic antecedents of meadian social psychology. *Symbolic Interaction* 7(1):44–65.

Sidney, Phillip. 1970. *The Defense of Poesy*. 1595. Ed. Lewis Soens. Lincoln: University of Nebraska Press.

Simmel, Georg. 1950. In *The Sociology of Georg Simmel*. 1908. Ed. and trans. Kurt Wolff. Glencoe: The Free Press.

———. 1968. On the concept and tragedy of culture. Trans. K. Peter Etzkorn. In *Georg Simmel: The Conflict in Modern Culture and Other Essays*, 1911, ed. Etzkorn, 27–46. New York: Teachers College Press.

Siniavski, Andrei. 1984. The joke inside the joke. *Partisan Review* 51(3):356–66.

Smith, Sydney. 1869. Edgeworth on bulls. Review of *Essay on Irish Bulls*, by Richard Edgeworth and Maria Edgeworth. In *The Works of the Reverend Sydney Smith*, 1803, 75–78. London: Longmans, Green, Reader and Dyer.

Spencer, Herbert. 1910. The physiology of laughter. In *Essays: Scientific, Political, and Speculative*, 1860, 452–66. New York: D. Appleton & Co.

Spencer, Gary. 1989. An analysis of JAP-baiting humor on the college campus. *Humor* 2(4):329–48.

Stephenson, Richard. 1951. Conflict and control functions of humor. *American Journal of Sociology* 56(6): 569–74.

Stoppard, Tom. 1973. *Jumpers*. New York: Grove.

Stora-Sandor, Judith. 1991. The stylistic metamorphosis of Jewish humor. *Humor* 4(2):211–22.

Sully, James. 1902. *Essay on Laughter.* New York: Longmans, Green.

Suls, Jerry. 1972. A two-stage model for the appreciation of jokes and cartoons: an information-processing analysis. In *The Psychology of Humor,* ed. Jeffrey Goldstein and Paul McGhee, 81–100. New York: Academic Press.

Tanner, Stephen L. 1989. E. B. White and the theory of humor. *Humor* 2(1):43–53.

Tillyard, E. M. W. *The Elizabethan World Picture.* New York: Vintage Books.

Titters: The First Collection of Humor by Women. 1976. Ed. Deanne Stillman and Anne Beatts. New York: Collier Books.

Trilling, Lionel. 1972. *Sincerity and Authenticity.* Cambridge: Harvard University Press.

Ungar, Sheldon. 1984. Self-mockery: an alternative form of self-presentation. *Symbolic Interaction* 7(1):121–33.

Varsava, Jerry. 1990. Review of *The Contemporary American Comic Epic: The Novels of Barth, Pynchon, Gaddis, and Kesey,* by Elaine B. Safer. *Humor* 3(2):222–26.

White, E. B. 1941. Preface. In *A Subtreasury of American Humor,* ed. E. B. White and Katherine S. White. New York: Coward-McCann.

Wilson, Christopher. 1979. *Jokes: Form, Content, Use and Function.* New York: Academic Press.

Winston, Mathew. 1972. Humour noir and black humor. In *Veins of Humor,* ed. Harry Levin, 269–84. Cambridge: Harvard University Press.

———. 1978. Black humor: to weep with laughing. In *Comedy: New Perspectives,* vol. 1, ed. Maurice Charney, 31–43. New York: New York Literary Forum.

Workshop on Humor and Cognition (Synopsis), 1989. *Humor* 2(4):417–40.

Želvys, V. I. 1990. Obscene humor: what the hell? *Humor* 3(3):323–32.

Zijderveld, Anton. 1968. Jokes and their relation to social reality. *Social Research* 35(2).

Zucker, Wolfgang. 1969. The clown as the lord of disorder. In *Holy Laughter: Essays on Religion in the Comic Perspective,* ed. M. Conrad Hyers, 75–88. New York: Seabury Press.

Illustration Credits

Fig. 1 (Guindon). Reprinted by permission of Richard Guindon.

Fig. 2 (Harley Schwadron). Reprinted by permission of *Penthouse* magazine. © 1977.

Figs. 3 and 14 (Bizarro / Dan Piraro). Reprinted by permission of Chronicle Features, San Francisco, CA.

Fig. 4 (Full Disclosure / Szep). Reprinted by permission of Universal Press Syndicate, Kansas City, MO.

Fig. 5 (Callahan). Reprinted by permission of Debra Levin.

Fig. 6 (S. Gross). Reprinted by permission of Cartoonist & Writers Syndicate.

Figs. 7 and 11 (Pepper . . . and Salt). Reprinted by permission of Cartoon Features Syndicate.

Fig. 8 (Eldon Dedini). Reprinted by permission of *Playboy* magazine. © 1981 by Playboy.

Fig. 9 (Tom Meyer). Reprinted by permission. © San Francisco Chronicle.

Fig. 10 (J. B. Handelsman). Reprinted by permission of *Playboy* magazine. ©1987 by Playboy.

Fig. 12 (Laugh Parade / Bill Hoest). Reprinted by permission of Bunny Hoest and Parade Magazine. © 1992.

Fig. 15 (The Now Society / William Hamilton). Reprinted by permission of Chronicle Features, San Francisco, CA.

INDEX